Global Constructions
Of Multicultural Education

Theories and Realities

Sociocultural, Political, and Historical Studies in Education
Joel Spring, Editor

Global Constructions
Of Multicultural Education

Theories and Realities

Edited by

Carl A. Grant
University of Wisconsin—Madison

Joy L. Lei
Vassar College

2001

LAWRENCE ERLBAUM ASSOCIATES, PUBLISHERS
Mahwah, New Jersey   **London**

The camera ready copy for this book was supplied by the editors.

Lawrence Erlbaum Associates, Inc., Publishers
10 Industrial Avenue
Mahwah, New Jersey 07430

Cover design by Kathryn Houghtaling Lacey

Library of Congress Cataloging-in-Publication Data

Global constructions of multicultural education : theories and realities / edited by Carl A. Grant, Joy L. Lei.
  p. cm. – (Sociocultural, political, and historical studies in education)
  Includes bibliographical references and index.
  ISBN 0-8058-3597-0 (cloth : alk. paper) – ISBN 0-8058-3598-9 (pbk. : alk. paper)
    1.   Multicultural education—Cross-cultural studies—Congresses. I. Grant, Carl A. II. Lei, Joy L. III. Series.

LC1099 .G56 2001
370.117—dc21
                                                                          2001031516

Books published by Lawrence Erlbaum Associates are printed on acid-free paper, and their bindings are chosen for strength and durability.

Printed in the United States of America
10 9 8 7 6 5 4 3 2 1

This book is dedicated to Joy's parents,
with love and appreciation.

Contents

Foreword

Joel Spring, Series Editor
New School University, U.S.A.

Many educators are not aware of the worldwide significance of multicultural problems. In the United States multicultural and multilingual policies and problems are directly related to the international migration of populations resulting from colonialism and the current global economy. *Global Constructions of Multicultural Education: Theories and Realities* confirms the global importance of multicultural issues. Contrary to attempts by nationalistic 19th century European historians to portray nations as monocultural, most nations, including European nations, are multilingual and multicultural. Government leaders, educators, and others need to be aware of the interrelatedness of cultural and language problems around the world. This volume contains international examples that can be used in developing policies and educational methods for resolving multicultural and multilingual issues.

In their Preface, the editors recall that their interest in creating this volume was sparked while traveling in Taiwan. Taiwan is a good example of how global events have created multicultural and multilingual societies. Over the course of centuries, Taiwan has experienced Chinese, European, and Japanese colonialism. The result is a society divided by language and culture. Today, the Taiwanese government is attempting to maintain the languages and cultures of nine indigenous tribes. The survivors of this indigenous holocaust are demanding bilingual and bicultural education. In addition, older citizens, who experienced Japanese colonialism up to the end of World War II, remember being forced to learn Japanese. On call-in radio programs there are raging debates over the language of schools. "Why can't the schools use Taiwanese dialect in the classroom?" is a frequently asked question because of the imposition of Mandarin by the fleeing remnants of Chiang Kai-Shek's army in the late 1940s. In keeping with the growth of English as the global language and the domination of Mandarin, a new bilingual Mandarin and English elementary school has recently opened in Taipei. Political parties continue to be divided by language and culture.

Taiwan is only one example of the effect of colonialism and population movement in creating multilingual and multicultural societies. European colonialism sparked the diaspora of African and Indian populations to countries around the world. Adding to the complexities of these diasporas are the clashes of cultures that exist in Africa and India. In recent years, European nations have received many members of the African and Indian diaspora along with "foreign workers," particularly from Turkey. European nations must now formulate educational, cultural, and citizenship policies to meet the needs of these new immigrant populations. The Peoples Republic of China continues to wrestle with problems faced by their linguistic and cultural minorities.

The essays in this volume provide the reader with a comparative understanding of the global range of multicultural issues and the many approaches to resolving multicultural and multilingual issues. These essays will heighten the reader's awareness of the importance of developing sound multicultural policies for resolving internal and external national conflicts.

Preface

HOW AND WHY *THIS* BOOK PROJECT

The seed for this book was planted on a winding road in Taiwan. In 1997, several scholars of multicultural education, from four countries including the host country, were invited to participate in the "International Symposium on Multicultural Education: Theories and Practices" at the National Taiwan Normal University. The purpose of this symposium was to present to a mainly Taiwanese audience (educators, policymakers, community leaders) perspectives on the theories and practices of multicultural education, including problems and issues confronting the field. This 5-day symposium (May 29–June 2) also afforded the opportunity for the international group of scholars presenting papers to both have time to listen (and hear) one another, and to raise questions about the nature of multicultural education, including the conditions of multicultural education in countries not represented at the symposium.

Throughout the days these scholars spent together, it was often acknowledged that the discussions were richly informative, in part because they illuminated the fact that multicultural education, in some simple or complex form, was underway in many different countries, and in part because it became obvious that there was a great need for scholars of multicultural education to know and understand the conditions of multicultural education in a global context. It was during one of these discussions, particularly the one that took place on a bus traveling on a very windy road to visit some of Taiwan's schools and cultural sites, that the idea was proposed to continue these discussions the following year at the 1998 American Educational Research Association's (AERA) Annual Meeting in San Diego, California. It was also proposed that these discussions be enriched and expanded by including scholars on multicultural education from additional countries. Christine Sleeter, who had accepted the position as Program Chair of the 1998 AERA Annual Meeting and one of the scholars on the bus, embraced the idea and said, "Send me a proposal!"

"Conceptualizing How 'Multicultural Education' Is Being Played Out Globally: The Beginning of a Dialogue" was the title of the 1998 AERA symposium co-chaired by Carl Grant and Joy Lei. Quotation marks were purposely placed around multicultural education to acknowledge that it is a term widely used in some countries, but not the term of preference in other countries. The symposium brought together nine scholars, who addressed multicultural education in nine different geographical regions. These invited papers were enthusiastically received, but they also produced both feelings of frustration and a call to action. The feelings of frustration came about because the 2-hour symposium did not allow ample time (approximately 10 minutes per paper) for the presentation and discussion of the papers. Nevertheless, it did provide enough time for the audience and other presenters to know that they wanted to learn more about multicultural education in the regions discussed. They knew that the knowledge they were receiving about the current conditions of multicultural education in different global regions was not available in any published form. Material that addressed multicultural education from multiple international perspectives was rare, and the few publications that exist were published in the1980s. Both presenters and audience participants claimed that the knowledge about multicultural education they were receiving was something that their students, as well as other advocates of multicultural education, needed to know.

The presenters' frustration with having an inadequate amount of time to deliver their presentation was compounded by Carl holding up note cards at the 5-minutes, 2-minutes, and time-is-up mark. Ultimately, this frustration did serve a positive purpose of leading a call to action. It motivated the presenters to accept the invitation to prepare their paper for publication. To prepare the papers for publication, the presenters agreed to read each other's paper. Each presenter sent his or her paper to the other presenters in order for them to offer feedback. The presenters thus served as referees. They pointed out areas in the papers that needed additional work, for example, underdeveloped theoretical frameworks or clarification of language that would make the writing more user friendly to an international audience. This process of reading other presenters' papers also offered the author/reader ideas for his or her own chapter. The plan worked well—the authors provided each other with excellent feedback. Two of the chapter authors, however, were unable to continue to work on their paper due to other obligations and therefore decided to drop out of the project.

We (Carl and Joy) assumed the editorship of the book project, including finding a publisher and coordinating the review process. While waiting for the papers to be reviewed and for the authors to respond to the feedback, we identified additional authors in other global regions to contribute to the book. Originally, the hope was to have at least one chapter from a country within each of the continents. This goal, although not achieved because of time constraints, did allow us to discover from our discussions with potential authors that the ideals and realities of multicultural education exist in many countries throughout the world.

WHAT DO THESE CHAPTERS TELL US?

The chapters in this volume tell us about how various global regions are dealing with three major areas of concern within the field of multicultural education: (a) the conceptualization and realization of "difference" and "diversity," (b) the inclusion and exclusion of social groups within a definition of multicultural education, and (c) the effects of power on relations between and among groups identified under the multicultural education umbrella.

The chapters are informative of how different regions have been or are presently dealing with issues of "difference" and "diversity" in their educational system. Because each region has a different sociohistorical context, the chapters point to the different terminology used in varying regions in discussing the same concepts or ideals. They also tell how the various regions are approaching difference and diversity from distinct cultural and ideological perspectives, or if difference and diversity are receiving any attention at all. Additionally, these chapters tell us whether or not the various regions define difference and diversity in the same ways.

Which social groups are included under the multicultural education umbrella in particular global regions? Do all or most regions include, for example, gender and class when discussing or practicing multicultural education? Or is multicultural education exclusively about race and ethnic culture? In other words, does it mainly address anti-racist education? From reading the chapters we not only learn about the inclusiveness of the multicultural education umbrella in the different regions, we also discover in which countries these marginalized groups receive equal or fair support to achieve equality and equity. In other words, the chapter authors have not particularized multicultural education so that it focuses on only one dimension of diversity and/or "otherness."

Also, some critics of multicultural education have argued that discussions on the effects of power within the multicultural education discourse are absent or muted. The chapter authors in this book directly address how power relations between dominant and subordinate/marginalized/oppressed groups based on socially constructed markers significantly affect and differentiate the educational experiences of students.

Whereas the chapter authors do pay attention to the themes we just noted, they also bring their particular interest and perspective to the book. The chapters address issues such as linguistic, racial, ethnic, and religious diversity, class, educational inequalities, teacher education, conceptualizations of citizenship, and issues of identity construction. In addition, the authors offer both historical and social contexts for their analytical discussion on the ideals and practices of multicultural education in a particular region.

In summary, *Global Constructions of Multicultural Education: Theories and Realities* is not a book that tells us about multicultural education with an international "twist;" it provides readers with different ways to think, talk, and research about issues of "diversity," "difference," and the effects of power as they relate to education.

ARRANGEMENT OF CHAPTERS

The chapters in the book are arranged alphabetically, according to the authors' surname. By using this arrangement, we suggest that there is not one recommended order for reading the chapters. Instead, our recommendation is that the reader take a region (or author) that he or she knows pretty well and one that he or she does not know well, and compare and contrast the conditions of multicultural education in the two regions. Or, allow your scholarly interest to direct your choice.

ACKNOWLEDGMENTS

There are several individuals whom we wish to thank for their efforts in bringing this project to successful fruition. Christine E. Sleeter, as Program Chair of the 1998 AERA Annual Meeting, strongly endorsed the idea of a symposium on multicultural education in global contexts and saw to it that such a symposium became a part of the program. Jim Banks, as the President of AERA at the time, supported Christy's decision and noted that the symposium was in keeping with the Annual Meeting's theme, "Diversity and Citizenship in Multicultural Societies." Wen-jing (Peter) Shan and Jason Chang at the National Taiwan Normal University coordinated the "International Symposium on Multicultural Education: Theories and Practices" in Taiwan, where the idea originated, and gave us four great days to discuss multicultural education and to enjoy Taiwan's hospitality. Naomi Silverman of Lawrence Erlbaum Associates and Joel Spring, editor of the Sociocultural, Political, and Historical Studies in Education series, both deserve a big thanks for their enormous support, including shepherding the idea for this book though the publication process. We also thank Lori Hawver and Sondra Guideman at Lawrence Erlbaum Associates for their guidance during our preparation of the book manuscript. Much appreciation goes to Jennifer Austin, who did the countless little but important tasks to help bring about the publication of this book, and Corrin Rausenberger, who carefully completed the tedious task of the Author and Subject Indexes. Finally, and most importantly, we thank the contributors to *Global Constructions of Multicultural Education: Theories and Realities* for their intelligent and insightful chapters, their wonderful collegiality, and their patience and diligence throughout the publication process.

—Carl A. Grant and Joy L. Lei

Chapter 1

Sociocultural and Linguistic Diversity, Educational Theory, and the Consequences for Teacher Education: A Comparative Perspective

Cristina Allemann-Ghionda
University of Cologne, Germany

The dimension of cultural and linguistic diversity and its significance for education have been discussed in Europe especially after the Second World War, but much more intensely from the mid-1970s on, when migration became visible as a stable fact in many immigration countries. The role of international organizations such as UNESCO, the Council of Europe, OECD, and the European Commission was and is influential in this field, promoting both discussion and international cooperation on policies, theory building, and research on implementation (CDCC, 1986; Commission of the European Community, 1994; OECD, 1991; Sténou, 1997; Wagner, 1997). Many universities in immigration countries boast scholarship on migration studies and, particularly, on the relationships between migration, multicultural society, the importance of culture for the development of individuals, bilingualism, multilingualism, and the aims and contents of education.

This chapter focuses, in its first section, on the latest developments of the continental Western European theoretical discussion on intercultural approaches to education. To do so, the author had to select a part of the literature available and therefore concentrates on texts by German- and French-speaking scholars, thus providing examples from three countries with a long and rich experience with immigration and its effects on education, an experience starting from the late 1950s: Germany, France, and the French-speaking part of Switzerland. The discussion developed in Italy and the Italian-speaking part of Switzerland is also considered. The school systems of these regions had to react to a foreign-speaking immigration only from the late 1980s on.

The kind of "intercultural education" conceptualized in this area of Europe reflects a time and experience gap, but also different determinants: in the migrant population, in the structures of the education systems, and in the tradition of social research as well as of pedagogical research and development. The conceptions resulting from these different backgrounds are briefly outlined. Some arguments used in the criticism of intercultural education are also discussed in this section.

In the second section, it is argued that the intercultural approach is to be conceptualized as a core issue in general education. It is maintained that the cultural dimension of education is to be included in such a conceptualization, but in the framework of a broad and complex net of factors. A definition of an education respectful of sociocultural and linguistic diversity is given, and the aims and elements of such an education are outlined. In these two sections, the author's data and literature background is mainly supported by her own comparative, empirical, and qualitative research into the strategies developed in six school systems located in six regions of the four countries already mentioned: Germany, France, Italy, Switzerland,[1] as well as studies of the theoretical conceptions developed in the same area and beyond (Allemann-Ghionda, 1997a, 1997b; Dasen, 1997).

Finally, in the third section some conclusions are drawn as to the consequences that a concept of general education thus reshaped (i.e., including the dimension of sociocultural and linguistic diversity) has for the aims and contents of basic teacher education. Elements for a reformed curriculum (primary and junior high school teachers) are presented.

INTERCULTURAL EDUCATION: A PEDAGOGICAL UTOPIA IN AN INSTITUTIONAL VACUUM

The policies on the issue of multiculturalism in society and school in the different countries involved in this chapter cannot be presented here and are not the primary subject. This would be the topic of another paper, if not of several books (Todd, 1994; Wicker, 1997). However, it may be helpful to give some basic information in order to locate correctly the meaning and the possibilities of implementation of the pedagogical change intended by the scholars who promote "intercultural education."

---

[1] For detailed descriptions of the case studies and for the cross-case analysis, see the author's publications mentioned in the References.

To put it bluntly: None of the four European countries considered here has a governmental, official program to foster multiculturalism in society or in education. Of the four countries, France is the one most clearly against multicultural policies. Its official philosophy is that of integration and absorption of cultural differences. The latter are tolerated, but their reproduction is not encouraged (Haut Conseil, 1991). According to the policy of the 1990s, one of the aims of education is to promote a dominant role of French culture and language, as stated in the curricula (Ministère de l'Education Nationale, 1994). France is the only country that gives citizenship on the grounds of *ius soli*,[2] much like in the United States, although with a somewhat more restrictive rule. This is a fundamental detail, for a reason that is explained later. The other three countries, Germany, Italy, and Switzerland, do not have a state policy for multiculturalism. However, in laws and recommendations they claim to favor integration *and* to respect the right of minorities to keep contacts with their cultures and languages of origin, much more strongly than France does. These two principles are also stated in recommendations concerning "intercultural education" as well as in the curricula of many school systems,[3] in which teachers are encouraged to appreciate the variety of the cultures and languages represented by migrant children or, more generally, to develop a pluralist, in some cases even a relativist understanding of cultures and of history, and sometimes also of religion (detailed analysis in Allemann-Ghionda, 1999). Each of these three countries has a more or less restrictive way of granting citizenship to immigrants, their laws being more and less based on *ius sanguinis*: Italy undertook a reform in 1991 in order to make the procedure to obtain the citizenship easier for citizens of the European Union and harder for extra-Europeans (Caritas di Roma, 1997, p. 173). The difference in treatment on the issue of citizenship is crucial in order to understand the meaning of concepts like "migrant," "foreigner," and "cultural minority" in each of the countries discussed here. If a country allows and encourages migrants to become its citizens, integration occurs as a natural consequence of an institutional act, and the question of keeping one's original cultural identity alive is

---

[2] *Ius soli* means literally "right of soil" or "law of soil"—that is, a country gives citizenship to any child that is born on its soil. The opposite concept is *ius sanguinis*, "right of blood," which means that a person inherits citizenship from his or her parents. Germany recently (2000) modernized its law on the acquisition of citizenship, introducing a mixture of *ius soli* and *ius sanguinis*.
[3] The plural is used because Germany and Switzerland, both federal states, have respectively 16 and 26 different school systems.

regarded as secondary even by the former migrants themselves; or at least, this is the case in the European countries discussed here. In these countries, as soon as a migrant becomes a citizen of the immigration country, the topic of defending his or her cultural identity becomes almost irrelevant. The cultural identity of migrants is no major political issue, and no powerful movement of cultural or ethnic recognition of migrants or former migrants who became citizens of the immigration country is known in these countries. The quest for having a space recognized for cultures and languages of migrants has been put forward by few single associations representing some of the better organized ethnic groups, while the majority of the migrants remain isolated and silent in this respect. Yet the effectiveness of the few organized groups has never become so strong as to provoke durable legal and institutional reforms in any of the four countries. The question of the national, regional minorities in the four countries, their quest for recognition in society and education, and its meaning for intercultural forms of education might and should be discussed in a similar way (Allemann-Ghionda, 1998), but this topic cannot be dealt with here for space reasons. However, the literature on the language rights of national minorities usually excludes the issue of migrants' languages (see, e.g., Giordan, 1992).

As there is no affirmative policy in favor of multiculturalism, in none of the four countries is there a way to "force" school authorities and teachers to implement intercultural education by adapting the school structures and teaching contents, although the concept of intercultural education is mentioned in school policy documents (except in France, where this concept gradually disappeared from official policy documents). There is a gap between the official educational policies and the normal school reality, which mostly runs according to the principle of assimilation, not even integration. Some exceptions do exist in form of experimental projects (Allemann-Ghionda, 1995), but the duration of these innovations is mostly short. The weak reaction of schools to the challenge of multicultural issues is just one more example of how hard it is to change the "grammar of schooling," as Tyack and Tobin (1993) called the normal, routine functioning of schools. The current trend (especially strong in German-speaking areas) to give each school a large amount of autonomy, combined with the increasingly popular political fashion to run schools as if they were private enterprises, with the financial difficulties public institutions currently have to face, as well as with the dominance of market-oriented decisions in daily school policies, makes it even more difficult to implement any ideas expressed in policy documents, advanced as these may be. Nor do the central, or local authorities blame schools or the authorities at the level just below them for not carrying out what is recommended in policy documents. Yet, statistically speaking, the children of migrant families are subject to school failure more frequently and more severely than the children of natives, so that the absence of affirmative policies in favor of cultural and linguistic minority children, and the impossibility to have local authorities, teachers, and teacher educators take seriously any recommendations, is a major problem. The implications of this poor degree of implementation can hardly be underestimated, if only because of the percentages of migrant children in the schools of Switzerland (21%), Germany (11%), France (10%) and Italy (less than 1%) (these average percentages conceal the fact that in a single school there can be up to 90% migrant children), not to mention other facets of the concept of "intercultural education" beyond the ones related to migration.

Given the absence of affirmative policies to protect and foster the plurality of cultures and languages of migrants in society and in education, the theories of intercultural education developed in the different countries represent attempts to change a mainstream idea of education and of pedagogy that is historically still based on the concept of "one nation, one culture, one language." (In Switzerland, a country with four language regions, German, French, Italian, and Romansh, it will be: "one region, one culture, one language.")

But let us get back to the history of intercultural education in Europe, in order to see how these attempts to change a traditional, nation-based conception of education gradually developed.

The first decades of experience with children of migrants (roughly from 1955 to 1975) were informed by the "swim-or-sink" principle. Teaching these children the official language and aiming at their fast assimilation was the official and currently practiced strategy. Accordingly, the first "theories" about schooling migrant pupils essentially aimed at developing appropriate, scientifically based methods to teach migrant children the second language, that is, the language of the country they were presumably going to live in for a time long enough to require language skills. Such theories and methods were particularly developed in Germany (Apeltauer, 1987), where several universities installed chairs in this field. In France, a scientific approach to the teaching of French as a second language was much less developed, as the methods for teaching French as a foreign language were considered by many as adequate for a migrant public too (Pujol & Véronique, 1991). It eventually appeared to some that in spite of apparently sound theory and methods, this compensatory pedagogy did not prevent migrant children from being, on the whole, less successful in school than natives. It was clear that their belonging mostly to an underprivileged class was a major source of difficulty in school. But, additionally, the idea emerged that cultural and linguistic factors might be of importance in several respects. The practice of suppressing or simply ignoring the language and culture of the child's parents was more and more criticized.

The concept of "intercultural education" was first used in the mid-1970s in Germany and France, and some years later in Switzerland, when immigration was already a consolidated reality in these countries, and when it was evident that a schooling strategy merely based on assimilation was not effective (school failure) and, moreover, was contrary to the rights of minorities to have their cultures and languages respected. The term intercultural education was at that time associated with the presence of migrant children whose cultures and languages of origin were no longer to be excluded from school, but on the contrary were to be included at least by making the teachers aware of the specific backgrounds of the pupils. The active respect of "other" cultures passed, in this phase, through permitting and encouraging the teaching of the mother tongues of migrants in the schools of the immigration countries. The reason given was, at first, that in case of return to their countries of origin, the students would be able to attend schools in their own mother tongues. Later, mother-tongue teaching became an argument for better second-language learning. Finally, the identity argument was introduced. The principle of mother-tongue teaching found its way into official recommendations of the single countries from the early 1970s, then the Commission of the European Community took up the idea in its guidelines of 1977.

The conceptualization of intercultural education in Western Europe has several sources. One of them is that some scholars previously active in the field of second-language teaching became aware of the unsatisfactory results of this approach in schools. The other source is of a more theoretical nature. The emerging of the "cultural paradigm" in disciplines such as anthropology and psychology contributed to a first paradigm shift in pedagogy: from the paradigm of assimilation (based on a deficit hypothesis) to that of the recognition of cultural difference (based on a difference hypothesis). The influence of the North American discussion was considerable. As Dittrich and Radtke (1990) pointed out, the concept of "ethnicity" (an expression of the positive view of cultural difference), not used in Western Europe after the World War II because of its negative political connotations based on the persecution of ethnic minorities under the Nationalsocialist and Fascist regimes, began to be scientifically and politically acceptable in the same countries that had been ruled by those regimes (Germany and Italy) as well as in other countries, after it was reimported from the United States and Canada (and, particularly, Québec) and was attributed a new, positive connotation linked to the affirmative policies for ethnic minorities in these countries. One of the first theoretical laboratories for intercultural education was the Council of Europe, and more specifically its project Number 7 "The education and cultural development of migrants" (CDCC, 1986), in which scholars from many countries cooperated. The Council of Europe received the contributions of scholarships of many countries and gave back, in turn, conceptions and policy recommendations to the same countries. But where a country had no political orientation and no legal basis for multiculturalism, these theoretical frameworks and practical recommendations remained almost without consequences: a necessary pedagogical utopia in an institutional vacuum.

The analyses and conceptions developed in the Council of Europe were inspiring for the scientific communities of each country involved. So in a way intercultural education as it was conceptualized in Europe in the 1980s, represents a European discourse in that it contains a common core of ideas. Nevertheless, in each country the theoretical debate on intercultural education does have particular features, and in each national scientific community one can detect different positions, which does not simplify the task of description, analysis, and comparison. In the following, we attempt to characterize how intercultural education is presently conceptualized in the four countries, noting common features and differences. The aim is not to be exhaustive, but to show the main points as well as the most controversial issues.

To avoid a certainly long and maybe dull description, we make the comparison along the way in which in the four countries the intercultural dimension of education deals with two fundamental concepts: *cultural difference* and *multilingualism.*

As mentioned previously, the concept of cultural difference became relevant in European pedagogical discourses as a reaction to several stimuli, one of which was the adoption of the concept of "ethnicity" as it was known in the United States and in Canada in the 1970s and 1980s. The "old" immigration countries Germany and Switzerland, and, some years later, the "new" immigration country, Italy, developed conceptions of intercultural education based on a positive view of cultural difference and on the acceptance of ethnicity. The category of the ethnic, scientifically legitimized after it was positively connotated thanks to affirmative policies in the United States and in

Canada, became frequently mentioned in theoretical texts, policy documents, and even textbooks (Allemann-Ghionda, 1997c), either explicitly using the term of ethnicity (Nieke, 1995) or enhancing in other ways the positive value of cultural difference (Rey-von Allmen, 1996). The fascination of cultural difference and of ethnicity appears to be very strong in Italy, a country in which immigration from abroad came later, and it was and is an immigration mostly from extra-European countries. So in the Italian discussion we find a dominance of the topos of getting acquainted with "the Other," which is perceived both as a necessity and an exciting experience, as "the Other" appears to be utterly different in his or her looks, speech. and lifestyle. Cultural difference seems to still have an absolute and unquestioned position in the Italian discussion (Secco et al., 1992).

In the old immigration countries, however, the cultural paradigm is not totally unquestioned, but on the contrary, subject to criticism. This is the case especially in France, where the research tradition is characterized by a *répugnance à l'interethnique et au minoritaire*, as De Certeau (1987, p. 191, note 5) pointed out. The roots of this aversion against everything ethnic and against cultural particularism are to be seen in the centralist tradition, in the anti-republican past of autochthonous minorities, as well as in the structuralistic Marxist orientation of the social sciences, predominating up to the 1980s—an orientation in which the socioeconomic aspect is the main and essential criterion to analyze society. Accordingly, some authors in France warn against the emphasis put on cultural difference, because this would encourage a form of cultural, neo-differentialist racism, not less dangerous than the traditional biology-based racism (Taguieff, 1985). So in France, the conception of intercultural education, which was included in policy documents in the mid-1970s, was gradually thrust into the background and is now considered obsolete by many authors; the nation-based, conservative education policy of the 1990s is complementary to this development in theory. The criticism of the fostering of cultural difference and of intercultural education leads to a pedagogy in which the equal rights of all children as citizens are to be central, regardless of any cultural specificity (Costa-Lascoux, 1992).

Parallel to the discussion in France, a similar discourse developed in Germany. According to Radtke (1995, p. 46), intercultural education has encouraged a culturalist and ethnicist point of view of the professional educational thinking that now leads attention away from internal structural problems of the organization of schools to cultural determinants external to schools. Instead of talking about cultural differences, educationalists should concentrate on the equality of opportunities and treatment, and on eliminating the barriers to integration. An equivalent of the French anti-culturalist sociology would be the position expressed by Bukow and Llaryora (1993). For them, cultural difference is but a fallacious construction. Only the socioeconomic position of a person and of a group are relevant. Whereas in France intercultural education has almost completely disappeared from the theoretical and policy discussion, this is not so in Germany. The criticism of the cultural paradigm, on the contrary, encourages a more differentiated conceptualization of intercultural education, both in theories and in policy documents: a conception in which culture matters, but the social and economical determinants of a child's life matter also. A similar evolution can be observed in Switzerland.

Why is cultural difference so important in the discourse of many German, Swiss, and Italian scholars (and in official policy documents)? And why is the criticism of intercultural education so harsh in the theory (and policy) discussion of France? Whereas the research tradition of France is strongly influenced by structuralist and Marxist positions, the research traditions of the other countries owe their arguments to equal or more strong influences favorable to the recognition of the specificity of minority languages and cultures. Especially after the Second World War, many scholars in Italy and Germany endeavored to develop or revitalize pedagogical theories open to internationalism and to the respect of different cultures, languages, and points of views, as a sort of moral commitment to the democratic ideals that had been mortified during the totalitarian regimes. In Switzerland, the openness for interculturalism in research may be seen as a facet of the pluralism of opinions and the search for consensus deeply rooted in society and in politics, as an aspect of the plurality of cultures, which (at least in part) neutralizes nationalist ideas about culture in pedagogy, as an influence of the German and Italian pedagogical discussion on interculturalism, and as the pedagogical outcome of the discussion in the international organizations, some of them located in Geneva. A further factor of differentiation may lie in the principles that rule the organization of the common life of different cultural and linguistic groups. Germany, Italy and Switzerland's constitutions all mention the protection of language and cultural as well as religious minorities, whereas France's constitution only mentions the equal rights of all citizens (not communities). France has a centralist government system (as does Italy), but Germany and Switzerland are governed according to a federal system that allows leeway for many different accommodations to regional specificity. The Italian centralism, however, is mitigated by the constitutional principle and by laws favorable to minorities, including migrants; in those texts cultural difference is mentioned as a positive element. The variety contained in and resulting from federalism theoretically offers a favorable background for the idea of tolerating or even appreciating cultural and linguistic difference. In practice, though, local specificities can generate parochialism in language issues. Generally speaking, none of the four countries treat national and foreign minorities equally.

Beside cultural difference, *multilingualism* is an equally important topic in the discussion about intercultural education. Many authors think that, in order to open education to an intercultural dimension, as well as to appreciate the specific culture and needs of migrants, it is wise and necessary to value the bilingualism of migrants and of any other bilingual person. This assumption, however, is not equally strong in the four countries, nor is it developed in the same way everywhere.

Generally speaking, the language issue in intercultural education is stronger in Germany and Switzerland, and weaker in France and Italy. In Germany and in Switzerland, the arguments include: (a) the importance of allowing migrant children to continue to learn the language of their parents, so that they may strengthen their personal and social identity as well as become better speakers of the second language, and bilingual speakers altogether; and (b) the idea of making all pupils or students familiar with the variety of languages, so that they may learn to respect the persons and cultures represented by those languages. Good examples of a synthesis between theoretical approaches and curriculum development for multicultural schools have only recently been published (Kuhs & Steinig, 1998). Both in Germany and Switzerland, the favorable attitude of many researchers toward the language issue may be influenced by a relatively strong attention to foreign language teaching in the school systems.

In France and Italy, the language issue is much less discussed, but for quite different reasons. In France, the strong assimilating philosophy and institutionalized intended integration (especially through citizenship), along with the policy to strengthen the French language and culture, leads to underestimating the importance of the languages of migrant children in public education, even if a minority of researchers claims to defend a space for mother tongue tuition, and some migrants' languages are included in the offer of "foreign languages." In Italy, it is essentially the kind of migration that determines the small attention given to bilingualism and multilingualism in intercultural education. Migrants come essentially from African and Asian countries, and they speak "exotic" languages or dialects. The heterogeneity of immigration makes it even more difficult to imagine the inclusion of any other language beside Italian and the foreign language taught in a particular school, although the policy documents declare openness to the languages of migrants. For similar reasons, migrant languages are not much considered in the Italian-speaking part of Switzerland. Both in France and in Italy, the theoretical discussion seems to be unfavorably influenced by the scarce attention given to foreign language teaching in the school systems until very recently.

In the pedagogy of the four countries, European integration is now a powerful stimulus to pay more attention to the questions related to cultural difference and multilingualism in education, but not necessarily and in no case only related to migrant students.

Where the intercultural discussion has not been drawn back by a severe criticism and rejection of cultural specificity in the name of what we might call an *equity hypothesis*, the current discussion on intercultural education is evolving. After a first paradigm shift, a transition from a paradigm of assimilationism (informed by a *deficit hypothesis*) to a paradigm of cultural difference and ethnicity (informed by a *difference hypothesis*), a second paradigm shift might be characterized by the evolution towards the paradigm of heterogeneity and pluralism (informed by a *diversity hypothesis*). Finally, a third paradigm shift appears to take place in theory: In the early 1990s, more and more authors of texts in general pedagogy (Heyting & Tenorth, 1994) have recognized that the plurality of cultures and pluralism in education are not marginal issues concerning a special pedagogy for migrants and minorities or maybe for multilingual and multicultural environments, but that they are core issues concerning general pedagogy, regardless of the characteristics of the students involved. The next section of this chapter develops the contents of the evolution of the intercultural education, particularly the two last paradigm shifts described previously.

SOCIOCULTURAL AND LINGUISTIC DIVERSITY AS A CORE ISSUE IN GENERAL EDUCATION AND PEDAGOGY

Why does culture matter in education? In the theoretical conceptions of intercultural education we find that the factor "culture" is mentioned as relevant at one or more of the following different levels:

- The cultural and social backgrounds of students, teachers, and parents should be taken into account in order to understand their attitudes, actions, and learning problems as well as personal and social needs.
- The international and multicultural character of society as a consequence of migration and other phenomena related to globalization should be included as topics in order to change the cultural contents of the curricula.
- The cultural contents of education should be revised altogether in the name of a universalist idea of education, free from any form of ethnocentrism, so the contents include different perspectives and educate for pluralism and relativism.

In the first conceptions (1970s), intercultural education was primarily a matter of the first level: an approach to help migrants coping with school, and schools coping with migration. The discussion gradually widened toward the general question of preparing young people to live in a multicultural, socially heterogeneous environment; in this context, the European integration became more and more an argument for intercultural integration. Finally, the question of pluralism and relativism was discussed as a question for the philosophy of education, independent from the kind of students involved in a particular setting.

As we saw, some critical positions argue that the cultural factor is of no importance whatsoever, because it is the result of a social and scientific construction, it hides the factors of differentiation that really matter in society (i.e., the social and economic situation of individuals and groups), it can be misused for discriminating against these persons and groups, and it does not change the negative situation of migrants in school for the better.

To such criticism, one may answer that feelings of cultural identity are not only the product of heteronomous attribution, but are also or even more subjective realities (and realities nevertheless) that determine an individual's life and may lead him or her to express belonging and loyalty to a group, and to experience the effects of difference. Moreover, sociopsychological research has provided objective evidence for the fact that cultural difference affects the communication between individuals and groups (Camilleri & Vinsonneau, 1996; Gudykunst, 1993). From a pedagogical point of view, we have to consider two main points: On the one hand, a total exclusion of all topics of cultural and linguistic variety in school eventually leads back to a conception of education identical to that of the nation-based education systems of the 19th century. Social justice will not arise out of this, but ethnocentric and nationalistic ways of thinking will be supported on the side of the cultural majority, and discrimination will result for minorities. On the other hand, a well-founded dealing with cultural factors (differences, variety) will not conceal the factors of the social, economic, and political forces that rule human relationships, but will integrate them in the elaboration of a conception.

So the conceptualization of education in a society marked by globalization and by multiple relationships between cultures needs to pursue reflection about the role of the cultural factor. However, the theoretical discussion about intercultural education seems to be stuck at present. One reason may be the difficulty to implement theories. Theories are difficult to implement if the political and institutional framework is not favorable (lack of policies for multiculturalism). A further question must be asked: Are the school systems compatible with intercultural approaches? In other words, the discussion about how to take into account cultural factors in education should link the theoretical discussion with a close and critical look at the structures of the education systems as they actually are, particularly focusing the questions of selection and exclusion or inclusion.

At this point, we refer to the *second* and *third paradigm shift* in the discussion.

The *second paradigm shift* implies that the definition of education should not focus merely on the cultural difference, but on a complex set of differences that may be encountered in a classroom and a school, exactly as is the case in any larger group of persons That is, there are differences in culture, language, religion, social and economic position, and gender, to mention some differences of the collective kind; but there are also differences basically related to the individual, such as psychological or character or physical features, opinions, sexual orientation, health, and social behavior. All of these contribute to make groups in most schools heterogeneous in many respects, and not only when and because migrant or other minority students are present. The pedagogical consequence of this statement would be that the teacher or the teaching team should be able to work on the grounds of a school organization, with a curriculum and teaching methods respectful of this heterogeneity. In the present situation, this is often not possible because some school systems do not respect heterogeneity as a "normal" fact of society and of school. For example, going back to the four countries examined in this chapter, we find that some school systems (Germany, German-speaking part of Switzerland) are highly selective and segregating. They have many forms of separating students considered apt for higher qualifications from those whose school career and working life are due to be more modest ones, and students regarded as "different" from those held to be "normal."[4] The result is a complex system of differently qualifying types of junior high school, and of special classes such as special education for mildly and for severely disabled children, and classes for migrant pupils who do not speak the second language yet. Strangely enough, migrant students tend to be placed in the classes for special education and in the less qualifying types of high school even when their only "difference" is that of belonging to a cultural minority and socially underprivileged family, often combined with an insufficient command of the second language. So the discriminating use of cultural, linguistic, and social difference is very much supported by the very structural orientation of the school systems. On the contrary, the school systems of Italy, of France, and of the Italian-speaking part as well as some of the French-speaking cantons of Switzerland, have altogether a more inclusive orientation. This favorably affects the academic achievement of migrant students, although a problem of school failure still exists. The structural differences between school systems suggest that a "positive discrimination" on the basis of cultural factors can only be successful in systems organized and conceived for the inclusion and best possible integration of all forms of "difference." If the question of integration or segregation is not tackled globally, the integration of cultural difference can only remain a sterile cosmetic exercise. A cultural reform of education needs to be pursued in the framework of structural changes toward inclusive structures, where these have not yet taken place. And, where the school systems are inclusive, the cultural and linguistic issue should be tackled specifically: It is a specific form of difference that requires pedagogical attention in order to guarantee a just treatment.

If the second paradigm shift just described is about going beyond a cultural view of difference toward a comprehensive view of heterogeneity, and about questioning the structural barriers that may hinder a just treatment of differences, the *third paradigm shift* can be described as the transition from a discussion that takes place in a scientific subcommunity (the intercultural educationalists) to a discussion led in general pedagogy. So we have again the question of trespassing artificial and excluding boundaries, this time in the realm of the very definition of education, which is the basic preoccupation of pedagogy. The many effects of globalization concern all young people, teachers, and planners involved in education, regardless of their own cultural identity. The theoretical discussion in general pedagogy ought

---

[4] The reforms that have been gradually making some of the school systems in these countries more permeable and inclusive cannot be discussed here.

to be interested in reflecting on the aims, contents, and possible changes that are necessary in order to make education a meaningful help to grow up in a world that is globally interdependent, to be able to analyze events in this context, and to communicate in it.

These very roughly defined finalities need to be made precise. In doing so, the whole possible range of students is to be kept in mind: young people belonging to a majority or to minorities, native or foreign. The following elements for an education respectful of sociocultural and linguistic diversity are suggested:

- Subjective and objective support of the identity of sociocultural and linguistic minority students.
- Constructing curriculum contents implying and reflecting the positive value of the plurality of cultures and languages.
- Building communicative, action-oriented skills.
- Accepting sociocultural diversity and the plurality of ideas as a challenge for democracy.

Subjective and Objective Support of the Identity of Sociocultural and Linguistic Minority Students

One of the core ideas of intercultural education is that it traditionally aims at strengthening the cultural identity of minorities. But how can this goal be reached if there is almost consensus about narrow and one-sided culturalistic approaches being contraproductive? It is not by encouraging students perceived as members of a minority to exhibit their origins and particularities, that their identity will be strengthened and their rights respected. It seems more urgent to bring about a kind of education in which the specific life background and knowledge of minority students is kept in mind and inspires the setting and contents of teaching at all times by surrounding them with an atmosphere of respect and consideration. A concrete consequence of such respect and consideration will be that the teaching is free of cultural, social, religious, linguistic, or any other prejudice, as well as ethnocentrism, not to mention racism. Even more concretely, the languages of migrants and other minorities must have a definite place in the curriculum, along with the cultural contents they express. This place will be different according to the organizational possibilities of the school and to the staff available, and the arrangements will vary from formal teaching of all languages represented (if the minorities concerned agree), to bilingual classes or schools, to forms of partial immersion involving some subject matters, to more informal and less structured approaches of language and culture awareness (Byram & Morgan, 1994). In the European countries considered in this chapter, the connection between language and culture is usually very tight in each community of migrants. The language of origin is therefore the vehicle to express consideration for culture. Thus, a pedagogy attentive to the plurality of cultures must be aware and create awareness of the plurality of minority languages. Such a pedagogy will be inscribed in the broader framework of an education that is respectful of sociocultural and linguistic diversity. Respect for sociocultural and linguistic minorities will go along with respect for any other form of difference in the classroom. Respect will be a matter of attitude to be fostered through education, but also a matter of teaching styles, of learning opportunities, and of equity of treatment.

Constructing Curriculum Contents Implying and Reflecting Over the Positive Value of the Plurality of Cultures and Languages

The principle of respect and consideration of the cultures and languages of minorities can be broadened and extended to become a general pedagogical principle. Even beside and beyond the presence of minority students in a classroom and the concern not to offend, but on the contrary to strengthen their identities, the curriculum contents and the methods of presenting and discussing such contents can be modeled in such a way that the plurality of cultures and languages is constantly present and becomes evident to every student. The plurality of perspectives (pluralism), combined with the exercise of critical analysis, is a pervading principle that can be applied to any topic or subject matter. Here again, language teaching (revisited) can be a very rich experience. Choosing appropriate literary texts or material of everyday situations, a teacher can lead students to sharpen their perception of difference in the meanings given to concepts and things, and in ways of life. In subject matters like history, geography, art history, history of religions, politics, and biology, and also by interdisciplinary projects, the choice of meaningful topics, "key-topics" as Klafki (1993) called them, can be helpful. Such meaningful topics can embrace the problems that are relevant for society in a general manner (not only for minorities), and at the same time contain international or intercultural dimensions that allow to point at issues that involve the power relationship between majorities and minorities in a town or country (or between North and South, East and West), or the acceptance of different ways of thinking and of living.

Building Communicative, Action-Oriented Skills

Besides fostering a basically open attitude to difference, and transmitting contents carefully chosen to support openness, a definition of education adequate for a society in which sociocultural and linguistic diversity is the rule should also contain a set of skills in the realm of communicative competence in a sense larger than the language-based one. Given the assumption that virtually any individual in our world is confronted with other individuals with backgrounds and ways of expressing themselves different from his or hers, and that, moreover, any individual is asked to react mentally, often also verbally and with actions, to a firework of messages in codes not always known, such communicative skills must be considered as key qualifications. Such qualifications have a factual and cognitive component, in the sense that the individual should be able to analyze the messages conveyed by persons or things, and to reflect on his or her own thoughts, feelings, or reactions, instead of just reacting blindly to the irritations of difference. Theoretical models and empirical research findings in cultural psychology and intercultural communication (Bennett, 1986) can provide instruments that can be integrated into pedagogy and into teaching.

Accepting Sociocultural Diversity and the Plurality of Ideas as a Challenge for Democracy

Sociocultural and linguistic diversity implies a complex plurality of lifestyles and ideas. Misunderstandings and conflicts are likely to occur, power clashes may be the consequence, uncertainty about whether a value system can be accepted or not will occasionally disturb the relationship between people. Plurality is a challenge for democracy, and the institutions in which education takes place must meet this challenge in order to develop the students' sensitivity for a democratic way of coping with misunderstandings, conflicts, power clashes, and moral dilemmas. Such openness might be called pluralism. Developing such sensitivity may be the task of a subject matter designed for that, for example, philosophy. But education offers many more opportunities for exercising democracy in situations that occur in daily school life, or for discussing in school political events of more general interest. The question of value relativism should not be excluded from such discussions. A theoretical model for tackling differences is hard to find. If a single position dominates without having been discussed, then a kind of pseudo-universalism is imposed, in which the values of some minorities might be disregarded, and in which the ethnocentrism of the cultural majority is the real, if hidden, guideline (Todorov, 1989). If a total relativism of values is the rule, conflicts may arise. Discussion on values issues can only be fruitful if a consensus is the goal, and if such consensus is sought sincerely, without mental reserves about the superiority of any culturally inscribed ethic model, as is proposed by Gutmann (1993) in her concept of "deliberative universalism." A shared model and method of consensus finding is the necessary condition for the institutions (and in particular for schools) to construct conflict-solving strategies apparent to everyone.

The ideas expressed on how to shape education in school institutions imply adequate conditions that are often not given yet. This means that in many cases changes have to occur in the structure and organization of schools: minority cultures and languages can hardly be respected unless the timetable of a school, the staff, and the material facilities (rooms, etc.) are planned accordingly. Changes are also necessary, in many cases, in the official curriculum and in the textbooks provided by the authorities, or chosen by the staff, or made by single teachers. However, our analysis of the existing curricula in the four countries shows that the structural and organizational conditions are often open, indefinite, and flexible enough to allow many of the pedagogical changes proposed here. The curricula and textbooks can be integrated with further written and nonwritten material in order to attain the cultural change necessary for an education respectful of sociocultural and linguistic diversity, as in the four aims already outlined.

But the problem of change is not only one of adequate exterior settings and correct syllabi. Cultural change implying respect for sociocultural diversity and coping with the plurality of ideas is a matter of how the persons responsible for education, that is, teachers and school principals, are formed to bring about a paradigm shift in schools, complementary to the paradigm shift that is taking place in research. The application of such a pedagogy in everyday education in schools is still to be constructed, and the first generation of teachers has still to be educated in this perspective.

In the next section, an attempt is made to sketch the skills teachers (and school principals) need to acquire so that they may act in the sense of a pedagogy respectful of sociocultural and linguistic diversity and the pluralism of ideas.

THE CONSEQUENCES FOR TEACHER EDUCATION

The structures for the education of primary level teachers of the four countries have developed in systems outside the universities until very recent times. Many of these institutions were or still are schools at a secondary level, parallel to high schools. The first country to integrate the education of primary level teachers into university-level institutes (*Pädagogische Hochschulen*) and the universities from the 1960s on was Germany. In France, this kind of reform was implemented in the early 1990s (*Instituts Universitaires de Formation des Enseignants*). Italy is currently carrying out a similar plan, and in most parts of federalist Switzerland, a political discussion is taking place about whether or not, and how, to raise the academic level of teacher education by including it into universities or university-level institutions. Teachers for high school, however, receive an academic education in all countries; this education in the subject matters is not everywhere completed by a sufficient pedagogical education. For the primary level, the nonacademic heritage means that specific institutional cultures about how to define teacher education exist; they reflect different social realities. Where the institutes for teacher education are structures outside universities, the question of what place scientific knowledge has to occupy in teacher education is often treated as a minor one: Practical skills and teaching techniques are considered by the educators of teachers to be the most (or only) necessary ones. On the contrary, where the education of teachers is predominantly an academic one, as is the case for the secondary level, pedagogical questions including the practical skills tend to be neglected. The relation between "theory" and "practice" is a core issue in the current discussion on teacher education, with the ideal model still to be found even where the reform is 30 years old (Radtke, 1996).

This premise is necessary in order to point at the structural and cultural conditions in which a structural and cultural reform of the contents of education has to be discussed. Recent research concentrates on the primary level teacher education, but many statements apply also to the education of junior high school teachers, especially the proposals for curricular contents (Allemann-Ghionda et al., 1999a, 1999b). One point is, that the lack of theoretical concern and consciousness produces but scant reflection in the institutions themselves, about the implications of multicultural society and schools for education in general, and for teacher education in particular. Another point is that the curriculum contents in the present institutions for primary teacher education in most cases do not contain systematic programs for taking into account the dimension of cultural and linguistic plurality. The curricula do contain some information and activities relevant to the problems related to migration, in some cases more generally related to sociocultural and linguistic diversity. Except for a few cases, this happens in an approximative way, depending on the good will of single teacher educators, not on a policy of the institution, nor of the school authority. The approach is often that of the early stages of the discussion on school and migration (deficit hypothesis). One exception is the University of Geneva, which has already taken over the education of primary school teachers and included in its curriculum the preparation for teaching in a multicultural perspective. Other examples of relatively systematic curricular elements in teacher education are found in Germany. This state of affairs of generally poor consideration of the issue known as "sociocultural and linguistic diversity" may change, and research results may contribute, especially in those regions that have not yet completed the reform of teacher education for its curricular part.

Referring to the aims and contents of an education respectful of sociocultural diversity, the following consequences for the contents of teacher education may result:

> *Aim 1.* The subjective and objective support of the identity of sociocultural minority students requires teacher education to be rich in carefully chosen knowledge on the background and implications of migration and, in general, of sociocultural and linguistic diversity as it appears in schools. Several disciplines should contribute to constructing this knowledge: sociology, psychology, social psychology, psycholinguistics, and sociolinguistics. According to an empirical inquiry into the contents of primary teacher training in Switzerland, for example, the curricula contain no systematic information, and often no information at all, about bilingualism, in the scope of any taught subject. Many more examples could be quoted for other topics that are crucial to understanding what happens in a multilingual class with migrant students. If this kind of factual knowledge and theoretical reflection is lacking, the teachers are likely to misunderstand many events in the classroom and at meetings with parents. The results will very often be misplacement of migrant students in poorly qualifying classes or school types, unconscious discrimination within the classroom due to unreflected projection of negative prejudice on ethnic grounds, production of school failure due to the well-known Pygmalian effect, or reduction of every "wrong" word or action of a migrant student to "cultural" or "ethnic" causes. To avoid all these facts resulting from missing contents in teacher education, the teacher students must be formed to attain a level of analysis of the class accurate enough to enable them to make hypotheses about the children's situation, previous knowledge and skills (and not only ignorance and incapacities), language, culture and

religion background, as well as social environment. Especially the language issue demands much more and better study and training in several domains, ranging from knowledge about social, institutional, and individual multilingualism and bilingualism, to the development of teaching methods adequate for classes with different levels and qualities of language skills. Even beside the variety of language skills a class may have, teaching in heterogeneous classrooms requires a variety of teaching methods and the know-how to let the children learn at different speeds and according to different learning styles. The art of teaching with individualized and differentiated methods got lost along with the preindustrial custom to organize school in multi-aged groups. The growing heterogeneity in classrooms calls for such individualized methods and for better ways of practicing an inclusive and at the same time differentiated pedagogy.

Aim 2. Constructing curriculum contents implying a plurality of cultures and languages requires that teachers be able to reshape the curriculum contents in a pluralist way, given the assumption that in many cases the official curriculum and the textbooks will not meet this condition. To be able to reshape curriculum contents, implies a strong emphasis on training in text analysis and in curriculum research. Text analysis means, in this case, the method of examining given curricula and textbooks applying criteria to detect representations that might contain, for example, ethnocentric views. Curriculum research means, in this case, a method that will enable the teacher to complete the available selective information contained in the textbooks and the whole amount of information he or she has constructed in the course of time, with new information (texts, resource persons, films, etc.), and to arrange the contents in order to provide different cultural perspectives and instruments for critical appraisal. Both methods, text analysis and curricular research, are necessary particularly at this stage, in which intercultural education or, more broadly, an education respectful of sociocultural diversity and of the plurality of ideas as it may be discussed in educational theory, has hardly been transferred into curricula and especially into textbooks.

Aim 3. Building communicative, action-oriented skills requires from teacher education that it be enriched with specific elements of cultural psychology and social psychology, giving special attention to systematic work on the cultural biography of each teacher student. The teachers are to get acquainted with theories concerning communication, and specifically communication between individuals and groups with different social and cultural backgrounds. The typically occurring stereotypes and reactions are to be studied, and possible ways of acting and reacting to the practical part of the teacher education are to be imagined and "rehearsed," with the help of role plays and other methods apart from the mainly cognitive approach to texts.

Aim 4. Accepting sociocultural diversity and the plurality of ideas as a challenge for democracy requires from teacher education restructured curricular contents in the subjects philosophy and politics, or general pedagogy if such subjects are not taught. The capacity to communicate and act appropriately in heterogeneous groups because of the social, cultural, religious, and linguistic background of the students, is to be enhanced by working on the personal and social skills the student teacher has (Aim 3). A further step is to explicitly discuss, in teacher education, the issue of value conflicts of ethical, religious, or political nature. If the pedagogical aim is that schools be able to develop coherent strategies for solving conflicts based on ethical, religious, or political issues, teachers and school principals must have the theoretical background in order to grasp the meaning of such strategies and to participate in their construction. Analyses and models on the issue of pluralism and relativism, and reports on actually occurring conflicts (e.g., the prohibition to wear a scarf as a religious symbol in French schools) are the topics to be discussed. If the students in schools are to become responsible persons, capable of discussing issues democratically, those who teach them must have tools to propose arguments and examples to them and to lead them to use those arguments and examples in discussions on the topics chosen.

In the present situation, the issue of sociocultural and linguistic diversity is often taught in separate timeslots like "Africa weeks" or "The integration of foreigners," and in specific seminars or lectures on "intercultural" or migration-related topics. More often than not, topics related to this issue are the object of optional courses or minicourses, which students can easily avoid attending. This is especially the case in the German-speaking part of Switzerland, where teacher education is partly based on an elective curriculum. If general pedagogy discusses more and more in terms of an education respectful of sociocultural diversity and aware of pluralism, these dimensions are not any more the particular task of a special section of pedagogy. Following the same logic, they must also become core issues in teacher education. The ongoing structural and curricular reforms of teacher education (particularly in Italy and Switzerland) should not underestimate the question of including curricular elements into the compulsory part of teacher education and of rewriting the single disciplinary tables of contents, instead of confining migration and diversity topics into separate and optional formats.

CONCLUSION

The immigration countries Germany, France, and Switzerland have been leading a theoretical discussion about intercultural education since the mid-1970s, Italy from the mid-1980s. Theory was developed against the background of an institutional vacuum, in the sense that none of the countries has an official policy for multiculturalism. If this institutional reticence is one of the reasons for the poor implementation rate of intercultural education in schools, the second reason is the missing link between theorization on one side, and reflection on the aims of educational reforms on the other. A third reason is the general tendency to let school policies become private, market-oriented matters. Given the assumption that state school policies are necessary, it is argued in this chapter that inclusive education systems are more receptive for taking intercultural approaches than segregating ones. The theoretical discussion will be more convincing and more effective in practice if the goal of integrating all forms of difference into school structures will be pursued. Taking into account not only cultural but also social, linguistic, and any form of personal diversity, is not a case for a special subpedagogy, but should be perceived as a core issue of general pedagogy. More and more authors not identifiable with the scientific community of the "interculturalists" have begun conceptualizing diversity and pluralism. A concept of education respectful of sociocultural diversity and inclusive of pluralism needs teachers and school principals who will construct it in schools. This has consequences for the contents of teacher education. Coherently with the assumption that an inclusive orientation of the school systems is the condition sine qua non to effectively cope with sociocultural and linguistic diversity, this dimension must be fully integrated and become compulsory in the curriculum of teacher education.

REFERENCES

Allemann-Ghionda, C. (1995). Implementing European strategies for language and culture diversity. A cross national comparison based on six case-studies. *EERA* [European Educational Research Association] *Bulletin, 1*(3), 12-22.

Allemann-Ghionda, C. (1997a). Interkulturelle Bildung [Intercultural education]. *Zeitschrift für Pädagogik, Supplement 36*, 107-149.

Allemann-Ghionda, C. (Ed.). (1997b). *Multiculture et éducation en Europe* [Multiculture and education in Europe] (2nd rev. ed.). Bern, Switzerland: Lang.

Allemann-Ghionda, C. (1997c). Ethnicity and national educational systems in Western Europe. In H.-R. Wicker (Ed.), *Rethinking nationalism and ethnicity: The struggle for meaning and order in Europe* (pp. 303-318). Oxford, United Kingdom: Berg.

Allemann-Ghionda, C. (1998). Les langues minoritaires nationales et de la migration dans les systèmes scolaires d'Italie et d'Allemagne: Politiques égalitaires, pratiques hiérarchisantes [National minority languages and migration languages in the education systems of Italy and Germany: Egalitarian policies, hierarchic practices]. In S. Pérez (Ed.), *La mosaïque des langues* [The mosaic of languages] (pp. 129-164). Paris, France: L'Harmattan.

Allemann-Ghionda, C. (1999). *Schule, Bildung und Pluralität: Sechs Fallstudien im europäischen Vergleich* [School, education and plurality: A European comparison based on six case-studies]. Bern, Switzerland: Lang.

Allemann-Ghionda, C., Goumoëns, C. de, & Perregaux, C. (1999a). *Pluralité linguistique et culturelle dans la formation des enseignants* [Language and culture plurality in teacher education]. Fribourg, Switzerland: Editions Universitaires.

Allemann-Ghionda, C., Goumoëns, C. de, & Perregaux, C. (1999b). *Curriculum pour une formation des enseignant(e)s à la pluralité culturelle et linguistique*

[Curriculum for a teacher education that is inclusive of language and culture plurality]. Berne, Switzerland: Fonds national de la recherche scientifique, Programme National de Recherche 33.

Apeltauer, E. (Ed.). (1987). *Gesteuerter Zweitspracherwerb. Voraussetzungen und Konsequenzen für den Unterricht* [Guided second language education: Its premises and consequences for the curriculum]. Munich, Germany: Hueber.

Bennett, J. M. (1986). Modes of cross-cultural training: Conceptualizing cross-cultural training as education. *International Journal of Intercultural Relations, 10*(2), 117-134.

Bukow, W. D., & Llaryora, R. (1993). *Mitbürger aus der Fremde. Soziogenese ethnischer Minderheiten* [Citizens from abroad. Social genesis of ethnic minorities] (2nd ed.). Opladen, Germany: Westdeutscher Verlag.

Byram, M., & Morgan, C. (1994). *Teaching-and-learning language-and-culture.* Clevedon, United Kingdom: Multilingual Matters.

Camilleri, C., & Vinsonneau, G. (Éds.) (1996). *Psychologie et culture : Concepts et méthodes* [Psychology and culture : Concepts and methods]. Paris, France: Armand Colin.

Caritas di Roma. (1997). *Immigrazione. Dossier statistico '97* [Immigration: Statistics 1997]. Rome, Italy: Anterem.

CDCC [Council for Cultural Co operation]. (1986). *Rapport final du groupe de travail. Projet Nr. 7 du CDCC: L'éducation et le développement culturel des migrants* [Final report of the project n. 7 Education and cultural development of migrants]. Strasbourg, France: Council of Europe.

Certeau, M. de. (1987). Economies ethniques: Pour une école de la diversité. In OECD [Organisation for Economic Co-operation and Development] (Ed.), *L'éducation multiculturelle* [Multicultural education] (pp. 170-196). Paris, France: OECD, CERI [Centre for Educational Research and Innovation].

Commission of the European Community. (1977, July). *Guidelines on the schooling of the children of migrant workers, No. 486.* Brussels, Belgium: Commission of the European Community.

Commission of the European Community. (1994). *Report on the schooling of migrants' children in the European Union.* Brussels, Belgium: Commission of the European Community.

Costa-Lascoux, J. (1992). L'enfant, citoyen à l'école [The child, a citizen in school]. *Revue Française de Pédagogie, 101,* 71-78.

Dasen, P. R. (1997). Fondements scientifiques d'une pédagogie interculturelle [Scientific foundations of intercultural education]. In C. Allemann-Ghionda (Ed.), *Multiculture et éducation en Europe* [Multiculture and education in Europe] (2nd rev. ed.) (pp. 263-284). Bern, Switzerland: Lang.

Dittrich, E. J., & Radtke, F. O. (1990). Der Beitrag der Wissenschaften zur Konstruktion ethnischer Minderheiten [The contribution of sciences to the construction of ethnic minorities]. In E. J. Dittrich & F. O. Radtke (Eds.), *Ethnizität. Wissenschaft und Minderheiten* [Ethnicity, science and minorities] (pp. 11-40). Opladen, Germany: Westdeutscher Verlag.

Giordan, H. (Éd.). (1992). *Les minorités en Europe. Droits linguistiques et droits de l'homme* [Minorities in Europe. Language rights and human rights]. Paris, France: Kimé.

Gudykunst, W. B. (1993). *Towards a theory of effective interpersonal and intergroup communication: An anxiety/uncertainty management perspective.* Newbury Park, CA: SAGE.

Gutmann, A. (1993). The challenge of multiculturalism in political ethics. *Philosophy & Public Affairs, 22*(3), 171-206.

Haut Conseil à l'intégration. (1991). *Pour un modèle français d'intégration. Premier rapport annuel* [For a French model of integration: First annual report]. Paris, France: La documentation française.

Heyting, F., & Tenorth, H. E. (Eds.). (1994). *Pädagogik und pluralismus. Deutsche und Niederländische erfahrungen im umgang mit pluralität in erziehung und erziehungswissenschaft* [Pedagogy and pluralism. German and Dutch experiences in dealing with plurality in education and educational science]. Weinheim, Germany: Deutscher Studienverlag.

Klafki, W. (1993). Allgemeinbildung heute—Grundzüge internationaler Erziehung [Liberal education today: Fundamentals of an international education]. *Pädagogisches Forum 6*, 21-28.

Kuhs, K., & Steinig, W. (Eds.) (1998). *Pfade durch Babylon. Konzepte und beispiele für den umgang mit sprachlicher vielfalt in schule und gesellschaft* [Paths through Babylon: Concepts and examples for dealing with language plurality in school and society]. Freiburg, Germany: Fillibach.

Ministère de l'éducation nationale. (1994). *Le nouveau contrat pour l'école. 158 décisions* [The new school contract : 158 decisions]. Paris, France: Ministère de l'éducation nationale [Ministry of national education].

Nieke, W. (1995). *Interkulturelle erziehung und bildung. Wertorientierungen im alltag* [Intercultural education and formation: Value orientations in daily life]. Opladen, Germany: Leske & Budrich.

OECD [Organisation for Economic Co-operation and Development]. (1991). *Education and cultural and linguistic pluralism. Synthesis of case studies. Effective strategies and approaches in the schools.* Paris, France: OECD, CERI [Centre for Educational Research and Innovation].

Pujol, M., & Véronique, D. (1991). *L'acquisition d'une langue étrangère: Recherches et perspectives* [The acquisition of a foreign language: Research results and perspectives]. Geneva, Switzerland: Cahiers de la Section Education de la Faculté de Psychologie et de Sciences de l'éducation de l'Université de Genève.

Radtke, F. O. (1995). Demokratische diskriminierung. Exklusion als bedürfnis oder nach bedarf [Democratic discrimination: Exclusion as a need or as required]. *Mittelweg 36*, 32-48.

Radtke, F. 0. (1996). *Wissen und Können. Grundlagen der wissenschaftlichen Lehrerbildung* [Knowledge and skills: Foundations of a science-based teacher education]. Opladen, Germany: Leske & Budrich.

Rey-von Allmen, M. (1996). *D'une logique mono à une logique de l'inter. Pistes pour une éducation interculturelle et solidaire* [From a logic of "mono" to a logic of "inter": Tracks for an education that is intercultural and promotes solidarity]. Geneva, Switzerland: Cahiers de la Section Education de la Faculté de Psychologie et de Sciences de l'éducation de l'Université de Genève.

Secco, L. (Ed.) (1992). *Pedagogia interculturale. Problemi e concetti* [Intercultural pedagogy: Problems and concepts]. Brescia, Italy: La Scuola.

Sténou, K. (1997). Expériences et projets de l'Unesco dans le domaine de l'éducation interculturelle [Experiences and projects of the Unesco in the field of intercultural education]. In C. Allemann-Ghionda (Ed.), *Multiculture et éducation en Europe* [Multiculture and education in Europe] (2nd rev. ed.) (pp. 83-93). Bern, Switzerland: Lang.

Taguieff, P. A. (1985). Le néo-racisme différentialiste. Sur l'ambiguïté d'une évidence commune et de ses effets pervers: l'éloge de la différence [Differentialist neo-racism. On the ambiguity of a common evidence and on its perverse effects: The praise of difference]. *Langage et société 34*, 69-98.

Todd, E. (1994). *Le destin des immigrés. Assimilation et ségrégation dans les démocraties occidentales* [The destiny of migrants: Assimilation and segregation in western democracies.] Paris, France: Seuil.

Todorov, T. (1989). *Nous et les autres. La réflexion française sur la diversité humaine* [We and the others: The French reflection on human diversity]. Paris, France: Seuil.

Tyack, D., & Tobin, W. (1993). The grammar of schooling: Why has it been so hard to change? *American Educational Research Journal, 31*(3), 453-479.

Wagner, A. (1997). Orientation and Work of the OECD [Organization for Economic Co-operation and Development] in the Field of Intercultural Education. In C. Allemann-Ghionda (Ed.), *Multiculture et éducation en Europe* [Multiculture and education in Europe] (2nd rev. ed.) (pp. 95-100). Bern, Switzerland: Lang.

Wicker, H.-R. (Ed.). (1997). *Rethinking nationalism and ethnicity: The struggle for meaning and order in Europe*. Oxford, United Kingdom: Berg Publishers.

Chapter 2

The Rise and Fall of Multicultural Education in the Australian Schooling System

Desmond Cahill
RMIT University, Melbourne, Australia

Prior to the mid-1970s, the political philosophy of multiculturalism and the allied notion of multicultural education were both unknown on the Australian sociopolitical and educational scene. Their genesis was, of course, generated by Australia's massive post-World War II immigration movement, another Golden Age of Migration that has now come to an end even though immigrants and refugees continue to arrive on Australian shores in significant numbers despite public disquiet on environmental and unemployment grounds.

The government policies and programs attached to the umbrella term of *multiculturalism* fundamentally have been an attempt to incorporate the "immigrant other" into the Australian polity. Multicultural education has been the response to deal with the realities of classrooms containing students from a range of cultural and linguistic backgrounds even though its aims were, as shall be seen, always broader. Underlying the debates that continue unabated, especially from the 1996 resurgence of the ever-present racism that lies at the heart of the European invasion and settlement of the Australian continent and the formation of the Australian nation in 1901, has been the failure of Australian society to resolve in a satisfactory and constructive way the diminishing but still potent legacy of the British colonialist and White European supremacist mindset, the failure to deal with the claims of the Aborigines, and the failure to construct an assured self-identity as a multi-ethnic nation hovering uneasily on the Asian periphery. Fundamentally, it has been a failure of national leadership, and the failure to articulate and communicate a national vision.

It is important to note that the multicultural education movement was initially less focused on race and racial differentiation than on overseas birthplace, language, and ethnicity. This may seem surprising for a nation whose White Australia policies were hammered out in the land of "the New Gold Mountain" of the 1850s. They were then enshrined for more than half a century in the first legislative acts of the Australian Parliament until their complete repudiation in early 1973. It was not an accident that very soon after that the concept of a multicultural Australia emerged, as the impact of the post-War immigration program was fully felt across most parts of the nation and as Asians, beginning with the Anglo-Indians in the mid-1960s, began their various emigratory movements together with the movements of Islamic peoples, especially from Lebanon and Turkey in the late 1960s and early 1970s.

To understand both the rise and recent fall of the multicultural education movement, we need to appreciate the changes in both the immigration/cultural diversity and educational landscapes.

CHANGES IN THE IMMIGRATION AND CULTURAL DIVERSITY LANDSCAPE

Australia has increasingly been held up as a multicultural lighthouse because of the massive transformation of its demographic profile, notwithstanding the recent step back from government commitment to multicultural policies. The Australian Bureau of Statistics in its five yearly censuses has never collected data on the basis of race except in relation to the Aborigines and Torres Strait Islanders, Australia's indigenous groups. Information has been collected in terms of (a) birthplace, (b) parental birthplace, (c) language regularly spoken, and (d) religion. Table 2.1 outlines Australia's multicultural profile at the time of the 1996 census in terms of birthplace, language, and religion.

TABLE 2.1

Australia's Multicultural Profile (in percentages)

Top 20 Birthplaces		Top 20 Languages		Top 20 Religious Groups	
1. Australia	73.9	1. English	82.0	1. Roman Catholic	27.0
2. United Kingdom	6.0	2. Italian	2.1	2. No religion**	25.2
3. New Zealand	1.6	3. Chinese*	1.9	3. Anglican	22.2
4. Italy	1.3	4. Greek	1.5	4. Uniting Church***	7.5
5. Vietnam	0.8	5. Arabic	1.0	5. Presbyterian	3.7
6. Greece	0.7	6. Vietnamese	0.8	6. Orthodox****	2.6
7. China	0.6	7. German	0.6	7. Baptist	1.7
8. Germany	0.6	8. Spanish	0.5	8. Lutheran	1.4
9. Philippines	0.5	9. Macedonian	0.4	9. Islam	1.1
10. Netherlands	0.5	10. Tagalog	0.4	10. Buddhism	1.1
11. India	0.4	11. Croatian	0.4	11. Christian	1.0
12. Malaysia	0.4	12. Polish	0.4	12. Jehovah's Witness	0.5
13. Lebanon	0.4	13. Turkish	0.3	13. Judaism	0.5
14. Hong Kong	0.4	14. Maltese	0.3	14. Pentecostal	0.4
15. Poland	0.4	15. Dutch	0.2	15. Salvation Army	0.4
16. South Africa	0.3	16. French	0.2	16. Church of Christ	0.4
17. Ireland	0.3	17. Serbian	0.2	17. Hinduism	0.4
18. Malta	0.3	18. Hindi	0.2	18. Assembly of God	0.4
19. USA	0.3	19. Russian	0.2	19. 7th Day Adventist	0.3
20. Croatia	0.3	20. Korean	0.2	20. Latter Day Saints	0.2
Others	10.0	Others	5.9	Others	2.2
TOTAL	100.0	TOTAL	100.0	TOTAL	100.0

Note. Source: Australian Bureau of Statistics, August 1996 census.

*Chinese includes Cantonese as the largest Chinese-speaking group together with Mandarin plus small numbers of Hokkien, Hakka, and Teochew speakers.

**No religion means those who said they had no religion or nothing was stated on the census form. Their numbers have risen very considerably in the last decade.

***The Uniting Church is the result of a union of the former Methodist and Congregationalist Churches and some Presbyterians in 1975.

****Orthodox includes the Greek Orthodox as the largest, together with, in order of size, the Macedonian, Serbian, Russian, Coptic, Ukrainian, and Romanian Churches.

Since 1947, the Australian population has increased from approximately 7 million to close to an estimated 19 million in 1999, about half through natural growth and the other half through migration. At every census in the post-War period, the percentage of overseas-born Australians has increased to total 26.1% in 1996. This implies that an estimated 40% of the population either is born overseas or has at least one parent born overseas. Of this number, about two thirds are from countries where English is a foreign language (Italy, Vietnam) or an associate language (Malta, the Philippines). Migration is thus a central fact in Australian social, political, and religious life, and, in the view of Foster and Stockley (1984), multiculturalism was devised as a systems management mechanism to handle and defuse the immigrant question.

The first two post-war decades (1950s–1970s) were focused on European migration, but since then there has been an increasing influx from the Asian countries, initially from India, East Timor, Hong Kong, and Vietnam, and more recently from countries such as China and the Philippines. In the 5-year period from 1991–1996, increases in aggregate numbers were in respect of China (+32,119 persons), Vietnam (+28,799), the Philippines (+19,506), New Zealand (+15,543), Hong Kong (+9,497), and South Africa (+6,149), with decreases for the United Kingdom (-46,051), Italy (-16,678), Greece (-9,615), and the Netherlands (-7,811), principally as a result of mortality. Although immigration continues from the three main English-speaking countries (New Zealand, United Kingdom, and South Africa), representing just over one third of the intake, in 1997–1998 the largest source countries, in order, were China, Hong Kong (still retained as a separate category), India, the Philippines, Vietnam, Bosnia-Herzogovina, and Indonesia.

Another aspect of Australia's multicultural mosaic is religious affiliation with, as the largest religious group in 1996, the Roman Catholic church (4.8 million), followed by the Anglican (3.90 million), the Uniting Church (1.33 million), the Presbyterian/Reformed (0.68 million), and the Orthodox (0.50 million). A large group is the atheist and agnostic group (25.2%), so prevalent that in late 1998 Pope John Paul II described Australia as "a culture of secularism." In the 5- year intercensal period, the fastest growing religious groups were the Buddhist (an increase of 42.9%) and the Islamic (35.8%). Hence, Australia is very much part of the growing religious diasporas across the world, and, at the schooling level, this has been reflected in the recent increase in non-Christian schools.

Another perspective is given by the language figures (Table 2.1), which include the second generation group (i.e., those born in Australia with at least one immigrant parent) and perhaps subsequent generational groups. Reflecting not only the birthplace data but also the fact of language shift across to English, in aggregate numbers between 1991 and 1996 there were significant rises in the number of English, Chinese, Vietnamese, and Arabic speakers, and speakers of

Australia's indigenous languages, with very sharp decreases in speakers of European languages except for Macedonian and Croatian, though the increase is more apparent than real because of the shift in self-description of "Yugoslav" language speakers from the 1991 census. It is anticipated that after the next census in 2001 the Chinese languages (mainly Cantonese and Mandarin) will be the most widely spoken languages in Australia after English.

Table 2.2 contains the first- and second-generation figures for the largest groups, though it must be pointed out that groups such as the Italians and Greeks are now moving into their third and fourth generations. Crisscrossing this has been the increasing rate of intercultural and interfaith marriages. The old Chinese saying that "a chicken does not marry a duck" is increasingly irrelevant in Australia though, like the differential rates for language shift across to English, the rate of intermarriage varies enormously across ethnic communities.

TABLE 2.2

Australia's First- and Second-Generational Groups

Birthplace	1st-Generation	2nd-Generation	Total	% of Pop.
U.K.	1,072,514	1,444,620	2,517,134	14.2
Italy	238,216	333,880	572,096	3.2
New Zealand	291,381	199,928	491,309	2.8
Greece	126,524	153,913	280,437	1.6
Germany	110,332	139,319	249,437	1.4
Netherlands	87,898	142,528	230,426	1.3
Vietnam	151,085	46,848	197,933	1.1
Lebanon	70,237	82,526	152,763	0.9
China	110,987	40,163	151,150	0.9
Ireland	51,462	95,097	146,559	0.8
Philippines	92,933	35,160	128,093	0.7
Malta	50,871	77,191	128,062	0.7
India	77,522	43,640	121,162	0.7
Poland	65,119	55,640	120,759	0.7
Malaysia	76,221	30,710	106,931	0.6
Croatia	47,015	41,179	88,194	0.5
Hong Kong	68,437	19,415	87,852	0.5
USA	49,526	36,724	86,250	0.5
South Africa	55,717	28,157	83,874	0.5
FYROM	42,181	28,470	70,651	0.4

Note.   Source: Australian Bureau of Statistics, August 1996 census.

As a consequence, there has been a whole range of cultural, religious, and linguistic encounters not only at the national level but especially at the level of local suburbia—in the neighborhood, in local community structures, in the workplace, and especially in the schools, right from the late 1940s (Martin, 1978). In Australia, there are virtually no ghettoes in any strict sense of the term, and the ethnic concentrations that were present in the poorer inner suburban areas were dispersed to middle and outer ring suburbs in the large cities such as Sydney and Melbourne. The inner suburbs have been transformed, meanwhile, by the process of gentrification over the past quarter century through the replacement of migrant and other poor families by middle class, double income couples who want to be close to the city's central business district and other cultural amenities.

All this made the necessity for a multicultural educational process more than evident but the dispersal also made it more difficult to deliver in practical terms at the local level.

Since 1980, changes in the immigration intake policy have had a direct impact on schooling systems and their strategies for educating arriving students. In addition, all systems have had to cope with much greater numbers of first-, second-, and third-generation students at various stages of the shift from first language to English as a second language that occurs in all non-English speech communities and with varying levels of bilingual proficiency. These changes have been:

Diversification in the Immigrant Intake. With each decade in the post-War period, significant changes have occurred in the source countries with a proportional decline in the number of immigrants where English is the first and official language such as the United Kingdom and the United States, and an increase in the numbers from non-English-speaking countries, as has been documented earlier.

As well, intake categories have changed. During the 1980s, family reunion numbers increased, but with the extended family component being significantly cut during the past decade, now being about 10% of the intake in 1997 (DIMA, 1997). At the same time, there has been a very significant rise in nuclear family migration, especially as a result of intercultural marriages. Skilled migration has also been cut because of the economic circumstances though this has been offset by the increase in business migration. During the 1990s, the source countries for the refugee and special humanitarian program have shifted from Vietnam and Timor to countries such as Afghanistan, Bosnia, Ethiopia, Iraq, Sri Lanka, and Somalia.

Although schools have been appreciative of the consequent cultural richness of this diversification, their student populations became more multilingual than previously. This in particular had an effect on the employment of bilingual teaching aides and adequately trained interpreters and translators. This multilinguality made it more difficult to employ a greater range of these personnel and, in a climate of funding cutbacks, response capacity became limited.

Changed Patterns of Dispersal. Students from families where English is not the main language are now more dispersed across Australia and within each school system than previously. The dispersal was caused by (a) the influx of well-educated and financially well-off specialist workers and business migrants into more affluent areas that previously had not received significant numbers of immigrants, (b) the gentrification of inner-suburban metropolitan areas that has forced recently arrived families to find accommodation in the cheaper middle-ring and outer-ring suburban areas, (c) the movement of refugee families into country areas, usually under the auspices of the government's Community Refugee Settlement Scheme, and, most importantly, (d) the movement of first-, second-, and third-generation families away from former areas of ethnic concentration and zones of transition, typically in lower socioeconomic status areas, to a broad range of suburbs across each of the major cities.

The result was to make education service delivery more difficult, especially in the allocation of teachers of English as a second language (ESL) across a greater range of schools, in the provision of English language intensive schools for newly arrived immigrant and refugee students, and in the establishment of language maintenance programs. In general, the available resources had to be spread more thinly across the schools.

Cuts in the Immigrant Intake. The constant shifts in immigration intake policy, especially the cutbacks during the 1990s, have had considerable structural impact as they resulted in the closure of many language reception centres for newly arriving immigrant students and the laying off of some teachers. However, the general effect was to increase the precarious nature of the ESL strategy and of ESL employment. For school systems, it rendered planning difficult, and forced most systems to employ teachers on a temporary basis, given that the funding was Commonwealth-based. Yet it must be said in passing that even though the percentage of the ESL teaching force employed on a temporary basis is high, they are a most committed group of teachers.

Increasing Numbers of NESB Students. Since the high figures of the late 1980s, the immigrant intake has declined. This led to the perception that the number of children from non-English-speaking families has declined. This perception seems to have been strongly held in national bureaucratic circles in Canberra where the focus has always been upon the newly arrived, and partially contributed to their undermining of the ESL program that began in the mid-1980s under the Labour Government and was finally to succeed in 1997 under the Liberal conservative coalition government. It was and remains a wrong perception. First, there has been the pipeline effect over several decades of the second-generation cohort; that is, the children of immigrants who arrived either as adults or as children themselves. As well, the third generation cannot be discounted. The state of South Australia, which has traditionally been the leading state in multicultural education, has had the broadest definition to include this group and in 1992–93 the third generation who did not speak English at home comprised a not insignificant 12.6% of the total number of students from a non-English-speaking background (NESB). As well, the retention rate of students from immigrant backgrounds increased. Overall, although the numbers may have plateaued in some states such as South Australia because of the relatively low immigrant intake over more than a decade in that state, the number of NESB students using the traditional definition increased overall, especially in the largest state, New South Wales, as has the NESB proportion of the total student population, again especially in New South Wales and in Sydney particularly.

Special Groups of Permanent Ethnic Minority Students. As another change agent, the immigrant intake profile has produced new sub-categories of ethnic minority students in addition to the older ones such as rural-based immigrant students whose needs were found by a national study (Cahill, 1996) to be less well met than a decade previously. The children of business families from Confucian-heritage countries such as Hong Kong, Singapore, and Taiwan have constituted a new element in the multicultural mosaic of Australian schools, standing in stark contrast to the lowly unskilled immigrant of the past and the penniless refugee of past and present. Whereas these parents are highly educated, successful, and socially astute, there is also the downside of suicide, unemployment, and depression as a result of the move to Australia. Schools praised the studiousness and task commitment of these children but were concerned about the many cases where adolescent children were left on their own to fend for themselves while the parents commuted overseas to supervise their business interests or to attend to family matters; in some cases the teenagers became involved in minor criminal behavior (Cahill, 1996).

Refugee and traumatized immigrant children have always been present in Australian schools, but the increase in numbers from a fairly wide array of refugee contexts and as a proportion of the overall intake has generated additional pressures for schooling systems, even though the educational and health care systems have cooperated fairly well in coping with the needs of these usually resilient children who know so much about the brutalities of life. There tend to be two broad groups: children who have been exposed to acute traumatic events followed by relatively stable family and communal care, and children who suffer additional adversities through losing their homes, possessions, and friends and, often, parents and siblings (Boothby, 1992). To this group must be added the children of political asylum claimants, an issue that in Australia has been highlighted by the presence of Chinese nationals and their dependent children and by the saga of the Cambodian and Sino-Vietnamese boat people who arrived illegally on northern Australian shores and now are held at special detention centers. The detention of children in these centers without adequate educational provision has presented a *prima facie* case that Australia is in contravention of the international conventions on children, migrants, and human rights.

Within the system there are illegal immigrant children whose number is unknown because there are significant problems in matching the arrival and departure data for children. However, their number is probably very low. It was also clear that systems and school personnel show a strong resistance to acting as compliance officers for the Australian government. Catholic school personnel in particular showed a particularly strong resistance, maintaining that the Church had a humanitarian tradition towards the poor, the outcast, and the exiled. This attitude has now materialized in the formation of the Sanctuary movement to provide support for refugees, especially the East Timorese, to whom the government has refused to grant permanent residency because they are seen, somewhat improbably, as the responsibility of Portugal.

Other groups that are increasing in numbers are the second migration or *pendolare* children whose families move them back and forth between Australia and the home country and across the globe, with parents sometimes making these decisions with scant regard for their children's educational welfare and, secondly, the children of intercultural relationships. Price (1994) has documented over a long period the rise in intercultural marriages that in Australia has been highlighted at a public level by the Filipino bride controversy (Cahill, 1990; Chuah, Chuah, Reid-Smith, & Rice, 1987) and the recent priority given to Serbian-Croatian intermarried families from the Balkans conflict. Another small group is the immigrant adoptee children, approximately 500 of whom enter Australia each year, usually as babies or as small children, as the adopted children of Australian parents.

The listing of these different groups of children together with their increasing numbers highlights the complexity of the task that schools and systems have had to confront in implementing a multicultural educational perspective. Usually their needs are apparent, yet it is in meeting their needs that the less obvious needs of other NESB students, such as second- and third-phase English language learners, have not even partially been dealt with. With the changes since 1996, their situation has become even more problematic.

Temporary Migration Children. Temporary migration has grown exponentially since 1985, principally because of the tourist boom and the overseas student influx. The various cohorts of long-term (i.e., more than 1 year) temporary school students include full fee-paying overseas students (FFPOS), studying at primary and secondary schools; dependent children of consular officials and staff; dependent children of FFPOS university and technical education students; dependent children of temporary workers with specialist skills; and dependent children of parents on probationary 2-year visas in marriage or de facto relationships.

In 1993 there were 7,964 secondary school FFPOS students and 182 primary students, whereas by 1996, the numbers had more than doubled with 14,450 secondary and 2,733 primary FFPOS students, mainly from Indonesia (2,517), South Korea (1,921), Taiwan (1,606), Japan (1,430) Hong Kong (1,139) and Thailand (960). These children represent a new element in the cultural diversity profile of the Australian schooling population even though they are concentrated in the elite independent school sector.

CHANGES IN THE EDUCATIONAL LANDSCAPE

The Era of Educational Assimilationism: Late 1940s to Mid-1970s

When immigrant children from the United Kingdom and the displaced persons' camps of continental Europe began arriving in Australia immediately after World War II, the various Australian governments made no special provision for their schooling and appeared to have little interest in it. As a result of the baby boom, students staying longer at school, and the immigrant influx, educational authorities in all systems were barely able to cope with the "education explosion" in the immediate post-war period.

Australia is a federated nation of six states and two territories that individually have constitutional responsibility for educational provision. Except at the university level, education is thus administered at the state/territory level. When the states were unable to cope with the education explosion of the 1950s, the Australian government stepped in in the early 1960s to provide funding for special programs and school building programs.

In each state and territory, the schooling system operates on a tripartite basis between:

1. The *government school system*, completely funded by the government, which educates, according to the 1996 census figures, 73.9% of students at the primary or elementary level and 65.2% at the high school level.
2. The *Catholic school system*, which began in the 1820s as an Irish Catholic system in opposition to the WASP establishment and which now educates 19.8% of the nation's school students. Catholic schools are funded by both federal and state governments on a gradated basis from almost total funding for schools in low SES areas to considerably less in high SES areas.
3. The more loosely aligned *independent school sector* ranging from elite Protestant and Jewish schools to Christian Biblical schools run by fundamentalist groups to, in more recent times, full-time ethnic community and ethnoreligious schools. They are funded on the same gradated basis as Catholic schools.

As well, in all states and territories, there are the part-time ethnic community schools sponsored by community or religious groups and even by entrepreneurial individuals, which are attended by the children of immigrant parents or grandparents to study their cultural and language heritage and, in many cases, to take religious education classes. The Greek community sponsors by far the largest number of such schools, which have been a key factor in the maintenance of the Greek language in a nation that contains the world's third largest Greek-speaking city, namely Melbourne. All these part-time schools receive a very small government subsidy together with assistance for their teacher training needs.

Historically for more than 100 years, government financial assistance to private schools had been a sensitive issue until its resolution in the early 1970s with a final rapprochement between the British Protestant and Irish Catholic sectors, though some on the extreme left continue to mumble against government funding for Catholic and independent schools. Any government that attempted to deny funding to Catholic and Independent schools would be committing political suicide. Such is the change that the discourse now speaks of the Anglo-Celtic majority pitched against the multicultural minority. The pluralist schooling system is now perceived as reflecting Australia's egalitarian tradition, as any community group, once they meet the financial and educational threshold standards, are able to receive government funding to establish a full-time school. Hence, more than ever, a veritable smorgasbord of schools exists in response to parental choice and community initiative.

No other institution was as affected nor affected as quickly by the immigrant influx as the schooling sector. The 1950s has become stereotyped as the era of Menzies, the pro-British Prime Minister; it was the era of assimilationism and Anglo-conformism, publicly accepted with no recognition of cultural maintenance and unquestioned even by the incoming immigrants and refugees, preoccupied as they were with survival in a new environment. The discourse was not of "the other," but of making them "the same;" hence, they were to become "new Australian children" who were deigned to fit easily into the schooling system. No statistics were kept; virtually no research studies were conducted; and the notion of multicultural education, even if it were on the horizon, would have seemed either laughable or utopian. There were no interpreters nor bilingual aides nor special programs.

By the late 1960s, the presence of large numbers of non-English-speaking children from poorly educated, low-skilled families had led to a distinct shift of emphasis from student "success" to student "failure." The paradigm shift also resulted from public concern about education in general and the movement from a teacher-centered to a child-centered philosophy of education. Small-scale studies documented the handicaps besetting students from immigrant backgrounds.

The Australian Department of Education and Science belatedly took the initiative with the introduction of the Child Migrant Education Program in 1970, which eventually became known as the English as a Second Language (ESL) Program. It dovetailed with the Adult Migrant Education Program for adult immigrants, which has remained in place since that time although in 1997-1998 it was privatized as a consequence of the application of economic rationalist principles.

The Australian ESL program remained as the nation's central strategy for more than a quarter of a century. It was totally oriented towards ESL teaching and initially conceived as a stop-gap measure to cope with the backlog of immigrant children who had a handicap in English. Not surprisingly in the early 1970s, it opened a Pandora's box of new realizations, greater difficulties, fresh insights, and new initiatives (Cahill, 1996; Martin, 1975). Within 4 years, with the political punch of the immigrant communities, the program was greatly expanded, major research projects were being planned, and teacher education colleges were beginning to grapple with the issue of educating children in a multilingual and culturally pluralist society. Educationalists began reflecting on the cultural imperialism implicit in Anglo-conformism, but also on the curriculum implications of Australia's heterogeneous population and the squandering of the cultural and linguistic resources of immigrant peoples. The late 1970s was essentially a period of transition to the flowering of multiculturalism and multicultural education during the 1980s.

The Era of Multicultural Education: Late 1970s to Mid-1980s

The years 1979 to 1986 represent the high-water mark in immigrant and multicultural education, when it was the center of intense national focus and interest. The centerpiece of the response used to be the Commonwealth English as a Second Language Program with its two elements, namely, the on-arrival element for newly arriving students and the general support program for students in schools across each system.

The research activity of the 1970s continued into the 1980s and indeed burgeoned. Particular focuses were immigrant children and social mobility, the educational performance of particular ethnic groups, the educational and social experience of ethnic minority female students from immigrant families, bilingualism, and teaching strategies for ESL children.

In 1979, the Australian Multicultural Education Program was established, and as a national program it functioned for 7 years until it was axed in 1986. It gave a certain national cohesion to immigrant and intercultural education that culminated in the stillborn document, "Education in and for a Multicultural Society," the final publication in 1987 of the National Advisory and Coordinating Committee for Multicultural Education, and the last time that immigrant minority groups had a formal role in educational policy advice at the national level.

A group of educationalists led by McNamara prepared a report that was to serve as the guiding document for the implementation of the Multicultural Education Program (Commonwealth Schools Commission, 1979). Its concept of multicultural education was based on the belief that the various cultural traditions represented in Australia had something of value to share with other traditions and something of value to learn from them. The report identified six interrelated elements within the school program as the core of *education for a multicultural society*:

1. General programs or studies that aim at fostering in all students an appreciation of the dignity of the contribution made by the cultures that exist within Australian society;
2. Particular programs or studies that aim to present to all students an opportunity to study the historical, social, aesthetic, literary, and cultural backgrounds and traditions of particular ethnic groups resident in Australia;
3. International and intercultural studies that aim at fostering in all students an appreciation of the dignity of the contribution made by the cultures that exist within Australian society;
4. Community language programs that aim to give the opportunity to all children to study an Australian language other than English;
5. English as a second language programs that are aimed at enabling students from non-English-speaking backgrounds to learn English to a level of competence to ensure that the students can participate both in the work of the schools and the activities of the wider community; and
6. Bilingual education programs that allow students to learn conventional subjects in an Australian language other than English.

The McNamara Report was broad in its scope, placing the emphasis both on English and on languages other than English, including emphasis on transitional bilingual education programs. The efforts in this select bilingual education area were to be generally shortlived, mainly because it was unusual to have an elementary school with a sufficient concentration of children from a particular language group to warrant such programs. Schools were, and remain, almost always characterized by multilinguality.

The Report emphasized that the multicultural perspective was applicable to *all* students in *all* Australian schools, in the formal curriculum and in the "hidden" curriculum. Embedded in this thinking, though it has never been accepted at a public discourse level, was the notion that all Australians, whether from a mainstream or minority background, had an ethnic background. The Report was later to be criticized for placing too much emphasis on a so-called "lifestyle" approach to education inasmuch as it concentrated on cultural and linguistic maintenance and studies in ethnic diversity and neglected the notion that multicultural education is primarily about *life chances*, about increasing the chances for all children, especially those from immigrant minority backgrounds, to have access to the full range of occupational, educational, economic, political and aesthetic opportunities, although it was argued that this life chance aspect was more or less covered by its sister program, the much larger ESL program.

Another issue was terminology in referring to children and adolescents from immigrant family backgrounds. There has been, and there remains, no nationally accepted terminology. Documents from the early 1970s usually referred to "migrant children," a term that did not distinguish between those who came from homes where English was spoken and those who did not, although it usually referred to the latter. The most widely used phrase has been "non-English-speaking background" or NESB. But in some systems, its use was actively discouraged in favor of LOTE (language other than English) because there was disquiet about the negative implications of NESB, which was said to reflect a dominant monolingualism and a lack of appreciation of bilingualism.

Even in official statistics, the acronym NESB is differently defined, thus making comparisons difficult. A plethora of replacement acronyms were developed: MLOTE (main language other than English), LOTE (language other than English), LBOTE (language background other than English) and CBOTE (cultural background other than English). This was partly a reflection of the lack of national cohesion since the mid-1980s and partly mirrors the complexity of the immigrant intake. There are also practical difficulties: For example, should an immigrant child raised by English-speaking Burgher parents in Sri Lanka or a child born of an English-speaking man and Filipino woman be included in the NESB category? Behind this dispute lay a funding issue insofar as states and territories were funded on the basis of the NESB category (i.e., a child born in a non-English-speaking country or with at least one parent born in a non-English-speaking country) so it was in their interests to keep the definition as broad as possible. There was much talk about one Australian family—that of the Australian Labor Prime Minister, Paul Keating (1991-1996) who had married a Dutch-born airline stewardess and whose four children technically came under the NESB category.

Lack of standardization has implications for data collection and identification of needs, especially language needs. During the 1990s, attention has focused on a definition revolving around the notion of "main language other than English spoken in the home," but this has also been criticized because the linguistic situation in immigrant homes is often complex, and it is not easy to say which is the main language spoken in the home because of the language shift occurring in the family and community.

The Multicultural Education Program always had its opponents. The concept of multiculturalism in education had been strongly debated within Australia with scholars such as Bullivant (1981) being openly contemptuous of the whole multicultural enterprise because it did not deal explicitly enough with the concept of race and, because in terms of school achievement, lower class White Anglo-Australians were said to be the group most at risk rather than the children from immigrant families with their high aspirations and cohesive family patterns. Thus in 1983, the Australian Schools Commission commissioned a review of the program (Cahill, 1984, 1986).

The *Review of the Multicultural Education Program* (Cahill, 1984, 1986) found that although it had many lasting achievements, it had not brought about substantial and lasting change in the Australian schooling system. The review team concluded that the program had provided a base for implementing and testing the multicultural education philosophy and had sharpened the debate about multiculturalism in Australian education, but it also illustrated how difficult it was to shift the perceptions of teachers and students and how much time it took to develop expertise and program sophistication. Programs succeeded when aims were clear, realistic, and achievable, were supported and implemented by knowledgeable and skilled staff, and when the program was accompanied by teaching staff education. Noteworthy was the randomness of the process notwithstanding the constant emphasis on multiculturalism.

Overall, 14 % of Australia's 10,000+ schools had at that time received at least one grant from the Multicultural Education Program, but very few schools with low numbers of children from non-English-speaking backgrounds applied for funds. Underlying this pattern was a perception that "multicultural" equalled "immigrant" or "non-English" and, further, a failure to explore the dimensions of the different ethnic heritages of British and Irish peoples within the multicultural framework. Its non-English heritage character was interpreted, albeit unfairly, as anti-English.

The Multicultural Education Program during its short life till its 1986 axing provided a springboard for later initiatives. But by 1986 the pressure for change was building. Implementation failures were found in the ESL Program, and, as already suggested, there was the questioning of the whole multicultural enterprise. Even those who were sympathetic felt that the program needed to confront more openly the issues of racism, that it was based on narrow definitions of ethnic culture and an individualistic notion of ethnicity, and did not sufficiently address the need for a total reformulation of Australian history and the evolving identity of the Australian people (Kalantzis & Cope, 1984; Rizvi, 1986; Singh, 1998a).

Nor did it address sufficiently issues of citizenship or civics education. In fact, citizenship has never been a contentious issue from an educational perspective. Citizenship is available relatively easily in Australia, now after 2 years of permanent residency; permanent residents from the moment they arrive in Australia are entitled to all the benefits of the state except for the right to vote and public service employment, though their social security entitlements have now been curtailed for 2 years under the current conservative government. Very late in the 1980s civics education came onto the public agenda, and some initiatives have taken place though controversy has been generated from left and right perspectives as to curriculum content (e.g., should a civics education include details about trade unions and their history and contribution to Australian society? Should it acknowledge the Aborigines as prior occupiers of the Australian landmass?, etc.)

However, right throughout the 1980s the philosophy of multiculturalism was being enacted in many different ways at both national and state level. At the state level, ethnic affairs or multicultural commissions were established by every state government designed to show its large immigrant electorate that their concerns and aspirations were to the fore in government thinking. These commissions continue to function despite the setbacks that have occurred nationally.

At the national level, the Office of Multicultural Affairs was established and located in the Department of the Prime Minister and Cabinet, principally to oversee the implementation of the Access and Equity Strategy that required every public service department to ensure that its services met the needs of ethnic minority groups, both indigenous and immigrant. Needless to say, this did not make the Office popular within the Canberra bureaucracy with its right to peruse every Cabinet submission. It was established in response to the community outcry at the cuts in 1986 but it was eventually to disappear finally in 1996 as the climate changed in the mid-1990s. It remained a contested proposal with the Labour opposition in 1999 promising to establish a revamped Office of Multicultural and Citizenship affairs if elected to office.

The principal accomplishment of the Office of Multicultural Affairs was to develop the official definition or description of multiculturalism as articulated in the *1989 National Agenda for a Multicultural Australia*. The 1989 formulation brought together and synthesized the three strands of thought that had competed against each other through the 1980s, namely, the emphasis on ethnicity and the politics of identity and cultural maintenance, the emphasis on life chances and the need to create a society where everyone has the opportunity to develop their talents and succeed, and the need for productive diversity whereby the talents and skills of immigrants could be fully utilized for the common good of the nation.

The 1989 definition was built around the notions of commitment to the nation and equality of opportunity, and acceptance of basic structures and values including the Constitution and the rule of law, tolerance and equality, parliamentary democracy, freedom of speech and religion, English as the national language, and equality of the sexes. It is based on eight underlying principles:

1. All Australians should have a commitment to Australia and share responsibility for furthering national interests.
2. All Australians should be able to enjoy the basic right of freedom from discrimination on the basis of race, ethnicity, religion, and culture.
3. All Australians should enjoy equal life chances and have equitable access and an equitable share of the resources that governments manage on behalf of the community.
4. All Australians should have the opportunity fully to participate in society and in the decisions that directly affect them.
5. All Australians should be able to develop and make use of their potential for Australia's social and economic development.
6. All Australians should have the opportunity to acquire and develop proficiency in English and languages other than English, and to develop cross-cultural understanding.
7. All Australians should be able to develop and share their cultural heritage.
8. Australian institutions should acknowledge, reflect, and respond to the cultural diversity of the Australian community.

It revolves around three dimensions:

1. The dimension of social justice: the right of all Australians to equality of treatment and opportunity, and the removal of barriers of race, ethnicity, culture, religion, language, gender, or place of birth.
2. The dimension of cultural identity: the right of all Australians, within carefully defined limits, to express and share their individual cultural heritage, including their language and culture.
3. The dimension of economic efficiency: the need to maintain, develop, and utilize for Australian economic development the skills and talents of all Australians regardless of background.

In a further evolution in April 1999, the conservative Australian government without much fanfare, after much delay and to allay the fears of the ethnic community lobby, adopted a new meaning of Australian multiculturalism as "a united and harmonious Australia built on the foundations of our democracy, and developing its continually evolving nationhood by recognizing, embracing, valuing, and investing in its heritage and diversity" (National Multicultural Advisory Council, 1999, p. 37). This new meaning was built around, first, the ten values of commitment to Australia, freedom, a fair go, democracy, rule of law, tolerance, mutual respect, political equality, equal opportunity, and nondiscrimination and, second, the four principles for living with cultural diversity:

1. The Principle of Civic Duty—whereby all Australians are obliged to support and commit themselves to the basic structures and principles of Australian society, which guarantee freedom, equality, and the flourishing of diversity.
2. The Principle of Cultural Respect—which, subject to the law, gives the right to express one's own culture and beliefs and a reciprocal obligation to allow others to do the same.
3. The Principle of Social Equity—which gives all Australians the right to equality of treatment and freedom from discrimination, no matter what their race, culture, religion, language, location, gender, or place of birth.
4. The Principle of Productive Diversity—which encourages the cultural, social, and economic dividends from the diversity of the population for the well-being of all Australians.

The revised definition, although welcomed after a long period of government ambivalence, placed greater emphasis on democracy and citizenship, implying an unstated fear that the social policy of multiculturalism was in fact a de facto policy of separatism and division. It also implied a resistance to the notion of dual citizenship.

Toward a Culturally Inclusive Curriculum: Mid-1980s to Mid-1990s

In 1986 a series of Australian budgetary decisions, motivated by the imperatives of national deficit reduction and the beginning of the application of Thatcherite economic rationalist principles, severely jolted the multicultural education area. The ESL Program was severely cut and the Multicultural Education Program was axed, as previously noted.

Since that time, the educational landscape has changed in which schools have been asked to provide a higher quality of service on the basis of reduced funding. There has been much rhetoric about efficiency and quality when quality has clearly diminished. From the immigrant and multicultural perspective of this paper, the most critical of these changes have been:

1. the downsizing of the teaching force in many systems as governments have sought to rein in their budgets as the principles of the economic rationalist philosophy have been applied, resulting in greater efficiencies, higher teacher-student ratios, greater stress for schooling staff and the shift toward principals becoming engaged in fund-raising and marketing exercises to ensure the viability of their school;

2. an accompanying discourse in education and its commodification with new terminology such as "the educational product," "customers and clients," "quality assurance," "schools of the future," "schools of the new millenium," and "navigator schools" while the notions of "access" and "equity" that were the catchcries of the multicultural movement in the late 1980s are no longer in vogue;

3. school devolution and autonomy, and, at secondary level, the abolition of zoning with a consequent movement towards elitism in many systems in such schemes as selective schools and schools of the future;

4. the introduction of information technology and the various curriculum changes, with the shifts in priorities toward such things as computer education and Asian languages of commercial importance, and away from the languages spoken by immigrant communities;

5. the increased retention rate of students into the upper secondary levels since the early 1980s and the changes in final school year and university requirements;

6. the growth of the part-time and full-time ethnic schooling sector and its growing interface with the mainstream systems, and a push from some sections, especially in the state of Victoria, to privatize all schools by abolishing the distinction between government and non-government schools.

The data from the national *Immigration and Schooling* study (Cahill, 1996) revealed a troubled educational landscape. When interviewed in 1993 and 1994, the survey of teachers found that teachers, although generally satisfied with their teaching positions, were low in morale in many government systems. All teachers are less than impressed by the government changes, especially those of state governments, which they have been required to endure and to implement. However, the overwhelming majority believe that over the years the schooling system has responded well, if not very well, to the needs of children from LOTE family backgrounds, though there is an important dissenting minority, especially those working in language education. Moreover, less than half felt that the response has been good in regard to refugee children, especially those partly schooled.

Comparison between studies done in 1983-1984 and 1993-1994 revealed the increasing professionalism of the teaching force, the greater competence of specialist teachers of immigrant students, and the leadership of more confident and knowledgeable principals. Schools are better fitted and equipped than a decade previously. Nonetheless, as will be documented, many of the gains of the 1980s are now clearly in reverse; there is a sense of stepping back from the enthusiasm and the energies of the early 1980s to respond to the needs of the immigrant and refugee students as a certain tiredness and smugness and covert hostility have crept in. In 1996, the hostility became much more overt.

The paper, *Education in and for a Multicultural Society: Issues and Strategies for Policy Making* (NACCME, 1987), is the last national document wholly focused on multicultural education. Moving away from the 1979 McNamara Report, this report developed the notion of "equitable multiculturalism" as distinct from the earlier "pluralistic multiculturalism," the latter described as concerned in the main with the "celebration of difference." Equitable multiculturalism revolved around the three key elements of equity, understanding, and identity. Applied to education, these elements were concerned with issues of equality of access and participation for ethnic minorities, intercultural education, and the development of cultural and ethnic identity. The emphasis also changed to the concept of "mainstreaming" which firstly involved ensuring that ethnic minority students were appropriately initiated into the mainstream of Australian life and that the perspective of mainstream Australian children from Anglo-Celtic backgrounds was broadened to be multicultural, that is, cross-culturally knowledgeable and attuned and recognizing that the Australian identity is very broad, implying that there are many ways of being an Australian, not just the White Anglo-Australian way. Otherness was to be celebrated as a virtue.

Hence, the early 1980s approach gave way to a culturally inclusive or cultural learnings approach across the curriculum. The social context in which the shift has occurred included a growing questioning of the possibility of the multicultural ideal, particularly during the Gulf War in 1991, the Greek-Macedonian dispute that had a rather nasty ethnocentric content in Australia, and especially the rise of the Hanson phenomenon in 1996. The Hanson phenomenon was initiated by a Queenslander, Pauline Hanson, who portrayed herself as an antipolitician and won election to the Australian parliament in 1996 as part of a move to the right in Australian political life, though she lost her seat at the election late in 1998 in which her party, however, won about 8% of the vote. In the eyes of some, she represents perhaps, as the last elected bigot, the final gasp of White Australia. Others are less sure, given the "yellow peril" fear that lies deep in the Australian psyche. Her rise to prominence stemmed from many factors including the recent successes of the Aboriginal land rights claims, the success of Asian countries, and the growth of the Asian communities in Australia. To all these, she was opposed. She has been vociferously opposed to multiculturalism, arguing that "all Australians should be treated the same." This mantra appeals to many Australians—the other is to become the same.

Hansonism represents the rise of the racist right in Australia as a reaction against the very real progress in changing Australian attitudes and against globalization generally. The growing concern over racial violence that should not be exaggerated led the shift away from a shallow multiculturalism. The previous approach in recent times was criticized as being based on too individualistic a notion of ethnicity and failing to come to grips with powerful globalization forces that are flattening cultural differentiation (Singh & Gilbert, 1992). They have argued that despite its worthy ideals, racism rather than egalitarianism has been European Australia's defining characteristic. More recently, Singh has strengthened his critique. "Simply infusing the existing curriculum with anti-racist and anti-sexist perspectives may merely add novel content to an outdated imperialistic, patriarchal framework. Additionally, it is not clear on what and whose terms ethnic minority interests and perspectives are to be included in the curriculum" (Singh, 1998b, p. 321).

Working within this reformulated historical approach, Singh and Gilbert built on previous theoretical work (Kemmis, Cole, & Suggett, 1983; Rizvi, 1986) to develop the notion of "cultural learnings," an approach that places less emphasis on the personal clarification of individual and social identity but enables students to clarify and evaluate public and private discourse in terms of the sociopolitical and economic place of racial and ethnic minority groups. The aim of educational programs is to create, first, skilled, reflective, and qualified workers for Australia's well-being and, second, active citizens, informed on Australia's traditions and cultural heritages. "There has been an identifiable racial order which has linked the apparatus of power and control to the racial clarification of individuals and groups. It may, therefore, not be simply a matter of including 'race' and ethnicity in the curriculum, but there may be a need to rearticulate the way in which they are presently represented" (Singh & Gilbert, 1992, p. 28).

Over the past decade, many curriculum reforms, especially in the area of social education, have been implemented across the different levels of the schooling system. It is fair to say that almost without exception they included a "culturally inclusive" approach based on the recognition of Australia as ethnically diverse. Although driven by Australia's immigrant dimension, it has also been focusing on the development of Asian literacy and the aspiration that Australian students develop the necessary cultural understandings for interaction with the Asia-Pacific region, an aspiration only partly shaken by the Asian financial crisis.

Cultural diversity and inclusivity has also been broadened to characterize difference in ethnicity, class, gender, socioeconomic status, geographical location, religion, sexual preference, and age, and is an all-encompassing concept, to be related to the global, community, workplace, education, and individual contexts.

Nonetheless, there are several issues that have emerged that are of grave concern to the multicultural lobby. First is the issue of Asian studies and Asian language studies in schools for which there is a 15-year implementation plan that in a sense replaces the earlier emphasis on a multicultural approach that was highly European focused. It has been driven by economic imperatives toward Japan, China, Korea, and Indonesia, while neglecting the languages of other Asian communities in Australia (e.g., Vietnamese). Singh (1995) expressed concern about the tendency to see Asia as undifferentiated, and has strong reservations that Asian curriculum projects can adequately give representation to "the diversity of authentic Asian voices."

A second issue concerns the growth of private, full-time ethnic and ethnoreligious schools. In the past few years, the two major states of New South Wales and Victoria have seen the establishment of primary and secondary schools by the Arabic, Armenian, Coptic Orthodox, Greek and Greek Orthodox, Islamic, Jewish, Lutheran, Maronite, and Turkish Muslim communities. It is claimed they are socially divisive, creating ethnic and educational enclaves and being the antithesis of multiculturalism. The other viewpoint is that they express Australia's religious and cultural pluralism. All are English-language schools though they may teach their heritage or religious language. Invariably they are staffed by Australian-trained teachers. Immigrant parents choose these schools because of their dissatisfaction with government schools. Rightly or wrongly, they perceive their local government schools as lacking discipline, giving too little homework, and not insisting on traditional values regarding adolescent sexuality. Questions have been raised about their lack of contact with other types of Australian schools, their quality of education, and their curriculum content, for example, what do Islamic schools teach about Arabs and vice versa? Singh (1998b) worried that the separation of community-based schools may dilute both critiques of the educational system and the garnering of support for overcoming the educational disadvantages suffered by the disadvantaged. In any case, a well-formulated policy to deal with this new element in the smorgasbord of Australian schools is totally lacking.

Multiculturalism and Multicultural Education: The late 1990s

The emergence of Hansonism in 1996 was not a new phenomenon for it had been slowly building up in a zigzag fashion over the previous decade. What was different was the lack of national leadership. Prime Minister Howard with his theory of political correctness unfortunately borrowed from the United States and reinforced with a mantra that Australians cannot feel guilt for the disadvantages of indigenous groups created the political space for Hansonism to flourish. The immediate factors behind Hansonism were the favorable land rights decisions in 1992 and 1996 for indigenous groups on which both the Labour and Liberal governments had failed to inform the people with a thorough public education campaign, and the need to expunge Australia's long and deep racist heritage. Portrayed as such, the issue was never guilt, but justice and appropriate accommodation to the legitimate aspirations of the Aboriginal peoples.

Another factor was the declining support for the immigration program even though successive governments have never followed public opinion on immigration. They have always been ahead of it. There have continued to exist the false perceptions of uncontrolled and illegal immigration and of widespread immigrant welfare fraud. A third factor has been the influence of environmental fundamentalism even though environmentalists by and large are very opposed to the Hanson agenda. Nonetheless, the impression has been created that "Australia is full" and cannot take more immigrants, even though the Australian birthrate is now below replacement levels.

The Hanson phenomenon has highlighted the growing gap between the educated classes, both left and right—the so-called "chardonnay set"—and general society. The former have a different vision of a pluralist, globalized Australia and the directions it ought to move whereas the latter remain unconvinced.

Beneath these trends is that the support for the Hanson vision of a fortress and racist Australia has come principally from downwardly mobile groups in both urban and rural contexts who have lost out in the globalization process, and from other groups, often middle class, who fear losing out in job competition, underpinned by a general fear about losing their social status and identity. Xenophobia and prejudice can be "interpreted as ways of reassuring the national self and its boundaries, as attempts of making sense of the world in times of crisis" (Wimmer, 1997, p. 27). The downwardly mobile and the insecure no longer feel themselves to be the "legitimate owners" of the state. They want to keep reserved their place in the social fabric, especially now that the promises of the welfare state may no longer be able to be kept. The dominant mood of this mobilization has been that of resentment: resentment against the city, resentment against the political elites, resentment against globalization, and resentment against any other convenient scapegoats, such as Asian immigrants.

In a scapegoat mechanism, the resentment shifts in the job competition stakes to the rivalry between more established groups and the minority groups. As Wimmer (1997) has documented so well, it subsequently aligns itself to the cultural differentness argument that suggests that selected foreign cultures are incompatible with the mainstream. They are too different, they are too "other." The argument goes on to suggest that those from the Third World, even more so than those from the Mediterranean world, are incapable of assimilation. There is the phobia of being swamped, the phobia of intermarriage and racially mixed grandchildren, the phobia of a non-English world, the phobia of being bypassed in status and wealth. It is a kind of moral panic. There is also much talk about "ghettoes" for cultural incompatibility is said to lead to ghettoization, even though in Australia there are no ghettoes. The others, who become "strangers in our midst" or "the intruders" into our ideal community, the mythical Anglo-Saxon Australia, are perceived as preventing the state from accomplishing its true task, namely, to look after the well-being of its "owners" (Wimmer, 1997). Advocates of a multicultural society and a perceived divided society are thus seen as traitors to the common national cause of looking after Anglo-Australia.

The Demise of the ESL Education Program. During the 1980s, there was a spirited and critical debate that had strong ideological overtones regarding the relationship between immigration, education, and social and occupational mobility. It centered around the educational performance of students from immigrant backgrounds, the impact of performance on vocational attainment, and the subsequent social and economic mobility of students from immigrant heritage families. Entry into university was often used as a surrogate variable for occupational and educational mobility though evidence never focussed on the type and level of tertiary course. The parameters of the debate were (a) access to all levels of the education system by immigrant students compared to students from mainstream monolingual backgrounds, and their relative performance within each stage of the educational process; and (b) the transfer of educational attainment into university entry, career outcomes, employment opportunities, and occupational and economic status for ethnic minority students compared to students from mainstream backgrounds.

Researchers such as Bullivant, Birrell, Seitz, and Williams began to argue in the mid-1980s that contrary to the received wisdom of the previous two decades, ethnic minority children had done well in "the educational race." Birrell and Seitz (1986) attributed their success to the strong and disciplined family support system, the peasant core value to survive in the face of adversity, and their ethnic pride and cohesiveness. Bullivant (1988) spoke of the ethnic success ethic, suggesting it was no longer possible to speak of educational inequality in respect of NESB students and that more focus had to be given to lower class Anglo-Australian students.

However, Jakubowicz and Castles, among others, argued that previous analyses had failed to address the existence of an underclass. They suggested that "while Birrell's Monash University may have significant numbers of sons of Italian and Greek working class fathers in universities, so too do the dole queues" (Jakubowicz & Castles, 1986, p. 9). Kalantzis and Cope (1986) at the height of the debate argued that it was dominated by the use of aggregate data, and important subcategories within the collectivity of so-called migrant children were glossed over.

The National Equity Program for Schools (NEPS) was introduced in 1993 by the Keating government, bringing together under this program various special programs such as the Disadvantaged Schools' Program and the Country Education Program. The rhetoric said it was to maximize the educational outcomes for disadvantaged students and equalize educational outcomes for targeted groups affected by factors such as poverty, isolation, disability, family breakdown, drugs, violence, and non-English-speaking background. The ESL component represented more than a third of the Program in funding terms. The "broadband" nature of the program implied that funds in subprograms such as the Special Education or Student at Risk components could be transferred between subprograms to target disadvantaged groups nominated by the Commonwealth. However, the ESL component was effectively protected through being quarantined.

One view at the time suggested that NEPS was taking account of the intersecting disadvantage of class, ethnicity, gender, and so on, and permitted resource shifts in response to changing needs or priorities. An alternative view was that it became a de facto form of recurrent funding, giving greater scope to education systems to shift funds as they pleased in response to vaguely enunciated priorities or to vociferous pressure groups. With the election of the Howard government in 1996, it became a transitional arrangement to the abolition of the general support element of the Commonwealth ESL Program after 26 years of existence and its meshing with other equity programs (DSP and STAR) into the Early Literacy Program, which has become the Literacy Program, which has, in turn, become the Literacy and Numeracy Program.

Whatever the administrative maze games, the result is a downgrading of ESL focus and funding. If the nation is at the crossroads with the rise of Hansonism and the failure of national leadership, so is ESL education in schools. The de-quarantining must also be seen in the broad context of the cut of immigrant services generally. ESL teachers are being relocated, their professional specializations are not being recognized, and ESL support units in education systems are disappearing.

With the 1997 National Literacy Action Plan, the Ministers of Education across the nation have agreed that "by the end of primary school, all children will be numerate, and able to read, write, and spell at an appropriate level, and that the impetus of this will carry them forward into secondary schooling, post-secondary education, and employment" (DEETYA, 1998, p. 4). Literacy levels for Years 3 and 5 will be reported to parents against agreed national literacy standards, and, where appropriate, an individual student learning improvement plan will be implemented. From 1999, every child entering primary school will be assessed for their literacy needs with at-risk students being identified and special strategies put in place. Schools failing to meet agreed levels of student performance will be assisted to develop literacy improvement plans.

The Action Plan with its emphasis on early literacy clearly addresses one of the concerns of unmet need reported in the *Immigration and Schooling* study (Cahill, 1996). As well as the needs of the new cohorts of NESB students identified earlier, unmet need focused particularly on two groups: (a) those, both overseas-born and Australian-born, starting school for the first time at the age of 5 with virtually no capacity to speak English, and (b) the growing ESL need at upper secondary level as a consequence of the higher retention rate.

Students who had satisfactorily passed lower- and middle-secondary levels had their English-language deficiencies, especially in written English, exposed and unmasked as they moved into the upper secondary level. They were more likely to be identified as ESL learners. Literacy is not merely a Year 4 accomplishment as the Commonwealth Government is currently emphasizing—it is a process that continues beyond secondary schooling well into adulthood. One aspect of this has been that, although there are other factors involved, Chinese and Vietnamese students increasingly chose science and mathematics subjects where English language demand was seemingly less. However, the Commonwealth is intending to push ahead with assessment testing at Years 7 and 9 or 10.

Applying the (Total Quality Management) TQM and other similar management models, the Australian government emphasis is now on outcomes as performance indicators rather than inputs. It represents an opportunity for ESL professionals insofar as they can assist in setting nationally agreed benchmarks and subgoals in respect of different types of ESL learners, and insisting, with appropriate funding, that these benchmarks are achieved. In other words, the emphasis on assessment outcomes at Years 3 and 5 and eventually at Years 7 and 9 or 10 implies that ESL teaching skills ought to be much in demand. However, this is a big "but." In this deregulated market, the ESL professional lobby groups will need to define more carefully their core business as teachers and the specific skills they bring to Australian classrooms.

There are still two fundamental problems with the present strategy. First, the current Commonwealth approach assumes that ESL education and literacy education are interchangeable. Certainly they are not independent of each other, but are rather intersecting and, in another sense, ESL education is broader than first language education and its close relative, remedial education. In defining its core business, the ESL teaching is based on second language acquisition principles and, more broadly, that good ESL teaching addresses the cultural competency needs of second language learning children. Second, more and more, aside from the on-arrival element, ESL policy has become detached from settlement policy. The demise of the general support element of the ESL Program implies that the Australian government can no longer claim that it has a long-term settlement strategy for the children of immigrants—immigrants who for many decades were invited to settle in this country and who have contributed immensely to its development.

Why has there not been a strong reaction from the immigrant communities? In his 1984 review of the ESL Program, Campbell suggested that the ESL industry detach itself from the multicultural lobby represented by the ethnic communities. This in fact occurred after the 1986 crisis. In retrospect this was unfortunate. The main political support for the ESL school program in the Australian context can only come from the ethnic communities and perhaps from the teacher unions. Yet this detaching resulted in the ethnic communities losing interest in the schooling issue, perhaps because the children of middle class community leaders do very well at school or because the movement into the third- and fourth-generation by the children of the larger, longer established, and more powerful immigrants groups has diverted attention away from the greater complexity of the educational landscape. Instead, they have focused on other issues such as the ethnic aged. Yet arguing for a reallocation of resources directed at the real needs will not be easy. At the same time, many immigrant families have also been victims of globalization and economic rationalism. Many of the so-called Aussie battlers are immigrant—poor, defeated migrants who do not have the English language skills and the organizational skills within an Australian context to voice their discontent. Their voices have been drowned out, and voices such as that of FECCA (Federation of the Ethnic Communities' Councils of Australia) have been far from vocal.

Hence, in contemporary Australia, there is a struggle of titanic proportions occurring between a White Anglo-Australian restorationism and a pluralist, democratically based multiculturalism. This debate has left the advocates of a multicultural education in a state of tension, if not despair, as these contradictory and dialectical forces vie against each other. But the debate has brought home how foundational to the multicultural perspective is the reformulation of Australian history to incorporate the voices of the Aboriginal peoples as well as the voices of immigrants, women, and other voiceless minorities. In November 1999, the Australian nation rejected the opportunity to become a republic without Queen Elizabeth as head of state. This occurred because of deft political maneuvering by a monarchist Prime Minister and because the republican movement was divided over the type of republic it would endorse—in particular whether the president should be directly elected by the people or should be elected by a two-thirds majority of the Federal Parliament.

Now that public opinion has veered to the right with antidemocratic and racist shifts but is likely to return more to the center, the proponents of a multicultural education approach are in the process of regrouping and rethinking their traditional objectives within broader frameworks. Singh (1998a) has argued that it needs to be placed within the context of national identity with the present lack of distinctiveness of "Australianness" with an imitative Coca-Cola media output, a flag that still contains the Union Jack, and the national head-of-state belonging to the mother country. In particular, it needs to be framed within a democratic education framework that encourages a core dialogic component. This dialogue needs to incorporate the diverse voices and diverse histories, ensuring a voice of indigenous and immigrant minority groups, acknowledging the different interpretations of Australia's past, analyzing the situations of one's own identity groups, eliminating disadvantage and alleviating vulnerability, and developing citizen action competencies.

Additionally, Singh stressed the need for structurally disadvantaged groups to have objective knowledge and critical examination of the totality of their socioeconomic and psychoeducational milieu that both assists and hinders self-understanding, and diminishes ethnic self-concept. Curriculum content is of central significance in order to ensure ethnic minority students have the knowledge and skills for productive work in the post-industrial age. "For instance, they need to be taught about the nation's income and property distribution, the ownership of industry and commerce, and the implications for themselves of resource allocation and job opportunities" (Singh, 1998b, p. 327).

Kalantzis and Cope, who likewise have been leaders in the multicultural education field for close to two decades, have developed their thinking on multiculturalism in the context of work through their notion of "productive diversity" and their critique of cultural over-generalizations. Building on the notions of the centrality of culture in a globalized world and of the superiority of the culture-as-negotiated-differences metaphor rather than culture-as-sameness, Cope and Kalantzis (1997) developed a variegated and rich notion of productive diversity for a new global/local environment where local diversity and interconnectedness are more critical productive factors than ever in the post-Fordism period. They developed their model around five constructs:

1. flexibility, which allows for the productive integration of difference, entailing responsiveness, interactiveness, synergy, and the reflexive and complementary relationship of differences;
2. the resource of multiplicity, which includes not only the necessity of multiskilling but also quality and complementary relationships;
3. the operative principle of devolution, which is not mere dispersal but positive cohesion generated through diversity;
4. the principle of negotiation, where people develop and use multiple layers of identity and multiple ways of communication; and

5. the end product of diversity as a principle of social order and productive community.

Within this context, they develop the notion of citizenship not merely national, but corporate, global, and so on, and extend it to education that moves well beyond any civics education or any simplistic cultural inclusive approach.

In their most recent contribution, Kalantzis and Cope (1999) have critiqued previous conceptions of multiculturalism as "superficial pluralism" and have articulated "a critical, postpluralist, postprogessivist multicultural education," whereby the core culture is transformed by multilayered allegiances in an internationalized society that nonetheless retains its orientation to social equity. This implies a transformation of mainstream structures in response to diversity and a set of variant pedagogies for all students with the emphasis on enhancing life chances and on developing skills for diversity and socially powerful knowledge.

Hence, the newer approaches are not just concerned with difference or with the "other" as other, but with the other as belonging to the core of Australianness. The cultural inclusive approach has ensured that ethnicity and gender have not been marginalized. Essentially the Hanson phenomenon has not been about racism so much as about identity and citizenship, commitment and cohesion, and Australia's place in an interdependent world. These multicultural approaches will be concerned, not just with difference, but with the ongoing development and redevelopment of shared values (Singh, 1998a).

A particular feature of the multicultural education movement, as it positions itself and however it might eventually be labeled, has been the increasing rapprochement between the indigenous and immigrant perspectives in this repositioning. It is likely that in the immediate future it will be articulated in the context of three interrelated ideas (a) the globalization/localization interconnectedness, (b) cultural and linguistic diversity, and (c) international and crosscultural work practice.

What about the agenda of Australia's indigenous communities? Throughout the 1980s and 1990s, the advocates of Aboriginal education policies and of multicultural education policies have kept their distance, primarily because Aboriginal community leaders feared that their aspirations would be swamped by the much larger, immigrant-focused multicultural movement, given that Aborigines and Torres Strait Islanders represent about 2% of the population. They feared being seen as merely another ethnic minority rather than as the indigenous minority with special claims as the original inhabitants and explorers and discoverers of Terra Australia. However, in the emerging conceptualizations of Singh, Kalantzis, and Cope, the Aboriginal agenda is very much at the center of their curriculum framework though in practical political terms, Aboriginal and immigrant community leaders would see themselves more in competition for scarce public resources than in a cooperative relationship built around minority status.

CONCLUSION

Both the educational and immigration fields have undergone great changes in the past decade. The shift to corporatism in schools has endangered the educational pathways for at least some students from immigrant backgrounds and the education system has not responded appropriately to the changes in permanent and temporary migration and settlement patterns. The current danger in Australia is that a more sophisticated version of the old assimilationism is being constructed, operating in tandem with a nationalism that is more narrow than need be. The Hanson phenomenon illustrates and has exacerbated this trend, though in early 2000 Hanson's political movement became badly fractured as a result of ideological feuds and administrative incompetence. A new and perhaps stronger political splinter party has been formed though its future remains problematic. It has eschewed previous racist, anti-Asian policies and adopted an antiglobalization, protectionist stance, though all these extreme right wing groups are aggressively opposed to any concession to Aboriginal landright demands.

The challenge remains, but is more critical than ever, of creating pathways for students, regardless of their background, to become future citizens not only of Australia but also of the world, able to interact interculturally across national, religious, ethnic, language, and class borders. All this may be in jeopardy, especially at the secondary level. As one principal remarked, "If only both teachers and students had a little more help..." (Cahill, 1996). Educational inequality in respect of certain sections of the immigrant community is now reemerging as a greater issue, especially in lower SES, high/medium migrant density areas.

The sting of change is not in change itself but in responding assertively and appropriately to the changing circumstances. The Hanson debate has been not so much about racism as about moral values and a viable vision for Australia. It is time to exorcise the ghost of White Australia; it is time to proclaim that cultural and language differences can exist in an Australia formed around shared core values. If it is the debate that Australia had to have, it is also the debate that Australia has to win.

REFERENCES

Birrell, R., & Seitz, A. (1986). The ethnic problem in education: The emergence and definition of an issue. Paper presented at the 1986 National Research Conference on Ethnicity and Multiculturalism, Melbourne.

Boothby, N. (1992). Displaced children: Psychological theory and practice from the field. *Journal of Refugee Studies, 5*(2), 106 -122.

Bullivant, B. (1981). *Race, ethnicity and curriculum.* Melbourne: Macmillan.

Bullivant, B. (1988). The ethnic success ethic challenges conventional wisdom about immigrant disadvantages in Australia. *Australian Journal of Education, 32*(2), 223 -243.

Cahill, D. (1984). *Review of the Commonwealth Multicultural Education Program.* Canberra: Commonwealth Schools Commission.

Cahill, D. (1986) An evaluation of Australia's Multicultural Education Program. *Journal of Multilingual and Multicultural Development, 7*(1), 55 -69.

Cahill, D. (1990). *Intermarriage in international contexts.* Manila: SMC Press.

Cahill, D. (1996). *Immigration and schooling in the 1990s.* Canberra: AGPS.

Campbell, W., Barnett, J., Joy, B., & McMeniman, M. (1984). *Review of the Commonwealth as a second language program.* Canberra: Commonwealth Schools Commission.

Chuah, F., Chuah, L., Reid-Smith, L., & Rice, A. (1987). Does Australia have a Filipina brides problem? *Australian Journal of Social Issues, 22*(4), 573 -583.

Commonwealth Schools Commission. (1979). *Education for a multicultural society.* Canberra: Commonwealth Schools Commission.

Cope, B., & Kalantzis, M. (1997). *Productive diversity: A new Australian model for work and management.* Sydney: Pluto Press.

Department of Employment, Education, and Youth Affairs. (1998). *National Literacy Action Plan.* Canberra: Commonwealth of Australia.

Department of Immigration and Multicultural Affairs (Research and Statistics Unit). (1997). *Immigration update.* Canberra: DIMA.

Foster, L., & Stockley, D. (1984). *Multiculturalism: The changing Australian paradigm.* Clevedon: Multilingual Matters.

Jakubowicz, A., & Castles, S. (1986). The inherent subjectivity of the apparently objective in research on ethnicity and class. *Journal of Intercultural Studies, 7*(3), 5-25.

Kalantzis, M., & Cope, B. (1984). *Head or heart? Strategies for combating racism.* Wollongong: University of Wollongong.

Kalantzis, M., & Cope, B. (1986). Why we need multicultural education: A review of the "ethnic disadvantage" debate. *Journal of Intercultural Studies, 9*(1), 39-57.

Kalantzis, M., & Cope, B. (1999). Multicultural education: Transforming the mainstream. In S. May (Ed.), *Critical multiculturalism: Rethinking multicultural and antiracist education* (pp. 245-276). London: Falmer Press.

Kemmis, S., Cole, P., & Suggett, D. (1983). *Orientations to curriculum and transition: Toward the socially-critical school.* Melbourne: Victorian Institute of Secondary Education.

Martin, J. (1975). The education of migrant children in Australia 1945 -1975. In C. Price & J. Martin (Eds.), *Australian immigration: A bibliography and digest* (pp. 1-65). Canberra: Australian National University.

Martin, J. (1978). *The migrant presence.* Sydney: George Allen & Unwin.

National Advisory and Coordinating Committee on Multicultural Education (NACCME). (1987). *Education in and for a multicultural society: Issues and strategies for policy making.* Canberra: NACCME.

National Multicultural Advisory Council. (1999). *Australian multiculturalism for a new century: Toward inclusiveness.* Canberra: Commonwealth of Australia.

Price, C. (1994). Ethnic intermixture in Australia. *People and Place, 2*(4), 8-11.

Rizvi, F. (1986). *Ethnicity, class, and multicultural education.* Geelong: Deakin University Press.

Singh, M. (1995). The relevance of Edward Said's critique of Orientalism to Australia's "Asian Literacy" curriculum. *Journal of Curriculum Studies, 27*(6), 599-620.

Singh, M. (1998a). "It's not easy being Australian": Education in a multicultural and multi-racist society. In J. Smyth, R. Hattam, & M. Lawson (Eds.), *Schooling for a fair go* (pp. 245-276). Sydney: Federation Press.

Singh, M. (1998b). Multiculturalism, policy and teaching. In E. Hatton (Ed.), *Understanding teaching* (2nd ed.) (pp. 319-331). Sydney: Harcourt Brace.

Singh, M., & Gilbert, R. (1992). *Focus on cultural learnings in schools.* Queensland: Department of Education.

Wimmer, A. (1997). Explaining xenophobia and racism: A critical review of current research approaches. *Ethnic and Racial Studies, 20*(1), 17-41.

Chapter 3

Multicultural Education in India

Sveta Davé Chakravarty

Center for Education Management and Development, New Delhi, India

THE POLITICS OF IDENTITY

Historically, streams of racial, cultural, linguistic, and religious groups have come into the Indian subcontinent over the centuries. They all contributed to the "Indian" civilization, but not necessarily to a unified civilization. Two images of cultural identity coexist: an *organic* identity, with internal integrity, characterized by spirituality, transcendence, and otherworldliness, and a *composite* identity, which views Indian traditions as synthetic and adaptive, with a pluralistic character, tolerant, and inclined towards peaceful coexistence.[1] Both these images are constructs, invoked at different times to different ends. Both images fail to incorporate the underlying tensions in Indian society—the tensions underlying all multicultural populations.

The Constitution of India, formulated shortly after independence, provides for the protection of religious, linguistic, and cultural freedom to all communities. However, India was constituted as a union of states divided along linguistic lines, with the states themselves extremely heterogeneous in terms of cultural populations. Sharma (1997) defined "ethnicity" as a multilayered, multifaceted phenomenon comprised of complex identities including religious, linguistic, ethnic, caste, and racial and sectarian identities.[2] Kolhatkar (1992) pointed out that because the

---

[1] See S. L. Sharma for a comprehensive discussion of the issue of politicization of identity.

[2] Whereas religion is invoked most frequently as the divisive factor, and whereas minority groups might point to "*the* Hindu majority" as the most powerful and exploitative group, the Hindu population is by no means homogeneous, nor is it uniformly powerful. Moreover, policymakers have repeatedly been accused by upper-caste Hindus of reverse discrimination, that is, of favoring the traditionally backward groups by reserving seats in government services and

various groups have had varying access to resources, disparities between communities in both economic and educational development continued to increase after independence. In the realm of policy, the term "regional disparities" appears frequently, and is used to denote a multiplicity of issues that together contribute to a situation where there is an unequal distribution of resources and unequal access to development (economic, educational, human).

Further, the idea of the overarching structure of the modern "nation-state," which subsumes specific identities, has threatened cultural groups with a loss of identity through assimilation. The internal contradiction in the formulation of the Indian state became evident very early in independent India's history. Sharma (1997) pointed out that the constitutional obligation to grant cultural rights stands in direct opposition to the obligation of the Western model of the modern nation-state to build a civil society in which the civic culture of modern nationalism prevails over ethnic diversity. Genuine cultural pluralism cannot be viable in this framework. Extreme centralization and a tendency towards an increasing concentration of power at the center have served to generate disintegrative forces. Ethnic resurgence has thus been fueled by developmental distortions, unequal distribution of resources, marginalization of cultural groups, and perceived discrimination by majority powers.

The architects of the modern Indian State operated on the assumption that Indian society was characterized by infighting. This assumption of the leaders has over the years served to intensify the divide further. A clearly articulated ideology that values cultural diversity might have changed the way diversity has been perceived in the last 50 years. (This point is addressed later.) Meanwhile, it is important to note that the precarious balance achieved in this "nation-state" has been and continues to be upset repeatedly by political interests that capitalize on both "primordial attachments" and newly constructed group identities by pursuing the British colonial policy of "divide-and-rule" for quick political gain.

In the scramble for political supremacy, the groups with little political organization have been sidelined consistently, with the result that, despite the guarantees of the Constitution, the disparities in the distribution of resources have continued to grow. Empirical research studies have indicated an educational and social lag of women and girls, members of scheduled tribes and scheduled castes, and members of certain minority groups, especially in rural areas.

---

higher education institutions. Thus, the Mandal Commission recommendations for 50% reservation in 1989 caused widespread riots among upper-caste Hindus.

Minorities

The Constitution defines "minorities" as communities constituted on the basis of religion or language, even when the language does not have a separate script. The Constitution guarantees that "any section of the citizens, residing in the territory of India or any part thereof, having a distinct language, script or culture of its own shall have the right to conserve the same" (Article 29 [1]). Historically, minorities, including religious minorities—Muslims, Christians, Jains, Jews, and others—have not been able to access their fair share of resources and have sought, in recent years, to organize effective political lobbies to redress the balance.

Gender

Traditionally, women in most cultural groups in India have been discriminated against in terms of access to developmental resources, property, and inheritance rights. Even though women have voting rights, cultural politics have denied them a public voice. In recent years, a Constitutional amendment has guaranteed women 33% of the seats in village-level political bodies (*Panchayats*), and a bill granting them 33% of the seats in the national Parliament has been tabled and is being hotly contested in Parliament.

Scheduled Castes

India's caste system[3] is notorious the world over and forms a significant element in the stereotypes that contribute to the construct "India." Because scheduled castes are a part of caste society, these groups are an integral part of society all over India. Social access has been denied to these groups on the basis of traditional social hierarchies in villages.

Scheduled Tribes

India has the second largest tribal population in the world. According to the 1991 census cited by Shukla (1995), there are 613 scheduled tribes, 67.7 million people (8% of the total population), of which 62.7 million live in rural areas. The so-called tribes have little in common with each other. They have traditionally been distinct cultural groups that have evolved in isolation from the mainstream cultures. With heterogeneous social, economic, linguistic, and religious patterns, these tribes survived in isolation for centuries, until modern development led the mainstream to impinge on their world.

---

[3] The term *Scheduled Castes* refers to traditionally disadvantaged caste groups that were identified and listed in a schedule. Similarly, *Scheduled Tribes* were also tribes listed in a schedule.

The hierarchical sociological order has over the centuries had a significant impact on the distribution of all resources, including education. In recent years, education has been increasingly viewed as the tool to provide equal opportunity.

THE POLITICS OF EDUCATION

In the centuries-old caste system, education was available only to the upper castes, and the pattern established in colonial times had made formal education the domain of a small stratum of society, creating "forward" and "backward" classes. Thus, because existing systems of education had intensified the divide, the Constitution provides for a right of admission to educational institutions regardless of religion, race, caste, or language, and also for minorities to establish their own educational institutions. Additionally, the Constitution recognizes the need to promote the education of the disadvantaged communities, including Scheduled Castes and Scheduled Tribes.[4]

Medium of Education

The linguistic issue greatly complicates the picture, especially in the area of education. For education to be effective, the medium of instruction must be the mother tongue, but frequently it is not. Majumdar (1997) pointed out that a political distinction has been encoded in the terms "regional language" and "mother tongue." Whereas one is politically loaded, the other is not. Because a recognized regional language enables the group to claim certain rights and benefits as a cultural community, the number of regional languages has been limited and currently stands at 18, with other linguistic groups vying for inclusion. The medium of instruction beyond primary level is required to be one of the 18 regional languages in the Eighth Schedule of the Constitution.[5] However, in a

---

[4] Article 30 of the Constitution of India provides that all minorities, whether based on religion or language, shall have the right to establish and administer educational institutions of their choice. Other Articles of the Constitution relevant here are as follows: "no citizen shall be denied admission into any educational institution maintained by the State or receiving aid out of State funds on grounds only of religion, race, caste, language, or any of them" Art. 29 (2); "the State shall promote with special care the educational and economic interests of the weaker sections of the people, and in particular, of the Scheduled Castes and Scheduled Tribes and shall protect them from social injustice and all forms of exploitation" Art. 46.

[5] "it shall be the endeavor of every state and of every local authority within the state to provide adequate facilities for instruction in the mother tongue at the primary stage of education to children belonging to linguistic minority groups" Art. 350-A.

country of over 300 dialects, this means that for the children of groups that do not speak any of the 18 languages, education in an alien language becomes virtually meaningless. In recent years, educational policies have recognized the need for at least the first few years of schooling to be in the mother tongue. Ambasht's (1997) study of tribal communities concluded that the policy of the central government to impart primary education to Class III in the mother tongue, and to provide culture-specific education, has been mostly ignored by the States.

In discussing inequalities in education, it is important to study not only the problems created by the multiplicity of languages but also the role of language in the distribution of resources. Krishna Kumar (1997) has argued that English has a unique position in mediating the distribution of resources: "The ability to use English fluently has become a synecdoche, a socially understood shorthand, for general ability" (p. 53). He suggests that "in the atmosphere that English medium private schools construct, terms such as 'mother tongue' or 'first language' lose the meaning and status customarily accorded to them in academic discussions of language education" (p. 53). With rampant growth of English-medium, fee-charging schools in both urban and rural areas, the children populating state schools belong to the extremely disadvantaged communities that cannot give their children the perceived advantage of English-medium schooling. It is important to note that "English-medium schooling" does not guarantee the quality of English required to participate in "elite" professions. English is not merely a skill to be acquired, but rather a symbol of long-term advantages. For those whose home environment does not complement the English conceptual world, such schooling prevents real learning, requiring rote learning instead. Thus a child living in a Hindi-speaking "world" would be better educated in Hindi, yet the child runs after English as a status symbol. There is a real need to inculcate valuing regional languages by the education system. Currently, according to Kumar (1997), dependence on an Indian language has become a sign of deprivation and the disadvantaged groups must continue to suffer "from a chronically unfair compulsion to participate in the mainstream economy from a weak position.... Culturally, the disadvantage is expressed most sharply in the fact that language has ceased to be a means of sustaining collective self-identity and morale" (p. 58).

Kumar (1997) pointed out that in the two-tiered educational system in India, whereas better English, self-confidence, assertiveness, and self-esteem are accrued by one set of students, absence of a name, a school tradition, pride of belonging, and a school culture add to the psychological disadvantages of belonging to a socioeconomically marginalized community. Conversely, those from the elite schools remain divorced from reality, the "world of the vernacular." Their learning remains theoretical and devoid of application to the real world.

Nevertheless, English remains privileged by industry and government in the belief that national interests and international commerce will profit by it.

The Goal of Multicultural Education

Disparities in education and other developmental resources relate also to multiple kinds of difference in population groups such as the rural/urban divide, gender, and so on. The Public Report on Basic Education states that "the unreached are in a number of categories, for example, child laborers, adolescent girls, tribal children, scheduled caste and scheduled tribe children, street children and children from slum colonies, children of migrant laborers, and physically and mentally challenged children" (PROBE, 1999, p. 28). For the purposes of this chapter, multicultural education refers to the education of the diverse groups that comprise the population of India. In this context, culture must be defined broadly as the "world" inhabited by each group, a world delimited by social, ethnic, religious, physical, linguistic, and economic characteristics that combine to create a collective identity distinct from other "worlds." The goal of multicultural education then becomes to provide high-quality education to all students, so as to equip them to function effectively both in their own "world" and in the larger multicultural world.

Education has a crucial role to play in addressing the complex politics of diversity in India. There is now a growing recognition that the fundamental rights of citizens of India include the right to religion and culture and therefore, by implication, the right to education in a culturally relevant setting. Majumdar (1997) pointed out that this has been upheld in the Supreme Court in several recent public interest litigation cases and so is likely to be enforced more and more. The task, however, is herculean, the numbers formidable, and the multicultural complexity overwhelming.

THE PUBLIC SYSTEM OF EDUCATION

In trying to meet the challenge of the Constitution to provide education for all, the government of India has made formidable advances in terms of sheer quantity of educational institutions; both the system of higher education and the systems of primary and secondary education have grown extremely rapidly. Historically, education in India had been developed primarily under the patronage of caste and religious associations. Whereas this provision remains, there has also been a move to strengthen national interests. The Kothari Commission on Education (1964-1966) advocated a common school system of public education, with the idea that the educational system could become a powerful tool of national development, and of social and national integration. This system was envisaged as one

- that will be open to all children irrespective of caste, creed, community, religion, economic conditions, or social status;
- where access to good education will depend not on wealth or class but on talent;
- that will maintain adequate standards in all schools and provide at least a reasonable proportion of quality institutions;
- in which no tuition fee will be charged; and
- that would meet the needs of the average parents so that they would not ordinarily feel the need to send their children to expensive schools outside the system.[6]

Exacerbation of Inequality

In the rapid expansion of the public school system over the last 50 years, both quality and the ideal of cultural freedom have been compromised. Thus, Ganguly-Scrase (1997) argued that in creating a common school system, "equity in curriculum has more often than not implied the effacement of cultural difference altogether, and has thereby perpetuated a class and gender bias in both educational practice and content" (p. 107). Both academics and policymakers are beginning to realize that education, which was to serve as an instrument of equality, has in fact tended to exacerbate inequalities. Factors that contribute to educational inequality include: poverty, which prevents children from going to school as there is an opportunity cost for sending children to even "free" government schools; limited access, as some areas still have no schools; and, according to R. P. Sinha (1997), a difference in standards of educational institutions. R. P. Sinha maintained that "in the pursuit of creating an egalitarian educational system, intervention by the bureaucracy and the State has in actuality introduced two separate and independent educational edifices: (one of) 'nominal and notional education' and one of high-quality education" (p. xxi). A. Sinha (1998) suggested that in pursuing the legacy of colonial India, with the Macaulayan system of formal education, India has continued to attempt to produce generations of clerks, whose education is based on memorization and little or no development of higher order thinking skills. A multilayer education system has come into being with elite schools catering to a small percentage of the population that continues to corner the best jobs.

---

[6] Report of the Education Commission 1964-1966; p. 10, 1.38, quoted in A. Sinha.

Kumar (1997) introduced the concept of "sponsored mobility" to refer to the phenomenon in which those who attend the elite schools get admission to elite higher education institutions and then move into the best jobs in the country. "Formal education, instead of being a Great Equaliser, has become the Great Sorting machine" (Singh & Prabha, 1997, p. 38). Also, according to Kumar, as decision makers continue to manipulate policy to favor the elite, reservation of seats for the minority groups is the "single major means of entry to the elite service through which the downtrodden sections of society have been able to send their sons [sic]" (quoted in R. P. Sinha, 1997, p.xx). Further, because emphasis has until recently been given to higher education, and the public school system does not prepare students effectively for the entrance tests to higher education institutions, there continues to be a built-in mechanism that prevents the students of the public school system from improving their lot in life.

The situation has had a powerful impact on the attitude of teachers and principals and Kumar (1997) argued that "the state-run school teacher [now has] the justified feeling that his [sic] job is to look after children who have nowhere else to go" (p. 49). The outcome is of course extremely damaging for the students from already marginalized communities:

> In its worst form, the cynicism of state school teachers is directed toward children of the most deprived sections of society, who are usually first generation learners. These children are faced with negative feedback for every act they commit. Sooner or later, they get caught up in the vicious cycle of the self-fulfilling prophecies rooted in the teachers' prejudices and cynicism.... The run-down ethos of state-schools and the indifference of teachers add to the reproductive nature of our divided education system. Early streaming of children into two kinds of schools translates into advantages for the better off and disadvantages for the poor. (p. 50)

The situation calls to mind James Banks' definition of the latent curriculum: "It is that powerful part of the school culture that communicates to students the school's attitudes toward a range of issues and problems, including how the school views them as human beings" (Banks, 1997, p. 21). Our system disempowers children further by affirming that they are not welcome even in the schools that no student would attend by choice.

Recent data show clearly that despite mammoth efforts to increase access and enrollment figures, the goal of universal elementary education articulated in the Constitution 50 years ago is still far from being achieved. Whereas the national gross enrollment ratio was 90% in 1997-1998, net enrollment ratio was merely 60.3%, which is indicative of the extremely high dropout rate. The net enrollment ratio for girls was

48.8% and for boys 71%, indicating a high differential between the genders. The variation between states is considerable; for example, in Rajasthan, the net enrollment ratio for girls is 47% lower than that of boys. In the country as a whole, 56% of enrolled children complete Class V, and Learning Achievement is not up to Minimum Levels of Learning for those who do finish. Teacher absenteeism stands at 33%.[7] In the year 2000, 39 million children between 6 and 11 years and 7.28 million outside that age group need to be brought into schools in order to universalize primary education. The figures for elementary education are still higher. Elementary education (to age 14) is widely accepted as the most effective way of improving the standard of living, thus the most urgent need in Indian education is to provide effective elementary education to all groups.

Policy Measures Toward Equality in Education

Though policy in the early years focused on national initiatives, later 5-year plans indicated increasing awareness of the need to develop specific policies for various hitherto marginalized disadvantaged communities.[8] Reservation of seats in institutions of higher education and in the civil services have long been a part of policy in India. Recognizing that the reservation policy did not address the problem of access to basic education, the *Program of Action*, 1992, a revised version of the *National Policy on Education*, 1986, listed the following priorities: focus on women's education, education of minorities and of scheduled castes and scheduled tribes, education of the disabled, and adult and continuing education. The *Program of Action* spelled out the strategies to be adopted for each of the major groups.

Gender. In recognition of the critically important relationship between women's education and the country's development, special emphasis is being given since the last 5-year plan (1992-97) to the education of the girl-child.[9] Nayar (1995) has pointed out that the *National Policy on Education* of 1986 went substantially beyond the equal educational opportunity and social justice (equity) approach and expects education to become an instrument of women's equality and empowerment. The following passage appears in the *National Policy on Education*: "The national education system will play a positive, interventionist role in the

---

[7] Data from *EFA 200 Assessment: Core EFA Indicators*, UN 1999, quoted in Shanti Jagannathan, GO-NGO Partnerships.
[8] See Kolhatkar for a discussion of the shifting priorities and strategies of the 5-Year Plans.
[9] See Education for All: The Indian Scene for a discussion of the immensely successful *Mahila Samakhya* program, initiated in many states towards empowering women.

empowerment of women. It will foster the development of new values through redesigned curricula, textbooks, the training and orientation of teachers, decision-makers and administrators, and the active involvement of educational institutions" (Paragraph 4.2, p. 10).

The *Program of Action* (1992) spelled out the need for the entire educational system to be alive to gender and regional disparities. Gender sensitivity is to be reflected in the implementation of educational programs, with educational personnel sensitized to gender issues. The *Program of Action* recommends that all teachers and instructors will be trained as agents of women's empowerment. Common core curriculum and textbooks were to be revised and made gender sensitive. Similar strategies are suggested so as to build the capacity and sensitivity of the educational system to issues pertaining to minorities, scheduled castes, scheduled tribes, and other disadvantaged groups.

Minorities. In keeping with the constitutional right of all minority groups (see footnote 4), the *Program of Action* revised and developed further the Fifteen-Point Program for the Welfare of Minorities, 1983, in acknowledgment of the fact that the implementation of the guarantees to these groups has been uneven.

Scheduled Castes. Singh and Prabha (1997) noted that some scheduled castes are far ahead of others on various indicators of educational indices. The proportion of students from these groups is rising in government schools due not only to the efforts to increase enrollment, but also to increased awareness and demand for education, and to the fact that students from slightly higher income levels are moving to fee-charging private schools.

Tribes. According to Rao (1987), the first study of educational problems of scheduled tribes in India was made in 1944 by Professor Furer-Haimendorf, who conducted an empirical study among the Gonds of Adilabad district of Nizam's dominion of Hyderabad and highlighted problems of language and script and teachers. For the first time it was pointed out that an education program for tribals has to be in consonance with their habitat, economy, and culture. Subsequently, Article 46 of the Constitution of India directed that special attention be paid to the educational and economic interests of scheduled tribes and scheduled castes. However, as is apparent from the table below (from Shukla, 1995), there is a significant disparity between literacy levels of the general population and of tribal populations.

Literacy Percent	Total	Males	Females
Total Population	52.11	63.86	39.92
Scheduled Tribes	29.60	40.65	18.19

The *National Policy on Education*, 1986 and the *Program of Action* of 1992 recognized the need to take affirmative action toward increasing the participation of tribal communities in the educational system. Priority would be accorded to opening primary schools in tribal areas, and special funds were mobilized to construct school buildings. Residential schools would be established on a large scale, curricula and instructional materials would be developed for the early stages with arrangements for transition to the regional language, incentive schemes would be formulated for the scheduled tribes (including scholarships for higher education), tribal youth would be trained and encouraged to become teachers, and preschool centers, nonformal, and adult education centers would be opened on a priority basis in areas predominantly inhabited by tribes. A number of schemes were initiated and implemented in some tribal areas.

In the *Program of Action*, 1992 the goals of educating all these and other traditionally disadvantaged groups were to be met by the following strategies:

1. integrated educational plans, linking preschool, nonformal, elementary, secondary, and higher education;
2. adoption of alternative channels of schooling where formal schools are inaccessible;
3. microplanning through involvement of teachers and community to design a family-wise, child-wise plan of action for universal access and participation;
4. making parents aware of their responsibility for ensuring the completion of elementary education by their children and for providing the necessary support;
5. introduction of Minimum Levels of Learning (competence-based achievement and assessment;)[10]
6. improvement of school facilities through revamped Operation Blackboard, a nation-wide project to improve the infrastructure of single-room, single-teacher schools, and connecting it to the Minimum Levels of Learning strategy;
7. decentralization of education management for making the schools function toward ensuring universal enrollment, retention, and achievement;
8. revision of process and content of elementary education to make teaching-learning child-centered, activity-based, and joyful;
9. introduction of continuous and comprehensive evaluation with focus on remedial measures;

[10] Adoption of Minimum Levels of Learning Competencies is designed to promote equity, measurability, and evaluability in issues of curriculum. See A. Sinha, p. 42.

10. modification of teacher training programs in view of changed strategies;
11. improvement of monitoring system for Universalization of Elementary Education;[11] and
12. launching a national mission to achieve the goals envisaged in the revised policy. (Summary cited in A. Sinha, 1998).

FROM POLICY TO IMPLEMENTATION

As mentioned earlier, the *Program of Action* was drafted to expedite the implementation of policies spelled out in the *National Policy on Education*. Following the adoption by Parliament of the *Program of Action*, 1992, special schemes were launched for the girl-child, for scheduled castes and scheduled tribes, for illiterate adults, and for Basic Education for the Child, which put into one large category all those unreached children who belong to the many unclassified categories and are marginalized due to their socioeconomic conditions. In the wake of the Jomtien Declaration of Education for All (1990), of which India was a signatory, the first Basic Education projects were launched in Bihar and Rajasthan (*Lok Jumbish*—People's Movement, see footnote 15), two of the most educationally backward states in India. The goal was to identify and enroll (in formal or nonformal schools) every child up to the age of 14 and retain them for at least 5 years to ensure they attain at least minimum levels of learning (MLLs). Special emphasis was given to the education of the girl-child and scheduled castes and tribes. A great deal of effort was put into mobilizing the community (especially women), nongovernmental organizations were involved in management and implementation of the programs, and teacher training institutes were established at the district level (District Institute of Education and Training, DIET). There was a rise in enrollment in all the target groups. More significantly, the program resulted in children from hitherto unreached groups, such as scavengers' children, being enrolled in schools. However, the gains from all the initiatives were nowhere near the targeted numbers.

DPEP: A Model for the Future?

The District Primary Education Project (DPEP) emerged in 1994 as a large program that incorporated much of the philosophy and strategies of the Basic Education Programs, with "a focus on sustainability, equity, and local ownership." Its objectives were based on the policy provisions

---

[11] Universalization of Elementary Education, a program developed to ensure education for all up to the age of 14 (Grade VIII), is still—in the year 2000—a distant dream.

of the *National Policy on Education* and the *Program of Action*, 1992. DPEP
supported replicable, sustainable, and cost effective program
development and implementation in order to:

- reduce differences in enrollment, dropout, and learning
  achievement between gender and social groups to less than 5%;
- reduce overall primary dropout rates for all students to less than
  10%;
- raise average achievement levels by at least 25% over measured
  baseline levels by ensuring achievement of basic literacy and
  numeracy competencies and a minimum of 40% achievement levels
  in other competencies by all primary school children;
- provide access for all children to primary schooling or its
  nonformal education equivalent.

DPEP also sought to strengthen the capacity of national, state, and
district institutions and organizations for the planning, management,
and evaluation of primary education.[12] The program will cover 209
districts in 18 states, that is, 39.7% of the country.

Problems of access to schools and access to learning have long been
known, and even strategies to alleviate them have been understood and
listed in various planning documents over the 50 years since
independence. For instance, the objectives of educational planning
spelled out in the *Program of Action* (listed earlier), if implemented
effectively, would create the equality of opportunity that is desired, as
well as raise India's Human Development Index to a respectable level.
However, implementers have not been able to overcome the problems
that inevitably arise in the process of implementation. The heart of the
problem lies in poor management of initiatives. Whereas several smaller
initiatives have recognized the need for participatory processes to
mobilize the community and the need for capacity building to empower
functionaries at the grassroots level, DPEP is the first major program to
understand the need for capacity building at all levels for management
and supervisory functions, so that innovations can be supported and
institutionalized.

Decentralization is the cornerstone of the DPEP model, with the
district as the locus of decision making and local-specific planning at the
block level, where the block covers a group of villages and 50 to 60
schools. Resource centers for clusters of schools further localize the
management of the program and Village Education Committees manage
the program at the village level. DPEP has mobilized vast resources for
primary education and has been able to fund a great deal of work in

---

[12] For the basic premises of the District Primary Education Program, see *DPEP
Assessment and Challenge*, as well as the document of the Joint Review Mission,
November 1999.

training and curricular innovations. However, if the program is to serve to reform primary education in India, a great deal needs to be done to consolidate its gains and institutionalize changes being made. In order to ensure its sustainability the parallel structures created by the program must be mainstreamed.

The program is discussed at length here because of its promise to revolutionize public education in two thirds of India. The path-breaking feature of the model lies in the decentralized institutions for management and academic support, which, unlike the government of India's administrative structure on which DPEP was modeled, would actually devolve power to the district, block, and village levels. Thus, the concept of the block resource center and the Village Education Committee gives a special decentralized focus to education that was formerly lacking. In order to bypass the monolithic bureaucracy of the state system of education, DPEP created parallel structures: a DPEP cell in the national Ministry of Human Resource Development, a society for the program at the state level, the State Institute for Education Management and Training (SIEMT) to parallel the existing State Council of Educational Research and Training (SCERT), and a separate wing for Planning and Management in the existing District Institute of Education and Training (DIET). The following diagram represents the structure:

NATIONAL GOVERNMENT DPEP CELL

State Government
SCERT   SIEMT

District Level
DIET   Planning & Management Wing

Block Level
Block Education Officer   Block Resource Centers (BRCs):
Planning + School Inspector: Organizing, coordination,
Supervisory function in 30 to 50   administration, monitoring and
schools.   follow-up, plus academic activities
                                      such as development of materials and
                                      teaching-learning processes.

Cluster Level
Panchayat: May be a cluster of villages;   Cluster Resource Centers (CRCs):
Elected *Sarpanch* as member of   Conduct of training programs, follow-
committees.   up & school support visits to schools,
                                           networking of teachers & VEC
                                           members, environment-building
                                           activities, data collection, information
                                           generation.

Village Level Committees	Village Level Village Education Committees: Community mobilization, construction activities, local resource generation, running preschools and alternative schools, utilization of school grant and so on.

However, once DPEP resources dry up, the question will arise whether these structures established at each level are sustainable. The agreement with the government of India, which provides 85% of the funding for the 5 to 7 project years, requires that the states increase their share of the financial cost annually, until at the end of the period they bear the entire cost of sustaining the program or structures—for example, the Block and Cluster Resource Centers—established at various levels. Sustaining the momentum after the national government's funding ceases—in the year 2000 for Phase I and 2003 for Phase II—will be critical to the program's long-term success. In bypassing the state bureaucracy, however, and creating a parallel management system, the program has undercut its own policy of generating state ownership of the initiative. Decentralization in this case resulted not in the empowerment and role clarity of each level, but in the bypassing of one level to reach the next.

Further, in many cases, the capacity of the district level institutions, the DIETs, to provide state-of-the-art training in innovative teaching and curriculum development, has not been built. Instead, the bank of consultants at the national level has taken on the training of the local functionaries, a point also raised by Jagannathan (1999) in an essay on the partnerships between government and nongovernmental organizations (NGOs). There is also some concern that though the Block and Cluster Resource Centers could be of immense value in maintaining the momentum of the program, it is not clear that they will continue to serve as resource centers. Currently, the DIETs have no real linkages with Block Resource Centers, and Cluster Resource Centers have by and large remained a brilliant but unimplemented idea. Jagannathan maintained that the devolution of powers and capacity building are "woefully inadequate," that Block Resource Centers are primarily administrative units and need to be academically strengthened. Further, "even though participatory planning at village and block levels takes place, ultimately the aggregate district plan is fitted into a DPEP framework that has set certain norms and procedures. Decentralization, surveys, and even formation of VECs are carried out as per government orders, rather than through a community consultative process" (p. 41). In suggesting that DPEP guidelines are restrictive and "sometimes go contrary to actual bottom-up planning," Jagannathan has identified the major weakness of a scheme that could hold tremendous promise for equitable education in India for all groups.

In summary, DPEP has thus far privileged a strategy of creating a parallel administrative structure rather than empowering existing state structures. It has also not been able to effectively build capacity of the levels to which power was ostensibly devolved so that the structures created could function as regional resource centers. DPEP seems to be falling prey to the government of India's feudal mentality of holding on to central power even as it creates structures to decentralize it, a mentality that thwarts the translation of policy into projects toward universalizing elementary education in India.

Centralization has indeed been the source of the current dysfunctional state of the Indian system of education and decentralization is its only hope of recovery. In denying people the right to make decisions about their education, the state both devalued and disempowered them. The promise of DPEP is its planned use of participatory processes that involve all stakeholders in decisions that affect their lives. Effective use of participatory processes would rejuvenate the gasping system of education. For this to happen, a paradigm shift in the bureaucracy's attitude to community participation is the critical first step. It is not clear that the bureaucrats in charge of DPEP and indeed the policymakers who authored and continue to propound the beliefs of the *National Policy on Education*, 1986 and the revised *Program of Action*, 1992 have made that shift.

Imaginative programs of educational development, such as *Lok Jumbish*, "People's Movement,"[13] are being threatened by a deep malaise

---

[13] *Lok Jumbish*, the Rajasthan Basic Education Project, is a case in point. On July 16, 1999, 12,000 villagers from the hinterlands of Rajasthan—educationally one of India's most backward states—gathered in Jaipur in front of the offices of the state government. It was a rally to protest the government decision to bureaucratize a people's movement for education, *Lok Jumbish*. The flexible, nonformal education program covering 13 districts in Rajasthan was started in 1992 by the state government in collaboration with external funding agencies. In keeping with the policies propounded in the Program of Action (1992), the goal of the project was to provide equitable education to the socially and educationally disadvantaged and to create structures that would make education an instrument of equality. Necessary modifications to the content and process of education were made for each community, to relate the education to the environment, people's culture and living conditions. The fundamental premise of the program was the empowerment of communities to review, plan, and manage their education.

Among the people who spoke at an elite gathering of intellectuals in New Delhi subsequent to the rally was 16-year-old Sonapa, who until a year before had spent her time grazing livestock, until her parents had been convinced of the in Indian politics and governance: short sightedness and short-term political interests that subvert the persistence and continuity necessary for any project to succeed and to be upscaled. The corollary to this problem is the deeply rooted unwillingness to devolve power to the grassroots level, where development and change must take place.

The 73rd and 74th Amendments to the Constitution of India made provision for *Panchayati Raj* Institutions to be established at the village level and for funds to be made available by the State Finance commission for village level activities.[14] Thus, community participation has been institutionalized through the *Panchayati Raj* system. The system could theoretically empower communities to take ownership of governmental initiatives. The extent to which power has actually been devolved to the *Panchayati Raj* Institutions varies by state, with tremendous progress having been made in a few states, such as Kerala, but most states have in fact done very little to empower the village level institutions. Decentralization, contextualization, and microplanning require a participatory approach that is alien to the rigid hierarchical structures of government. The reluctance of the civil service bureaucracy to hand over power to democratically elected village bodies is standing in the way of development.

---

need to give her the opportunity to learn. In six months of a nonformal primary education program under the aegis of *Lok Jumbish*, Sonapa achieved Grade V competencies and was able to enroll in the Government Secondary school. The moving public speeches of women in support of education—in a heavily patriarchal, feudal society in which women usually appear in public with faces veiled—attested to the success of *Lok Jumbish*. The movement had so completely won the hearts of the communities it had touched, that villagers—an old peasant woman, a Muslim clergyman, a fiercely feudal farmer—appealed passionately to state officials to let it continue as their movement, their only hope of improving the lives of their children.

When the external funding agency withdrew its support to the project in the wake of India's nuclear explosions in Spring 1998, the State Government started looking for alternative funding and alternative methods of running the program. The very success of the movement—which has brought education to every home in 6,000 villages, provided innovative teacher training programs for existing schools, prompted the formation of women's groups to advocate women's education, raised the literacy rate of Meo Muslims from 28% for boys and 11% for girls to 82% and 57% respectively—seems to be jeopardizing its existence as the government attempts to place it under the World Bank's District Primary Education Program (DPEP), already functioning in 26 districts of the state, with uniform rules and regulations for all the districts. The fate of *Lok Jumbish* still hangs in the balance.

[14] The *Panchayat* is the centuries old village governing committee, traditionally comprised of village elders, and in its new incarnation, of elected members, including reservation of 33% of the seats for women.

Similarly, participation of the community in the form of Village Level Committees and *Panchayati Raj* Institutions is not always effective. Unequal power structures and traditional social hierarchies prevent the Panchayats from being truly representative. The Panchayats are not always democratically elected and sometimes vested interests prevent equitable distribution of resources, including education. The poor therefore are often alienated from the forms of intervention such as subsidies that mostly do not reach them. A. Sinha (1998) sounded a cautionary note: "We will also have to remember that the increase in allocations and subsidies do promote leakages of all kinds and the poorer regions have a high propensity to misutilise [resources], as the inequalities in the power structure are more marked in these regions" (p. 97). At the village level, social stratification is a fact of life.[15] Homogeneity exists, according to Sinha, at the level of the hamlet; therefore, interventions have to be at that level: "the poor alone can deliver programs for themselves and we will have to concentrate on levels of solidarity and homogeneity, the *tola* or the hamlet, for the achievement of basic needs and to institutionalize this level of participation" (p. 97).

The government of India's model of administration—adopted by DPEP in form for management of the project—would work if decisionmaking is actually moved down to regional and local levels, and capacity built at each level to make informed decisions. Thus, the role of *Panchayati Raj* Institutions must be understood by all stakeholders to be to represent the interests of the community in overseeing the functioning of all local service organizations in healthcare, education, and infrastructural development. The goals of multicultural education would be served when the decentralization of powers becomes effective, and local communities make decisions about their own educational needs.

THE ROLE OF EDUCATION

Sinha (1998) emphasized the importance of school education in India:

> In a hierarchical and stratified society like ours, the primary school emerges as a progressive social institution that questions status by ascription or accidents of birth and promotes status by achievement. The inability to provide quality primary schooling to all children, irrespective of their poverty or assetlessness, can lead to a process of promoting elitism and inequality. A common school system, on the

---

[15] See diagrams of social structures of caste based and tribal villages in A. Sinha, Figs. 1 & 2, p. 199.

other hand, can play a major role in reducing economic disparities and social inequalities. (p. 41)

Thus, he suggested that in challenging social reproduction by accidents of birth, education enables a sweeper's daughter, born into one of the "lowest" castes, to become something other than a sweeper.

Growth in the Indian education system has not been accompanied by the democratization of education. Government-led initiatives such as *Universal Elementary Education* and *Education For All* assume that regional disparities are eliminated at least at the level of basic education. But such initiatives presuppose equality without addressing equity. That is, they tend to assume that the same content delivered in the same way will result in a uniform level of achievement throughout the country. Further, due to their extreme centralization and, more importantly, due to the lack of an ideology and strategies to deal with the existing diversity, such initiatives cannot have the necessary reach. A plurality of strategies must be promoted in order to address the needs of a diverse population.

Access to Education

The definition of access to education includes making education accessible to all types of learners and interesting enough to retain every child. Debunking the widely held belief that illiterate parents do not want education for their children, and especially not for girls—who are considered *paraya dhan*, the property of (and possible income-generator for) the future husband's family—the PROBE survey of four educationally backward states indicates that 98% of parents wanted education for their boys and 87% for their girls. In a different survey, one of the most striking findings was "the strong desire of parents to get children educated. Education is perceived as an empowering influence in the lives of children and as a way to break the bondage of poverty and ignorance" (A. Sinha, 1998, p. 51).[16] Clearly, demand exists for the supply of good quality education. And Jagannathan (1999) pointed out that in the experience of the MVF program to eradicate child labor, "MVF's communities not only withdrew their children from work, they have contributed in cash and kind to the schooling of their children" (p. 28).

Revisiting the Content and Delivery of Education

Given the clientele of the public system of education, there is every need for the nationally determined focus of education to be life skills, defined by the Kothari Commission as literacy, numeracy, work experience, and

---

[16] See A. Sinha for discussion of a field investigation carried out by 231 officer trainees of the IAS, IPS, IFS (Indian Administrative, Police and Foreign Services) and the Indian Forest Service in 1995 in 16 districts of Rajasthan, Madhya Pradesh, UP, and Bihar, educationally among the most backward states in India.

social service. Work experience needs to be included in order to relate education to productivity and social service to promote social integration. This approach of promoting life skills rather than mere learning skills has been used successfully in the curriculum of the BRAC program in Bangladesh and the Escuela Nueva in Colombia. Education has to be defined broadly as human development in order to provide dignity to the lives of children who might today be scavenging in garbage dumps. We must understand that though the population of the public school system as it exists is diverse in terms of cultural backgrounds, it is homogeneous in its need. For most of the children in these schools, the education the school provides is the only vehicle to an improved quality of life.

Jagannathan (1999) suggested that whereas it is imperative to recognize that the demands on even highly motivated teachers are very high, urgent attention is needed to address the high nonlearning and dropout rates. Even though policy declarations in the *Program of Action* of 1992 attest to the understanding that disadvantaged children must receive special attention, the gap between the expectations of teachers in the formal schools and the reality of the children populating them has not been addressed effectively.

Lockheed et al. (1991) have pointed out that teachers need to understand that children from a disadvantaged home environment may not know how to behave in a classroom setting and will lack the exposure to books, maps, puzzles, crayons, and other developmental materials, in addition to abstract and representational use of language and complex verbal directions. Because children from disadvantaged communities have home environments that provide little or no support for them to learn, they are frequently unable to relate to the school environment and drop out of school. The same is true of children with special needs such as slow learners.

In order for education to fulfill its role, schools must attract and retain students from socioeconomically marginalized groups. For this to happen, the content of education and the method of delivery need to be looked at very carefully. Jagannathan (1999) suggested that "quality in school education [needs to be] defined in a much broader context than just learning outcomes of children in terms of reading and writing abilities." She maintained that the school is a place where children from deprived communities find means of self-expression and interact with each other and with society with dignity, and that the definition of education by some NGOs as a socialization process must become integral to the public systems of education. Several innovative programs are focusing exclusively on evolving ways to understand the needs of children from disadvantaged communities and preparing teachers to meet those needs.[17]

In discussing the need for high-quality education to serve the diverse groups that constitute the multicultural population of India, we must consider the dual problem of: (a) a stratified system in which mass public education does not fulfill its function of providing the primary path to an improved quality of life; and (b) the inaccessibility of this public system of education to certain groups. The primary need in the Indian educational system—and our definition of multicultural education—is therefore to provide effective education within the common school system and ensure that it is accessible to all.

---

[17] The issue of access has also been innovatively addressed by three distinctive initiatives. The objective of the *Bodh Shiksha Samiti*, which operates in the slums of Jaipur, Rajasthan, is to make the curriculum accessible, by evolving "such pedagogic practices and processes which would enable children [in a fragile socio-economic fabric] to receive appropriate, equitable, quality education, based on community participation and initiatives." In keeping with the fundamental belief that the teacher must share the worldview of the children, teachers are youth from the community who receive intensive training. The process used in the slum schools has been upscaled to a pilot in 10 municipal schools. With a Bodh resource teacher, a limited class size of 30, and a school-community contact program, dropout rates fell from 60% to 20%, and children of Class III were found to have Class IV competencies. The model of community schools is being replicated in all of urban Rajasthan. It is important to note that the focus is on the process of understanding the needs specific to a community.

To increase access to educational facilities, the state government of Madhya Pradesh launched a scheme—the Education Guarantee Scheme—whereby it promised the basic resources to open a school: teaching-learning materials and an honorarium for a teacher, to be provided within 90 days of demand from a community that did not have a school within 1 km. 25,000 such schools were set up in 2 years. Additionally, teacher training equivalent to the in-service training for regular government teachers was provided.

Another innovative program to increase access to education was launched by the Rishi Valley Foundation, an enlightened educational organization. It has evolved a satellite schools program to serve isolated hamlets with no access to schooling. Its model of multigrade, single-teacher schools promotes ecological interests, and has resulted in reviving village communes by providing a locus for community activities. The organization developed the "School-in-a-Box": teaching-learning materials for multigrade, multilevel schools, which allow children to proceed at their own pace. This is now a patented product, available in different Indian languages. Teacher training is provided in the use of the multigrade kit, and evaluations have been developed to complement the kit. The program has been used by the Tribal Development Authority of Andhra Pradesh to establish cluster resource centers for 2,000 Tribal schools, in Tamil Nadu slum schools, and in DIETs' capacity building in Uttar Pradesh. Jagannathan pointed out that the model has enormous potential for replication because a majority of rural schools are multigrade, single-teacher schools.

Education must be culture specific in order to reach every child, and must be broad enough to inculcate the valuing of diversity. It would then serve both as an integrative force in the nation and as a tool for the development of every individual's potential. We are arguing here for the need both for centralized policy guidelines and for contextualization of education to the population it serves.[18]

CENTRALIZED POLICY VERSUS DECENTRALIZATION

In the realm of education, two issues need to be addressed right away: one, how can educators ensure that the value systems and voices of "other" groups are included in the system of education; and two, how can culturally relevant education be planned for each cultural group. Ambasht (1997) suggested that because education is socialization into the culture in which the individual is expected to function, tribal education should mean transaction of a culture-specific curriculum. The question then arises: In an increasingly global environment, can a cultural "world" remain closed? And, if not, what kind of balance is needed and how can it best be achieved? For example, Ambasht (1997) argued that because traditional math in various tribal systems is to the base 5 or 20, it is not necessary to induce a shift to base 10. Accepting that the system is valid and must be taught as such during primary years, it could be argued, however, that the transition to the more universal base of 10 would be essential to function in the larger world in which most tribes also participate. Not to equip them to function effectively in this world would be to handicap them in the name of preserving tradition. As a corollary, the core curriculum could be enriched by including ways in which different communities use different systems of mathematics. Whereas education within one's own cultural context is necessary for reinforcing self-esteem initially, education to participate as equals in the multicultural national context is essential for sustained well-being. How can the curriculum be defined to include cultural specificity as well as multicultural understanding?

---

[18] The example of Delhi that, with its large and steadily increasing migrant populations, is a microcosm of India, will serve to clarify the argument. Though the area is divided into 11 districts, the system of secondary education is highly centralized, with not only policy matters but also functional ones being decided at the top. Because schools serve highly localized populations, our argument would be for increasing the autonomy of schools, so that they may make culturally appropriate functional decisions based on the larger policy articulated at the top. Thus, whereas shared values would be the larger goal, there must be space for them to be interpreted in local-specific ways.

Whereas education policy in the last 20 years has focused on making education accessible to diverse groups, "multicultural education" is not a term used in policy in India. Further, attempts to broaden the curriculum to make it inclusive have bordered on tokenism. Oza (2000) emphasized this point: "Guided by the apex body at the national level, the curriculum aims to incorporate all kinds of diversities. It also attempts to include all information indiscriminately. This has resulted in a curriculum which is not contextual to address the needs of the child, and there is an information overload" (p. 2). The burden of an unwieldy and fragmented syllabus uniformly applicable to all students is now acknowledged as a major factor in compromising achievement levels of all students, and especially of students who do not have the advantage of socioeconomic support from the home environment.

The Concept of Universal Design

In addressing the need for a common curriculum broad enough to serve diverse populations, the principle of "Universal Design" might be considered. Though the concept was developed for the inclusion of technology-based solutions towards making the curriculum accessible to disabled learners, its application to populations of diverse learners is clear. Orkwis and McLane (1998) gave a working definition:

> Universal design means the design of instructional materials and activities where the learning goals are achievable by individuals with wide disparities in their abilities to see, hear, speak, move, read, write, understand English, attend, organize, engage, and remember. Universal design for learning is achieved by means of flexible materials and activities that provide alternatives for students with wide disparities in abilities and backgrounds. (p. 7)

Curriculum. For the architects of the Indian education policy, this would mean understanding that an "inclusive curriculum" entails not inclusion of the many cultural worlds that make up the multicultural population of India—which would amount to tokenism or to a curriculum so unwieldy as to be unusable—but rather *flexibility*, so that it can be tailored to the needs of the group it serves as well as the mode of delivery (i.e., distance education,[19] alternative education,[20] etc.). Thus, in

---

[19] Distance education and interactive radio broadcasts have also been identified as effective ways of supplementing the teaching of less-trained teachers. The use of communication technology may be the only means of addressing the vast needs of developing countries of the size and complexity of India. In order to use resources optimally, points of maximum leverage need to be identified. There are few villages and hamlets in India that have not been reached by radio and television, thus these media could be employed most effectively in the delivery of education to remote regions. Here too, although guidelines for the use of the

the example given, the curriculum for Grade 5 math would state: "Students will be able to compute" and would make no reference to the base (5, 10, or 20). Having learned the one, students would be in a position to pick up the other easily when the opportunity arises. Content, means of representation of the content, means of expression available to students, and means of engagement of students with the content *all* need to be flexible in order for the principle of universal design to serve its purpose of universal accessibility.

Textbooks. Further, when we speak of the need for appropriate textbooks, we must first address the issue that the quality of existing textbooks needs to be improved so that, as Lockheed et al. (1991) suggested, they are consistent in approach and method, clear in presentation, of an appropriate level for the students, are motivating for students, and can be used with ease by less-qualified teachers and also

medium may be formulated at the national or state level, programs would have to be developed at the district level with input from local communities, in order that they be local-specific and appropriate to needs of the communities they serve.

[20] The National Policy of Education accepted nonformal education as an alternative path to formal education and suggested that the nonformal education system be extended to the whole country. The belief underlying the system is that education of a standard comparable to that of the formal education system can be provided even outside primary schools, with flexible hours for working children, a shorter learning day, in a locality of the learner's choice, with textbooks specially prepared for such learning centers. Following the international Jomtien Declaration on Education for All, nonformal education became a major strategy to reach the unschooled, with children to be mainstreamed after Class V. A total of 850 agencies were funded by the government to run nonformal education centers. However, the concept of nonformal education has been discredited by several critics, including Jagannathan. They maintain that there is little evidence that children from centers of nonformal education get absorbed into regular school and that it cannot be an avenue for full-fledged education: "By accepting that certain children cannot come to regular schools, the program effectively dichotomized the provision of education for the normal and the underprivileged children" (Jagannathan, 1999, p. 37). Jagannathan stated that the nonformal education centers have been repackaged as "Alternative Schools" with unclear policies and no learning from the nonformal education experience. However, the successes of *Lok Jumbish* and other nonformal education programs including *Deepalaya* in Delhi, which runs schools in 1,000 slums, indicate that the problem lies not with the concept of nonformal education, but rather with its implementation in some places. Indeed, the use of para-teachers from the community, possible thus far only in the nonformal system, if implemented in a planned way, with appropriate training and supplementary support—structured learning materials, interactive radio broadcasts, and so on—is possibly the most viable means of reaching the unreached.

allow for good teachers to expand on them. Policy guidelines would be required to ensure this part. Secondly, we must ensure that both content and approach are relevant to the culture they address. Decisions concerning content and medium of textbooks would therefore have to be decentralized to the context they are to serve—the district or even block level. DPEP states have made a promising beginning in restructuring textbooks to make them more accessible to children (see Oza, 2000). The critical next step would be for the apex national body (NCERT) to use the experience of DPEP to make the best textbooks available to the rest of the country to be adapted for use in different contexts.

Teacher Training. In teacher-training programs, the quality of the program needs to be ensured in terms of state-of-the-art methods, innovative technologies proven in the field, and so on, as well as in terms of the relevance of the content to the context the teachers will serve. Currently, archaic teaching practices hamper student learning, for example: lectures by teachers with students copying from the blackboard, memorization rather than discussion of information, and little ongoing monitoring and assessment. A centralized framework for effective teaching might include policy guidelines for practical methods for covering each subject, adapting the curriculum to the social and physical environment of the pupil, understanding how children learn, evaluating teaching and learning, managing classrooms, and building effective parent-teacher and community relations. Guidelines for follow-up and feedback need to be institutionalized if the training is to lead to sustained improvement. However, training in effective practices for local conditions—for example, for large classes in urban areas and multigrade in rural—has to be designed and delivered at district or block level. Such training, with on-site follow-up, would constitute a significant step towards effective teaching.

Decision-Making. The experience of DPEP has shown that when education management is shifted to the ground level, the community becomes involved in school improvement, local-area planning, and in assuring quality. As understood by the policymakers of the Program of Action, 1992, the involvement of community needs to be a central strategy towards equalizing access to quality education.[21] Jagannathan (1999) pointed out that, "involving mothers as mobilisers has a very salutary effect on the schooling of children" (p. 32), and the concept of para-teachers has been shown, as in the initiatives of Pratham, MVF, and

---

[21] Also, the role of the community in mobilizing resources when government resources fall short has been repeatedly proven by various experimental programs. Yet community resources have been largely ignored by public programs.

Bodh, to be effective. However, if the local bodies such as the Panchayati Raj institutions and the Village Education Committees or the Parent Teacher Associations are to be effectively empowered to manage the education of their children, it is imperative to build their capacity to take on the task; and until capacity is built, to provide them with the access to appropriate training for teachers and teaching-learning materials, and tools for monitoring. We have argued here that these tasks need to be undertaken by district and block level agencies.

Systems Approach. Banks (1997) has argued for a whole-school approach to reform: "Multicultural education views the school as a social system that consists of highly interrelated parts and variables. Therefore, to transform the school to bring about educational equality, all the major components of the school must be substantially changed" (p. 23). We need to go a step further and define institutional development as school-based reform that focuses on the school as a whole as well as the state system of education of which the school is a part. This systems approach to public education would entail ensuring that all parts of the system are developed together to work in tandem. Thus, programs of reform must include a relevant curriculum, structured learning materials, need-based teacher training, appropriate teaching-learning processes, a supportive environment, and adequate infrastructure.

Sharma (1997) has argued cogently that there is a complementary relationship between decentralized democracy and ethnic diversity. In the realm of education, the top-down strategy of policymakers has not borne fruit.[22] Also, as Hallinger (1999) pointed out, the high-power distance in Asian societies has prompted leaders to assume that orders from above will be implemented unquestioningly. Hallinger argued that, as in the case of public education reform in Hong Kong, even in Asian societies ownership and commitment at the level of implementation are essential because "passive acceptance of orders [from above] to implement the innovation is neither a guarantee of support nor a predictor of success" (p. 15). Privileging diversity entails empowering and building the capacity of communities to evolve their own solutions.

---

[22] The initiative of vocational education in the Delhi Government school system serves an example of the problem with top-down initiatives. Policymakers have recognized the need for vocational education and put it into the Program of Action of 1992. However, whereas vocational education exists in the public school system at the senior secondary level (Classes 11 and 12), it exists as a nominal implementation of the policy. With part-time teachers and inadequate planning and resources, the program attracts few students, who at the end of the course are not equipped to get even basic jobs in their chosen fields. With this as with other top-down initiatives, teachers and principals remain disengaged from the idea even as they implement it.

Until decision making is brought to the level of those who have to implement the decision, lack of ownership and of commitment will subvert all attempts at reform.

The need to provide effective learning in the systems of public education entails the articulation of a coherent vision of effective schools and of strategies and detailed action plans to attain that vision. The critical difference will be made when there is a clear understanding of the *roles* of the different levels of the public system of education. Thus, policymakers must be content to make policy decisions, leaving executive decisions to the levels closer to the ground reality. By defining broadly what students should be able to achieve at each stage and by laying down policy guidelines for the adoption of the concept of universal design in the preparation of instructional materials and policy guidelines for teacher training in the use of the universal design, policymakers would fulfill their obligation to provide a curriculum that is accessible to every learner.

Creating provision for the institutionalization of the learning of pioneering programs would be one way of using centralized governance effectively. The role of policymakers must be not only to evolve policy guidelines but also to create mechanisms whereby the model of programs so evolved—from the bottom up—may be replicated and their learning institutionalized. Though the *National Policy on Education* of 1986 states that, "The curriculum at all stages of education will be designed to create awareness of the rich cultural identity of the tribal people and also of their enormous creative talent," mechanisms for including diverse content and sensitizing teachers toward it[23] need to be put in place in a systematic way, instead of token additions that continue to marginalize the groups they represent.[24]

---

[23] The Campus Diversity Initiative, funded by the Ford Foundation, is using curricular and cocurricular interventions to address the need on campuses around India to increase sensitivity to and empathetic understanding of diversity. The first phase of the project, launched in 23 colleges, has produced a significant impact in terms of levels of awareness of the value of difference in both faculty and students. In order to upscale the learnings of Phase 1, in Phase 2 the project will develop the capacity of teacher-training institutes. The model used in this initiative could be replicated to ensure the integration of multiple voices and the sensitivity to understand them into the curriculum. The goal is not merely to provide a balanced or representative curriculum, but rather to inculcate an understanding of many cultures, developing cross-cultural skills whereby individuals acquire the ability to participate empathetically in other "worlds."

[24] The promotion of pluralism in both the content and delivery of education must be supported by research at the microlevel. Ganguly-Scrase (1996) called for educational research at the microlevel to "help us to evaluate critical and reflexive approaches to pedagogic practice and avoid middle-class bias and

Points of Leverage. In view of the magnitude of the task of operationalizing the strategies suggested by the *Program of Action*, 1992, policymakers must first identify and use the points of greatest leverage. Teacher recruitment policy, one of the mechanisms in the hands of policymakers, is one such point of leverage. A. Sinha (1998) suggested that, as the proportion of scheduled caste/scheduled tribe teachers is far from representative, proactive recruitment be pursued. In the interim, information concerning the model of para-teachers, youth from the community trained to serve as teaching aides in the regular government schools, could be made available nationally. Also, more women teachers need to be recruited if more girls are to be enrolled. Thus, whereas the policy exists nominally in the *Program of Action*, 1992, the implementation of the strategy of adopting contextually relevant recruitment policies so that motivation levels are high entails capacity building of regional recruitment programs.

Similarly, another point of leverage would be the institutionalization of innovative methods of teacher training in pedagogy and the development of appropriate teaching-learning materials, such as those evolved by *Bodh* and others. That is, these methods must become an integral part of the regular in-service and pre-service training programs conducted by SCERTs and DIETs. As mentioned earlier, DPEP is struggling to find ways for such institutionalization. Planning at the initial stages must include processes that facilitate the institutionalization of innovative ideas so that they do not remain one-of-a-kind initiatives. Structures must be built to support the use of new models on site once the training is completed. The DPEP model of Block Resource Centers and Cluster Resource Centers was designed to serve the purpose of academic and supervisory support at the ground level. The model, whose urban counterpart would be Zonal Resource Centers, has great potential for decentralizing decision making and capacity building of school stakeholders. However, ensuring that the linkages to the training institutions are functioning smoothly is crucial to the effectiveness of this model.[25]

---

prejudices" (p. 131). Ambasht (1997) also made a plea for more interdisciplinary studies in education and social anthropology, asserting that people trained in social anthropology and pedagogy are required to develop materials for each major tribal area in consonance with the national curricular framework and with linguistic and cultural background of tribes.

[25] For example, the Bridge approach used by two innovative programs has proved very effective in helping to prepare children from disadvantaged communities to join the mainstream school system, one dealing with child labor, the other with children from urban slums. The MV Foundation, a private, charitable Trust in Andhra Pradesh uses bridge courses in regular schools to help

CONCLUSION

Critical to any effective strategy for dealing with multiculturalism in the Indian context is the need for a coherent ideology that recognizes the value of diversity and the role of education in realizing the ideals of

---

the children make the transition easily. It has also mobilized the community to contribute to problem solving in the formal schools, to contribute resources ,and to require accountability of the schools. The MV Foundation uses education to address the larger problem of child labor and, in the case of bonded labor, to break the cycle. Since 1991, 80,000 children have been withdrawn from work and enrolled in school, including 4,000 children who were freed from bondage. The project operates in 500 villages in which now 90% of children are enrolled in primary education. The MVF uses microplanning processes to eliminate child labor and mainstream the children into government schools. In the first stage, first-generation educated village youth conduct a house-to-house survey to identify children out of school. A residential camp is then planned for a 3-month bridge course before the children join the local government school. The same volunteer is trained as a para-teacher in the school to strengthen PTAs so as to keep the community involved and the school accountable.

MVF's policy of using education to eradicate child labor and its strategies of using the community resources to complement the government system have been adopted by both the Social Welfare Department of AP and by DPEP in AP. MVF serves as a resource agency for the state governments of Tamil Nadu, Madhya Pradesh and West Bengal, and NGOs in these and several other states have adopted the camp approach towards mainstreaming children from disadvantaged groups, including the urban deprived, child laborers, and girl children.

A variation of the bridge approach is used by the *Pratham* Mumbai Education Initiative, which focuses on preschool education as the bridge to enrollment of slum children in regular schools. Forty percent of India's urban population lives in slums, which are often unauthorized settlements with no public services. Most slums do not have government schools and in most slums, more than 50% of children out of school, either unenrolled or not attending. The *Pratham* Mumbai initiative aims to make the government education network understand the schooling needs of deprived communities. It uses a low-cost, community-based model of preschool education to prepare such children to move easily into the formal school system. Youth from the community receive training as instructors and appropriate teaching-learning materials are developed. The program operates from resource centers within Municipal (county) schools in Mumbai, and the network is to be handed over to the Municipal Corporation. In the second phase, the program is spearheading the setting up of Education Advisory Committees in all schools to build in community participation in schooling process. These Education Advisory Committees will take responsibility for micro planning in their catchment areas and so ensure universal enrollment. This strategy of using preschool to make the bridge to the formal system has proved very effective in increasing enrollment in the public school system and is expected to reduce dropout rates. The model is being replicated in parts of Delhi, Jaipur, Chennai, and Patna, and in other districts of Maharashtra.

cultural pluralism. Though the problem of disparities in educational development is starting to be addressed, this is being done in a fragmented way, with no integrated plan to harness the richness of pluralistic development. The whole issue of the role of education in preserving diversity has to be rethought. A great deal of advocacy is required to inculcate the belief that it is important to keep diversity alive. Such advocacy has to lead to the development of a critical mass of decision makers who believe that cultural diversity must be preserved and who will make the decisions necessary for it to happen.

ACKNOWLEDGMENTS

I am greatly indebted to my colleagues at the Center for Education Management and Development, Nuzhat Parveen, M. S. Selvanathan, Lena Kapoor, Nimeran Sahukar, Smruti Jena, and the Director of CEMD, Jayshree Oza, for their help in identifying issues, developing ideas, and locating information for this chapter.

REFERENCES

Ambasht, N. K. (1997). Inequalities in education—The case of tribal communities. In R. P. Sinha (Ed.), *Inequality in Indian education* (pp. 97-114). New Delhi: Vikas.

Banks, J. A. (1997). Multicultural education: Characteristics and goals. In J. A. Banks (Ed.), *Multicultural education: Issues and perspectives* (3rd ed.) (pp. 3-31). New York: Wiley.

Department of Education (1986). *National Policy on Education.* Ministry of Human Resource Development.

Department of Education. (1992). *National Policy on Education, 1986: Program of Action, 1992.* Ministry of Human Resource Development.

Department of Education. (1993). *Education for all: The Indian scene.* Ministry of Human Resource Development.

Department of Education. (1998). *Three years of DPEP: Assessment and challenge.* Ministry of Human Resource Development.

Ganguly-Scrase, R. (1997). Social justice and the micropolitics of schooling in India. In T. J. Scrase (Ed.), *Social justice and Third World education* (pp. 107-132). Garland.

Hallinger, P. (1999, June). *Learning to lead educational change: Seeing and hearing is believing, but eating is knowing.* Paper presented at the Conference on Professional Development for School Leaders, Centre for Educational Leadership, Hong Kong University.

Jagannathan, S. (1999). The role of NGOs: New partnerships for primary education. A study of six NGOs in India. Manuscript submitted for publication.

Kolhatkar, M. R. (1992). Planning strategies for removal of regional disparities in educational development: Past experience and future perspective.

In S. Nuna (Ed.), *Regional disparities in educational development* (pp. 201-217). New Delhi: South Asian.

Kumar, K. (1997). Educational inequality and language. In R. P. Sinha (Ed.), *Inequality in Indian education* (pp. 47-60). New Delhi: Vikas.

Lockheed, M. E., Verspoor, A. A., Bloch, D., Englebert, P., Fuller, B., King, E., Middleton, J., Paqueo, V., Rodd, A., Romain, R., & Welmond, M. (1991). *Improving primary education in developing countries.* London: Oxford University Press.

Majumdar, T. (1997). Intercultural education in India. In D. Coulby, J. Gundera, & C. Jones (Eds.), *International education world yearbook of education* (pp. 113-121). London: Kogan Page.

Nayar, U. (1995). Gender issues in primary education. *Indian Educational Review, 30*(1), 220-241.

Orkwis, R. & Mclane, K. (1998, Spring*). A curriculum every student can use: Design principles for student access.* ERIC/OSEP Topical Brief. ERIC/OSEP Clearinghouse on Disabilities and Gifted Education, Council for Exceptional Children.

Oza, J. (2000) *DPEP: School-level change.* Manuscript submitted for publication.

The PROBE Team. (1999). *Public report on basic education.* New Delhi, India: Oxford University Press.

Rao, V. N. (1987). Perceptions and problems of scheduled tribe school students: Implications for mental health programmes. In G. Pfeffer & D. K. Behera (Eds.), *Contemporary Society, Vol. II* (pp. 236-241). New Delhi: Concept.

Sharma, S. L. (1997). Ethnic threat to India's pluralist integrity: A plea for a culturally responsive polity. Unpublished manuscript.

Shukla, N. (1995). Effectiveness of various interventions for improving tribal education: A research study. *Indian Educational Review, 30*(1), 175-189.

Singh, R. P. & Prabha, S. (1997). Equality in education: Present position and future trend. In R. P. Sinha (Ed.), *Inequality in Indian education* (pp. 32-46). New Delhi: Vikas.

Sinha, A. (1998). *Primary schooling in India.* New Delhi: Vikas.

Sinha, R. P. (1997). Problematique of equality in Indian education: General introduction. In R. P. Sinha (Ed.), *Inequality in Indian education* (pp. xv-xxxiv). New Delhi: Vikas.

Chapter 4

What Can Multiculturalism Tell Us About Difference? The Reception of Multicultural Discourses in France and Argentina

Inés Dussel

Latin American Faculty for the Social Sciences (FLACSO), Argentina

Reading Carl Grant and Gloria Ladson-Billings' account of the journey of multicultural education in the United States, from its censorship and marginalization to the seemingly central position it has today, one can not help but celebrate that the 1998 AERA Annual Meeting was devoted to multiculturalism (Grant & Ladson-Billings, 1997). Forged through much struggle and pain by those who suffered and challenged multiple forms of oppression, multiculturalism has clearly become one of the most successful contemporary educational discourses not only in North America but worldwide.

However, this more central position for multiculturalism has not been without problems and indeed, as Grant and Ladson-Billings have described, there is always the risk of turning it into a sterile, pasteurized, and superficial pedagogical discourse. In this chapter, I focus on two cases in which the reception of multiculturalism has been weak, or has been contested in the name of democracy and equity: the French debate on the Muslim girls' veil and the Argentinean experience with school uniformity.[1] I claim that multiculturalism discourses are

---

[1] I consider these cases as *events*, that is, as discontinuous unities that cannot be reduced to generalizations (Foucault, 1972). Against the modern project of comparative education as the revelation of the rules and laws of education across the world (as described in Kazamias & Schwartz, 1977), I attempt to place discontinuity at the center of my research, not to render things unintelligible but to question the narratives that have subsumed the singular in the general. Following Samuel Weber, I claim that the singular is "what is left over after all the powers of generalization have been exploited to the fullest and their potentialities both realized and exhausted" (Weber, 1996, p. 213). The singular is that "which does not fit in," but paradoxically this definition refers to a certain generality that is exceeded. The notion of "event" then provides a grid of intelligibility that enables one to pose relations and interruptions between diverse elements. Comparability

regulatory ideals that prescribe how identity and difference should be conceived of and dealt with, which articulate historical and social North American constructions. After presenting the cases of France and Argentina, I advance the hypothesis that the reception of multiculturalism is shaped by national traditions that address the construction of identity/difference in particular ways and that play a remarkable role in how multiculturalism discourses on this issue are read. Also, I argue that uneven international power relations cause multiculturalism to enter into different language games, attaching new meanings in different contexts.[2] I conclude my contribution reflecting on what we can learn from these cases, which address the question of this book about the possibilities of a dialogue across different experiences.

MULTICULTURALISM AND THE REGULATION OF IDENTITY/DIFFERENCE IN NATIONAL SETTINGS

The spread of multiculturalism as a global discourse, one which celebrates diversity and pluralism and appears to be the postmodern heir to the Enlightenment's humanism,[3] is probably related to the fact that it addresses central problems of contemporary societies. As political scientist William Connolly (1996) asserted, multiculturalism

> speaks to a distinctive time when declining empires find former colonial people migrating to the imperial centers; when the globalization of economic life enables affluent workers to cross national boundaries at a faster rate and propels large numbers of "guest" workers into alien states; when television and other electronic media draw diverse cultures into closer proximity; when the acceleration of *speed* in practices of communication, war, fashion, and political mobilization makes the contingent and constructed character of what we are a little more palpable. (p. 53)

In this scenario of crisis of former identities and relations, the search for new integrative ideals that account for these shifts and new patterns of regulation has found, in a notion of multiculturalism that addresses diversity while reclaiming equality, a charming appeal.

---

can thus be established on the basis that one assumes continuity and discontinuity at the same time.
[2]I use the notion of language game, borrowing it from Wittgenstein, and particularly from Rosa Nidia Buenfil Burgos, a Mexican educator (Buenfil Burgos, 1997).
[3]The last sentence may seem oxymoronic to many, as postmodernism seems to be opposed to humanism—as to all universalisms. I chose the word "heir" to emphasize the conflictive relation of most of multiculturalism to the legacy of humanism, which for many social theorists and educationists still seems current: *egalité* and *liberté*. See, among others, Derrida (1992) and Laclau (1996).

But what does multiculturalism stand for? Multiculturalism involves the authorization and legitimation of particular assumptions on identity and difference (Modood & Werbner, 1997; Zizek, 1997).[4] In other words, it functions as a regulatory ideal that shapes the way in which individuals should think, feel, and behave, and it entails the internalization of rules and ways of acting that are hereafter presented as "natural" (Butler, 1993; Rose, 1997).[5] Through its emphasis on pluralism, multiculturalism comes to replace exclusivist national identities that assume an ethnic, religious, and linguistic homogeneity.

There are, however, many multiculturalisms (Grant & Ladson-Billings, 1997). Its mainstream version, originated in the United States, has been described as a celebration of diversity that has tended to reproduce the "saris, samosas, and steel bands syndrome" (Donald & Rattansi, 1992). Highly influential in the education field, this strand of multiculturalism has been a powerful rhetoric for school reform, developing new curricula and goals that are to be "culturally sensitive." This reform has been led in many cases by a "logic of aggregation" of cultural contents to the established ones (McCarthy, 1998a).

This dominant version of multiculturalism intends to reconcile the demands for recognition of minorities with the nation-form, advocating for a national protection of these minorities. Reifying culture and ethnicity and conceptualizing racism as a psychological prejudice, mainstream multiculturalism has failed to address the continuing hierarchies of power and legitimacy that exist among different centers of cultural authority. In that respect, it has not challenged the political logic of assimilation, as it has maintained a center of culture against which the rest of the ethnic groups should be organized as exotic or "simply different." William Connolly (1996) called this reasoning "the arboreal imagination": the nation (the common self) has been thought of as a tree with a central trunk of common mores rooted in

---

[4] I follow here Cameron McCarthy's (1998b) perception of multiculturalism as "a set of propositions about identity, knowledge, power, and change in education, a kind of normal science, a form of disciplinarity of difference in which the matter of alterity has been effectively displaced as a supplement." He goes on to say that multiculturalism has turned into "a discourse of power that attempts to manage the extraordinary tensions and contradictions existing in modern life that have invaded social institutions... . At the heart of its achievement, multiculturalism has succeeded in freezing to the point of petrification its central object: 'culture'" (p. 1).
[5] The almost compulsory need for U.S. minorities to organize as minor nation-states within a larger territorial one, with specific readings of history, traditions, and mores, is but one example of the ways in which multiculturalism disciplines cultural values and perceptions.

White Christianity, with many branches or racial minorities coming out of it. This reasoning, which can be traced back to Rousseau and Tocqueville, can still be found in milder versions in today's liberal pluralists such as Charles Taylor and Jürgen Habermas.

There are, also, other possibilities within multiculturalism, such as those represented by the writings of some contemporary feminists, and gay, lesbian, and African-American scholars (Butler, 1993; Gilroy, 1993, McCarthy, 1998a). They reject the wish to universalize a minor nation-state and propose instead a "democratic state of multiple minorities contending and collaborating with a general ethos of forebearance and critical responsiveness" (Connolly, 1996, p. 61). In these other multiculturalisms, the notion of "minorities" is challenged through asserting multiple possibilities of being across and within states, in what Connolly called a "rhizomatic" model of pluralism with flows connecting in multiple directions. Culture itself must be thought of as a radical hybridity, embedded in power relations, always being rewritten, and not as the "authentic" outcome of a particular group (McCarthy, 1998a; Spivak, 1997).

What happens when these multiculturalism discourses, predominantly performed by North American and other Anglo-Saxon scholars, are re-staged in different national settings, which have their own ways of dealing with difference within the nation-state? I advance the hypothesis that its reception is profoundly related to the distinctive national and local patterns of constructing notions of identity and difference. Multiculturalism is read differently in different contexts, according to particular histories and traditions (Modood & Werbner, 1997).

Simplifying a complex history for the sake of this argument, I would say that in the United States, difference has been primarily articulated in terms of race (Winant, 1994). As stated before, the "arboreal imagination" of multiculturalism posits the homology between the nation and a tree with a central trunk of common mores rooted in White Christianity (Connolly, 1996). The very notion of minorities, which on the one hand has been so productive socially and politically for the Civil Rights movement, has nonetheless tended to perpetuate the affirmation of a center majority that was White, male, and Anglo-Saxon, and also to essentialize racial affiliation as a "natural" line. (Grant & Ladson-Billings, 1997; McCarthy, 1998b).

On the other hand, in most European countries, nations were thought of as homogeneous and continuous entities, and the only "visible" difference was in terms of social class. In the common sense, but also in scholarly work, "race" was something that existed down there, in the colonies, and has become important only recently, due to the new immigration waves (Noiriel, 1996). In Latin America, one could sketch two broad types: the Andean countries that have been sensitive to ethnic issues (due to the fact that a larger Indian culture has survived the genocide of conquest), and the Southern Cone societies (like Argentina), with weaker Native groups who were almost exterminated right away. This second group has tended to be more European-like in their patterns of inclusion and exclusion, and was organized around class lines. In both regions, multiculturalism discourses have entered the educational field only in recent years, and mostly related to the translation of Anglo-speaking authors.

How, then, has multiculturalism been received in countries with uniformizing national imaginaries? I approach this question by way of analyzing two cases in which multiculturalism has been contested as a universal rhetoric for educational reform. Both experiences, however divergent they might be, speak to the need to take into account particular histories and traditions that shape the way in which multiculturalism is read. Also, they urge us to be more cautious about its spread across the globe, acknowledging that the many multi-culturalisms that populate the Anglo-Saxon world seem to be blurred and confused in its dissemination.

THE FRENCH CASE: (UN)VEILING SCHOOLS

In 1989, three Muslim teenagers were forbidden to wear their veils at their lycée in Créil, a Parisian suburb. At the onset of the conflict, the girls and their families accepted the ban, but some weeks later, after receiving the advice of organized Muslim groups, they decided to fight for their right to attend schools with their veils. The conflict soon spread to other schools, and the issue gained relevance in the news and in the French public sphere. Initially there was a tolerant policy from the national government, but the advent to power of the Islamic guerrillas in Algeria increased the fear of Islamic fundamentalism. In 1994, the State Council (the court of arbitration for conflicts between the state and the citizens) finally dictated that the "ostentation" [sic] and proselytizing of religious symbols in schools should be prohibited, alleging that French schools are secular (laïque) and no religious symbols should be allowed in them. The words "ostentation" and "proselytizing" are the key terms in here, for they provide a way of distinguishing the veils from the Catholic crosses and Jewish David stars, which children are allowed to wear in schools. Also, the authorities appealed to feminist discourses, which have denounced the veil as a symbol of oppression for women [I come back to this argument later]. Despite this defeat, Muslim groups are still advocating for their cause. The struggle has been displaced to the local schools in which every principal decides whether or not wearing the veil implies "ostentation" or "proselytizing."

The *affaire des foulards* has shaken the grounds of the political and educational system. The French Republic was constituted on particular notions of nationalism and citizenship that stressed equality, enlightenment, and freedom. But this "common self" (as Rousseau called it) should be achieved through the giving up of particularisms, egotistic drives, and earlier traditions. One is not born French, but one becomes French through individually accepting these common rules and culture in a republican contract (*pacte republicaine*). One of its basic premises is that there cannot be a group affiliation more powerful than the nation; cultural pluralism, thus, becomes threatening and dangerous (Audard, 1996). This is the reason why France does not see itself as a multicultural society, despite the fact that the rate of foreign population has been traditionally equal to or even higher than that of the United States.[6]

The school was a privileged place in which this "Frenchness" would be achieved, and that is why it was structured following the patterns of homogenization and centralization. The school system assumed from the beginning that uniformation was the best means to achieve equality and a common morality. This homogenization pervaded all aspects of daily life in schools. Through the action of inspectors, teacher training schools, textbooks, and journals, the teaching practice was regulated with great detail.[7]

---

[6]In a provoking and rigorous book, Gerard Noiriel argued that France has received proportionally at least as many immigrants as the United States, but whereas the latter has tended to inflate the role of immigration (which took place parallel to the formation of the nation), the fascination with origins in France (the republican myths established by the French Revolution) has made immigration invisible for scholars and for the common sense (Noiriel, 1996).

[7]For example, in the famous *Dictionnaire Pédagogique* by Férdinand Buisson (1911), an encyclopedic textbook that was distributed to all schools, many pages are devoted to regulating the appearance of teachers and children and their daily rituals. Teachers should make sure that every child appear properly dressed and cleaned when arriving at class, as well as establish regulated movements for entering and exiting schools. It also prescribed general movements for the children, such as the following: "students should march on line, their bodies straight, their arms uniformly positioned, be it crossed over the school desk or behind their backs with their hands shaken" (Crubellier, 1993, p. 104, my translation).

The school system constructed a particular notion of "equity" that was defined as a common dignity of pertaining to a grand nation with unlimited possibilities (Nique & Lelievre, 1993). As it was remarked by Jules Ferry, the Minister for Education in the 1880s responsible for the secular laws, rich and poor should sit altogether in the school's desks; talents would emerge clearly out of this common education, effacing the traces of social origins (Ognier, 1988). Gender, racial, and class differences would be left outside the school building, in whose inside everyone would be "just a teacher or a pupil."

Religion was to be left aside as well. The common morality was grounded on a powerful secular myth in which the state and the nation took the place of God. In this constitution of citizens "from the top," the state monopolized the space of "the public." "The private" was equated to backwardness, religious sectarianism, traditionalism, whereas "the public" represented the republican ideals of homogeneity and equity. Secularism turned into a "reason of state" (Köker, 1996).

Despite the events of May 1968, the broad consensus on which the uniformizing action of the school was based seems to have gone unchallenged until the emergence of the veil affair, which questioned the construction of secularism as opposed only to the Catholic church (Ognier, 1993). The equivalence between "secularism" and "national state" was shaken by the emergence of new immigrants who insisted on their right to be different, who wanted to have a non-French cultural identity (Beriss, 1990). For the first time in many years, groups that refused to be assimilated in such ways emerged, and posed challenges that are still being processed by the French society.

With this background, I now discuss how the event of the veiled Muslim girls in schools was constructed in the public debates in its two peaks (1989 and 1994), in which negative appeals to multiculturalism were made to refuse the right of the Muslim girls to wear their veils. The mainstream French press has presented it as a battle between universalism/democracy ("France") and integrism/fundamentalism ("the Muslims" and the ghost of "Iran")—a construction that prevents, from its very beginnings, the inclusion of the other in a nonsubordinated way. After the passing of the State Council dictum that forbade the "ostentation" of religious signs in schools, Le Nouvel Observateur titled its special edition "The Resistance to Integrism" (Alia, 1994). L'Express warned about "How the Islamites infiltrate France" through the "conspiracy of the veil" (Stein, 1994). But that has also been the position of several intellectuals. At the onset of the conflict, some well-known scholars like Elisabeth Badinter, Régis Debray, and Alain Finkielkraut, published an open letter to the National Minister for

Education entitled: "Teachers, do not capitulate!" [to the Islamic pressures] (*Le Nouvel Observateur*, 1989). Emanuel Todd and André Glucksmann have also spoken out defending the school's position to reject the veiled girls and urging society "to invite the immigrants to become French." In 1993, the leading Hungarian-French feminist Julia Kristeva published a book, *Strangers to Ourselves*, in which she significantly recaptures the biblical story of Ruth as the "good," assimilated immigrant, to pose it as a model for contemporary migrant women. The woman who collaborates, who leaves behind her own culture, who can no longer be recognized by her former relatives, condenses the qualities Kristeva and other intellectuals want the immigrants to have. The veiled women then, are not being "good immigrants," nor even "good women," in their acceptance of oppressive signs (for a critique of this position, see Honig, 1997; Spivak, 1997).

Through these discursive strategies, the veil has become the site of a struggle between conflicting values and cultures. According to the French National Ministry for Education, in 1989 there were 15,000 veiled girls attending schools; by the end of 1994, the total seemed to sum up 860 (Stein, 1994, p. 24). In this powerful movement, the discourse of the veil has rearticulated old discourses and policies on women and the Orient common to the Orientalism described by Edward Said (1978).

However, this Orientalist view neglects the complex history of the veil in Muslim societies.[8] Associated in the first place with the family of the Prophet, the use of the veil gradually included women from all strata of society. It is said that it allowed women to go out of the domestic space and engage in public activities. Although the protection of the women's body, the construction of her sexuality as something hidden, or reserved for the household, did certainly have implications for the maintaining of patriarchal structures, it also gave women the possibility of circulating around, seeing while not being seen. For some scholars, this gave the women a particular gaze, which is absent in most theorizations.[9] Due to this place, the veil has functioned as a

[8]As Trinh-Minh-ha remarked, "if the act of unveiling has a liberating potential, so does the act of veiling. It all depends on the context in which such an act is carried out, or more precisely, on how and where women see dominance" (Trinh Minh-ha, 1986-1987, p. 5). Although I do not completely agree with her appeal to a "liberating potential," as if this "potential" was already inscribed in the act itself and was not an effect of discursive and political articulation (Buenfil Burgos, 1997), Trinh Minh-ha's comments seem fruitful for reflecting on the complexity of the veil as a cultural and political sign.
[9]Some feminists, such as Leila Ahmed and Homa Hoodfar, criticize the Western view that the "veiled" status of Muslim women was "worse" or "more

screen on which colonial desires and fantasies about the sexuality of women have been projected, as has been the case with the harem (see Grewal, 1996).

In most Muslim countries, the unveiling has been perceived as a measure of Westernization and modernization, at least since the 19th century. Leila Ahmed recounted how travelers to Egypt and Egyptian pro-Western reformers constructed it as symbol of backwardness and oppression in the late 19th century (Ahmed, 1992). Assia Djebar, an Algerian writer, traced the images of Muslim women in Western painting, from Délacroix to Picasso, that presented them in the harem or veiled, always with forbidden sights, mainly as passive victims (Djebar, 1986/1987). An analysis of the history of compulsory unveiling of women during the Shah's regime in Iran, and the equally compulsory veiling since the Islamic revolution in 1978, shows to what extent the veil has condensed contradictory dynamics in terms of gender, class, and religious democracy. Instead of regarding it as an emancipating measure, the work done by an Iranian-Canadian scholar shows that the effects of compulsory unveiling of women in the Shah's regime in 1930s Iran had disastrous consequences for the women from lower classes, as it implied losing the possibility of getting into the streets, working at the weaving factories, or even attending schools, without achieving any compensatory gain (Hoodfar, 1986). In all these studies done by "Third World" feminists,[10] it is made evident that Western feminism became a part of the colonial discourses, producing an equivalence that is still difficult to disentangle for postcolonial feminists.

Ironically, thus, it is the colonial/Western discourse that has given new meanings to the veil, and has turned it into a contested symbol. Women in the Algerian struggle for independence used to hide guns under their veils and transport them around the city. After some bomb attacks, the French authorities attempted to forbid their use but as strong opposition emerged, the law was never fully put into practice. As Franz Fanon remarked, the French occupier was so occupied about unveiling Algeria that the veil became a symbol of resistance (Fanon, 1967).

---

oppressive" than the "unveiled" one of Western women. Also, they have pointed out the contradictions of many of the colonial functionaries who advocated for the unveiling of Muslim women in the colonies but were opposed to women's suffrage in the metropolis.

[10] I use the category of "Third World" for lack of a better one, although I am not comfortable with many of the implications invoked by it. I would like to acknowledge through it the work done by feminists who write from their "oblique, ex-orbitant" position to the transnational world order (Spivak, 1997).

One can hypothesize that the uses of the veil in contemporary France probably produces flashbacks of the experience of Algiers in collective memory, although significantly this is never mentioned. Despite the fact that they are predominantly Moroccan and Algerian, the immigrants are presented as "Iranian," and are said to be manipulated by fundamentalist groups.

What have been the positions articulated by the Muslim groups on this respect? There is almost no information in the mainstream journals and newspapers on this.[11] I refer to a sociological study done on the suburbs of Paris that interviewed several veiled girls from 1990 to 1993 (Gaspard & Khrosrokhavar, 1993). The teenagers claim to be choosing to wear the veil for very different reasons. Some of them perceive it as a way to protect themselves from the pressures of their families and to facilitate the transition to the adult world in Western societies. In that respect, it is an escape from the patriarchal structure of their families. Others conceive it as a marker of their menaced identity. It has been said that, after the Rushdie affair and the Gulf War, racism has provoked the behavior that Muslims do not intermingle with Whites as before, and in that respect do not experience as they did before—at least in their daily life—the conflicting values of both cultures. According to some studies,

> ...with the racial lines drawn and the Muslims as a community threatened, many amongst the youngest generation found that they had no choice other than returning to the fold and suspending any criticism of the veil. They have chosen to return to Islam, the religion that offers them a sense of identity, of belonging not only to a small community, but to a vast, vibral and vocal community, an *umma* that is prepared to defend the cause against all odds. (Afshar, 1993)

Even though they do not explicitly mention multiculturalism as their goal, the Muslim groups' defense of their right to difference is read as an affiliation and a consequence of the spread of multiculturalist ideals. In that respect, it is important to point out that the spread of educational discourses across the globe does not occur in a vacuum or in dialogue among equal partners. Educational fields are shaped by uneven and unequal international relations in which the

---

[11] In my doctoral research, I am trying to fill in this gap with other cultural texts, as popular music, literature, and movies. As an example of such materials, I instance the film "Salut, cousin!," shot in 1995 by Merzak Allouache, which tells the story of one young man coming from Algeria to Paris to do "some business" (smuggling clothes) for a couple of days. While he stays at his cousin's, a pop singer willing to be assimilated to France, the visitor learns about the daily life of immigrant Algerians. The movie provides a rich text about the multiple ways of being "Algerian" in France.

United States occupies an extremely influential economical and cultural position. It should not surprise us, then, that multiculturalism is read in different countries as the spread of Americanism and (to put it extremely) as a neocolonial project.

Thus, American multiculturalism has come to play the role of the "other" against which France must preserve itself. Multiculturalism is equated with tribalism, differentialism, and political correctness, all of which are seen as dynamics that threaten the achievements of the French republic (Scott, 1997). Gilles Kepel, a sociologist, claimed that the French assimilationist model of integration is largely preferable because the Anglo-Saxon way leads to ghettoization and tribalization (*Le Monde*, November 30, 1989, p. 14). Also, the Minister of Defense, Jean-Pierre Chevènement, warned against the charm of the American model that "hides the danger of balkanization" (*Le Monde*, November 9, 1989, p. 1). The anthropologist Emanuel Todd remarked that "there is a naïve reappraisal of the American discourse in favor of difference." The naïveté, in his view, implies that those who advocate for the right to difference ignore that the American society is a "machine of assimilation." Moreover, they lose sight of the fact that the French republican values are the most diverse way of life and belief of the world [sic] (*L'Express*, November 24, 1994, p. 28). Todd asked, why should we adopt multiculturalism if the French Republic is already cosmopolitan by itself? Maybe he should ask himself to what extent this cosmopolitanism is the expression of colonial *epistemes* and desires. In any case, he presents multiculturalism as a neocolonial discourse that tries to impose the experience of the United States on other countries, just as Eurodisney or McDonald's are doing.

In summation, I have argued that the construction of a homogeneous national identity, with roots in a public school system that has equated secularism to universalism, is being currently challenged by the insistence of Muslim girls to wear their veils at schooling. Whereas it seems clear that the French way to national integration needs to be rethought and remade to allow room for difference, it also can be argued that the religious affiliation proposed by the Muslim groups presents the same limits that Cameron McCarthy finds in current politics of racial affiliation in the United States. It assumes an indelible line of separation between one group and the other, and believes that culture and religion are some kind of property indisputably owned or possessed by a particular group. In that respect, it does not give us more help than traditional nationalisms to learn how to live with each other in a world of difference (McCarthy, 1998a), nor does it speak to the critical responsiveness that William Connolly advocates for.

However, I understand that this case provokes us to think about the importance of finding democratic grounds on which to articulate differences, a point that is not trivial and that multiculturalism also has to face at some point. Moreover, I find that these debates reflect in contradictory ways an effort to challenge the spread of global discourses and global solutions irrespective of national traditions and problems. What remains deeply problematic from my standpoint is that this contestation of a globalized discourse that appears as a new regulatory ideal for everybody is expressed in nationalistic terms, reaffirming the foundational myths of the republic and leaving unchallenged the roots of the injustice and exclusion that were made evident in the gesture of unveiling the girls.

THE ARGENTINEAN CASE: THE WHITE APRONS

Argentina shares with France and the United States a history of mass immigration that shaped in significant ways the construction of the nation. Initially colonized by the Spaniards, the Southern country was a marginal settlement and achieved its independence in 1810. The national state was built during the second half of the 19th century, at the same time that a genocide was committed against the nomad tribes of Native people. Also, local elites at the provincial states had to subject themselves to the power of a centralized oligarchy, and provincial identities, which up to that point had been the primary collective identities, had to be abandoned (Chiaramonte, 1989). From 1860 to 1930, 6 million people came to the country, most of them European, but also Middle Eastern immigrants, accounting for 75% of the total population growth in Argentina. The great majority settled down in Buenos Aires, the capital city, where almost 80% of the population were immigrants or children of immigrants by 1914 (Sarlo, 1993).[12]

To integrate this disparate population, a key factor was the organization of a national educational system. The "literate citizenship" (Sábato, 1992) educated by the schools would be the pillar of the republican order and the national union imagined by the founding fathers, most of them subscribers of a loose liberalism (Schwarz, 1977). Public instruction was conceived of as the best guarantee that the sovereign people would exercise its duties in the right way. As in

---

[12]Even in 1936, foreigners accounted for 36.1% of the total population of the big cities of the Littoral provinces (Sarlo, 1993, p. 12).

France, secularism became an important feature in the common culture created by schools. Everyone should be socialized on the same grounds, irrespective of their national and social origins or religion, and these grounds were seen as "neutral," "universal" terrain that would embrace all peoples.

Thus conceived, the public school turned into a formidable machine of assimilation of the immigrant and provincial population. The extension of elementary schooling and the introduction of a centralized teacher training system were the means through which this heterogeneous mass became integrated into Argentine society (Tedesco, 1986). Literacy rates soon achieved the levels of Western European countries, and a large reading public emerged that consumed textbooks, magazines, and books.[13] It is interesting to note that the popular literature had many points of contact with "high culture," and it was usual to find the writings of Borges or of European philosophers in the magazines that were bought massively by these newly literate (Romero & Gutiérrez, 1992). In the collective myths that forged the national imagery, Argentina was presented as a melting pot in which everyone would be welcomed and could move up in society and in culture.

However, the patterns of inclusion brought along other exclusions (Popkewitz, 1998). Like the French republican pact, the Argentinean common national self required rejecting particularisms and liberal individualistic programs. In order to become national subjects, immigrants should abandon their languages, mores, heroes, and costumes. The school system participated actively in this campaign (which was called the "Patriotic Crusade"), policing the boundaries of "proper Spanish," "proper memories," and "proper rules." Through the adoption of a medicalized pedagogy, children were "normalized" and subjected to strict disciplinarian rules and rituals (Puiggrós, 1990). Teaching practices were supposed to follow scientific methods that could be replicated across the country.

To illustrate this imagery that combined uniformity with progressive claims to equality and social progress, I refer to the introduction of white aprons (*guardapolvos*; literally, dusters) as school uniforms in the late 19th century—an event that I find becomes more relevant to the United States due to the current debates on school uniforms in several school districts. To avoid social differentiation by appearance, the educational authorities decreed that children should

---

[13] As early as 1930, 95% of the population of Buenos Aires was literate, and 30% attended high schools (Sarlo, 1993; Tedesco, 1986).

attend schools wearing an identical white cloth or apron over their clothes. This uniform, which resembles the one worn by medical doctors or nurses, also had some prophylactic aims, so as to prevent germs and bacteria from spreading throughout schools (Amuchastegui, 1995). Soon after, the teachers were obliged to wear them as well. Again, there are visible links between uniformity, particular notions of equity, and a medicalized pedagogical discourse.

What is intriguing is that this use of white aprons has survived to date. As many readers may know, Argentina has undergone a series of military dictatorships in this century. Generally speaking, every time a democratic government was elected, liberalizing policies were effected. However, the white apron not only has been kept as a uniform but also has gained new relevance recently in the heat of political struggles to defend public schooling.

What is it that makes it so resilient to changes? As with the veil in France, the white aprons condense multiple meanings. Like all uniforms, they imply that the individual should be addressed as a member of a particular group, which implies a series of behaviors and rituals that are expected to be performed by this uniformed subject. In other words, it has a particular readability as a sign that other clothes often do not (Lurie, 1981). In that respect, white aprons can be considered as another way of normalizing and disciplining children, of writing the laws in the bodies of the subjects, as Michel de Certeau has said (De Certeau, 1984).

However, there are other meanings as well. For many immigrants and children from low-income families, the possibility of an abstract equity and of hiding their backgrounds was appealing, for it implied a temporal release of the markers of difference. Whereas it can be argued that these markers remained in their language and habitus notwithstanding the uniformation, their narratives speak of inclusion and equity (Sarlo, 1997).

The current educational reforms in Argentina, which combine efficientism, World Bank recipes, and populist philanthropism in varied ways, have represented an abrupt interruption of these imageries (Dussel, Tiramonti, & Birgin, 2000). The notion of a uniform system has been replaced by compensatory programs that focus on "target populations," classifying the school children as "normal" or "needy" (those needing special assistance). The enactment of overt differentiation through lunch snacks and special aids to poor children has transformed the landscape of schools, breaking the tradition of uniformation. In many cases, classrooms and even schools have been closed due to the lack of funding. Competition among schools for the scarce resources has been implemented as a rule.

In this context, white aprons have become important as markers of inclusion within particular groups of the social field. The uniform locates the individual within a hierarchy; sometimes it even gives information about his or her achievements (Lurie, 1981). It is a symbol of distinction, of social inclusion in a different class of people, and in that respect it is more fiercely defended by those who have to rely on this acquired cultural capital for success (Bourdieu, 1984). This is expressed clearly by a 16-year-old teenager who lives in a low income neighborhood. She said: "I feel comfortable going to the school with my apron, because it means that you are a person in progress, in the making, it means that you are a student" (quoted in Duschatzky, 1998, p. 58). She recalled her pride in walking down the streets of her neighborhood wearing her apron, as a symbol that distinguishes and protects her from gangs and "lazy kids," as she called them.[14]

Moreover, white aprons have become the distinctive symbol of public schooling in the Teachers' Union protests. Since the beginning of 1997 the Teachers' Union has placed a white tent in front of the National Congress in Buenos Aires and its members have rotated themselves in fasting, denouncing their low salaries and complaining about the way in which the educational reform is being carried out. Interestingly, they have given away white aprons to people who visited them as a symbol of their claims, and have been wearing them all the time. Uniforms have become invested with new content, defending the tradition of a common schooling against recent trends to reshape it.

Given this background, it is not surprising that the reception of multiculturalism has been weak so far. As in France, multiculturalism is perceived as a "North American discourse" that cannot account for national traditions. On the part of the national government, the enactment of an overt differentiation in the compensatory programs recalls some aspects of the positive discrimination present in the affirmative action policies; for example, the targeting of a particular group on the assumption that current differentiation will lead to a leveled playing field in the future (Taylor, 1994). However, there is no appeal to the need to rethink the patterns of integration and

---

[14]This is consistent with the findings of an ethnographic work done in elementary schools in another district, also located in a low-income population (Redondo & Thisted, 1999). Parents put special emphasis on getting their children's aprons, and devote a large part of the subsidy they receive from the government to get them.

differentiation. Neither has there been an addition of "multicultural" contents to the curriculum in its recent reform.

Those who defend public schooling as it was before the current reforms, like the teachers and the students from low-income population who are in danger of being expelled from the school system, emphasize narratives of inclusion. The ideals of emancipation still organize the utopian dreams of those who want "their share of the cake," and difference appears to entail the threat of segregation, balkanization, and social schism. Another teenager from a low-income population expressed this judgment in the following way:

> When I finish high school I will study to become a history teacher. My head was blown by the French Revolution, the mixture of ideas, the will to emancipation. Instead, when studying the North American Revolution, I couldn't feel involved...they (the United States) invade you with their language. Kids now say "OK" instead of "sí." I don't like their culture.... You know, in the U.S. there are barrios for Latinos, Chinatowns, Black neighborhoods, they do not mingle with each other. (quoted in Duschatzky, 1998, p. 64)

Again, as in the French case, the resistance to multiculturalism discourses is posed in nationalistic terms, although this time it is expressed from the bottom of the social scale. However, this antimulticultural position tells something important about the need to link issues of difference to issues of inclusion. The national imagery of social inclusion is still powerful, and organizes the perception of children and teachers who feel, rather correctly, that they have a lot to lose in contemporary educational reforms. Regretfully, this "resistant" position has not implied any rearticulation of the notions of identity/difference, and has left unchallenged the traditional exclusions of alterity that have shaped the school system in Argentina.

CONCLUSION

Throughout this chapter, I have intended to show that multiculturalism implies the authorization and legitimation of particular assumptions of identity and difference, rooted mostly in the Anglo-Saxon experience. I have distinguished between a mainstream multiculturalism and an emergent "rhizomatic" one, which no longer is based on the affirmation of a cultural center. Despite these differences, when spread globally, multiculturalism discourses enter into different language games, national traditions, and political fields, which make them assume different meanings.

Both in France and Argentina, the tradition of school uniformity and universal secularism associates difference and diversity with danger and social split. In France, the emergence of a significant Muslim minority has challenged the republican consensus on a homogeneous national culture, and has started a wide debate on the grounds on which social integration should take place. United States multiculturalism has been attacked by advocates of the national tradition as bringing in balkanization and tribalism. In Argentina, the current reforms proposed by the government, which intend to reshape the public school system along the lines of social differentiation, meritocratic legitimacy, and compensatory programs, have been resisted in the name of uniformity and democracy. The traditional white apron, the school uniform that distinguished public schools students and teachers, has become a symbol of the struggle for defending a common schooling, and multiculturalism and difference are being associated with tribalization and U.S. neocolonialism.

What conclusions are to be drawn from these cases? I would like to point out just a few of them, which I find relevant for the international dialogue toward which this book is gesturing. It would be easy to dismiss these contestations, saying, as somebody has in a graduate class, that the French and the Argentineans are authoritarian and do not know anything about civil rights. But that would also prevent any dialogue from beginning, and would shut and compress positions that are complex and multifarious (Said, quoted in Simoes de Carvalho, 1998, p. 17) and that need to be disentangled in order to construct a more receptive ground for a rhizomatic multiculturalism.

First, we must remind ourselves that the spread of multiculturalism, as it has been said before in this chapter, does not occur in a vacuum. Educational fields are shaped by uneven and unequal international relations in which the United States occupies an extremely influential economical and cultural position. Dialogue, then, does not take place between equal partners, nor is it free from power relations. Any attempt to bridge over this differential reception of multiculturalism must take this fact into account.

Second, multiculturalism is read from within national imageries that are structured by particular constructions of identity and difference. Multiculturalism discourses, understood as regulatory ideals about how we are to live with each other in our contemporary world, intersects and interrupts these imageries. This juncture, if it is to avoid becoming a monologue on each part and promote an interchange, always entails some violence. To pretend a smooth, global adoption of multiculturalism rhetoric will not help in the construction of a common understanding.

Third, it is important to understand that multiculturalism's heterogeneity in the U.S. field is generally not perceived as such worldwide. In that respect, the narratives of inclusion that appear at the center of contestation against multiculturalist discourses in France and Argentina should not be trivialized nor considered part of a "false consciousness" by those who speak them, in some sort of "collective deceit." In the circulation of multicultural discourses in the countries I have analyzed, the right to be different seems to be opposed to the narratives of inclusion. If that is something that minorities have struggled against painfully and dramatically in the United States, this struggle is nonetheless blurred and almost missed in the way in which multiculturalism is being disseminated across the globe.

Given these conclusions, is it then possible to maintain a dialogue that cuts across national experiences and that does not establish a new supremacy, called Americanization or whatever? I feel that a starting point should be to give up the pretension of building a new universalism against which we should measure all other experiences (Simões de Carvalho, 1998; Zizek, 1997). Instead, we should remind ourselves that power relations are deeply inscribed in our discourses, even when they are formulated by the minorities or by the periphery of the world-system.[15] This does not mean, however, that the quest for a democratic ground be abandoned. On the contrary, it posits again the old question about the translatability of cultures, which compel us both to strive for common grounds and to accept that ultimately some parts of a foreign culture might remain an irreducible alterity for ourselves (Donald, 1992). As Sanford Budick (1996) asserted, "even if we are always defeated by translation, culture as a movement toward shared consciousness may emerge" from this defeat (p. 22). What may be perceived initially as a pitfall can ultimately be a source of strength for cultural and political renewal.

Finally, this quest for a dialogue across experiences on how multiculturalism is being played out globally also implies a new responsibility, that of looking to what has been excluded and forgotten

---

[15]Paul Gilroy offers one of the best, to my knowledge, accounts of these power relations in the differences around how to define "Blackness" and "Africanness" between African-Americans, Black British, Caribbean Blacks, etc. (Gilroy, 1993). Also, Gloria Anzaldúa analyzes the frictions between Chicanas and Mexicanas in her *Borderlands/La Frontera* (1987). For me, these cases speak about the need to leave this space of universalism open and to continually challenge every attempt to fix it as a given, immutable place (Laclau, 1996).

in our present struggles. Although nationalisms have caused and are still causing terrible pains to human beings (and I am certainly not interested in resuscitating them), those who contest multiculturalism in terms of national traditions may be speaking today about the need to re-articulate difference and inclusion in new ways, and in that respect, I find they challenge us to provide even more vigorous narratives of multiculturalism that account for diversity as well as for social justice.

ACKNOWLEDGMENTS

This chapter is part of my fieldwork for my Ph.D. dissertation. I would like to thank Gustavo Fischman for his help in developing some of these ideas. Also, Tom Popkewitz has provided me with a challenging and encouraging intellectual environment at the University of Wisconsin-Madison, and I am grateful to him for that.

REFERENCES

Afshar, H. (1993). Schools and Muslim girls: Gateway to prosperous future or quagmire of racism? Some experiences from West Yorkshire. In R. Barot (Ed.), *Religion and ethnicity: Minorities and social change in the metropolis* (pp. 56-67). Kampen, Netherlands: Kot Pharos.

Ahmed, L. (1992). *Women and gender in Islam*. New Haven & London: Yale University Press.

Alia, J. (1994, December 8-14). Islam: La résistance à intégrisme [The resistance to integration]. *Le Nouvel Observateur*, 4-9.

Amuchastegui, M. (1995). Los rituales patrióticos en la escuela pública [Patriotic rituals in public schools]. In A. Puiggrós (Ed.), *Discursos pedagógicos e imaginario social en el peronismo (1945-1955)* [Pedagogical discourses and social imaginary during the peronist governments (1945-1955)] (pp. 13-41). Buenos Aires: Galerna.

Anzaldúa, G. (1987). *Borderlands/La frontera: The new mestiza*. San Francisco: Aunt Lute.

Audard, C. (1996). Political liberalism, secular republicanism: Two answers to the challenges of pluralism. In D. Archard (Ed.), *Philosophy and pluralism* (pp. 163-175). Royal Institute of Philosophy Supplement: 40.

Badinter, E., Debray, R., Finkielkraut, A., de Fontenay, E., & Kintzler, C. (1989, November 2-9). Lettre ouverte [Open letter]. *Le Nouvel Observateur*, pp. 9-10.

Beriss, D. (1990, Winter). Scarves, schools, and segregation: The *Foulard* affair. *French Politics & Society, 8*(1), 1-13.

Bourdieu, P. (1984). *Distinction: A social critique of the judgment of the taste*. Cambridge: Harvard University Press.

Budick, S. (1996). Crisis of alterity: Cultural untranslatability and the experience of secondary otherness. In S. Budick & W. Iser (Eds.), *The translatability of cultures: Figurations of the space between* (pp. 1-22). Stanford, CA: Stanford University Press.

Buenfil Burgos, R. (1997, June). Is ambiguity synonymous with non accountability? Postmodernism and discourse political analysis. Paper presented at the 1st Annual Conference Reclaiming Voices: Ethnographic Inquiry and Qualitative Research in a Post-modern Age, University of Southern California, Los Angeles.

Butler, J. (1993). *Bodies that matter: On the discursive limits of "sex."* New York & London: Routledge.

Chiaramonte, J. C. (1989). Formas de identidad en el Río de la Plata (1810-1850) [Forms of identity in the Rio de la Plata area (1810-1850)]. *Boletín del Instituto de Historia Argentina, 1*(2), 13-30.

Connolly, W. (1996). Pluralism, multiculturalism, and the nation-state: Rethinking the connections. *Journal of Political Ideologies, 1*(1), 53-73.

Crubellier, M. (1993). *L'école républicaine, 1870-1940: Esquisse d'une histoire culturelle* [The republican school, 1870-1940: Towards a cultural history]. Paris: Christian.

De Certeau, M. (1984). *The practice of everyday life.* (S. Rendall, Trans.) Berkeley & London: University of California Press.

Derrida, J. (1992). Force of law: The "mystical foundation of authority." In D. Cornell, M. Rosenfeld, & D. Gray Carlson (Eds.), *Deconstruction and the possibility of justice* (pp. 3-67). New York: Routledge.

Djebar, A. (1986-87, Fall-Winter). Forbidden sight, interrupted sound. *Discourse, 8,* 39-56.

Donald, J. (1992). *Sentimental education.* London: Verso.

Donald, J., & Rattansi, A. (Eds.). (1992). *Race, "culture" and difference.* London & Newbury Park: Sage.

Duschatzky, S. (1998). *El valor simbólico de la escuela para jóvenes de sectores populares* [The symbolic value of schooling for low-income students]. Buenos Aires: Fundación Banco Patricios.

Dussel, I., Tiramonti, G., & Birgin, A. (2000). Decentralization and recentralization in the Argentine educational reform: Reshaping educational policies in the '90s. In T. S. Popkewitz (Ed.), *Educational knowledge: Changing relationships between the state, civil society, and the educational community* (pp. 155-172). Albany: SUNY Press.

Fanon, F. (1967). *A dying colonialism* (H. Chevalier, Trans.). New York: Grove Press.

Foucault, M. (1972). *The archeology of knowledge & the discourse on language* (A. M. Sheridan Smith, Trans.). New York: Pantheon.

Gaspard, F., & Khrosrokhavar, F. (Eds.). (1995). *Le foulard et la République* [The veil and the Republic]. Paris: La Découverte.

Gilroy, P. (1993). *The Black Atlantic: Modernity and double consciousness.* Cambridge: Harvard University Press.

Grant, C., & Ladson-Billings, G. (Eds.). (1997). *Dictionary of multicultural education.* Phoenix, AZ: Oryx Press.

Grewal, I. (1996). *Home and harem: Nation, gender, empire, and the cultures of travel.* Durham & London: Duke University Press.

Honig, B. (1997). Ruth, la modèle immigrée. *Political Theory, 25*(2), 112-136.

Hoodfar, H. (1986). The veil in their minds and on our heads: The persistence of colonial images of Muslim women. *Resources in Feminist Research, 22*(3/4), 5-18.

Kazamias, A., & Schwartz, K. (1977). Intellectual and ideological perspectives in comparative education: An interpretation. *Comparative Education Review, 21*(2 & 3), 153-176.

Köker, L. (1996). Political toleration or politics of recognition: The headscarves affair revisited. *Political Theory, 24*(2), 315-320.

Laclau. E. (1996). *Emancipation(s).* London: Verso.

Lurie, A. (1981). *The language of clothes.* New York: Random House.

McCarthy, C. (1998a). *The uses of culture: Education and the limits of ethnic affiliation.* New York: Routledge.

McCarthy, C. (1998b, April). All-consuming identities: Race and the pedagogy of resentment in the age of difference. Paper presented at AERA Meeting, San Diego, CA.

Modood, T., & Werbner, P. (Eds.). (1997). *The politics of multiculturalism in the new Europe: Racism, identity, and community.* London & New York: Zed Books.

Nique, Ch., & Lelièvre, C. (1993). *La République n'éduquera plus. La fin du mythe Ferry* [The Republic will no longer educate: The end of the ferry myth]. Paris: Librairie Plon.

Noiriel, G. (1996). *The French melting pot. Immigration, citizenship, and national identity* (G. de Laforcade, Trans.). London & Minneapolis: University of Minnesota Press.

Ognier, P. (1988). *L'Ecole républicaine française et ses miroirs* [The French republican school and its mirrors]. Bern, Switzerland: Peter Lang.

Ognier, P. (1993, Août-Décembre). Ancienne ou nouvelle laïcité? Après dix ans de débats [Old or new secularism? After 10 years of debates]. *Esprit, (194),* 202-220.

Popkewitz, T. S. (1998). *Struggling for the soul: The politics of education and the construction of the teacher.* New York: Teachers College Press.

Puiggrós, A. (1990). *Sujetos, disciplina y curriculum en los orígenes del sistema educativo Argentino (1885-1916)* [Subjects, discipline, and curriculum at the origins of the Argentine educational system, 1885-1916]. Buenos Aires: Galerna.

Redondo, P., & Thisted, S. (1999). Las escuelas primarias en los margenes [The schools in the margins]. In A. Puiggros (Ed.), *En los límites de las educacion formal: Niños y jóvenes de fin de siglo* [Imagining the future: Educational prospective and utopia] (pp. 143-190). Buenos Aires: Homo Sapiens, Rosario.

Romero, L. A., & Gutiérrez, L. (1992). Ciudadanía política y ciudadanía social: Los sectores populares en Buenos Aires, 1912-1955 [Political and social citizenship: Low-income groups in Buenos Aires, 1912-1955]. *Indice,* (5), 12-25.

Rose, N. (1997). Identity, genealogy, history. In S. Hall & P. du Gay (Eds.), *Questions of cultural identity* (pp. 128-150). London & Thousand Oaks: Sage.

Sábato, H. (1992, August). Citizenship, political participation and the formation of the public sphere in Buenos Aires: 1850s-1880s. *Past and Present, (136).*

Said, E. (1978). *Orientalism.* New York: Pantheon Books.

Sarlo, B. (1993). *Borges: A writer on the edge.* London: Verso.

Sarlo, B. (1997). Cabezas rapadas y cintas argentinas [Shaved heads and Argentine emblems]. *Prismas: Revista de Historia Intelectual, 1*(1), 187-191.

Schwarz, R. (1977). As idéias fora do lugar [Misplaced ideas]. In *Ao vencedor as batatas* [Potatoes for the winner] (pp. 13-25). Sao Paulo: Duas Cidades.

Scott, J. (1997). "La querelle des femmes" in the late twentieth century. *New Left Review, 226,* 3-19.

Simões de Carvalho, P. (1998). Failing to marvel: The nuances, complexities, and challenges of multicultural education. *Multicultural Education, 5*(3), 14-17.

Spivak, G. (1997). Diasporas old and new: Women in the transnational world. In A. Kumar (Ed.), *Class issues: Pedagogy, cultural studies, and the public sphere* (pp. 87-116). New York & London: New York University Press.

Stein, S. (1994, November 24). Le complot [The plot]. *L'Express,* p. 24.

Taylor, Ch. (1994). The politics of recognition. In A. Gutman (Ed.), *Multiculturalism: Examining the politics of recognition* (pp. 25-73). Princeton: Princeton University Press.

Tedesco, J. C. (1986). *Educación y sociedad en la Argentina (1880-1945)* [Education and society in Argentina, 1880-1945]. Buenos Aires: Hachette.

Todd, E. (1994, November 24). Invitons-les a devenir françaises [Let's invite them to become French]. *L'Express*, p. 28.

Trinh   T.   Minh-ha.   (1986-87,   Fall-Winter).   Introduction: She,   the inappropriate/d other. *Discourse, 8*, 3-9.

Weber, S. (1996). *Mass mediauras: Forms, technics, media*. Stanford, CA: Stanford University Press.

Winant,   H.   (1994).   *Racial   conditions: Politics,   theory,   comparisons*. Minneapolis & London: University of Minnesota Press.

Zizek, S. (1997). Multiculturalism, or, the cultural logic of multinational capitalism. *New Left Review, 225*, 28-51.

Chapter 5

Fashion or Compensation: The Developments of Multicultural Education in Taiwan

Chuen-Min Huang
National Taiwan Normal University, Taiwan

The ideal and movement of multicultural education has existed in Taiwan for only about one decade. It is still in the infant stage if compared with the United States. However, as Gay (1992a, 1998a) pointed out, the major goals of multicultural education should apply in all settings, but the operational practices should be appropriately contextualized in different individual geopolitical and sociohistorical milieus. In other words, the development and implementation of multicultural education in different settings represent individually a unique case that needs to be carefully examined in its own historical, social, cultural, and political background. It is important to know how the developments of multicultural education in different settings are affected by different geopolitical and sociohistorical contexts.

Taiwan is definitely not a monolingual or monocultural society, although the percentage of the four ethnic groups that comprise the island's population is widely disparate. They are 73.3% Southern Min, 13% Mainlanders, 12% Hakka, and 1.7% aborigines (X. F. Huang, 1994). The people in Taiwan view the nine aboriginal tribes that belong to the Malayo-Polynesian Austronesian linguistic family as racially different from the dominant Han people, who belong to the Sinitic (or Sino-Tibetan) linguistic family. Even though the Hakka and Southern Min people, who immigrated from Mainland China in the 17th and 18th centuries, belong to Han ethnic groups and have largely adopted the Chinese characters as the written orthography, their various languages are not mutually intelligible. Nor are Hakka and Southern Min comprehensible to the different dialects of Mainlanders or Mandarin. Furthermore, many Taiwanese are familiar with Japanese because compulsory 6-year Japanese education was put into effect from the 1930s to 1945 during the Japanese occupation in Taiwan (1895-1945).

The major purpose of this chapter is to examine the developments of multicultural education in Taiwan. It is important to know why there is a need for multicultural education, what the background of multicultural education is within Taiwan's geopolitical and sociohistorical context, how different factors affected the evolution of multicultural education, what have the developmental characteristics of the multicultural education movement been like in Taiwan, and what are the future concerns.

Data derived from documentary reviews and instructional material analyses[1] provide information and explanation to indicate the developments of multicultural education in Taiwan around language, ethnicity, and gender issues. The documents used in producing this chapter included the policies, regulations, and official acts on the issues of language, ethnicity, and gender from the late 1940s to the present. Instructional materials analyzed here include curriculum standards,[2] national textbooks,[3] approved textbooks,[4] mother tongue teaching books,[5] and homeland culture books.[6] Before 1996, all textbooks used in schools for Grades 1 to 9 were national textbooks, which followed the 1968 and 1975 curriculum standards. After 1996, the approved textbooks, which followed the 1993 curriculum standards, were allowed to be published by commercial agencies. The first textbooks were released in 1996 and 1997. Also, after 1993, seven DPP (Democratic Progressive Party) governing counties[7] have compiled their own materials for homeland culture and mother tongue teaching in schools.

---

[1] Part of the data used in this chapter were based on the author's dissertation, *Language Education Policies and Practices in Taiwan: From Nationism to Nationalism* (1997), College of Education, University of Washington.

[2] There are two types of curriculum materials in Taiwan. One is curriculum standards and the other is textbooks. Curriculum standards are the guidelines for writing textbooks, and textbooks are the edited outcomes based on curriculum standards.

[3] Before 1996, textbooks were edited, compiled, and published by the National Institute for Compilation and Translation (NICT), an affiliated organization of the Ministry of Education.

[4] After 1996, textbooks published by commercial agencies or the NICT need to get approval from the Ministry of Education.

[5] As part of the homeland culture teaching, mother tongue teaching, such as Southern Min, Hakka, and aboriginal languages, has been promoted by several local county governments because Mandarin, the national language, is not the first language/mother tongue of most Taiwanese people.

[6] "Homeland culture" here refers to Taiwan-centered recognition rather than China-centered recognition, which was the focus of previous curricula.

[7] The DPP was founded in 1986. Since then, it has won more seats in the election of legislators, representatives, and county governors. It had governors in seven counties in 1993. All of them are much involved in the promotion of mother tongue curriculum and instruction. They were Kaohsiung, Penghu, Pingdong, Taipei, Yilan, Xinzhu, and Zhanghua.

SOCIOHISTORICAL CONTEXT

The defeat of the Nationalist government by the Chinese Communists in 1949 led the Nationalists to retreat to Taiwan "temporarily." The Nationalist government in Taiwan, which viewed itself as representative of all of China, vowed to return to the Mainland and reunify China. There was a belief that since Mandarin was adopted as the national language in the late 1920s on the Mainland, Taiwan, as a province of China from 1885 and as the official residence of the Nationalist government, should also adopt Mandarin. Therefore, the Nationalist government, which did not acknowledge the existence of multilingualism and the diversity of ethnicity and culture, strongly promoted a Mandarin-only policy and China-centered politics in Taiwan.

This situation did not change until the period of 1985 to 1989. Recent rapid economic development and growing democratization in Taiwan have initiated many changes. An opposition party was founded in 1986, and martial law was lifted in 1987. Since then, people have been expressing their individual and ethnic rights in the political and educational arenas. Ethnic revitalization has led to increased efforts to maintain local/Taiwanese languages, and to promote the rights of ethnic groups and Taiwan-centered politics.

In order to reveal the three dimensions of multicultural education in the development process, this section briefly described the sociohistorical context of multicultural education in Taiwan. Detailed contextualization and analysis of political, economic, social, historical, and cultural relationships within which multicultural education developed is provided in the following section.

DEVELOPMENTS AND PRACTICES

The origin of multicultural education in Taiwan was initiated by arguments about the relations of ethnicity, language, and national identity among the KMT (Kuomingtang[8]), aboriginal groups, local groups, legislators, provincial/national representatives, and the opposition party. Conflicts between legislators, representatives, and government officials on language issues in the Legislative Yuan and the National Assembly during the transition period also presented confusion around languages and dialects, and around language and

---

[8] KMT is the political party of the Nationalist government.

group identity.[9] The national governmental official assumed that those "dialects" were not national, official, or common languages, and did not allow them in public institutions. Some legislators and representatives, on the other side, thought that Southern Min and Hakka are the mother tongues of the 85% majority in Taiwan and therefore should be allowed in public use. Both sides were partially correct, because language alone is not sufficient to develop national unity and ethnic identity.

Theoretically, the developments of multicultural education in Taiwan from the late 1940s to the present can be divided into three different periods: predevelopment (1949-1985), transition (1985-1989), and after transition (1989-present). In the period of predevelopment, China-centered politics, Han dominant culture, and Mandarin-only policies were promoted. During the transition period, together with powers from economic development, growing democratization, ethnic revitalization, and local group activity movement, diverse voices from different ethnic, gender, and linguistic groups were allowed to speak out loudly. After the transition period, the improvements made by multicultural education around issues of language, ethnicity, and gender have gradually become evident in the related documentary policies and instructional materials.

Language

Together with culture, religion, and history, language has been regarded as a major component of nationalism. Fishman (1972, pp. 39-35) suggestsedthat a common vernacular or an ancestral group language serves as a medium for nationalism, a link to a people's "glorious past," a path to confirm one's authenticity, and as a means to help construct a "contrastive self-identification." He contended that language in nationalism is used to pursue "the nationalistic unity, priority, or superiority of sociocultural aggregate," because it represents "the continuity of a Great Tradition with all of its symbolic elaborations in terms of ideologized values and goals" (Fishman, 1968a, p. 9; 1968b, p. 43). Obviously, there is a close relationship among language, history, culture, and identity. At a general level, ethnicity is viewed as a "sense of group identity deriving from real or perceived common bonds such as language, race or religion" (Edwards, 1977, p. 254). Furthermore, ethnic identity must persist by some sense of a group boundary that "can be sustained by shared objective characteristics (language, religion, etc.), or by more subjective contri-

---

[9] After the 228 Incident in 1947, the KMT was equal to the Mainlanders and people who cannot speak Taiwanese. After the establishment of DPP in 1986, the DPP was equal to the Taiwanese who were not Mandarin origins.

butions to a sense of 'groupness,' or by some combination of both" (Edwards, 1985, p. 10).

From this discussion, there is no question that the relationship between language and ethnic/national identity is an important one. But language is not the prerequisite of ethnic identity or national unity. Language is not the only feature of group identification; nor is it alone sufficient for affiliative bonds or nationalist sentiment (Cheng, 1979; Edwards, 1985; Fishman, 1972). However, Hung (1995) pointed out that language is a marker of ethnicity in Taiwan, and that mother tongue identity is equal to ethnic identity. He contended that, "Physique is the character of race; culture is the character of nationality (minzu) and language is its concrete character. In Taiwan, losing language is equal to the death of nationality" (Hung, 1992, p. 29). The political conflicts in Taiwan, as X. F. Huang (1994) stated, involved the explicit display of Mainland-or-Taiwan-origin concerns and resulted from an inappropriate language policy and its related political ideology. This means the political conflicts in Taiwan have complicated relations with ethnicity, language, and national identity.

During the predevelopment period, from the late 1940s to the 1980s, several characteristics of language policy were summarized according to the author's analyses (C. M. Huang, 1997). First, the Nationalist government, as a newcomer to Taiwan, used Mandarin promotion as a solution to language problems, an enhancement of societal stability, and a retention of legitimacy. Second, Mandarin promotion was a feasible choice that could reap the most benefit for the least cost because Mandarin-only promotion could save more money and time than bilingual programs. Third, the choice of a Mandarin promotion movement was a "good enough" rather than "best" option for solving pressing problems, avoiding disturbance to the new regime, and enhancing the governmental organization's stability. Fourth, the compromise between the ideal of bilingual programs and the reality of Mandarin promotion was a choice made by the government with consideration of the distribution of scarce materials and/or symbolic resources. Finally, after more than 40 years of promotion, Mandarin prevailed as the dominant language, and learning Mandarin was conditioned by the symbolic language images of it as a powerful tool for education, accessing economic and political resources, and facilitating upward social mobility.

Following the founding of the opposition party (DPP) in 1986 and the lifting of the martial law in 1987, the political climate in Taiwan gradually moved toward the process of democratization. This kind of movement, however, also created political tensions and other attached conflicts among different interest groups because the political conflicts in Taiwan involved issues of language, ethnicity, and national identity. Particularly, many language events and conflicts took place among different groups in the late 1980s, the transition period. The aboriginal and local groups founded some associations, societies, centers, and magazines to promote their pursuits. On the other side, the legislators and representatives began to question the Act of Radio Broadcasting and Television Programming (RBTP),[10] which required local languages on television programs and news reports, and began to challenge the status of local languages in school curriculum and instruction. The government, however, still insisted on the Mandarin-only policy and rejected the proposals from the local groups, legislators, and representatives to revise the Act of RBTP. After Martial Law was lifted in 1987, 20 minutes of news reporting in Southern Min and a half hour of programming in Hakka on one television channel were allowed. Another important event is the elimination of punishment for speaking non-Mandarin languages on all public school campuses.

From this description, it is clear that the reaction of the government to these language events and conflicts during the transition period is a kind of "choice of no choice." This kind of passive reaction toward all kinds of language issues included curriculum reform, mother tongue teaching and homeland culture education, the deletion of section 20 from the Act of RBTP, non-Mandarin language programs and news report on televisions, and the elimination of punishment for speaking non-Mandarin languages at schools. The initial motivation for these changes came from aboriginal and local groups' ethnic revitalization, but the contribution of legislators cannot be ignored. The creation of the opposition party (DPP) in 1986 and its increasing members in the Legislative Yuan, the National Assembly, the Municipal and Provincial Council, and the county government represented the accumulation of political resources to oppose the Mandarin-only language policy and China-centered politics from the government. Unlike the Mandarin-only period from the 1940s to the 1980s, legitimizing the new regime in Taiwan was not the main focus after the transition period. Instead of concentrating on the issues of geopolitical integration and widespread Mandarin use, the issues of sociocultural unity through recognizing mother tongue rights, ethnic identity, and homeland authenticity have become more important.

The development of changes in language policies was also reflected in instructional materials. The national language (Mandarin), which was the only language subject and material taught in schools before 1993, was a symbol of monolingualism. It served as a functional choice for the ideology of geopolitical integration quite well. The publication of mother tongue teaching materials by county governments since 1993

---

[10] The Act of RBTP was approved by the Legislative Yuan in 1976. In section 20, it stated that "the major language for domestic broadcasting is Mandarin, and dialects should decrease yearly."

was a major sign that different ethnic groups' authenticity and identity can be voiced through their own mother tongues. This also indicated the growing involvement of local governments in efforts to improve language policies. These new efforts included the creation of phonetic alphabets by some ethnic groups and the introduction of ethnic cultures in their own languages. They symbolized a move toward gradual sociocultural integration of Taiwan's multicultural population instead of a more political integration.

Ethnicity

As mentioned earlier, language and ethnicity are closely related. This is particularly true in the developments of multicultural education in Taiwan because political conflicts involved language, ethnicity, and identity. Language not only served an instrumental and practical function, but also as symbolic, psychological, and authentic affirmation. The promotion of the Mandarin-only policy and China-centered politics did solve communication problems, enhanced societal stability, and retained political legitimacy, but it deeply hurt the affirmation of the Taiwanese majority's ethnic identity.

During the predevelopment period, the rights of different ethnic groups were ignored because of the strong ideology of China-centered politics and Han culture domination. First, ideals and realities were not matched. For example, following the examination of the ROC (Republic of China) Constitution, articles 5, 159, 168, and 169 declared that all ethnic groups are equal, all people have equal educational opportunity, and that minority groups' legal status, culture, and education should be protected and supported. Ideally, the spirit of the Mainland-edition Constitution[11] on protecting minority groups' rights is high. However, this high spirit was not implemented in the reality of Taiwanese society. As a new regime from the Mainland, the KMT government internally needed to regulate conflict over the distribution of scarce materials and/or symbolic resources in ways that retained its legitimacy. Externally, in the middle of the 1950s, the battles over Quemoy (Jinmen)[12] with the Chinese Communists required an expensive and large-scale military offensive. Faced with threats to national security and regime legitimacy, the KMT government needed to make a choice between an ideal and a reality. However, under the

---

[11] The original ROC Constitution was approved by the National Assembly in 1946, when the Nationalist government still controlled the Mainland.
[12] Quemoy (Jinmen), a name of small islands located on the Taiwan Straits and very close to Fujian Province of Mainland China, had many battles with the Chinese Communist in the 1950s.

ideology of Han-dominant culture and China-centered politics, the government might not even have had the extra energy and resources to pay attention to issues such as minority rights. In other words, the Taiwan authorities promoted a strong assimilationist policy.

Second, unrealistic policies were put into effect. The KMT government in Taiwan, which viewed itself as representative of all of China, vowed to return to the Mainland and reunify China. After the retreat from the Mainland in 1949, they adopted the Mainland-edition Constitution for Taiwan. The Council for Tibetans and Mongolians, following the Mainland-edition Constitution, was founded at the Executive Yuan even though there was no Tibetan or Mongolian minority in Taiwan. Both the aborigines and Hakka are the demographic, political, and economic minority in Taiwan. However, no council for the aborigines and/or Hakka was created. The reality of diverse ethnicity in Taiwan was ignored under China-centered politics.

The rights of different ethnic groups in Taiwan continued to be ignored until the late 1980s, the transition period. Ethnic revitalization led to increased efforts to maintain Taiwanese culture and to promote the rights of ethnic groups and Taiwan-centered politics. Therefore, the assimilation policy and China-centered politics have been gradually changed. Several improvements on ethnic group rights provide evidence for this. First, the Committee for Aboriginal Education at the Ministry of Education, which is in charge of general education issues of the aborigines, was founded in 1988. Second, the Council for the Aborigines at the Executive Yuan, which is responsible for specific aboriginal education and cultures, was founded in 1996. Third, the Research Center for Aboriginal Education was established in five Teachers Colleges[13] in the early 1990s. Fourth, the Educational Reform Council of Executive Yuan (1996) proposed recommendations for the improvements of aboriginal education. Fifth, a constitution amendment in 1997, which claims to protect and develop the aboriginal languages, cultures, education, legal status, political participation, and other social welfare, recognized the multicultural reality of Taiwan. Finally, the Legislative Yuan approved the Act of Aboriginal Education in 1998 based on the 1997 constitution amendment. It is the first legal protection of aboriginal education in Taiwan.

From the analyses of instructional materials, several changes also illuminated the ideological shifts from a geopolitical emphasis to a recognition of diverse ethnicities. These changes were evident at both levels of structure and substance. Structurally, the shift from old curriculum standards (1968 and 1975) to new standards (1993), from

---

[13] They are Hualien, Pingdong, Taidong, Taizhung, and Xinchu Teachers' Colleges.

national textbooks to approved textbooks after 1996, and from national textbooks to homeland culture and mother tongue teaching materials indicate significant changes in cultural and ethnic priorities.

Substantial changes in ethnic and cultural policies were also evident in the content of the instructional materials. From the 1960s to the 1980s, the emphases of the political boundary of "China" had gradually shifted to the idea of China unity and peaceful unity between the Straits. However, the political ideology was too dominant to allow space for ethnic issues. Since the early 1990s, understanding Taiwan and homeland recognition have become hot topics. Instead of the previous emphasis on geopolitical integration, more attention is given to the emotional feelings of ethnic groups and their identities. Descriptions about the lives and cultures of ethnic minorities have become more accurate and detailed in textbooks. These developments are receiving important support, from the addition of "Homeland Instruction Activity" to regular elementary instructional materials, and the publication of homeland culture and mother tongue instructional materials. In addition, books about the cultures of different ethnic groups are being published, including ones about the aborigines, Hakka, and Southern Min. Generally speaking, more important and complete issues about ethnic groups such as their origins, histories, mythologies, religions, models, festivals, arts, songs and dances, and proverbs are presented.

Gender

Unlike language and ethnicity, gender[14] has seldom been connected with the movement of multicultural education in Taiwan. Most people in Taiwan rarely make the connection between gender issues and multicultural education. Some even do not consider gender as an important dimension of multicultural education. The reason could be that the issue of gender is not directly related to political conflicts and national identity, which were the stimulus for the initiation of multicultural education in Taiwan during the transition period.

Gender issues have become a nationwide topic after a famous feminist in Taiwan was sexually assaulted and killed in 1996. Immediately after that event, the Legislative Yuan passed the Act of Sexual Violence Protection, which had been in development for several years. The Act requires that all students at every grade level take courses on sexual violence protection for a minimum of 4 hours. In

[14] Special thanks are given to Professor Wen-jing Shan. His unpublished article on gender equity education in Taiwan provided many recent event documents on this issue.

1997, the Ministry of Education organized the Committee of Gender Equity Education[15] to promote gender equity, gender equity education, and education for sexual violence protection. Furthermore, several private and official journals have published special issues on the topic of gender equity education. From 1996 to 1999, the official policies on gender issues and gender equity education have made a great improvement.

Although gender concerns have been a nationwide issue for only a few years, the attention to gender equity can also be found in course selection and instructional materials. Before 1996, courses like home economics, nursing, handcraft arts, and martial arts training were designed for male and female students separately. Gender bias, prejudice, stereotypes, inequity, and the invisibility of females were prevalent in the narrative texts and visual images (Hsieh, 1999; C. M. Huang, 1993). Also, the language tone was often from the male perspective. After the establishment of the Committee of Gender Equity Education in 1997, the decision of including gender equity education in the New Guidelines for Grades 1 to 9 Curriculum was made. According to the New Guidelines for Grades 1 to 9 Curriculum (Ministry of Education, 1999), gender awareness, relationship, equity, role learning, and rights will be major concepts in the new curriculum, which will be implemented in 2001. More substantial integration of gender issues into the instructional materials are expected in the future.

DEVELOPMENTAL CHARACTERISTICS

The descriptions of language, ethnicity, and gender issues in Taiwan from different data sources indicate that the developments of multicultural education in Taiwan from the late 1940s to the present have been shifting from the predevelopment period to the after-transition period. Some features of the developments are presented here.

A More Open Government

Several developments in the official policies and practices of multicultural education have occurred that indicate the emergence of

---

[15] Five divisions of the Committee were included: teaching and teacher education, curriculum and instructional materials, research development and assessment, crisis treatment, and social and parental education.

more governmental openness and flexibility toward cultural diversity. The Committee for the Promotion of Mandarin, established in 1945, has to adjust its role and duty to better respect and honor the languages of different ethnic groups. Section 20, which is against the language freedom of television broadcasting, was deleted from the Act of RBTP in 1993. The first television company that is not affiliated with the government was allowed to open in 1997. This means that language freedom in television broadcasting has been advanced. Also, the Minister of Internal Affairs indicated that discrimination against people's mother tongues was inappropriate and that the government should begin to respect them.

The Council for Tibetans and Mongolians still exists following the original Mainland-edition Constitution. The Council for the Aborigines was finally founded in 1996. This indicates a compromise of ideal and reality for the KMT government after the transition period. The reality is that the pursuit of geopolitical integration has been changed to an emphasis of sociocultural integration since the transition period. To fulfill the practical needs of Taiwanese society, the original Mainland-edition Constitution was amended. The first legal protection of aboriginal education, the Act of Aboriginal Education, which was based on the 1997 Constitution amendment, was approved. For improving aboriginal education in Taiwan, the Committee for Aboriginal Education, the Council for the Aborigines, and the Research Center for Aboriginal Education were also founded.

Improvements on gender issues in Taiwan occurred later than those around language and ethnicity. However, within a short period, the Act of Sexual Violence Protection and the Committee of Gender Equity Education, which promote gender rights and gender equity education, were put into effect. This is indeed a great improvement.

All these developments in the policies of language, ethnicity, and gender demonstrate that a more open and flexible government has been evolving, although it is a passive reaction to the input of local groups and the demands from legislators and representatives. The first opposition party founded in 1986 and the elimination of martial law in 1987 were two significant political events that led to these governmental changes. Cultural and linguistic revitalization from different ethnic groups also played an important role.

More Voices Presented in Instructional Materials

Structurally, several improvements in instructional materials have been made. The 1993 Curriculum Standards encouraged, for the first time, loving one's homeland. Approved textbooks were allowed to be published by commercial agencies and are replacing national textbooks gradually. Several counties published their own materials for mother tongue teaching. Multicultural books, including ones on the aboriginal, Hakka, and Southern Min cultures, were published and incorporated into regular classroom instruction.

Substantially, improvements have been made as well. Formerly, introduction of aborigine cultures in the national textbooks was limited and they were discussed almost exclusively from the Han perspective, which possessed subtle discrimination. Unlike the national textbooks, the homeland culture materials include information about the Southern Min, Hakka, and aboriginal cultures, and the presentation is more detailed and fair. Also, some traditional Chinese culture is included along with Taiwanese cultures, such as the Chinese (lunar) New Year, Dragon Boat Festival, and Ancestor Worship Festival. Furthermore, the latest curriculum standards mandate that three new subjects be added to regular textbook content and classroom instruction. They are "Homeland Instruction Activity" in elementary school (Ministry of Education, 1993), and "Homeland Arts Activity" and "Understanding Taiwan" in junior high school (Ministry of Education, 1994). Therefore, language books of Holo, Hakka, and other aboriginal languages were published and taught in schools. The national language (Mandarin) is no longer the only language subject and material taught in schools since 1993. The county government thought that by teaching students to speak their languages and to understand and love their homeland, this would help them to develop more love for their country and the world. Cheng (1979) pointed out the importance of loving one's homeland and language loyalty, and "the cultivation of confidence in and respect for one's own community, culture, and people" (p. 565). His statement was finally put into effect in Taiwan after 20 years.

The invisibility of females and gender bias, prejudice, stereotypes, and inequity were prevalent in national textbooks. However, since the Committee of Gender Equity Education was founded and the New Guidelines for Grades 1 to 9 Curriculum were approved, the concepts related to gender equity education will be implemented in the new curriculum in 2001.

These changes illustrate that more appropriate and accurate voices of different linguistic, ethnic, and gender groups are being presented in instructional materials. But, more improvements are still needed. First, in textbooks a greater balance in the content allocated to different ethnic groups should be attained. This can be achieved by either incorporating more chapters or publishing separate books for each ethnic group, as is beginning to happen for the Bunun tribe. Second, rather than books being written in Mandarin, future texts should use the language of the ethnic group for which they are about or be bilingual, using both Mandarin and the ethnic group's language.

More Accurate Linguistic, Ethnic, and Gender Knowledge Is Available

For many years all the non-Mandarin languages in Taiwan were called "dialects." This phenomenon did not change until recently, as can be seen from the language that appeared in official documents. This was due to two reasons. First, the government did not know the distinction between languages and dialects, and assumed that Southern Min, Hakka, and the aboriginal languages were "dialects" of Mandarin. Second, in order to achieve political unity, all languages were unified as "dialects" under the national language of Mandarin. From the perspective of sociolinguistics, neither of these reasons is acceptable. Two language assumptions from Cheng (1979) explain why. First, language planning should include sociolinguistic goals, strategies achieving these goals, and nonsociolinguistic goals like political unity and national harmony. But linguistic unity is not a prerequisite for achieving political unity. Second, language serves as a communication tool and a symbol of group identity, but it is not the only criterion for group identity. Non-linguistic variables such as geographic, cultural, and institutional features also affect it. Hung (1992) also contended that it is reasonable to claim that Southern Min and Hakka are "sublanguages" or "dialects" of old Sino-Tibetan language, but they and the aboriginal languages are not the "dialects" of Mandarin.

Under the ideology of national unity and China-centered politics, not only was the speaking of non-Mandarin languages prohibited, but the fact that Taiwan is a multiethnic and multicultural society was ignored. Knowledge about different ethnic groups like the aborigines, Hakka, Southern Min, and the ones from the Mainland around the year of 1949 was either limited and with bias or not available. Gradually, misunderstanding about languages and ethnic identities was generated among the common people. Subsequently, some non-Mandarin-origin speakers felt ashamed of acknowledging their own ethnic and cultural identity. After the transition period, the greater emphasis on Taiwan-centered politics and sociocultural integration has led to the availability of more knowledge about ethnic groups and their languages and cultures.

Although gender issues have seldom been connected with multicultural education in Taiwan, like language and ethnicity, there have been more efforts at decreasing gender bias, prejudice, stereotype, and inequality, as well as increasing gender equity education. In the future, more accurate knowledge about gender rights and gender equity education will be generated.

The improvements on increasing accurate linguistic, ethnic, and gender knowledge are together contributing to the future developments of multicultural education in Taiwan. These improvements include: the publication of a Southern Min and Hakka dictionary; the establishment of the society for Taiwanese language and literature studies; the founding of a Taiwanese culture college, five research centers for aboriginal education, an institute of multicultural education and an institute of ethnic relations and culture; courses about multicultural education offered in some universities; conferences held on native language education, gender equity education, aboriginal education, and multicultural education; reports on mother tongue education from the Ministry of Education and the DPP; the publication of mother tongue teaching materials; the emergence of more sociolinguistic research; and the publication of special issues in some journals on language, mother tongue teaching, aboriginal education, and gender education.

FUTURE CONCERNS

This presentation of the developments of multicultural education and the analysis of its developmental characteristics in Taiwan provide a clear picture of how multicultural education in a particular setting has been affected by the geopolitical and sociohistorical contexts, and what kinds of issues and problems have been faced. They also raise some key points for future concerns. Four of these are discussed here.

Conceptual Dissemination

Multicultural education is not *one* course or educational program in actual practice, but a term used to describe "a wide variety of programs and practices related to educational equity, women, ethnic groups, language minorities, low-income groups, and people with disabilities" (Banks, 1993, p. 6). Although developments of multicultural education in Taiwan have been occurring from the predevelopment period to the after-transition period, some confusion still exists and needs clarification. For example, some scholars and educators who have blinded themselves to the truth claim that Taiwan is not a multicultural society and no multicultural "something" is needed. Others who care about their own political interests and regime legitimacy blame the idea of multicultural education for dividing the national unity. Even worse is that multicultural education has been equated with the DPP, the opposition that has been promoting Taiwanese independence. Furthermore, multicultural education has been equated exclusively with aboriginal education by some people. Whenever multicultural education is mentioned, these individuals think only of aborigine issues. The reason is that the initiation of multicultural education in Taiwan has a strong relationship with ethnic revitalization, which was directly related to the linguistic and cultural groups--the aborigines. Also, the implementation of multicultural education has focused on elementary-level education. Multicultural education is not a movement limited to elementary level only. It is a continuing reform at all school levels. As mentioned before, whether from a racial, ethnic, linguistic, or cultural perspective, Taiwan is indeed a multicultural society. The accurate and appropriate conceptions of multicultural education need to be disseminated with care.

Empowering Multicultural Teachers

Gay (1977) pointed out that the public school system has had a negative impact on minority students' self-esteem and psychological well-being. "For too long schools have perpetrated the sin of society by making many ethnic students ashamed of their ethnicity and encouraging them, in both overt and subtle ways, to reject and/or deny it" (p. 9). It seems that, from the perspective of the school, there is always an unbridgeable gap between school and home cultures. From the perspective of multicultural education, however, home and school cultures should not be in conflict with each other. Banks (1985) even contended that it is hard to develop students' positive attitudes toward other groups and a strong national identification unless they develop their first-culture identification first. Gay (1977) also identified that "however hard we may try to repress our ethnicity, it cannot be done entirely," and that "throughout life ethnicity continues to be a critical variable in our identification process, whether through affirmation or rejection" (p. 9). The existence of multicultural education is challenged to help students from diverse backgrounds mediate their home cultures and the school culture. To enhance the classroom participation of culturally different students, Gay (1992b) suggested that teachers in the classroom need to change their teaching and speech styles to reflect the cultural backgrounds of different students. And for these changes, future and in-service teachers need to be prepared with the competence of multicultural education (Gay, 1998b). However, the development of multicultural education in Taiwan has only been for about one decade. Not many teacher-training institutes offer courses on multicultural education. In order to achieve effective teaching and learning, knowledge about linguistic, ethnic, gender, and cultural diversity, and skills for mutual communication and respect need to be incorporated into teacher training programs in Taiwan.

Total School/Education Reform

Multicultural education is total school/education reform rather than merely a curricular change, which was one of the major goals in its inception. As the multicultural education movement continues to mature, the reform score also has expanded from the primary demand of curricular reform to all aspects of the educational environments. In regard to a process of educational reform that demands a systemic approach to total educational change, Sleeter and Grant (1994) have recommended six typical elements of schooling for practice. They are curriculum, instruction, evaluation, home/community/school relation-ships, staffing, and extracurricular activities. The development of multi-cultural education in Taiwan is still in the infant stage, and has not been mature enough to extend to all aspects of educational reform. But it is on the way. It has focused on curriculum reform, mother tongue teaching, and homeland culture recognition. Although the curricular reform in Taiwan has gradually led to more inclusion of the voices of women and ethnic groups, the tone of the texts is still presented from the perspectives of politically and culturally dominated groups rather than from the perspectives of women and ethnic groups. Also, the curricular reform is limited to the descriptions of ethnic foods, holidays, cere-monies, customs, ethnic heroes, and the contributions of ethnic groups. Therefore, the curricular reform in Taiwan has been occurring with a contributions and additive approach and not a transformation and social action approach if evaluated with Banks' (1997a) "levels of integration of multicultural content" (C. M. Huang, 1999). For the future development of multicultural education in Taiwan, the reform needs to expand from curricular changes to total school reform, namely to the dimensions of content integration, knowledge construction, prejudice reduction, an equity pedagogy, and an empowering school culture (Banks, 1997b).

Academic Resources Integration

In the 1990s, under the influence of western conceptions of multicultural education and internal political compensation, several related institutes of multicultural education were established. These include the Graduate Institute of Multicultural Education at the Hualien Teachers College, the Research Center for Aboriginal Education at five Teachers Colleges, the Institute of Ethnic Relations and Culture at the Donghua University. All of these institutes concentrate more on the issues of aboriginal education, which echoes the initial realities of multicultural education in the transition period. Also, the Institute of Taiwanese Languages and Literature Education, which focuses on the studies of aboriginal languages, Hakka, and Southern Min, was founded at the Hsinchu Teachers College. The establishment of all these institutes is a result of the political compensation of the government toward its ethnic minorities. However, the integration of multicultural education into academic resources has seldom been promoted. Also, the importance of multicultural education for effective teaching and learning has been recognized gradually, but the teacher training institutes and the teacher training centers at the comprehensive universities are offering very few multicultural education courses. For future development, more exchanges on multicultural teaching and research resources, student training courses, and related conferences and activities need to be promoted. Also, the integration of these related academic resources is needed to advance the progress of multicultural education in Taiwan in the new millennium.

CONCLUSION

The developments of multicultural education in Taiwan from the late 1940s to the present can be divided into three periods: predevelopment, transition, and after-transition. The ideological changes of these developments include: from geopolitical emphases to sociocultural integration, and from China-centered politics to Taiwan-centered politics. The factors of rapid economic development, growing democratization, and ethnic revitalization were together contributing to the developments of multicultural education in Taiwan after the transition period. The political conflicts in Taiwan during the transition period, which involved the display of Mandarin-or-Taiwan-origin concerns and resulted from the inappropriate Mandarin-only policy and its related political ideology, were the stimulus of the initiation of multicultural education in Taiwan. The influences of the western conceptions of multicultural education and the debates about the relations of ethnicity, language, and national identity among the KMT, the DPP, aboriginal groups, local groups, legislators, and provincial/national representatives were the forces that pushed the government to make some changes on the issues of multicultural education. The reaction of the government toward these forces to change, however, has been passive and compensatory. Whether the initiation and developments of multicultural education in Taiwan are a fashion from the western society or a political compensation to its ethnic minorities, its implementation needs to be contextualized in Taiwan's geopolitical and sociocultural settings. It is not only a short-term fashion or political compensation, but a long-term contribution and commitment.

REFERENCES

Banks, J. A. (1985). Ethnic revitalization movements and education. *Educational Review, 37*(2), 131-139.

Banks, J. A. (1993). Multicultural education: Characteristics and goals. In J. A. Banks & C. A. M. Banks (Eds.), *Multicultural education: Issues and perspectives* (2nd ed.) (pp. 3-28). Boston: Allyn & Bacon.

Banks, J. A (1997a). Approaches to multicultural curriculum reform. In J. A. Banks C. A. M. Banks (Eds.), *Multicultural education: Issues and perspectives* (3rd ed.) (pp. 229-250). Boston: Allyn & Bacon.

Banks, J. A (1997b). Multicultural education: Characteristics and goals. In J. A. Banks & C. A. M. Banks (Eds.), *Multicultural education: Issues and perspectives* (3rd ed.) (pp. 3-31). Boston: Allyn & Bacon.

Cheng, R. L. (1979). Language unification in Taiwan: Present and future. In W. C. McCormack & S. A. Wurm (Eds.), *Language and society: Anthropological issues* (pp. 541-578). The Hague, The Netherlands: Mouton.

Educational Reform Council of Executive Yuan (1996). *Educational reform report.* Taipei, Taiwan: Executive Yuan.

Edwards, J. (1977). Ethnic identity and bilingual education. In H. Giles (Ed.), *Language, ethnicity and intergroup relations* (pp. 253-282). London: Academic Press.

Edwards, J. (1985). *Language, society, and identity.* New York: Basil Blackwell.

Fishman, J. A. (1968a). Sociolinguistics and the language problems of developing countries. In J. A. Fishman, C. A. Ferguson, & J. Das Gupta (Eds.), *Language problems of developing nations* (pp. 3-16). New York: Wiley.

Fishman, J. A. (1968b). Nationality-nationalism and nation-nationism. In J. A. Fishman, C. A. Ferguson, & J. Das Gupta (Eds.), *Language problems of developing nations* (pp. 39-51). New York: Wiley.

Fishman, J. A. (1972). *Language and nationalism: Two integrative essays.* Rowley, MA: Newbury House.

Gay, G. (1977). Changing conceptions of multicultural education. *Educational Perspectives, Journal of the College of Education, 16*(4), 4-9. University of Hawaii.

Gay, G. (1992a). The state of multicultural education in the United States. In K. A. Moodley (Ed.), *Beyond multicultural education: International perspectives* (pp. 41-65). Calgary, Alberta: Detselig Enterprises.

Gay, G. (1992b). Effective teaching practices for multicultural classrooms. In C. Dias (Ed.), *Multicultural education for the 21st century* (pp. 38-56). Washington, DC: National Education Association.

Gay, G. (1998a). *Multicultural education in geopolitical and developmental context.* Paper presented at the Graduate Institute of Education, National Chung Cheng University, Chiayi, Taiwan.

Gay, G. (1998b). *Multiculturalizing teacher education.* Paper presented at the Department of Education, National Taiwan Normal University, Taipei, Taiwan.

Hsieh, H. C. (1999). *Gender education in Taiwan.* Paper presented at the International Conference of Gender Equity Education, Taipei, Taiwan.

Huang, C. M. (1993). Content analyses and developmental trends of elementary textbooks in Taiwan. *Bulletin of National Institute for Compilation and Translation, 6*(3), 24-27. Taipei, Taiwan: National Institute for Compilation and Translation.

Huang, C. M. (1997). *Language education policies and practices in Taiwan: From nationism to nationalism.* Doctoral dissertation, College of Education, University of Washington.

Huang, C. M. (1999). *Aboriginal education: A multicultural curriculum design.* Paper presented at the Symposium of Aboriginal Curriculum Developments and Teaching Strategies, Hualien, Taiwan.

Huang, X. F. (1994). *Language, society, and ethnic ideology: The studies of sociolinguistics in Taiwan* (2nd ed.). Taipei, Taiwan: Crane.

Hung, W. J. (1992). *Language crisis in Taiwan.* Taipei, Taiwan: Qian-Wei.

Hung, W. J. (1995). *The analysis of language conflicts and tactics in Taiwan.* Paper presented at the meeting of the First Symposium of Taiwan Local Culture, Taipei, Taiwan.

Ministry of Education. (1993). *The curriculum standards for elementary education.* Taipei, Taiwan: The Ministry of Education.

Ministry of Education. (1994). *The curriculum standards for junior high school.* Taipei, Taiwan: The Ministry of Education.

Ministry of Education. (1999). *New guidelines for Grades 1-9 curriculum.* Taipei, Taiwan: Ministry of Education.

Sleeter, C. E., & Grant, C. A. (1994). Multicultural education. In C. E. Sleeter & C. A. Grant, *Making choices for multicultural education: Five approaches to race, class, and gender* (2nd ed.) (pp. 167-207). New York: Macmillan.

Chapter 6

Language, Culture, and Identity in the Schools of Northern Scandinavia

Leena Huss
Uppsala University, Sweden

In this chapter,[1] northern Scandinavia is seen as comprising the northernmost parts of Finland, Norway, and Sweden, mainly the parts beyond the polar circle. One of the historical minorities in this area are the Sami who are an indigenous people and whose traditional territory, *Sapmi* or the Sami Land, has been split into four parts by national borders. The other populations taken up in the chapter are two regional minorities speaking a variety of Finnish, the Tornedalians, living on the Swedish side of the Swedish-Finnish border, and the Kven, living scattered in small villages by the North Norwegian coast.[2]

The aim of this chapter is to illustrate how three groups of formerly stigmatized minorities in Scandinavia try to rid themselves of the negative aspects of their past and create a new and more positive minority identity. The Kven, the Tornedalians, and the Sami have all experienced a long period of harsh assimilation policies but today there is among all these groups a strong wish to maintain their own languages and cultures and to transmit them to the following generations. For the schools in northern Scandinavia this has come to mean that they have to meet the needs of the minority children to a much greater degree than they have been accustomed to and to create an education that enables the children to achieve an additive bicultural situation: to be integrated in their majority peer group and the society

---

[1] This chapter is a summary of the themes addressed in Huss, 1999.
[2] Part of the Sami live in Russia but they are not included in this study. The total number of the Sami is estimated to approximate 70,000, with 40,000 living in Norway, 20,000 in Sweden, 6,500 in Finland and 2,000 in Russia. The number of Tornedalians is estimated to be 40,000 to 50,000 whereas the number of the Kven is unknown. According to linguistic criteria, there are approximately 2,000 speakers of Kven Finnish left, whereas the total number of people of Kven descent is probably much higher.

at large without having to abandon their family culture and identity. In this chapter, cultural revitalization in school is seen as an opportunity to integrate these minority groups into the rest of the society on more equal premises than before, which in turn will contribute to the rehabilitation of stigmatized minority identities in northern Scandinavia.

In Scandinavia, the schools typically are majority-controlled and majority-financed institutions and cultural revitalization thus pre-supposes support from the majority. What is happening today is that the Scandinavian majority societies are increasingly accom-modating the wishes put forward by historical minorities. This is part of a growing international consensus about the need to support the cultural rights of minorities as expressed, for instance, in the Council of Europe Charter for Minority or Regional Languages and the Council of Europe Frame Convention for the Support of National Minorities. It has been claimed that if the state shows generosity and loyalty to minority populations, it "can expect loyalty in return from them as they will have a stake in the stability and well-being of that state" (OSCE, 1997, p. 37). In consequence, if the state allows its minorities to develop a strong cultural identity, the minorities will have a chance to see themselves as participating members of the society and it will be in their own interest to support the continuation of that society. In that way it is possible to abolish the division between "us" and "them" that has turned out to be destructive in so many connections.

THE PAST

The Sami, the Kven, and the Tornedalians have a long history of discrimination and racial prejudice from the part of the majority populations (e.g., Huss, 1999; Wingstedt, 1998). The case of the Sami is particularly striking, as they, not unlike many other indigenous peoples in the world, have traditionally been regarded by the majorities as a kind of museum piece, picturesque and on their way to extinction because they do not fit in the modern world. These kinds of views date back to the Social Darwinist views that dominated at the turn of the century in the Nordic countries, according to which the Sami were an inferior race. In Sweden, Social Darwinism led to a paternalistic way of thinking: The reindeer-herding Sami population in Sweden was to be protected against the evils of civilization, among other ways by giving them a shorter, specially tailored school education. This idea is evident in a classic quotation of Vitalis Karnell, a school inspector in the North of Sweden in 1905.[3] "Do support the Lapps by all means, make them virtuous, sober and just sufficiently educated people, but do not let them sip from the chalice of civilization, or it is bound to remain just a sip, and it has never been nor will ever become a blessing. Lapps should remain Lapps."[4]

In Norway and Finland, Social Darwinism resulted in the opposite opinion as it was thought that the only way to save the Sami from extinction was to assimilate them as soon as possible to the majority population. Also, school education was supposed to be the means to achieve that goal and the result was that a severe policy of assimilation was launched. The Sami language was banned from classrooms and schoolyards and pupils who violated the rules were punished in different ways. In Sweden, the normal language of education was Swedish, but the use of Sami on school premises was not as rigorously prohibited as in Finland and Norway and certain aspects of Sami culture (handicraft, reindeer-herding, etc.) were taught in the special Sami schools that existed and still exist today. However, a great number of children were educated in other schools where Sami language and culture had no standing at all.[5]

The situation of the Tornedalians and the Kven during the period of assimilation was like that of the Sami with the exception that the Finnish language, including its Tornedalian and Kven Finnish varieties, was considered a political security hazard during the time when the present Finland was under Russian rule (1809-1917). It was feared that the Russian emperor would use the minority populations as an excuse to annex northern Finnish-speaking areas in Sweden and Norway. This resulted in an even more rigorous assimilation policy directed towards the Tornedalians and the Kven, with a mistrust toward anybody who showed any interest in the Finnish language and culture on the Swedish and Norwegian sides of the border.

The Home

During the age of open assimilation politics in northern Scandinavia, many parents wished to spare their children from the negative experiences they themselves had had as minority language speakers, by choosing the majority language as the means of communication a t

---

[3] Source: A Swedish journal called *Dagny* in 1905, as quoted in Ruong (1982, p. 190).
[4] All quotes from non-English sources in this article are translated into English by the author.
[5] See Svonni, 1998, for a more detailed description of the education of Sami children in Sweden.

home. The choice was considered by society as a normal and wise one that parents made "for the best of the child" (Huss, 1999; Huss & Lindgren, 1999). As described by Balto (1997), the Norwegian Sami children learned from early on that Sami was the "bad language" and there were examples of parents who never learned Norwegian themselves but nevertheless acted as Norwegianizers vis-à-vis their own children. For them, Norwegian language and culture were the symbols for the "good life" and the opportunity to go to another place and live like Norwegians, forgetting the failure that being a Sami represented for them (Balto, 1997, p. 116). Marainen (1996, p. 16) mentioned similar views among the Swedish Sami. In Tornedalen, the villagers who had moved southward and came back for holidays were admired for their new accents and for their difficulty in finding words in Tornedalen Finnish (Westergren & Åhl, 1997, p. 4). The Swedish language and culture were seen as belonging to the future, with Tornedalen Finnish belonging to the past.

The assimilative pressure typically broke the continuous transmission of culture from generation to generation. Jernsletten (1994, p. 64) described how this affected the Norwegian coastal Sami families. In the traditional Sami community, the first important linguistic and cultural impulses had been transmitted to children by the grandparent generation. As their experiences from the past and their knowledge of Sami folklore were tied to the Sami mother tongue, the transmission now failed because of linguistic reasons. The Norwegian of the elders did not allow for story telling, and the children did not understand Sami. Similar fates were common in the Tornedalian and Kven environments as well.

The School

As mentioned earlier, during the period of assimilation the main task of spreading national cultures and languages among the entire population was given to school teachers. For most of the minority children in the North, the start of school therefore came to mean a sudden breakup from their earlier lives and the introduction into a totally unknown world, with values and goals different from those that prevailed in the homes of the children. The curriculum was often meaningless in the eyes of the parents as it did not contribute to the knowledge and skills required in the everyday life of the community (Huss, 1999). Hoëm (1994) described how impossible it was for the Sami in Norway before the 1940s to accept the view of school as work or as a useful activity. What the school stood for was viewed as "a play, and often a tedious play, something that everybody stopped doing when they were confirmed and became adults" (p. 50). Indoor activities and writing was not something that the Norwegians could subsist on, it belonged to the alien world outside the community (Hoëm, 1994, pp. 50-51). The school also clearly discriminated against the cultural knowlege and skills obtained within the Sami community, and in order to avoid the social pressure in school and the wider society, the Sami pupils had to learn to suppress or to hide such knowledge when they were outside home (Jernsletten, 1994, p. 56). Similar sentiments are expressed by the Swedish Sami Johannes Marainen (1997); "Everything I learnt at school felt useless and foreign to my Sami way of life. As it was in no way associated with my own culture and my Sami community I never really took it seriously. I just accepted it and learnt what I was told to learn. When I finished school it would no longer be a reality to me" (p. 13).

Many parents also saw school as a threat as it could entice the children to leave their communities and join the majority society. Success in school could be seen as detrimental, as the school gave the children qualifications for another form of life than that of the local community. Bad school results could therefore be seen as welcome because they did not qualify for a career outside the community and the child could instead acquire the skills needed for local life (Hoëm, 1976, p. 328).

The feeling of "otherness" among the pupils was accentuated by the fact that the mother tongues of the children were forbidden languages on school premises. The teachers held the pedagogical view that a fast and complete switch of language was the best way to learn a new language The following excerpt is found in the memoirs of a former school inspector describing the situation in the Tornedalian village schools, as quoted in Klockare (1982):

> In the school of this particular teacher I also noticed that when entering the classroom, all the children put up their hands. When I asked why they did that the teacher answered that they in that way wanted to show that they had not spoken Finnish during the break. Who checked that they didn't? Probably the teacher's helper was to act as an informer. The methods in the battle against Finnish varied. The teachers competed amongst themselves in inventing efficient methods. (p. 34)

There is some information about individual teachers who seem to have been conscious of the psychological effects that an early suppression of the mother tongue could cause the children and some of them seem to have tried to alleviate the effects (Johansson 1997, pp. 52-53; Westergren & Åhl, 1996, pp. 4-5). Nevertheless, using the child's own language as a teaching aid in school was not favored as it was believed that a child's head (especially a minority child's head) would not have room for two languages.[6] Usually the "parrot method" described by Klockare (1982) was used: The pupils were to imitate the pronunciation of the teacher when reading aloud and they were to memorize texts and psalms regardless of if they understood what they were reading or not. Klockare mentioned that some teachers tried to illustrate the text by showing pictures and objects, but this was difficult in relation to abstract concepts. Klockare argued that the prohibition to translate considerably slowed down the Swedicization in Tornedalen, as the content matter, due to inefficient teaching, remained foreign to the children (p. 26).

Eidheim (1989, p. 57) analyzing the situation of the Norwegian coastal Sami in the 1950s and 1960s wrote that the school aimed exclusively at communicating the current values in an idealized Norwegian society, having for generations had the implicit and sometimes also explicit goal to Norwegianize the Sami communities. Norwegian teachers and the few Norwegians who had married into the community typically assumed the role of agents in the process of Norwegianization. The forbidden language as well as the culture connected to it were downgraded to something shameful as opposed to the new language and the new world represented by the school, which became targets to strive for and to be proud of. The shame of belonging to the minority as comprehended by both pupils and teachers was so great that it was considered as impolite even to speak about it. Eidheim (1989) quoted a teacher saying: "I know that many of my pupils are Lapps,[7] but of course, I have the tact to not take notice of the fact" (p. 63).

For many people, the negative school experiences led to a low self-esteem and a lasting linguistic insecurity. Some of those who made their way to higher learning later on discovered that something had been lost on the way. A Swedish Sami, Johannes Marainen (1996), described his difficulty of embracing his own language culture anew, which for him, as well as for many others, has been even harder than denouncing it during times of assimilative pressure:

---

[6] These views probably were in part influenced by results from the bilingualism research dating back to the early 1960s and earlier. Results from that time typically pointed at worse linguistic and cognitive development and a lower intelligence among bilinguals. These studies were later criticized for severe methodological flaws.

[7] The ethnonym Lapp was formerly widely used but is now considered derogatory and the ethnonym Sami is used instead.

Realizing what Swedicization had caused me personally I felt compelled to go backwards and analyze my own development, my metamorphosis from Saami to 'Swede.' I forced myself to think back about all the bitter experiences that had made me choose and organize my life according to the requirements from my surroundings. It was necessary to live through all the painful memories in an endeavour to understand and accept the reality and not, like before, continuously try to make excuses or pretend as if it was a non-issue. (p. 18)

ETHNIC REVIVAL IN NORTHERN SCANDINAVIA

The ethnic revival among minorities in northern Scandinavia is part of a larger ethnic revival movement in Europe that became apparent in the 1960s and 1970s (Allardt & Starck, 1981, pp. 15-16). After World War II, the former Social Darwinist ideas had become obsolete and the official attitudes in the Nordic countries toward historical minorities, for instance the Sami, were changed. Governmental committees were assigned the task of improving the situation of the Sami populations in Finland, Norway, and Sweden, and although the work of these committees did not in practice change the situation, the general atmosphere had clearly changed. The Sami were the first minority group in northern Scandinavia to start an ethnic mobilization in a larger scale. It was first initiated by a small ethnic elite who had reached a relatively high level of education and integration in the majority society. In that way they had the tools and the position to utilize the possibilities offered by the Nordic welfare state and democracy. These activists played a key role in the ethnic mobiliza-tion of the Sami during the first years, by "implementing their knowledge of Sami language, ethnography and history to give substance to the idea that the Sami possessed something valuable and honourable to take care of—a heritage which had been taken from them and which had to be recaptured" (Eidheim, 1993, p. 76). The heart of the matter and, indeed, the most difficult task of the Sami movement, was therefore to give "the inspiration for the reassessment of the self-depreciating self-understanding which the majority/minority situation had forced upon the Sami population" (p. 76). Another challenge was to reach out to wider circles of the Sami population and also to make non-Sami aware and favorably disposed to the issue.

In the Sami movement, the Norwegian Sami have had a leading role ever since the late 1970s and early 1980s. At that time a conflict arose about a planned hydroelectric power station that was to be built in the core Sami area in northern Norway. A huge resistance movement comprising the Sami as well as numerous Nordic environmentalists and sympathizers gained a lot of public attention and made a wider Norwegian public aware of the fact that there was an indigenous people in their own country whose rights had been grossly neglected. Since that time, the general attitude in Norway toward the Sami gradually became more and more favorable, resulting in 1987 in a law that guaranteed certain basic cultural rights to the Sami. The Sami in the other two Nordic countries have naturally benefitted from the achievements of the Norwegian Sami, although the development of Sami language and cultural rights has been slower in those countries. In Sweden, the Sami language still has no official or semi-official position anywhere, and in Sweden as well as in Finland, opportunities of getting Sami medium instruction in the comprehensive school are rather limited. However, the official policy now in all three countries is supportive toward Sami culture, and on the municipal level, the situation has improved remarkably during the 1990s.

The ethnic revival movements among the Tornedalians and the Kven are of a later origin than that of the Sami. The ethnic mobilization among the Tornedalians first accelerated in the early 1980s when an organization was founded to support Tornedalian culture, and the Kven started their national organization some years later. The Sami may therefore be seen as the pioneers among the northern minorities as far as cultural revitalization is concerned.

The public reaction to revitalization efforts on the local level has varied from place to place and from one time to another. Part of the non-Sami have reacted negatively in some northern regions in Norway and Finland where elements of Sami language and culture have been made part of the curriculum for all pupils. Among the Sami themselves, as well as among the Tornedalians and the Kven, there have normally been several groups present in every community: those who strongly support the ethnic movement, those who have partly favorable attitudes toward it, those who are indifferent about it, and those who oppose it. According to Hyltenstam (1999, p. 133), the stronger the in-group opposition against cultural revitalization is, the deeper the stigmatization of the minority has been. Within parts of the various Sami populations as well as the Tornedalian and Kven ones, the opposition has initially been very strong and still today, in spite of a clear development toward wider and wider circles of supporters, some minority members still see cultural revitalization as "ripping up old wounds" (Huss, 1999).

Toward a Multicultural School

In the wake of the ethnic revival gaining force in northern Scandinavia in the 1960s and 1970s the role of the school was changed. Earlier, the school had been the motor of assimilation and for many, it had represented the greatest threat to minority cultures. When revitalization started, the greatest hope was once again put to the school. The official, more pluralistic policies toward minorities influenced the school authorities, and many schools now accepted the general idea that they should draw on local history and local circumstances in their work and acknowledge the fact that all children did not share the same cultural background. Part of the northern school teachers seem to have been especially sensitive to new currents in society. Winsa (1993, p. 20) mentioned that school teachers in Tornedalen, formerly the category who were most critical toward the local language and culture, today are those who are doing the most radical work for cultural revitalization. The same interest in cultural issues is apparent among the personnel in many schools and kindergartens in different Sami areas.

Among parents, however, the attitudes toward a school actively promoting minority culture vary from enthusiasm to indifference and even opposition. For some people who have been punished in school for speaking their own language and who have become linguistically and culturally assimilated, the change in attitudes may be a painful one. Others again may see it as a futile and even backward effort. Winsa (1993) quoted a middle-aged Tornedalian man saying "They teach our language because the teachers want it, the children do not want it" (p. 24).

As mentioned earlier, cultural revitalization typically does not reach all the different layers of population at once, or at all. Selecting a minority language as the family language or engaging in minority-cultural activities may first be seen as a very unorthodox choice, and part of the ethnic group as well as the majority may adopt a very reserved attitude towards it. Minority parents may also shy away from being labeled as ethnic activists and "doing politics." The Sami parents in Balto's study (1997) told the interviewer that they chose to speak Norwegian for ideological reasons. The choice of Sami was seen as a political action, with little relevance for ordinary people. She quoted one of them as saying: "I speak Norwegian because I am not a Sami activist" (p. 119). Such feelings could be strong, and in some families Norwegian was chosen despite the fact that it made communication between the children and their grandparents impossible.

Local authorities and school officials may oppose cultural revitalization efforts, even if a general pluralistic ideology on higher administrative levels may well support putting them into practice. For instance, in Jokkmokk, the old heartland of the Swedish Sami, activists had to fight for 14 years before the municipality finally agreed to found a preschool for Sami children in 1989. The reason, according to the municipality, was that a Sami profile preschool would mean segregation of Sami children. This was actually quite astonishing considering the fact that there already was a very long tradition of special Sami schools in Sweden.

A basic question in cultural revitalization is whether the minority group should establish its own schools partly or entirely financed by minority members, or whether some kind of special education should be developed within the majority school system. In Finland, Norway, and Sweden, tradition has favored the centralized school system and private schools especially designed for ethnic and linguistic minorities have been rare. As for Sami, the three countries today have state-financed systems of promoting instruction in and through the medium of Sami, with special Sami-agenda curricula to be pursued. As a supplement to the Sami Law of 1987 in Norway, special provisions for the Sami language were included in 1992 to promote the use of Sami in public domains. According to these provisions, all pupils in the obligatory school within the six municipalities covered by the Sami Law are entitled to receive instruction in or through the medium of Sami. In four municipalities in northern Norway, Sami is a compulsory subject for the non-Sami as well. In 1997/1998 the number of students studying Sami language and culture in Norway was 2,116, with more than 70% of them living in the Sami administrative area (the six municipalities in northern Norway where the Sami language has an official status).

In Finland, as in Norway, no special Sami schools exist and Sami children are educated together with other children. Sami as a school subject was introduced in the 1950s but it is only since the 1970s and 1980s that the teaching of Sami language and culture has accelerated. In the academic year 1996/1997, instruction in Sami as a subject was given in 31 schools situated in the official Sami area and in 6 schools outside this area including Helsinki and Espoo in the extreme south of Finland, comprising 570 pupils in total (Aikio-Puoskari, 1997). Sami medium instruction given mostly during the primary school (Grades 1 to 6) was in 1996/1997 offered in 12 schools and covered 115 pupils, some of whom were in the secondary school. Today it is possible to study Sami as a mother tongue or as an optional subject, or it can replace some other subjects or be studied as the first foreign language. Sami medium instruction is given mostly during the primary school years, and mostly in the Sami administrative area, that is the four municipalities in the north of Finland where the Sami language has an official status.

The total number of Sweden's Sami schools in 1997/1998 was 161. The rest of the Sami children go to mainstream comprehensive schools. The Sami schools comprise only primary school (Grades 1 to 6). Their head is the Sami School Board, which is a state authority. Since 1962, this school form has been optional for all Sami children, having up to that point been compulsary for the children of reindeer herders. Sami has been used as a medium of instruction in only one of these schools, the school in Karesuando,[8] and primarily in the three first grades (Svonni, 1998, p. 30). In the other schools, Sami has been taught as a subject. In some other schools, "integrated Sami instruction" is offered, implying the possibility of choosing Sami "home language instruction" and receiving Sami profile instruction in certain other subjects such as handicrafts, music, and social sciences.

A curriculum of Kven Finnish for primary and secondary schools has existed since 1997, when a subject called Kven/Finnish as a second language was permanently established in the Norwegian school.[9] Before that, this subject had been taught on a trial basis. The main variety taught in these schools has until now been Standard Finnish with the exception of one single school where Kven Finnish is favored.

Tornedalen Finnish so far lacks curriculum, if the general curriculum for all "home languages"[10] is not counted. Within the Tornedalen Finnish area, the schools offer the option of studying Tornedalen Finnish as a mother tongue or instead of a second or third foreign language, and there is the possibility for the school to adopt a Tornedalen Finnish profile with special emphasis on the local language and culture. In the municipality centre of Pajala, Tornedalen Finnish has been introduced as a compulsory subject in the first three grades of school, and in the village of Kangos, special emphasis is put

---

[8] Since 1979, when Karesuando Saami school was reopened.

[9] The number of interested pupils has risen from year to year and comprised in 1997/1998 a total of 750 children in northern Norwegian schools (Figenschau, 1998, p. 6).

[10] Since 1976, immigrants and other linguistic minorities have had a right to study their "home language" as a subject in the Swedish school. Sometimes this right has been seriously limited by lack of teachers and teaching materials, as well as by an unwillingness on the part of the individual school to organize such instruction. In the recent years, home language (since August 1997 called "mother tongue") instruction has been subject to heavy budgetary cuts.

on the local language and culture during the whole primary school (Grades 1 to 9).

As has been shown, different areas and individual schools in northern Scandinavia vary greatly as to the degree of minority culture support they are offering to the pupils. The different school forms where aspects of minority languages and cultures are part of the curriculum form a continuum where one extreme is traditional mainstream school instruction with sporadic instruction in minority language and culture as a subject, and the other extreme is special minority schools with instruction through the medium of the minority language with special curricula also for other subjects than minority languages. Revitalization efforts are also currently being carried out in extremely varying circumstances ranging from regions where the young people already are more or less assimilated linguistically and culturally (e.g., in the Kven villages in northern Norway and among the Sami in many parts of Scandinavia) to regions where minority language and culture appear to remain safe or indeed gain terrain (e.g., in parts of the Sami core area in northern Norway).

In the following, six examples of ongoing cultural revitalization efforts in different parts of northern Scandinavia are given (for more more details, see Huss, 1999). The approach chosen in these efforts vary from creating small, protected domains for an incipient local revitalization movement (Kangos, Skånland, Börselv), to changing and developing the ideological values or the goals of an existing minority education to match current needs (Sami profile schools, Swedish Sami schools, multicultural values). The efforts described in the first three cases are quite recent and unique in their environments, in fact they all represent a pioneering contribution to a revitalization movement that still has to show whether it will gain wider acceptance or not. The latter three examples are reassessments of established minority educational structures that have been criticized by the minorities themselves who have reached a later stage in the revitalization process.

Kangos, Sweden: When the Village Creates its Own School. In the wake of revitalization, some individual language communities have opted for private solutions. Some of them have lost faith in the general preschool or school system and its ability to cater for minorities, others again see the opportunity to unite the local community around an important common issue. The positive side of giving instruction in an endangered language and promoting the local culture is that it can create a great interest and enthusiasm among teachers, pupils, and parents, and often has positive sideeffects on the local community at large (cf. Dorian, 1987).

In the village of Kangos in Tornedalen, a semi-private school called the Kangos Culture and Ecology School was founded in 1993 to promote local language and culture.[11] Actually, the school was founded because of a municipal decision to close down the village's school for financial reasons, which would have forced the children to travel by bus to a larger school in a nearby village. When the decision was made to set up a private school, the local language and culture were chosen as its foundation. Kangos is an isolated village where Tornedalen Finnish has survived better than in most other Tornedalen areas, but Swedish had largely replaced Finnish as the language of communication between parents and children. The principle adopted by the school was that Swedish is the main language of instruction but Tornedalen Finnish is introduced when teaching subjects with a natural association to Tornedalen Finnish, such as handicrafts, music, local history, and geography, and so on. In addition, every student studies Tornedalen Finnish as a subject a couple of hours a week. The aim is to increase the lessons in Tornedalen Finnish gradually and to introduce Standard Finnish in the upper classes. The teachers emphasize that they want to maintain a relaxed attitude toward the use of Tornedalen Finnish in class. It is used as it is used in the community, where code switching between Swedish and Tornedalen Finnish is frequent and "loan words" from Swedish are accepted. Tornedalen Finnish and Standard Finnish are considered equal but at school Tornedalen Finnish has a special status as the ancient language of Tornedalen. This is to counteract the deep-rooted belief among many Tornedalians as well as non-Tornedalians that Tornedalen Finnish is a means of communication inferior to Swedish and Standard Finnish because it has incorporated many Swedish loan words and because it has not been subject to the same language cultivation and development as Standard Finnish in Finland. The pupils are given tasks to collect terms pertaining to traditional occupations and handicrafts, and they are encouraged to seek help from elder people. They also document old place-names and try to find out what old Tornedalen Finnish family names actually mean in Swedish.

The foundation of the school work is the rehabilitation of the local language and culture. The teachers stress the importance of making the parents feel that the school is theirs and that the culture of the home and the community is appreciated by the school. This is also a way of

---

[11] Lisbeth Mörtlund (personal communication, August 1993 and August 1998).

engaging the parent generation that still remembers the assimilative
school of their own youth where the Tornedalian culture was banned.
The school is also working actively to create positive attitudes toward
multilingualism and other minority groups. The teachers feel a need to
make the children aware of the fact that other groups, like the Sami,
are facing similar difficulties as the Tornedalians and that all
minorities should support each other as well as live in harmony with
the majority. Special days dedicated to Sami culture have been
arranged and Sami visitors have been invited to the school. Another
specialty is the Tornedalian amateur theatre that has engaged both
adults and children in Kangos. Every now and then, the school children
set up a play about a local theme. Swedish and Finnish both are used,
to give the play a local character and to train the pupils' Finnish.
Many children are receptive bilinguals. They hear people speak
Tornedalen Finnish but they do not speak it themselves.

The shortage of teaching material in Tornedalen Finnish has been a
main difficulty in the daily work of the school although the situation
now is far better than when the school first started. The children's
competence in Tornedalen Finnish varies a lot and the same is true
about the teachers. Most of them have had to study the language and to
learn to read and write it by themselves. A continuous effort is
necessary as the children advance to the upper classes and the
Tornedalen Finnish used by the teachers must advance as well.

According to the teachers, the results so far have been positive. The
local attitudes toward the teaching of Tornedalen Finnish that used to
be partly negative are nowadays positive. Since several years back,
the teachers no longer need to argue on behalf of the local culture—it is
considered self-evident to promote it at school. However, they
emphasize that Kangos is special and that revitalization here has
advanced more than in other areas in Tornedalen.

Skånland, Norway: When the Young Are Showing the Way.
Skånland is the southernmost region in Norway where North Sami is
still spoken. Norwegians and the Sami have a long common history
there and linguistic and cultural assimilation has resulted in a
situation where Sami is spoken as a mother tongue only by people who
are 50 years of age or older.

When Sami was introduced in the compulsory school in Skånland in
1987, it was done to accommodate the requests from individual pupils.
Revitalization efforts in the Skånland schools are indeed marked by
the very specific circumstances prevailing there: Children want to
have instruction in Sami language and culture but parents mostly are

against it (Skåden, 1996, p. 66). Sami lessons in the school and two private Sami kindergartens are the only Sami language domains available for children as they mostly come from homes where only Norwegian is spoken.

When Sami instruction was started in the two schools in the area, the shortage of local written material was apparent; instead, oral tradition was abundant. Contacts with the remaining elder mother-tongue speakers were established with the help of parents and teachers, and gradually a circle of people interested in telling the pupils about different subjects related to Sami traditions were engaged as informants. The pupils who had chosen to participate in Sami instruction were very motivated, which also affected their parents. The latter participated in excursions and small-scale Sami immersion organized by the class and were also active in the other parent activities. The teachers as well as local Sami activists supported the children in their endeavors.

The philosophy of instruction was founded in a number of specific modes of work chosen for the program. The local community, its history and cultural traditions, local religious values, and direct contacts between the school and the community were seen as central. Fieldwork in the community with overnight excursions during which only Sami was spoken functioned as efficient Sami immersion camps and they also resulted in self-made textbooks on various themes. The cooperation between pupils and informants lead to an accumulation of valuable oral material that otherwise would have been lost. Contacts between the Sami classes and the local informants were also enhanced by community meetings open to everybody, where mutual discussions about currents themes like the relation between the local dialect and Standard written Sami took place. During these meetings the pupils could also report on the results of their fieldwork and other activities and get feedback from their informants. Many of the latter were interested in hearing what the children had achieved. The pupils and teachers felt that they were not only getting something from the community but also giving something back to it (Skåden, 1996, p. 78).

Börselv, Norway: Taking Back the Kven Culture. Kven Finnish language and culture were included in the curriculum of the Børselv School in northern Norway in 1974. Børselv is situated in the municipality of Porsanger, which is part of the official Sami language area, but the Kven presence there is age-old and still stronger than in many other northern Norwegian communities. Børselv was one of the last two communities where the Norwegianization policy was introduced. According to Lindgren (1994, p. 34), the Kven children, even in the 1950s, started school without knowing any Norwegian, and the teachers knew neither Kven Finnish nor Sami. Børselv was also the first place in Norway where the Kven started an ethnic organization of their own and today, in 1999, a cultural center is being built there. According to the initiator Terje Aronsen, the "Kvæntunet," or the Norwegian Centre for the Kven Language and Culture as it is also called, will be a resource center for various cultural activities, including language courses and the production of educational material (Terje Areonsen, personal communication, June, 1997). The municipality of Porsanger has declared itself trilingual (with Kven, Norwegian, and Sami) and Kven Finnish place names and signs are visible in the municipality.

The person behind the Kvæntunet, Terje Aronsen, is also the teacher in Børselv school who initiated the instruction of Kven culture in the school more than two decades ago. His idea was that the language and culture were so closely linked together that if you wanted to rehabilitate the language you had to rehabilitate the local culture as well. Many aspects of Kven culture are included in the curriculum: local history, place names, Kven music and handicraft. Instruction in the language is given from Grade 1 and the aim is to teach the children speak and write some Kven. In the upper grades, Standard Finnish is introduced. The initial focus on Kven Finnish as opposed to Standard Finnish first triggered some controversy, but Aronsen's argument, "If we are to maintain something, we must maintain what we have and not what we do not have"[12] gradually gained ground.

The biggest practical difficulty in Kven Finnish instruction has been the total nonexistence of teaching material. The teacher himself has had to create everything himself, including school books and Kven Finnish maps and handicraft items needed, and all this virtually without any funding at all. The aim has been to produce material that enhances the ethnic awareness of the pupils and gives them an orientation in the history of their forefathers. Aronsen considered it extremely important to stress that the children in the school belong to the 10th or 11th generation of the Kven in Børselv and should not be viewed as immigrants, as the Norwegian state has done up to the 1990s.

Changing attitudes has been a difficult task. The idea of teaching Kven language and culture in school was first regarded as controversial. Today, the parent generation is generally positive to cultural revitalization and the younger children are eager to learn about Kven

---

[12] Field notes, August, 1994.

culture. There are also plans for kindergartens where the grandparent generation would function as language and culture teachers for the youngest children.

Emphasizing the Sami Profile of the Schools in the Norwegian Sami Area. Stordahl (1997, p. 152) wrote that education for the Norwegian Sami has been the key to winning back their history, culture, and language. It has given the Sami population the possibility of acquiring knowledge about their own history and traditions as well as about the Norwegian culture and society. In the Sami core area in Norway, particularly in Kautokeino and Karasjok municipalities, children have the possibility of receiving their compulsory education through the medium of Sami, and the secondary school also has integrated aspects of Sami culture in its curriculum. Nevertheless, the critique of these Sami-profile schools as well as other attempts within the Norwegian school system to cater to the Sami has been severe. A former teacher from Kautokeino compulsary school stated critically that the Sami curriculum is nothing more than a Norwegian curriculum translated into Sami. Some Sami subjects have been introduced, like yoik[13] and Sami handicrafts, but that is all (Svensson, 1994, pp. 5-6). According to him, the Western world only takes seriously the knowledge that is found in books and dissertations, whereas the Sami children are taken away from their families, who are the real sources of Sami knowledge. Similar views have been expressed by many others concerned with the state of the Sami school today. One of the greatest present pedagogical concerns is that only part of Sami traditional or empirically based knowledge can be integrated in the educational system because this system is outside the control of the Sami and steered by national and international standards. The big challenge to Sami education is to develop models of instruction where knowledge from both the Sami and the non-Sami world are combined (Stordahl, 1997, p. 152). Issues related to the kind of Sami knowledge that could be incorporated in the curriculum and the ways to realize this incorporation are treated in Balto (1997).

A profound question and a central concern of Sami reindeer herders is that their children are excluded from the reindeer herding work when they start school and therefore they miss an important introduction to the knowledge necessary to future reindeer herders (e.g., Jernsletten, 1997, p. 98). Although special seasonal leaves for reindeer herding are

---

[13] Yoik is the traditional song of the Sami and it differs both in melody and structure from the music of the rest of the Scandinavian people.

allowed in some schools, it is claimed that the school curriculum is not adapted to a sufficient degree to the needs and wishes of the Sami society. The Norwegian and European character of the school is reflected in its preference of theoretical knowledge, as opposed to Sami traditional knowledge, which gives the sort of insight and understanding that is tied to a physical approach and experience (Jernsletten, 1997, p. 99). Jernsletten proposesd "field courses" in local knowledge and practical working skills, arranged in some Sami village schools as well as summer mountain courses in reindeer herding areas (p. 100). Nevertheless, he argued that the instruction of this subject area must be given a solid foundation by developing it at the secondary school, college, and university levels. This is an urgent issue as traditional knowledge still is accessible through people who have grown up in the traditional Sami way. However, the number of those who can transmit to younger generations this knowledge and the Sami language tied to it is diminishing. Another difficulty is that this knowledge must partly be transformed to suit the modern media while at the same time keeping in mind that the use of the media cannot replace learning combined with practice (Jernsletten, 1997, p. 100-101).

Reforming the Swedish Sami Schools. The Swedish Sami school system dates back to the segregationist period around the turn of the century when the official goal was to keep the Sami children separate from other children and to protect them from being enticed to abandon the life of reindeer herders. Later on, the Sami schools were developed to conform to the mainstream education while some aspects of Sami life such as handicrafts, music, and some knowledge of Sami livelihoods were retained in the curriculum. The Sami language played in these schools a very marginal role, being a subject taught a couple of hours a week at the most. Only in one school Sami was used as a medium of instruction, above all in the first three grades.

In the early 1990s, the Sami School Board initiated a study of the state of Sami language in the Sami schools to be carried out as a joint project in cooperation with two Swedish universities. The aim was twofold: to assess the language instruction in the Sami schools, and to propose new models for this instruction. In connecton with the assessment, a dissertation focusing on the knowledge of Sami among the pupils of the Sami schools was published (Svonni, 1993). Svonni had studied the different components of the children's linguistic competence in Sami and come to the conclusion that a rapid language shift to Swedish was going on among these children. He also maintained that it would soon be completed if nothing was done to change the situation in the school. The role of the school in language development had become more important than before as Sami was no longer learned in the family.

After the assessment had been completed, it was decided that a special bilingual program would be started in three Sami schools and follow-up studies would be conducted continuously (Svonni, 1994, p. 42). The central idea of the programs is that both Sami and Swedish are used as media of instruction, both languages are taught as subjects, and the teachers adapt their own language use to the level of competence in the individual child. The experiences from the Canadian language immersion education as well as bilingual models used for language maintenance in Wales, Catalonia, and other countries, are used as sources of inspiration. Svonni (1994, pp. 42-43) emphasized the importance of bilingual education for Sami children who start school as monolingual Swedish speakers. If the school is able to give these children enough command of Sami so that they can use it with their grandparents and other relatives, the children's knowledge of their own culture will increase and the children's self-esteem rise. The children will also have a greater opportunity of choosing their future education and work. For the society as a whole, the enhanced use of Sami in the school will mean an increase in the use of Sami outside the school and a step toward language maintenance instead of language shift, Svonni concluded.

Regaining Multicultural Values From the Past. Johansson (1994, pp. 47-50) described his childhood in a multicultural area in northern Sweden. Of Sami and Tornedalian descent, he wrote of his childhood and the intimate contact between the Tornedalian settlers and the nomadic Sami. When state schools were established in the area, they gradually divided the population and raised walls that never had existed before between the Sami and the non-Sami. According to Johansson, the children had previously developed a natural understanding of the two cultures and it was self-evident for them that everybody needed each other and should and would know both Sami and Tornedalen Finnish. When the children of reindeer herders were placed in their own school, this understanding was lost. In the Sami school, the children got some support for their Sami, while Tornedalen Finnish became a forbidden language in all schools. Only Swedish was used and the absence of the Sami children from the regular school yards caused the bilingual children to lose their knowledge of Sami. Among the Tornedalen children, the rigorous Swedicization policy also resulted in the children developing their own priority order for the languages of the area. Swedish was placed on the highest level and then there was a large gap to Tornedalen Finnish, which was officially forbidden. Sami, which had virtually disappeared from the neighbourhood, was placed at the lowest level. Johansson (1994, p. 50) concluded that everything the experiences of generations of people had taught about the equality of languages and cultures was effectively destroyed by the school. Fjellborg (1994, pp. 68-71) wrote about a similar childhood as Johansson's in Tornedalen with three languages used in everyday life in a society where the Sami and the Tornedalen Finnish speakers were dependent on each other in order to survive. Today, this is no longer the case, but according to Johansson we still need the knowledge of how to manage a multicultural society (Johansson, 1994, p. 50). Johansson claimed that the experiences and knowledge from the old days are still available but they are never used.

Johansson (1997, p. 54), who has also studied a trilingual and tricultural Swedish-Sami-Tornedalen Finnish instruction project in a northern village in Sweden, emphasized the importance of attitudes and the "climate" in the classroom. He argued that they are sometimes even more significant than the question of which language is chosen as a medium of instruction or which teaching methods are used. The crucial thing is that children with diverse cultural backgrounds are allowed to find their way to knowledge by anchoring their schoolwork in their own background and minority situation. In that way the cultural tradition of the minority is made visible in the reality of the children.

CONCLUSION

The cultural revitalization movement in Scandinavia has been facilitated by many different factors. First, since the more pluralistic ideology replaced the assimilationist ideologies in Scandinavia, the general atmosphere has changed and various forms of societal support for language and culture maintenance efforts have become available for minorities. Due to a change in the general atmosphere, speaking a minority language is no longer felt to be as stigmatizing as it used to be. The value of minority languages is recognized officially and the younger generations have much fewer personal experiences of being ridiculed or marginalized because of language and culture than had their parents and grandparents. The shame that in the 1960s still made many Kven, Tornedalians, and Sami hide their language and ethnicity, is now much rarer, at least as far as the young are concerned. Instead, the young are now showing interest in the heritage of their parents and grandparents. This tendency has been enhanced by the spreading of information about the experiences of other minorities in the world. Another important factor is the modern bilingualism research and the recommendations emanating from it. The beneficial impact of bilingualism for language and identity development of minorities is emphasized as a tool to bring about a state of empowerment (Cummins, 1996; Genesee, 1994). This is quite the opposite of the results from earlier research where bilingualism was seen as an anomaly, with fatal implications for the individual. Instead of being forced to choose between the minority or the majority language and culture, minority members now are given the option of embracing both. The new recommendations are, as already mentioned, spread among minority parents via brochures, booklets, and videos where they are given advice about how to make their children bilingual.

The cultural revitalization movement among the northern minorities of Scandinavia reflects the fact that former policies aiming at a rapid language and culture shift among minorities did not work out satisfactorily either from a minority or a majority point of view. They left parts of the minority populations suffering from stigmatization and alienation and at worst broke the family continuity between generations. Now the minorities themselves are trying to rehabilitate themselves by means of cultural revitalization. For them it is a matter of human rights: They are now trying to recover what earlier was taken from them by force (Skutnabb-Kangas, 2000). As far as the school is concerned, revitalization has come to mean several things. As shown in the examples given, some schools are now trying to give the pupils the same kind of supportive sociocultural learning context that mainstream pupils have normally had. This is done by including minority languages and cultures in the curriculum and creating an additional bilingual situation (both minority and majority language) for the students instead of a subtractive one (replacing minority language by majority language). The children's background and previous knowledge is taken as a basis of further education, which in turn gives new possibilities of involving minority parents in school activities. In this way a cooperation between the school and the home as well as the local community is created instead of the former total separation of the two. The new bi- or multicultural-profile schools have turned out to be popular among both parents and pupils and because of their new locally anchored methods they are considered innovative and efficient. Whereas cultural support formerly tended to be directed from above, today minorities themselves are increasingly developing and steering their own educational support structures (cf. May, 1998). In this way a self-mending and rehabilitating process is going on in the North. That is also an important reminder to the current policy makers in Scandinavia who are searching for more efficient ways of integrating immigrants and refugees in the Scandinavian mainstream societies.

REFERENCES

Aikio-Puoskari, U. (1997). *Saamen kielen ja saamenkielinen opetus Suomessa* [Education in and through the medium of Sami in Finland]. Sodankylä: Sámediggi/Saamelaiskäräjät.

Allardt, E., & Starck, C. (1981). *Språkgränser och samhällsstruktur. Finlandssvenskarna i ett jämförande perspektiv* [Language borders and structure of society: The Finland Swedes in a comparative perspective]. Lund: Almqwist & Wiksell.

Balto, A. (1997). *Samisk barneoppdragelse i endring* [Sami child-rearing in flux]. Oslo: Gyldendal.

Cummins, J. (1996). *Negotiating identities: Education for empowerment in a diverse society.* Ontario: California Association for Bilingual Education.

Dorian, N. (1987). The value of language maintenance efforts which are unlikely to succeed. *International Journal of the Sociology of Language, 68,* 57-67.

Eidheim, H. (1989). *Aspects of the Lappish minority situation* (2nd ed.). Oslo: University of Oslo.

Eidheim, H. (1993, November). On the organization of knowledge in Sami ethno-politics. In T. Brantenberg, J. Hansen, & H. Minde (Eds), *Becoming visible: Indigenous politics and self-government.* Proceedings of the Conference on Indigenous Politics and Self-Government, Sámi Dutkamiid Guovddas, University of Tromsø.

Figenschau, T. (1998). Interessen for finsk öker [The interest for Finnish is growing]. *Ruijan Kaiku, 8,* 6.

Fjellborg, S.-E. (1994). Med alla sinnen närvarande [With all one's senses present]. Svarta stjärnor, gränslöst land. Om kulturmöten och rötter i Norrbotten. *Krut, 74,* 68-71.

Genesee, F. (Ed). (1994). *Educating second language children: The whole child, the whole curriculum, the whole community.* Cambridge: Cambridge University Press.

Hoëm, A. (1976). *Makt og kunnskap* [Power and knowledge]. Oslo: University of Oslo.

Hoëm, A. (1994). Samebarns oppvekstvilkår før [The terms of growing up among Sami children in the past]. In R. Erke & A. Høgmo (Eds.), *Identitet og livsutfoldelse. En artikkelsamling om flerfolkelige samfunn med vekt på samenes situasjon* (2nd unrevised ed.) (pp. 38-52). Kautokeino: Samisk Utdanningsråd.

Huss, L. (1999). *Reversing language shift in the far north: Linguistic revitalization in Northern Scandinavia and Finland.* Uppsala: Acta Universitatis Upsaliensis.

Huss, L., & Lindgren, A.-R. (1999). Minority languages and identity in the Nordic countries. In J. A. Fishman (Ed.), *Language and ethnic identity: Before and after the "ethnic revival." Comparative Disciplinary and Regional Perspectives* (pp. 300-318). New York & Oxford: Oxford University Press.

Hyltenstam, K. (1999). Begreppen språk och dialekt—om meänkielis utveckling till eget språk [The concepts of language and dialect—about the development of

Meänkieli into a language in its own right]. In K. Hyltenstam (Ed.), *Sveriges sju inhemska språk-ett minoritetsspråksperspektiv* (pp. 98-137). Lund: Student-litteratur.

Jernsletten, N. (1994). Om språket i samiske samfunn [About language in Sami communities]. In R. Erke & A. Høgmo (Eds.), *Identitet og livsutfoldelse. En artikkelsamling om flerfolkelige samfunn med vekt på samenes situasjon* (pp. 53-66). (2nd revised ed.). Kautokeino: Samisk Utdanningsråd.

Johansson, H. (1994). På kvällen lades renhud vid renhud [In the evening reindeer hides were laid side by side]. Svarta stjärnor, gränslöst land. Om kulturmöten och rötter I Norrbotten. *Krut 74*, 47-50.

Johansson, H. (1997). Ska barnen verkligen utsättas för nordsamiska och meänkieli skolan också? Om trespråkighet, urbefolkningar och kulturövergrepp [Are the children really to be exposed to North Sami and Meänkieli in school, too? On trilingualism, indigenous peoples and cultural oppression]. In E. Westergren & H. Åhl (Eds.), *Mer än ett spåk. En antologi om två- och trespråkigheten i norra Sverige* (pp. 41-55). Stockholm: Norstedts.

Klockare, S. (1982). *Norrbottniska språkstriden 1888-1958. Finska språket i Tornedalen* [The language struggle in Norrbotten between 1888-1958]. Stockholm: Finska språket i Sverige.

Lindgren, A.-R. (1994). Kvensk språk [The Kven language]. In A. Strøm (Ed.), *Rapport fra seminaret "Kvenene en glemt minoritet?"* (pp. 30-44). Tromsø: Tromsø Museum.

Marainen, J. (1997). Jag—en same i det svenska samhället [I—a Sami in the Swedish society]. In E. Westergren & H. Åhl. (Eds.), *Mer än ett språk. En antologi om två- och trespråkigheten i norra Sveriges* (pp. 12-25). Stockholm: Nordstedts.

May, S. (Ed.). (1998). *Indigenous community-based education. Special issue of language, culture, and curriculum 11:3.* Clevedon: Multilingual Matters.

OSCE. (1997, June). *The role of the high commissioner on national minorities in OSCE conflict prevention: An introduction.* The Hague: The Foundation of Inter-Ethnic Relations.

Ruong, I. (1982) *Samerna i historien och nutiden* [The Sami in history and today]. Stockholm: Bonnier Fakta.

Skåden, A. (1996) "Læreran, dem gjør egentlig ikkje nokka": Elevene og bygda som ressurser i samiskundervisninga ["The teachers, they don't actually do anything": The pupils and the community as resources in Sami instruction]. In J. Todal & M. Pope. (Eds.), *Våg å snakke: Kommunikativ metode i samiskopplæringen* (pp. 65-80). Kautokeino: Samisk utdanningsråd.

Skutnabb-Kangas, T. (2000). *Linguistic genocide in education: Survival of linguistic diverity?* Mahwah, NJ: Lawrence Erlbaum.

Stordahl, V. (1997). Sami generations. In H. Gaski (Ed.), *Sami culture in a new era: The Norwegian Sami experience* (pp. 143-154). Karasjok: Davvi Girji Os.

Svensson, R. (1994). Var fågel sjunger med sin näbb [Every bird sings with its own beak], Svarta stjärnor, gränslöst land. Om kulturmöten och rötter i Norrbotten. *Krut, 74*, 4-7.

Svonni, M. (1993). *Samiska skolbarns samiska. En undersökning av minoritetsspråksbehärskning i en språkbyteskontext* [The Sami language of Sami school-children. A study of minority language competence in a language shift context]. Umeå: Umeå universitet.

Svonni, M. (1994). Från språkbyte till språkbevarande [From language shift to language maintenance]. *Krut 1994/74, Svarta stjärnor, gränslöst land. Om kulturmöten och rötter i Norrbotten*, 38-43. Stockholm.

Svonni, M. (1998) Saami. In A. Ó Corráin & S. Mac Mathúna (Eds.), *Minority Languages in Scandinavia, Britain, and Ireland* (pp. 21-49). Uppsala: Acta Universitatis Upsaliensis.

Westergren, E, & Åhl, H. (1997). *Mer än ett språk. En antologi om två- och trespråkigheten i norra Sverige* [More than a language. An anthology of bi- and trilingualism in northern Sweden]. Stockholm: Nordstedts.

Wingstedt, M. (1998). *Language ideologies and minority language policies in Sweden: Historical and contemporary perspectives.* Stockholm: Centre for Research on Bilingualism, Stockholm University.

Winsa, B. (1993). Meän kieli ja torniolaisitten kakskielisyys: Täälä plandathaan sprookit [Our language and the bilingualism of the Tornedalians. Here we mix our languages]. *Virittäjä, 1*, 3-33.

Chapter 7

Multiracial Reality, White Data: The Hidden Relations of the Racial Democracy and Education in Brazil

Álvaro Moreira Hypolito
University of Wisconsin–Madison, U.S.A.

Brazil is the country that had the largest slave population in the Americas; it is also where the myth of racial democracy[1] still persists. Unlike the United States, for instance, where race relations were built under segregationist and supremacist traditions (Skidmore, 1991), race relations in Brazil have been developed through miscegenation—the elite has attempted an assimilationist perspective in which miscegenation would incorporate other racial groups through a process of "Whitening"(Skidmore, 1992).

The Brazilian elite can first be understood here as an aristocracy that is connected with Portuguese colonial interests. It included the state, the politicians, and the big landowners who produced sugar cane and coffee. They represented the political, cultural, and economic elite from the colonial period until the 1930s. Since then, the presence of the bourgeoisie is more evident among the dominant classes. Today the dominant forces include groups that represent the interests of financial capital, multinational industry, big landowners, and rightist and neo-liberal politicians who have developed conservative policies. In general, these political and economic groups, whose racial and ethnic backgrounds are White and of European origin, are what could be defined as the elite or dominant classes in Brazil.

As part of the process of Whitening the elite has strategically not included racial data in the Demographic Census or in the PNAD

---

[1] Racial democracy is a usual idiom used in Brazil to express that there is no racism in Brazilian society. The notion of racial democracy, a common sense historically built, is often presented in the mass media, in official discourses, in textbooks, and in everyday life. The ideological discourse of racial democracy in Brazil is frequently used to indicate Brazil as the best example of how race relations can be democratic in a given society. Because racial democracy in Brazil is not really democratic but an ideological discourse, I sometimes use this expression within quotation marks.

(National Household Survey).[2] Thus, Brazil does not have any known official study at either the national or regional level with quantitative data available to demonstrate clearly the strong inequalities that exist in different social areas such as education, among others.

This chapter demonstrates how this lack of quantitative data on race in Brazil has hidden the multiracial reality and has obfuscated the understanding about teachers' work, race, and curriculum. I point out, using official data from the Brazilian government, how the questions of race are profoundly hidden. Particularly, I am interested in knowing the race constitution of teachers in Brazil. This is important because the analyses from quantitative data present in this chapter might help to improve and implement qualitative studies on teachers, culture, and curriculum.

I have studied teachers' work with a comprehension of teachers as workers who are defined by social class and gender relations. In Brazil, as I demonstrated (Hypolito, 1995, 1997), teachers present, simultaneously and contradictorily, cultural and social characteristics of the working class and middle class. Furthermore, they have experienced a feminization process, and teaching in elementary school, at least, is currently considered a woman's profession. However, in these studies the racial issues were not developed. Given the multiracial reality of Brazil, it is absolutely necessary to add the racial aspects, besides gender and social class relations, in analyses of teachers' work.

The concepts and perspectives of multicultural education as they have been used in the United States (see, e.g., Banks, 1995; Grant & Tate, 1995) do not exist in Brazil. Although racial inequality has been addressed within the critical tradition, it has usually been subsumed under class inequality. In particular, the relationship between race and education has not yet addressed race as a phenomenon that implies racial and cultural identities. It is important to say that multicultural education is a recent concern among Brazilian scholars and educators. In Brazil, themes such as cultural and racial identities, multicultural education, and race have been insufficiently theorized. Although connected with social class and gender, race, as a specific category, should be considered in greater depth.

DATA ON RACE IN BRAZIL

One of the most important strategies of the dominant classes in Brazil to hide the information on race was the categorization used to classify people as White, Dark, and Black. Included among Whites are the Portuguese, European immigrants (from Italy, Germany, France, and

---

[2] When racial issues were included, it was in a politically, methodologically, and ideologically wrong way as I try to demonstrate in following paragraphs.

other nations), and people who may have African or Brazilian Indian origin but look White. Included among Darks are *Mulato, Mameluco,* or *Caboclo, Cafuzo,*[3] and Brazilian Indian, and among Blacks are people who have African origin or are miscegenated but look Black. Table 7.1 shows the racial constitution of Brazilian people from 1835 to 1980 classified as White, Dark, and Black. These official data have kept Whites and Blacks separated, and subsumed all other people of color under the category of Dark. The majority of the people included in the category of Dark are products of miscegenation between African people and other ethnic groups.

TABLE 7.1
Racial Constitution of Brazilian People (%)

YEAR	WHITE	DARK	BLACK	DARK/BLACK
1835	24.4	18.2	51.4	69.6
1872	38.1	42.2	19.7	61.9
1890	44.0	41.4	14.6	56.0
1940	63.5	21.2	14.7	35.9
1950	61.7	26.5	11.0	37.5
1960	61.0	29.5	8.7	38.2
1980	54.8	38.4	5.9	44.3
1988	56.5	37.3	5.6	42.9

Note. From Fiola, 1990,[4] and PNAD, 1988 (Brasil, 1989).

Today in the Demographic Census and PNAD (National Household Survey), people are classified as White, Black, Dark, and Yellow—that is, Japanese, Chinese, and all the people who have been declared to be yellow [sic] (Brasil, 1989).

In 1835, as illustrated in Table 7.1, Black people were the majority (51.4%) and White people represented just one quarter of the total population. If we consider Dark and Black people together, almost 70% of the Brazilian population in the early 1800s were non-White. In 1980, however, White people represented more than half (54.8%), while Black people represented just 5.9% and Dark people represented 38.4%, even though the largest Black slave population in the Americas was in Brazil. This suggests there was a Whitening process as result of three moves: (a) an intensification of immigration of White people from Europe (Italian, German, and others) during the 1800s and early 1900s; (b) a miscegenation process that people have experienced in Brazil; and (c) a

---

[3] These kinds of miscegenation are: *Mulato*–Black and White; *Mameluco* or *Caboclo*–Brazilian Indian and White; *Cafuzo*–Black and Indian.
[4] Quoted by Skidmore, 1991.

biased methodology of classifying and categorizing the information on race.

It is necessary to pay more attention to the last idea—the bias in the classification and categorization of information on race. The criteria used to classify people in the official Demographic Census and National Household Survey (PNAD)—White, Black, Dark, and Yellow—are, as I said before, completely inadequate and biased. First, these criteria, instead of empowering the different ethnic groups, will include people of different origins—such as Brazilian Indians and Africans—in a general category like Dark. Simultaneously, important groups that are a result of miscegenation are "forgotten." They are *Mulato*, *Caboclo* or *Mameluco*, and *Cafuzo*. This situation is clearer, for example, in North and Northeast regions, where these people currently constitute the majority of the Brazilian people in those regions.

Second, the criterion used to define who is White is absolutely questionable. If someone looks White, they are White. I am a paradigmatic example, among millions and millions of "White" people in Brazil. My maternal grandmother was Portuguese and Brazilian Indian, and my maternal grandfather was Portuguese and African Black. My paternal grandmother was Portuguese and Jewish, and my paternal grandfather was Italian. Consequently, there are people in my family with the most varied appearances: dark-haired, curly-haired, redheads, dark-skinned, and so on. But because I look White, I am considered White.

Although there is a discourse of racial democracy in Brazil, in terms of political power, social conditions, and ideology it is "better" to be White than Black or Dark in Brazilian society. Thus, as a result of political, social, and race relations, many people consider themselves as "White." This is a process that ensues from what Joyce King (1991) defined as dysconsciousness, "...an uncritical habit of mind (including perceptions, attitudes, assumptions, and beliefs) that justifies inequity and exploitation by accepting the existing order of things as given..." (p. 135).

According to the 1988 PNAD, which pays central attention to color aspects of the Brazilian population (Brasil, 1989), the estimated number of White, Black, and Dark people, respectively, was 56.5%, 5.6%, and 37.3% of the total population. That is, at least 43.5% of the people were not White. In effect, considering the reasons before presented (i.e., the biased methodology to categorize race, the ideological definition of White, and the notion of dysconsciousness) and adding this last observation, I think it is reasonable to infer that the reported number of White people is questionable and has been used to construct the ideology of "Racial Democracy" under White control.

THE DENIAL OF RACIAL DEMOCRACY

Although the dominant classes have been successful in imposing their ideology of racial democracy, the concrete reality shows us that there are many problems involving racial discrimination and social inequalities.

One of the ways that the "Racial Democracy" discourse has been constructed in Brazil is to talk about race as if there were no racial inequalities. But reality talks louder as shown in the next paragraphs.

The relationship between income and race shows a significant difference among races. Black and Dark people earn significantly less income than White people. The average income of Black and Dark men in 1990 corresponded respectively to 63% and 68% of White men's income. Black and Dark women occupy a similar position: Their income corresponded to 68% of White women's income.

Considering the regional aspects it is important to say that White people are more concentrated in South and Southeast regions, and Black and Dark people are more concentrated in North and Northeast regions. The social and economic development in South and Southeast regions is significantly greater than in North and Northeast regions. For example, in Brazil 30.2% of the total population is considered to be below the poverty line. However in South and Southeast regions the poverty percentage is 20.1% and 23% respectively, whereas poor people represent 43.2% in the Northern region and 45.8% in the Northeast region.

To further illustrate this situation, if we compare rural areas in the Northeast with São Paulo and Rio de Janeiro, in the Southeast, in terms of other social indicators, we find the following information respectively: family average size: 5.5 to 4; average number of children in the family: 2.9 to 1.7; children between 7 and 14 years of age that are out of school: 44.7% to 16.%; illiterate heads of family: 67.6% to 19.2%. Thus, it is evident that in regions where the White population is predominant, the social and economic conditions are more favorable.

As in other social life spheres, the educational situation in Brazil also presents strong racial inequalities. Considering the 1988 data on years of schooling, we find that 34.7% of the Black population have no schooling at all, 41.6% have from 1 to 4 years of schooling, and only 1.2% have 12 or more years of schooling (Barcelos, 1993). In other words, 76.3% of Black people in Brazil have 4 or less years of schooling.

A recent report on human development in Brazil (Brasil, 1996) shows that the average years of schooling, according to race, is: White people: 5.9 years; Black people: 3.3 years; Dark people: 3.6 years; and Yellow people: 8.6 years.

A broader longitudinal study that investigated all children born in 1982 in the city of Pelotas, Southern Brazil, has given support for a qualitative study that confirms the school failure of Black people. This study—a follow-up study with 84 of those children—showed significant rates of school failure among Black children. The risk of grade retention was, respectively, 1.7 times higher among Black girls and 2.8 times higher among Black boys than among White girls and boys (Silva, Barros, Halpern, & Silva, 1996). The study also looked at teachers' perceptions about grade retention within the group of Black children. Teacher's perceptions were investigated through an open-ended questionnaire. The sample included 84 teachers, 70 of whom were women, 14 were men; 63 of the teachers were White, and 21 were Black. The study found that teachers' responses suggest a strong racial prejudice, which is denied and appears in a hidden way. When the teachers were asked if they knew which children (Black or White) had higher school failure, their reaction included a wide range of responses: surprise, doubt, refusal to respond, indignation, or absolute belief that there is no difference among the children in these aspects. Then,

> ...after these initial reactions, the answers were of two kinds: either they said that there is no difference between Black and White children in terms of school failure (51%) or they did not know how to answer (23%). Thus, 74% of the answers express the lack of knowledge or the lack of perception about such differences. This kind of answer was expressed by 81% of the Black teachers. (Silva et al., 1996, p.6)

It is important to say that just 17% of the 84 teachers answered that the Black children presented higher school failure, and among them only three were Black teachers. It is very strange that the teachers did not know the Black failure rate, given the fact that the rate of school failure among Black children is very high. I think that the notion of dysconsciousness mentioned before is very helpful in understanding this phenomenon.

Even though the dominant social classes have been obscuring the inequalities, racial democracy is not a consensual ideology, as the Brazilian elite has attempted historically to demonstrate. We have today important groups that are organizing movements for cultural resistance, fighting against all forms of discrimination, and trying to move toward a real racial democracy. In a broader sense these movements can be identified as *Movimento Negro* (Pinto, 1993).[5]

In the last years, given the strong discriminatory situation and the claims of Black Movements and scholars engaged in an emancipatory perspective, studies about race and education in Brazil have been growing (Barcelos, 1993; Machado, 1991; Pinto, 1992, 1993; Silva, 1992). Many studies have had difficulties demonstrating the inequalities in a precise way because the data are imprecise and the categorization is ideological. For example, as I demonstrated earlier, it is impossible to

---

[5] In Portuguese language, particularly in Brazil, the word *Preto* (Black) can be more pejorative than Negro. Thus, the Brazilian Black Movement is called *Movimento Negro*.

know, using the official categorization of race, how many students in the Dark group are from African origin or Native Indian origin. Today we know that Black and Dark people fail more in schools than White people, but we cannot know how many *mulatos* and *cafuzos* there are among Darks.

We live in a multicultural reality where, in many regions, the different cultures are not clearly identified—for example, in the South and in some states in the Southeast region. We can identify that in some regions (Northeast, for instance), there is a higher concentration of Black people and the Dark people are mostly identified as people with African origins. Thus, the racial relations in places like Bahia State (Northeast) tend to be more explicit: (a) the racial inequalities are more evident because the Black and Dark population are majority but they are socially and culturally excluded; (b) although the African-Brazilian culture (music, religion, dance, etc.) is very strong and present in everyday life and the people identify with it, the public school curriculum is very "White;" and (c) the conflicts over racial interests are more frequent (for example, battles over inclusion/exclusion of contents identified with African-Brazilian culture in curricula[6] or battles of resistance over the acceptance of the *Capoeira* Dance[7]). Although the hegemonic discourse states a "Racial Democracy," the social, racial, and educational reality denies it.

TEACHERS AND RACE

It is difficult to obtain clear information about teachers and race from some of the official published data (for example, Brasil, 1983, 1989, 1991). At the same time, different themes, such as curriculum and culture, curriculum and race, national curriculum, and teachers and race are emerging quickly among Brazilian scholars and educators.[8] This can be demonstrated by the inclusion of racial issues in several graduate school programs and by the growing number of articles and publications in

---

[6] Jacira Silva (1992) found that the textbooks omit the participation of Black people in the history of Brazil, as well as the history of political Black resistance and the contribution of the African culture to the Brazilian culture.

[7] *Capoeira* is at the same time a dance and a fight that the slaves in Brazil created as a cultural and political form of resistance. Although currently *Capoeira* is broadly disseminated in all regions of Brazil, a few decades ago (1930s) it was illegal and is still not incorporated in schools as Physical Education.

[8] Although the debate on race and education is vigorous in the United States and there is abundant academic production, most of this intellectual production is not widely known in Brazil. However, studies in education such as some works of Michael Apple (1986, 1993, 1996; McCarthy & Apple, 1988), which were translated to Portuguese, have been very important in stimulating the debate about race and education.

important journals such as *Cadernos de Pesquisa.*[9] In spite of this growth, few works can be found on specifically teachers and race, and among these there is no research about teachers and their racial composition. Because of the fact that in Brazil the contemporary educational research is strongly qualitative, the majority of the existing studies on teachers and race have concentrated more on teaching, curriculum, resistance, and racial identity. Two studies provide a good example of this tendency: Silva's study (1992) analyzes an experience of cultural resistance in a public school in which students and teachers recuperate different aspects of the Black local culture, such as dance, music, and so on, and include them in the curriculum toward the empowerment of their cultural identity; and Gomes (1994), through a case study, analyzed the school life of Black women teachers to show how they have resisted and fought to maintain alive their cultural and racial identities.

In previous studies, I studied the relations among teachers' work, social class, and gender in the Brazilian reality (Hypolito, 1991, 1995, 1997). I studied teachers' work, relating aspects of its historical making with class and gender relations, within a discussion of the capitalist nature of this kind of work. I analyzed teachers as workers in education who have been submitted to a proletarianization process and submitted to a capitalist logic as to its organization and rationalization. In Brazil, teachers have a contradictory social class condition, presenting characteristics of both middle and working classes, although with a historical tendency to be members of the working class. As Apple (1986) has demonstrated in the situation in the United States, where teachers' work has gone through a deep process of feminization, I also have demonstrated that in Brazil the process of proletarianization is absolutely connected with a feminization process (Hypolito, 1995).

I have developed a critical balance of theoretical and academic production about teachers' work in Brazil where I stated that class and gender relations are central categories for an interpretation of teachers' work (Hypolito, 1997). I found out that there is a serious political and theoretical lack in all studies analyzed: Few texts include race as an important category to interpret teachers' work. I think that it is absolutely necessary to further studies that include, besides class and gender, teachers and race relations in Brazil, considering race as a central category for an interpretation of teachers' work.[10]

Considering the total population in Brazil, according to race, as I have shown before, the population is distributed as White (56.5%), Black

---

[9] *Cadernos de Pesquisa* is an important and respected journal of education in Brazil.

[10] I believe that the use of these categories—race, class, and gender—following the theoretical nonsynchronous parallelist model developed by McCarthy and Apple (1988) is appropriate.

(5.6%), Dark (37.3), and Yellow[11] (0.6%). Even if it shows that White people are the majority, it is important to emphasize again that this criterion to classify race in Brazil is completely inadequate, as I have pointed out in my previous arguments. Also, as mentioned earlier, the non-White people are 43.5%, which represents almost half of the total population. And much more important to consider is the fact that this does not represent the picture of all regions in the country. In two regions (North and Northeast) Dark people are the "majority" (71.3% and 60.6%, respectively), and White people represent one third of the population (Table 7.2). In the Southern region, where the immigrant colonization has occurred significantly, White people are more than 80% and in the Southeast region they are over two thirds of the population. Black people are more significantly present in the Northeast and Southeast, where slavery was stronger. In the Midwest region, the number of White and Dark people is almost the same, but if we consider Black and Dark people together they represent 50.5%. It is true to say that in the Midwest the miscegenation processes are strong and what is White there would often be considered Dark in the Southern region.

TABLE 7.2

Population According to Race in Brazil and Regions, 1988

COUNTRY/REGIONS   POPULATION %

	WHITE	BLACK	DARK	YELLOW	TOTAL
BRAZIL	56.5	5.6	37.3	0.6	100.0
NORTH	27.0	1.4	71.3	0.3	100.0
NORTHEAST	32.9	6.1	60.6	0.4	100.0
SOUTHEAST	66.2	6.7	26.1	1.0	100.0
SOUTH	82.8	3.2	13.5	0.5	100.0
MIDWEST	49.0	3.3	47.2	0.5	100.0

Note. From PNAD, 1988 (Brasil, 1989)

Considering data from PNAD (1988), among teachers that work in public elementary school,[12] 19.1% taught Grades 5 to 8, 76.2% worked with elementary grades (1-4), and 4.7% worked in other activities in school (supervisor, principal, etc.).

---

[11] Brazilians of Asian origin (officially considered Yellow), mainly Japanese, are concentrated in the state of São Paulo where they have played a significant role in the state's economic development. Although as a group their educational performance exceeds that of Whites, there has been an uncomfortable silence on this point. In the case of Asians, silence perpetuates the myth of "Racial Democracy."

[12] Elementary school in Brazil consists of eight grades. The first four grades correspond to elementary school and the 5th to 8th grades correspond to middle school in United States.

In terms of comparison between teachers and population, according to race, considering the general data of Brazil as a whole, the percentage of population and teachers is not significantly different referring to Dark and Yellow people, but referring to Black there is a distortion: Whereas the Black people represent 5.6% of the population, the Black teachers represent only 2.8% of the teachers (comparing data from Tables 7.2 and 7.3).

On the one hand, in most of the regions the Black teachers are less represented compared to the%age of Black people in the total population: In the Northeast it means 3.7% to 6.1%; in Southeast, 3.5% to 6.7%; in South, 3.2% to 1.9%; in Midwest, 3.3% to 0.7%; and in the Northern region the difference is not significant. On the other hand, in all regions White teachers are more represented than White people in the total population: North, 5.5% plus; Northeast, 6.7% plus; Southeast, 8.9%; South, 9.7%; and Midwest, 9.1%.

TABLE 7.3

**Teachers in Public Elementary School in Brazil
According to Region and Race, 1988**

% of Teachers According to Race

Place	White	Black	Dark	Yellow	Without Information	Total
North	32.5	1.6	65.5	0.4	-	100.0
Northeast	39.6	3.7	56.7	0.0	-	100.0
Southeast	75.1	3.5	20.1	0.9	0.4	100.0
South	92.5	1.9	4.8	0.8	-	100.0
Midwest	58.1	0.7	40.5	0.7	-	100.0
Brazil	59.0	2.8	37.6	0.5	0.1	100.0

Note. From PNAD, 1988 (Brasil, 1989).

There is also present a percent reduction for Dark people in all regions, varying from 3.9% (Northeast) to 8.7% (South), although in the Northeast and the North the teachers are predominantly Dark.

Even in regions where the Dark population is more representative, the relative number of White teachers increased. Although the "Racial Democracy" is a solid myth in Brazil, I think that racial reality, evidenced in previous paragraphs, demonstrates that White hegemony is a reality to teachers, education, and educational issues. In the South, which is the "Whiter" region and consequently more racist and segregationist,[13] we find the most evidence of this situation where 92.5% of the teachers are White.

The racial reality we find in education reflects the social and economic conditions that people in Brazil are submitted to. As I said before, there is a relation between poverty, race, and different regions in Brazil. It is very clear that Darks and Blacks live in poor regions and they are related to working class and poor people. It is important to make this relation because the teachers in Brazilian public elementary schools, as I have discussed (Hypolito, 1995, 1997), can be considered working class. The average monthly wage of the teachers in the public elementary schools in 1987 was US $192.89.[14] Also, although women represent more than 95% of the teachers in elementary schools, this average wage is different according to gender: men teachers average US $216.60, and women teachers average US $190.34. Besides this cruel salary position, it is crucial to consider that the teachers come from a working class background, they live where working-class people live, and they share the same culture (Hypolito, 1997, p. 67). I believe that it is important and significant to consider class, gender, and race connections to adequately interpret teachers' work (Ladson-Billings & Tate, 1995; McCarthy & Apple, 1988).

In terms of people education and teachers education, the situation is similar. In all regions White people have more opportunity to attend school and, consequently, they obtain more certification. White people have more opportunity to become teachers because they have more educational and social opportunities.

In Brazil it is possible to obtain teacher certification to teach in elementary schools with a high school degree (it is a specific type of course). But often there are teachers teaching in elementary schools who have not finished the high school level. Of course, this is more frequent in poor regions. The tendency is to require higher education to teach in public schools, but this situation will persist certainly for some more years. If the educational opportunities persist as it has been, and the requirements to teach in elementary schools must be obtained in higher education, the tendency could be worse in terms of class, gender, and race opportunities. Today, for teachers, the racial discrimination is a reality in elementary school, a cruel situation in high school, and absolute in higher education. The number of Black and Dark teachers in

---

[13] Although illegal, segregationist practices involving Black people can be found in some places in the Southern region. For example, in certain institutions, such as clubs, subtle mechanisms exist through which only white people are accepted as members.

[14] The Federal government is attempting to increase this average to US $300.00, but it is not a reality yet. Although this average information came from 1987, I think it is close to reality. In poor regions, certainly the teachers' monthly wage is less than US $100.00.

high schools is insignificant, and the number of professors in higher education is practically nonexistent.

Finally, it is essential to add that included in the hegemonic and conservative strategies are the neo-liberal educational policies in Brazil. Among them three propositions can provoke significant changes for teachers: External assessment system, national curriculum, and continuing education programs of teachers. The first two tend to intensify the standardization of teaching and define educational functions for society, while at the same time defining what should be taught to achieve the desired cultural model. The third one refers to teachers' education as required to reach the objectives of the assessment system and the national curriculum. Once again, these propositions might have important implications with a multicultural perspective in education, mainly because the national curriculum and its consequent standardization of teaching tend to eliminate other educational and cultural approaches. Teachers tend to be forced into a standardization of teaching by a dominant culture—centered in masculinity, Whiteness, Christianity, and Eurocentrism. From my point of view, race and education relations in Brazil must be understood critically as a statement of identities and differences—identities as social and political diversity, as a critical perspective that not only intends to identify the differences and the power relations but also intends to fight politically against all forms of discrimination to eliminate race, gender, and class privilege (Goldberg, 1995).

CONCLUSION

In this chapter, I demonstrated how the elite in Brazil has been erecting its White hegemony. I think that it has been constructed through the "Whitening" and "assimilationist" processes. It was obtained through the immigration of White people, the miscegenation process, and the myth of racial democracy.

The myth of Racial Democracy has been attained through different strategies aimed to hide the racial inequalities. I pointed out that the criteria to classify and categorize the official information on race in Brazil are deeply biased in terms of methodology and ideology. This procedure does not make clear as to who is defined as White or Dark. Then, the number of White people in Brazil is overestimated and the number of people who come from Black African origin is diluted in a general category called Dark. The same happens with Brazilian Indian people. Thus, the multiracial reality is hidden under abstract categories that are favorable to White interests. In spite of the fact that numerically White people are the majority in Brazil, they are concentrated in two regions—South and Southeast. In the three other regions—North,

Northeast, and Midwest—the majority of people are Dark and Black. Territorially, these three regions represent the bigger part of the Brazilian lands.

But through these shrouded facts, the elite has built its strong discourse of Racial Democracy. However, when the social and educational situation is seen in regional details, this discourse is concretely denied. The racial inequalities can be seen in terms of education as well as in terms of social and economic aspects. As I described, in Brazil, poor people, poor regions, and social and racial inequalities are strongly related. The Racial Democracy is not present in schools, in salaries, in curricula, in everyday life. The quantitative data analyzed here help to identify how this official data work against a true racial democracy.

The contents in textbooks and in curriculum do not reflect the multiracial reality and Dark and Black people are underrepresented in the teacher population compared to their numbers in society. These phenomena tend to reduce the influence to include racial issues in schools. As Silva et al.'s (1996) qualitative study shows, racial prejudice and discrimination, although shrouded, are very strong in public schools. This study also confirms that the school has the discourse of equality but does not respect racial and cultural differences.

Although the teachers say that they do not know which children fail more in school (Black or White), they have some expectations that work as prophecies. Through a process that could be called *tacit contract* between teachers, school, and system, teaching must be "Whitened" and Dark and Black children, in order to obtain success in school, must "Whiten" themselves.

ACKNOWLEDGMENTS

I thank Daniele Fernandes, who is developing a study on race and education in Brazil, for having provided crucial information for this chapter.

REFERENCES

Apple, M. W. (1986). *Teachers and texts*. New York: Routledge.

Apple, M. W. (1993). *Official knowledge*. New York: Routledge.

Apple, M. W. (1996). *Cultural politics & education*. New York & London: Teachers College Press.

Banks, J. A. (1995). Multicultural education: Historical development, dimensions, and practice. In J. A. Banks & C. A. M. Banks (Eds.), *Handbook of research on multicultural education* (pp. 3-24). New York: Macmillan.

Barcelos, L. C. (1993). Educação e desigualdades raciais no Brasil [Education and racial inequalities in Brazil]. *Cadernos de Pesquisa, 86*, p.15-24.

Brasil. (1983). *PNAD–1982. Educação* [National household survey: Education]. Rio de Janeiro: IBGE.

Brasil. (1989). *PNAD–1988. Cor da População* [National household survey: Color of the population]. Rio de Janeiro: IBGE.

Brasil. (1991). *PNAD-1990* [National household survey]. Rio de Janeiro: IBGE.

Brasil. (1996). *Relatório sobre o desenvolvimento humano no Brasil* [Report on human development in Brazil]. Rio de Janeiro: IPEA; Brasilia: PNUD.

FIOLA. (1990, January). *Race relations in Brazil: A reassessment of the "racial democracy" thesis.* Occasional Papers Series, *24.* Amherst: Program in Latin-American Studies/University of Massachusetts.

Goldberg, D. T. (1995). *Multiculturalism: A critical reader.* Cambridge: Blackwell.

Gomes, N. L. (1994). *A trajetória escolar de professoras Negras e sua incidência na construção da identidade racial: Um estudo de caso em uma escola municipal de Belo Horizonte* [School life of Black women teachers and the making of racial identity: A case study in a public school in Belo Horizonte]. Belo Horizonte: FaE/UFMG.

Grant, C. A., & Tate, W. F. (1995). Multicultural education through the lens of the multicultural education research literature. In J. A. Banks & C. A. M. Banks (Eds.), *Handbook of research on multicultural education* (pp. 145-166). New York: Macmillan.

Hypolito, Á. M. (1991). Processo de trabalho na escola: Algumas categorias para análise [Labor process in school: Some categories for analysis]. *Teoria & Educação, 4,* 3-21.

Hypolito, Á. M. (1995). Relações de gênero e de classe social na análise do trabalho docente [Gender and social class relations in the analysis of teachers' work]. *Cadernos de Educação, 4,* p. 5-18.

Hypolito, Á. M. (1997). *Trabalho docente, classe social, e relações de gênero* [Teachers' work, social class, and gender relations]. Campinas/São Paulo: Papirus.

King, J. (1991). Dysconscious racism: Ideology, identity, and miseducation of teachers. *Journal of Negro Education, 60*(2), 133-146.

Ladson-Billings, G., & Tate, W. (1995). Toward a critical race theory of education. *Teachers College Record, 97*(1), 47-68.

Machado, L. Z. (1991). O lugar da tradição na modernidade Latino–Americana: etnicidade e gênero [The place of tradition in Latin America modernity: Ethnicity and gender]. *Cadernos de Pesquisa, 77,* 34-45.

McCarthy, C., & Apple, M. (1988). Race, class, and gender in American educational research: Toward a nonsynchronous parallelist position. In L. Weis (Ed.), *Class, race, and gender in American education* (pp. 9-39). Albany: State University of New York Press.

Pinto, R. P. (1992). Raça e educação: Uma articulação incipiente [Race and education: An incipient articulation]. *Cadernos de Pesquisa, 80,* 41-50.

Pinto, R. P. (1993). Movimento Negro e educação do Negro: A ênfase na identidade [Black movement and education of Black people: The emphasis in the identity]. *Cadernos de Pesquisa, 86,* 25-38.

Silva, C. A., Barros, F., Halpern, S., & Silva, L. A. (1996). A exclusão escamoteada: Reprovação das crianças negras [Shrouded exclusion: the failure of black children]. *Cadernos de Educação, 7,* 47-59.

Silva, J. (1992). *Resistência Negra e educação: Limites e possibilidades, no contexto de uma experiência escolar* [Black resistance and education: Limits and possibilities in the school experience context]. Porto alegre: UFRGS.

Skidmore, T. E. (1991). Fato e mito: Descobrindo um problema racial no Brasil [Discovering a racial problem in Brazil: Fact and myth]. *Cadernos de Pesquisa, 79,* 5-16.

Skidmore, T. E. (1992). *Fact and myth: Discovering a racial problem in Brazil.* Notre Dame, IN: Helen Kellogg Institute for International Studies, University of Notre Dame.

Chapter 8

Multiculturalism, Diversity, and Education in the Canadian Context: The Search for an Inclusive Pedagogy

Carl E. James
York University, Canada

The Canadian Multicultural Policy, introduced by the federal government in 1971, established a framework that, over the years, has informed the ways in which educational institutions have come to recognize the cultural diversity of the Canadian population, and has initiated educational programs that address issues related to race, national and ethnic origin, color, and religion. Although some educators and writers claim that multicultural education as implemented in schools has been responsive to the needs, interests, and aspirations of the diverse population of students (Mansfield & Kehoe, 1994; Samuda & Kong, 1986), critics have argued that this approach to education has been limited in its capacity to do so particularly with regard to marginalized students. To support their point, the critics pointed to the situation where, even with the implementation of "multicultural education," low teacher expectations continue to contribute to the streaming of minority and immigrant students into low-level educational programs, resulting in alienation and high dropout rates (Cummins, 1997; Curtis, Livingstone, & Smaller, 1992; Dei, Muzza, McIsaac, & Zine, 1998; Lucas & Schecter, 1992). On this basis, multicultural education as practiced has been unable to ensure equality of educational opportunities and, still less, equity for *all* students within the Canadian education system.

In light of this situation, alternative pedagogical perspectives have been adopted, constructing a patchwork of educational policies and programs, all of which purport to have equality and/or equity as a central goal. But more than equality of opportunity—a tenet of multiculturalism—is the need for equity. As Evans and Davies (1993) contended,

> Equality in education has been defined purely as a technical concern with the distribution of opportunities amongst different social groups.... Equity "gauges the result of actions directly against standards of justice." It is used to determine whether or not what is being done is just.... It is crucial to uphold a distinction particularly between equality of opportunity and equity because the achievement of the former is no guarantee that the latter is also evident. (pp. 23-24)

This chapter explores a number of perspectives that have informed equity discourses in education in an attempt to address the needs, interests, aspirations, and issues of the diverse population of students. I show that the Canadian federal multicultural policy served to establish an equality rather than an equity discourse that has limited the way diversity has been understood and addressed.[1] Framing "culture" in terms of "difference" related to ethnicity, race, language, and accent, thus negating its complex, ambiguous, contingent, temporal, and hybrid nature (Spivey, 1998), the policy has helped to impose a notion of diversity that has inhibited the implementation of a multicultural education that would take into account the shifting, contextual, complicated, and interrelated identities of students based on social class, gender, ethnicity, race, language, (dis)ability, sexual orientation, and other factors. As a result, over the years, other perspectives focusing on race relations, anti-racism, and "redefined" multiculturalism have been presented as better able to inform educational programs that would more effectively respond to the issues, needs, and aspirations of *all* students, and minority students in particular.

In the following, I examine, first, the problematic nature of the federal multicultural policy/act and the forms of "multicultural education" that emerged over the years. Second, I discuss other educational perspectives and the extent to which the ideology of multiculturalism has limited their possibilities for initiating changes to the educational system. Third, as an example, I explore how diversity is being taken up today by some aspiring educators who are concerned with "being inclusive" in terms of taking into account gender,

---

[1] Srivastava (1997) argued that "What differentiates Canadian multiculturalism from other national forms of multiculturalism is not its often insidious cultural pluralism and relativism (which may be seen quite clearly in American, British, and Australian forms of multiculturalism) but its imaginative hold on its citizens" (p. 117). And as Moodley (1983) wrote, the Canadian multiculturalism policy articulates a range of conflicting understandings of "cultural differences which extolled and considered a hindrance to be removed in the interests of equal opportunity" (cited in Roman & Stanley, 1997, p. 228). Further, with reference to a textual analysis of the policy, Ng (1995) contended that multiculturalism is ideologically constructed as "a social fact"—a means by which the State regulates and governs the society with an increasing diverse minority population.

class, ethnic, race, linguistic, accent, and (dis)ability differences of students. In doing so, I make use of the dialogues of teacher candidates taken with permission from their on-line comments that are part of their activities in an urban education course I teach in the Faculty of Education at York University in Toronto, Canada.

CANADA'S MULTICULTURAL POLICY AND THE CONCEPT OF CULTURE: THE "MULTICULTURAL" CONTEXT

Canadians tend to boast of the fact that, unlike the United States, Canada is a multicultural society. Indeed, the Multicultural Policy of Canada, which became part of the Multicultural Act in 1988, points out that the Constitution of Canada "recognizes the importance of preserving and enhancing the multicultural heritage of Canadians; ...[and] the diversity of Canadians as regards race, national or ethnic origin, color and religion as a fundamental characteristic of Canadian society" (Multiculturalism Policy of Canada, 1988). And whereas it is understood that the multicultural program exists "within a bilingual framework" (English and French), there is no questioning of the fact, as the then Prime Minister claimed when he introduced the Multicultural Policy nearly three decades ago, that in Canada "there is no official culture, nor does any ethnic group take precedence over any other" (cited in Palmer, 1975, p. 136). Indeed there is the belief, again as the Prime Minister asserted, that this approach to diversity is "the most suitable means of assuring the cultural freedom of Canadians"(cited in Palmer, 1975, p. 136), and that equality of opportunity exists for all Canadians irrespective of their origin, color, and religion.

This notion of cultural democracy presupposes that the norms, values, and principles, including the laws and policies by which the state operates, are culturally neutral, and therefore citizens are able to fully participate in the society and institutions uninhibited by cultural background. This position fails to recognize the dominance of Anglo-Celtic Canadians as an ethno-racial group and the construction of the English and French as "real" Canadians (James, 1995a; Walcott, 1996). Alternatively, "cultural groups" (so identified in the multicultural policy) are constructed as "Other" Canadians—people with a "heritage" from elsewhere and whose "foreign" cultural values and practices remain static and based on their past experiences in other countries. This framing continues to exclude, as it did when the British and French came, First Nations or Aboriginal people as part of the "diversity" of the Canadian society.

Also, the multicultural policy articulates a discourse of "difference" that signifies that culture is primarily carried in and exhibited by "foreign bodies"—people who are from somewhere else, who are "linguistically different,"[2] and do not "look and sound Canadian." I am referring here to the popularly held notion that Canadians are phenotypically white and, apart from the French, one of the "founding groups," who are understood to have a "French accent," "Canadians" (read Anglo-Celtics) do not have accents (see Bannerji, 1997; James, 1995a; James & Shadd, 1994; Roman & Stanley, 1997; Walcott, 1996). The "likeness" or "sameness" in bodies, language, accents, and "look" contribute to the homogenization of the respective "cultural groups." This can be seen as a way of "managing" difference and dissension that come with diversity. It is this management of difference and dissension that prompted the federal government of the 1960s to establish the Bilingualism and Biculturalism Commission which recommended the multicultural framework. As McAndrew (1995) wrote: "The Canadian policy of multiculturalism can therefore be seen as a response to the major goals of political socialization in the turmoil that characterized Canadian society in the 1970s" (p. 168).[3]

Critics argue that this cultural approach to the management of difference ignores the history of oppression due to race, gender, social class, language, sexuality, (dis)ability, and other characteristics, and the socially constructed dominant-subordinate relationship between ethnic groups (Bannerji, 1997; Razack, 1997; Srivastava, 1997). As

---

[2] Non-English-speaking and "accented" Canadians. The French continue to argue that they are a "distinct" group and identify their language and "culture" as part of their distinction; and they enjoy the privilege of the claim to their position as one of Canada's two "founding" groups.

[3] As I indicate elsewhere the 1960s was a period when French Canadians were fighting for more recognition of their linguistic and cultural identity and historical presence in Canada. Aboriginals were insisting on settlement of land claims. And with the increased numbers brought about by immigration, ethnic and racial minority groups who had been in Canada for generations were demanding recognition and rights to equal participation in the society. Moreover, global events, particularly the civil rights movements in the United States, helped to influence the assertiveness, expectations, and demands for improved conditions and cultural recognition of racial and ethnic minority groups (James, 1995b, p. 34). The introduction of Canada's multicultural program, therefore, can be viewed as an attempt to address the social and political issues of the day. It was intended to assuage the French who were advocating for equal political rights and status to those of English (or Anglo-Celtic) Canadians. To this end, English and French were retained as the two official languages of Canada. And other ethnic groups were expected to believe that with "official" government recognition and support they would enjoy cultural freedom and equal opportunity.

Razack (1997) wrote: "What makes the cultural difference approach so inadequate in various pedagogical moments is not so much that it is wrong, for people are in reality diverse and do have culturally specific practices that must be taken into account." Rather, this approach to cultural diversity often leads "to a superficial reading of differences that makes power relations invisible and keeps dominant cultural norms in place" (p. 25).

It is this discourse of multiculturalism that was endorsed by the English-speaking provincial governments, starting with Saskatchewan in 1975 and followed by Ontario in 1977. In those early years, respective provincial ministries of education established multicultural education programs that were related to the demographics of their population. For example, the Western provinces of Alberta, Saskatchewan, and Manitoba offered educational instruction in languages such as Cree, French, Ukrainian, Russian, German, and Hebrew (Ghosh, 1996, p. 19). Also, Nova Scotia developed programs to serve the educational needs of its long-established black population. In addition, Ontario and British Columbia, which attracted most of the immigrants to Canada (hence making them two of the most diverse provinces) offered multicultural educational programs that took language (including dialects), race, and ethnic origin into account.

On the other hand, Quebec, Canada's French-speaking province, rejected the federal policy of multiculturalism because, according to Ghosh (1996), "equal status for all cultures implied that French culture was equal to other cultures," and this was seen as likely to undermine their struggle for cultural survival in a predominantly English-speaking North American continent (p. 20). In light of this, in 1974 the Quebec government introduced language legislation making French the official language of the province. Further, as Ghosh wrote:

> In 1977, Bill 101 gave further prominence to French in everyday life, in work, and in education; all children with few exceptions (such as those of British parentage), would have to be schooled in French. The legislation raised the question of individual rights of non-francophones versus the collective rights of francophones. The concern of immigrant families is that schooling in French would limit the educational and employment opportunities of their children in a continent where 98% of the population is English. (p. 20)

But as McAndrew (1995) pointed out, although the Quebec government rejected the Federal government's multicultural ideology, it nevertheless "committed itself to a series of similar interventions aimed at fostering unity and communication between groups" (p. 173). Some of these interventions included "increasing the accessibility and quality of French language instruction services and developing the use

of French among immigrant and Quebeckers from cultural communities"
to ensure "full participation" of all Quebeckers in the life of that
province (McAndrew, 1995, p. 178).[4]

The Aboriginal population also took the position that the
multicultural policy, which in fact made no reference to their language,
culture, and/or political status, did not apply to them. Indeed, as
Aboriginals assert, they are not part of the "foreign" constructed ethnic,
racial, or language group of Canada. In fact, the Indian Act has served
to construct not only their identities as Indians, but accordingly their
social, political, economic, and educational existence. Residing in every
province in Canada, Aboriginal people, as in the years of
colonialization, continue to struggle to obtain an education that is
respectful of their heritage and identities. Contributing to this struggle
is the fact that the Indian Act places services for Aboriginals as the
responsibility of the federal government. Hence, provincial
governments and local boards of education have provided less than
adequate support for education that would address the particular needs
and concerns of Aboriginal peoples. However, Aboriginals have long
demanded the right to control their education in terms of curriculum,
content, and pedagogy (see Adams, 1989; Haig-Brown, 1993; Haig-
Brown, Hodgson-Smith, Regner, & Archibald, 1997; Monture-Angus,
1995).

Insofar as diversity is conceptualized in terms of race, national and
ethnic origin, and religion, pertaining mainly to "cultural groups" or
minority members (with the exception of the French and Aboriginals),
it sets a framework for how popular notions of culture, diversity, and
difference get articulated in institutions and society in general. This
notion of diversity, as is demonstrated in the following section, tends to
limit the understanding of multicultural education to "difference,"
which does not take into account social class, gender, (dis)ability,
sexuality, and other factors. As Bannerji (1997) declared: "There is
little in the state's notion of multiculturalism that speaks to social
justice. More than anything else, multiculturalism preserves the
partisan nature of the state by helping to contain pressures exerted by
'others' for social justice and equity"(p. 36).

---

[4] Nuancing these developments somewhat, Schecter (1991) pointed out that Quebec
government language interventions should be read as more than reflections of
historically situated attitudes toward language groups: "They are also deliberate
attempts to specify, and sometimes rearrange, the roles and prerogatives of the
state, community, and individual in the complex relationship between language
and social space" (p. 49).

TOWARD A PROGRAM EQUALITY: FROM MULTICULTURAL EDUCATION TO TRANSFORMATIVE PEDAGOGIES

Since the introduction of multicultural education, there have been ongoing debates about its capacity to meet the needs, aspirations and issues of the diverse student population. Introduced in many English-speaking school boards in the late 1970s, multicultural education sought to promote sensitivity to and respect for ethno-cultural differences and the integration of minority students using "the dominant educational framework of a monocultural pedagogy in which other ethnocultural groups have been accommodated" (Ghosh, 1996, p. 1).[5] Within this context, therefore, one would find students studying "foreign" cultures, participating in "multicultural days," and going on field trips to "cultural communities" and community centers as a way of recognizing and representing the "cultures" of the students within the schools.[6] Here culture is understood as a set of information and observable items and practices that can be identified and communicated. In some cases, expressions of culture were represented in terms of food, "costume" (dress), art, dance, religious symbols and practices, and/or talks about the norms governing eye contact. Becoming "acquainted" with these symbols and practices of culture represents the "tourist approach"—the idea that these cultural expressions are "elsewhere" outside of Canada.

The Canadian multicultural policy holds that lack of contact between "cultural groups" results in ignorance that in turn reinforces prejudice, ethnocentrism, racism, and xenophobia among members of the society. Hence, like the policy advocates, multicultural education programs such as "multicultural days," field trips, "multicultural literature," and "heritage studies" provide information about "Other" Canadians that is expected to heighten awareness and thus counteract negative attitudes.[7] But the narratives that are engaged during these

---

[5] This is reminiscent of the practice of integrating Aboriginal people into the public schools. In the 1972 document *Indian Control of Indian Education*, their concern was expressed in the following way: "In the past, it has been the Indian student who was asked to integrate: to give up his identity, to adopt new values, and a new way of life" (p. 25).

[6] This served more to "exoticize" the culture of the country of origin as the emphasis was more on "difference." The culture was seen as representative of the "cultural minority" student. Hence, the multicultural days, field trips, and so on. were intended to expose students to the culture of minority groups. The majority group culture is never recognized.

[7] Roman and Stanley (1997), in their study of a high school in, Vancouver, found that "multicultural" events served "to encourage students to 'share their customs

interactions are ones that, on the one hand, construct the "cultural Other" as "foreign and exotic" and, on the other hand, emphasize similarities rather than differences; for to recognize differences would mean promoting segregation and divisiveness, which are considered counter-productive to the maintenance and building of the national identity. Difference, then, insofar as it exists, is regarded as something that "comes from away" and is to be tolerated rather than accepted or valued.

Within multicultural education, compensatory programs such as English as a Second Language and Heritage (now International) Languages were initiated as a means of assisting in the integration of immigrant students into school programs. In Ontario, particularly during the 1970s and 1980s, heritage language classes were held on weekend and/or after school.[8] These classes depended on having a significant proportion of students from particular ethnic and linguistic populations, and were offered on the request of community representatives and/or parents. In the 1990s, many of these classes were integrated into the school day and have become another language program. In this respect the current name, *international language*, is more fitting. The idea, then, of language classes promoting the maintenance of language and cultural identities has been lost.[9] However, when "heritage classes" existed teachers were unlikely to integrate cultural and language issues into their everyday curricula because it was perceived that these matters were dealt with in these "special" classes.

---

with their classmates and to invite their parents to 'speak about their traditions' or to bring objects from home that are representative of their 'cultural background'" (p. 211).

[8] It is interesting to note that there were significant debates and negotiation between school boards and members of the Black or African communities who wanted similar programs for their children. Parents and members of the community, particularly those who recently came from the Caribbean and Africa, argued that their children were also entitled to programs that would promote and maintain their language and culture identities. In some classes, in addition to promoting Caribbean languages, Kiwahili and other African languages were taught.

[9] Although many minority parents welcomed the integration of the heritage (international) language program into the school day, others were concerned with their lack of control and the idea that these classes would be taught by teachers who were not familiar with or interested in the objective of such classes. Further, in some school boards where the integration of the programs formed a compulsory part of the school program and resulted in the extension of the school day, as McAndrew (1995) pointed out, majority group Canadians voiced their "opposition to public schools assuming responsibility for the teaching of minority languages and cultures and to public funding of 'cultural divisiveness'"(p. 171).

In accordance with their policy of cultural integration, the Quebec Ministry of Education established special programs that were intended to integrate non-English and non-French minority immigrant students into French schools while at the same time subsidize (80%) of the heritage language classes held by ethnic minority communities, provided they met the "province's requirement for curriculum and language instruction" (McAndrew, 1995). One of the objectives of the programs was to ensure the survival of the French-speaking population. Authors such as McAndrew (1995) suggested that the intercultural education in Quebec fosters communication between Quebec's "three communities"—the Anglophones, Francophones, and Allophones (the ethnic/linguistic minority groups), and has set in place measures to address prejudice and the history of isolationism that have existed between the communities.

However, in Quebec as well as in English-speaking Canada, the multicultural education programs that were adopted by school boards proved to be insufficient in addressing the educational needs and situations of many of the ethnic and racial minority students. The goals of fostering students' self-confidence and the sense of belonging that were to be attained through multicultural education and compensatory programs in particular were not realized. Minority students continued to feel alienated from the school system. But whereas some racial minority students did well within the existing situation, many continued to be grouped by ability or "streamed," performed poorly, and eventually dropped out (BLAC, 1994; Dei et al., 1998; Codjoe, 1997; Haig-Brown et al., 1997; James, 1990; Tanner, Krahn, & Hartnagel, 1995; Yau, Cheng, & Ziegler, 1993). Their poor performance, some educators and parents argued, was not a result of cultural adjustment (a reflection of the fact that a significant proportion were immigrants) but of systemic racism. Hence, it was advocated that schools need to acknowledge systemic racism as a barrier to the students' participation in school, which contributes to their academic underachievement (James & Brathwaite, 1996).

In jurisdictions with a significant population of African Canadians (Toronto, Halifax, Montreal, Vancouver, Edmonton, Winnipeg), parents and educators argued that even in the era of multicultural policies and programs, "the Eurocentic curriculum which promoted conformity or assimilation to Anglo-Canadian values and norms, remained evident in the curriculum, teaching methods and materials, and students' assessment." This, then, did not address "the subtle and sometimes blatant forms of racism, particularly structural and systemic racism, that are inherent in the educational system..." (James & Brathwaite, 1996, p. 24). And, as Lee (1994) wrote:

> One can organize a unity and diversity club and deal with cultural holidays and host a Multicultural Week and yet not deal with racism. These events may present some information about cultural groups and focus on the exotic and leave many people with a nice feeling but do nothing to address the school's response or lack of response to the languages and faiths of students of color. They may leave intact the Eurocentric curriculum which students consume daily. (p. 24)

In response to arguments regarding race, some school boards, particularly those in urban areas with a significant population of racial minority students, initiated race relations policies and programs (Fisher & Echols, 1989; Toronto Board of Education, 1979). In these cases, race was acknowledged in terms of color differences and not as a political and social construct of Canadian society that resulted in low educational outcomes for racial minority students. Racism was seen to be a consequence of ignorance; and racial minority students' lack of success was seen to be the result of low self-concept, racial tensions in schools, and lack of role models—as represented in the teaching faculty and in learning materials (James & Brathwaite, 1996). On this point, I suggested in an earlier writing that,

> To address this problem of racism, educators believed that students' experiences in racially mixed groups provided awareness of, and sensitivity to, each other. Understanding gained through such interactions would help to prevent racism, therefore creating a school and classroom atmosphere in which racial minority students could participate and become successful. For this reason, we would hear teachers insisting that racial minority students should mix...and racial minority "successful" role models would be brought into schools to demonstrate that success is possible in this society irrespective of race. (James, 1995b, p. 37)

Whereas educators have sought to address the poor educational performance of racial minority students, cultural differences and lack of family support, rather than systemic racism, have been identified often as the basis for the students' outcomes (Cheng, Yau, & Ziegler, 1993; Curtis, Livingstone, & Smaller, 1992). Hence, the "coloring" of the school staff and resources—for example, having minorities on staff, bringing them into school as resource people, and having "multicultural literature"—were initiated as measures that would show students the opportunities and possibilities in the society if only they applied themselves. In some cases, texts or multicultural literature were chosen because they "told of the places from which the students or their parents have/had come." In other cases, the texts were chosen because they "represented" the social, economic, and cultural conditions of the students (see Allen, 1997). Invariably, these were U.S. American texts telling of Black Americans. It is not so much that texts about African Canadians did not exist in Canada, but the practice represents the general notion among many Canadians that racial identification and corresponding racial problems are more evident in the United States.[10] To admit that race influences educational opportunities in Canada is contrary to the multiculturalism policy and the long-held myth of the colorblindness of Canadians and specifically of teachers.

Since the late 1970s, in many parts of Canada, primarily in areas with a large Black population, Black History Month is celebrated. In many school districts, the month's activities represent a significant aspect of their race relations programs, and is, in some cases, the only time that the history and information about minority people's contribution to Canada is ever addressed in the school's curriculum. African-Canadian educator, Althea Prince (1996), referred to the observation of the month as the "great Canadian multicultural myth." She pointed out that she and other members of the community participate in the events because they see it as an "opportunity to share who we are, explore where we came from, [and] discuss where we are going" (p. 167). They thought that the recognition of the month "showed progress." But according to Prince, the month's activities "simply cannot redress these historical distortions in one fell swoop" and "psychological bandaids of stories of kings and queens and stories of the slaves' journey on the Underground Railroad to freedom in Canada" are unlikely to "empower our children" (p. 177). Prince also suggested that:

> Clearly, the history of African-Canadian peoples needs to be dealt with within the schools. A month is not the way. An inclusive curriculum is not only desirable, but clamors to be developed. It feels sometimes as if we are in a bind. For if we continue to enable the ghettoized version of our history as a people, allowing it to be relegated to one month, then we are complicit in the perpetuation of a hegemony that denies our existence. Yet if we do not take this Black History Month crumb that is offered, we may find that our children, and all children, for that matter, have no access to even this ghettoized version of the history of African peoples. (p. 169)[11]

---

[10] That Canadians tend to believe that racial problems exist in the United States and not in Canada is likely a product of Canadians' exposure to American rather than Canadian literature about race and racial problems, and a reflection of the extent to which American literature dominates Canadian students' education. This might also in part explain why many Canadian students, even today, say that slavery existed in the United States and not in Canada, information to which they might never have been exposed in their schooling. Further, this is also likely a reflection of the liberal ideology of colorblindness that Canadians like to maintain.

[11] Prince (1996) made the point that during the month resource people have to "travel" with materials in a "Black-History-Month-Kit" that contains

Clearly, race relations policies and programs have done little to address racial inequality, minority students' cultural identities and experiences, and the power relationships within the alienating educational system. Indeed, as McCarthy (1995) wrote of the U.S. context, their policies and programs, "the lack of critical perspective within the multicultural formulation—one that links school knowledge and the microdynamics of the classroom to structural inequality and differential social power outside the school—has meant that multiculturalism [and race relations] has been in many cases easily incorporated and sucked back (Swartz, 1988) into dominant curriculum and education arrangements" (p. 22). Noting this, educators, students, parents, and community members have advocated for educational policies and programs that recognize the impact of racism on the schooling experiences of racial minority students. To this end, *anti-racism education* was initiated.

As in Britain (Brandt, 1986; Gewirtz, 1991; Troyna, 1987), some Canadian educators have advocated for education policies, curricula, pedagogies, and practices to be conceptualized within an anti-racism framework. It is understood that there are differences between multicultural education and anti-racism education (James, 1995b; Mukherjee, 1993; Ng, Staton, & Scane, 1995; Roman & Stanley, 1997; Srivastava, 1997; Thomas, 1987). Multiculturalism has been interpreted as being based on a liberal-reformist notion of cultural democracy, ethnic absolutism, and the racialization, ethnicization, nationalization, genderization, and class-based understanding of "Other" Canadians. Anti-racism is conceptualized as a perspective that understands that students' experiences are structurally influenced and situated "within the social relations of unequal power" (Roman & Stanley, 1997). Race, a social construction, and racism are understood in relation to historical contexts that are rooted in the socioeconomic and political history of colonization and imperialism. As a hegemonic ideology, racism operates at the individual, institutional, and structural levels and is part of a contiguous system of oppression intersecting with class, gender, ethnicity, sexuality, and other factors.[12]

"everything" that the "customer wants." She said that they do this "in the name of the community and history, for our children, for ourselves, for our society. We want to see our faces, hear our voices, read our words and speak them" (p. 168).

[12] In articulating a framework that gives attention to the intersections of race, class, gender, and other factors, Dei (1996a) used the term "integrative anti-racism." Similarly, anti-racism feminism identifies the intersection of race and gender (Dua, 1999; Jordon & Weedon, 1995).

Anti-racism education, therefore, seeks to provide students with a critical understanding of their social situation and experiences in relation to power differentials in society and, in particular, the school context. Culture is understood to be complex and dynamic and cannot be represented simply by symbols, objects, and individual stories. Understanding their power in the classroom and the ways in which the school system has operated structurally to alienate and marginalize minority students, educators are expected to use their role to facilitate and enable the learning of *all* students, taking into account their experiences, interests, expectations, and aspirations, thus making education relevant to students through their active participation in the education process.

Within the anti-racism framework, African Canadian parents and educators have advocated for *African-centered* or *Afrocentric pedagogy* for African Canadian students who have been identified as one of the groups of students whose poor educational performance and alienating experiences needed to be more effectively addressed (Dei, 1994; Henry, 1992, 1994). According to Henry (1992), Afrocentric education refers to "those constructs, values, knowledges, and ways of being informed by an African heritage, reshaped in North American society, and sustained and reproduced in Black cultural continuities" (p. 392). Dei (1996b) argued further that African-centered schools might be the most appropriate way to deliver successful education to African children in the "Euro-Canadian/American contexts" in which schooling takes place. Such schooling, said Dei (1996b), would be in "recognition of the importance of providing education that speaks to the lived material and social realities of peoples of African descent in a white-dominated society" (p. 295). In collaboration with members of the African community of Toronto, the Toronto Board of Education in September, 1994 established a "Black Focus School"—*Nigana*. It was subsequently closed for about 2 years, and was reopened in January, 1998 with fewer than 20 students.[13] This number of students probably is reflective of the opposition to the idea of what is sometimes referred to as "segregated schooling."

Unlike multicultural education, anti-racism education did not receive widespread adoption from provincial governments and school

---

[13] It should be noted that the Board considered the Nigana program an experiment; hence, it was anticipated that in time such a program would not be necessary—surely a liberal political notion of accommodation, and a political gesture that would hopefully "satisfy" Black parents and community members. And insofar that it is short-lived, it would save the Board from the criticism by largely White parents who saw this as support of segregation.

boards despite the advocacy by parents and educators. Although a number of provincial governments and school boards implemented race relations policies in the 1980s (Fisher & Echols, 1989; James & Brathwaite, 1996; Mukherjee & Desai, 1996), only the Ontario government went on to introduce an anti-racism policy and program. It is instructive to examine briefly how one government interpreted and implemented programs based on a transformative pedagogy. The "Resource Guide for Antiracist and Ethnocultural-Equity Education," published by the Ontario Ministry of Education (Ministry of Education and Training, 1992), stated:

> Ontario schools have been populated by students from a variety of racial and ethnocultural backgrounds, but the school system...has been primarily Western European in content and perspective, reflecting the original patterns of settlement in the province. As a result some students of other than Western European background have not seen themselves represented positively. This failure of the system to give equal attention and respect to all groups has contributed to stereotyping of some groups. (p. 2)

In a follow-up document a year later, the Ministry published the guidelines that the Boards of Education were expected to follow in their development and implementation of anti-racism and ethnocultural-equity policies. It stated:

> The intent of antiracism and ethnocultural equity education is to ensure that all students achieve their potential and acquire accurate knowledge and information, as well as confidence in their cultural and racial identities. It should equip all students with the knowledge, skills, attitudes, and behaviors needed to live and work effectively in an increasingly diverse world, and encourage them to appreciate diversity and reject discriminatory attitudes and behaviors. (Ministry of Education and Training, 1993, p. 5)

The document goes on to say that "some existing policies, procedures, and practices in the school system are racist in their impact, if not their intent" and have consequently limited the opportunities of racial and ethnic minority and Aboriginal students and staff from fulfilling their potential and maximizing their contribution to society (Ministry of Education and Training, 1993). Racism is defined as "a set of erroneous assumptions, opinions, and actions stemming from the belief that one race is superior to another; and may be found in institutional structures and programs as well as in the attitudes and behaviors of individuals" (p. 44).

Although the institutional and individual nature of racism is acknowledged, the structural aspect is disregarded. Neither is the issue of power differences that contribute to the lack of access and inequality within education recognized. Racism then is seen as just another form of prejudice (James, 1995b). Also race, as socially constructed in Canada, is not made explicit. Neither is there the recognition that educational institutions are sites for reproducing societal inequalities (Dei, 1996a; Roman & Stanley, 1997). So, the disadvantages of Anglo-Canadian students are conceptualized in the same way as the disadvantages of racial minority students. Further, the idea of "ethnocultural equity" is premised on the multicultural ideology of ethnic or "cultural group;" that is, "Other" Canadians gaining "confidence in their cultural and racial identities" and learning about each other so that they can live and work in this diverse society. The dominance in terms of the power of one ethnic group over another is not recognized or questioned. And although the documents recognize the Eurocentric nature of current educational programs, they do not suggest that this situation must be interrogated in order to bring about equity in the curricula. What rings through in these documents are the notions of intergroup harmony, individual prejudice, and the attainment of educational success through cultural pride (James, 1995b).

The anti-racism perspective and its practices in schools were not without its critics.[14] Anti-racism is perceived by some as exclusionary and privileging race and color. In their article, "A Critical Examination of Anti-Racist Education," Mansfield and Kehoe (1994) argued that, with its focus on "celebrating and sharing heritage" and promoting intergroup harmony and understanding, multicultural education has been effective in creating "a more humane and human rights conscious society where there is a desire for equity and fairness for all" (p. 239). Although admitting that "some persistent concerns of recently arrived visible minorities" need to be addressed, Mansfield and Kehoe went on to propose that "the focus of multicultural education could be expanded to incorporate some important concerns of anti-racist education, such as institutional barriers, material inequalities, and power discrepancies between minorities and majority. What we do *not* suggest is that multicultural education adopt anti-racism's exclusionary emphasis of color-racism and capitalism, or its divisive, oppositional approach" (p. 426).

In what might be considered to be an attempt to address what Mansfield and Kehoe (1994) called the "persistent concerns" of racial minority students, multicultural educator Ratna Ghosh (1996) proposed what she refers to as "redefined multiculturalism." She stated that

---

[14] Elsewhere (James, 1995b) I argued that the practice of anti-racism was in fact a form of multiculturalism as it was difficult for teachers, schooled in the liberal ideology of multiculturalism, to actually conceptualize school practices as racist and contributing to inequality.

redefined multicultural education is "inclusive, integrated, student-centered, and is based on cooperative approaches to teaching and learning. It emphasizes a democratic classroom ethos and an ethical affective approach in which learners are active participants." Emphasizing that this approach to education is "relevant at the structural and individual levels of education," Ghosh also made the point that any system that supports discrimination "against specific groups on the basis of their difference from the dominant group is unacceptable and therefore needs radical change at all levels" (p. 34). On the aspect of difference, Ghosh wrote that

> ...there are several definitions of difference but they are not fixed in any one time and place (that is historically and across cultures). Multicultural education means recognizing that differences are constructed on the basis of the lack of power and the subordinate identity of people and groups. The implication of this for teaching strategies is that educators need to understand the social and historical construction of difference.... Educators must know the effects of practices that label, devalue, and exclude the knowledge of the "other," the minority ethnocultural groups and females. They must also evaluate how schools deal with differences in social and pedagogical interactions that influence the way teachers and students define themselves and each other. (p. 6)

As in the U.S. American literature, this conceptualization of "redefined multicultural education" makes explicit the fact that the experiences of marginalized groups in terms of race, class, gender, sexuality, and other factors are to be incorporated into the organization of school and the curriculum (Amber-Belkhir in association with 16 WUS & TSU faculty, 1996; Gay, 1997; Grant & Sleeter, 1989; Perry & Fraser, 1993; Sleeter, 1993). Also, it seems to be consistent with McCarthy's (1995) notion of "critical multiculturalism," which, in the tradition of critical pedagogy, is premised on the idea that "a critical approach to multicultural education must involve a radical rethinking of curriculum and pedagogical practices in schooling in ways that begin to take seriously the heterogeneous populations now present in urban school systems...." (McCarthy, 1995, p. 43). In the same way, then, in redefined multicultural education, Ghosh is pressing for educational practices in Canada that pay attention to the hegemonic construction of difference. But within the context of Canada's pervasive liberal multicultural ideology, the practice of redefined multicultural education is likely to result in a situation where, as McCarthy (1995) observed with the practice of multicultural education in the United States, materials and activities get "sucked back" into the "dominant curriculum and educational arrangements." Hence, redefined multicultural education will not change the situation for marginalized Canadian students.

Canadian scholars have sought also to introduce other critical theories into the discourse of diversity education. For example, Rezai-Rashti (1995) suggested that anti-racism educators could learn from critical pedagogy "how to relate to their students' experiences and how to take their needs and problems as the starting point" as well as engage students in critique and thinking about possibilities. Walcott (1996) suggested that "cultural studies" is a perspective that is likely to enable students to access education in a way that speaks to their histories and experiences. It "seeks to open up a discursive space so that a multiplicity of positions, ideas, opinions, and interpretations might take place in the classroom" (p. 285). But these critical perspectives have not been seen in many classrooms. In exploring the reasons for this, Rezai-Rashti (1995), with reference to critical pedagogy, stated that

> As a practitioner, I have come to the realization that although critical pedagogy promises a language of possibility, it does not discuss how actual classroom practices can lead to students' empowerment. As presently elaborated, critical pedagogy remains a highly abstract set of theoretical principles. Its language, conceptualization, and scope are difficult for lay people...to comprehend and grasp. (p. 17)

In summary, the point that I have tried to make in this section is that multicultural education in Canada is limited in the extent to which it has been able to respond to the needs and interests of the diverse student population. This limitation is due in part to the fact that Canadian multiculturalism, as Bannerji (1997) explained,

> ...arises at the convergence of a struggle between the state and otherized, especially non-White, subjects. Their demands for justice, for effective anti-racist policies and administration, for the right to substantive social and cultural life, are overdetermined by the agenda of the state. As long as "multiculturalism" only skims the surface of society, expressing itself as traditional ethics such as...ethnic food, clothes, songs, and dances (thus facilitating tourism), it is tolerated by the state and "Canadians" as non-threatening. But if the demands go a little deeper than that (e.g., teaching "other" religions or languages), they produce violent reaction.... (p. 35)

It is within this pedagogical and political context that teacher candidates today are preparing themselves to work in schools with a diverse population of students. In the following section, as an example, I explore the discourses of teacher candidates who took an urban education course with me in the Faculty of Education, York University, Toronto.[15] This examination is based on the on-line conference postings

---

[15] The calendar description of the course explains that the course is designed for teacher candidates who are doing their practice teaching in the Westview area

of approximately thirty 30 candidates[16] who, as part of the course assignment, engaged in conversations on-line about issues that emerge from the class materials, discussions, teaching practice and community materials, and observations. The assignment also asked participants to "demonstrate in their discussions how we might consider making education in the urban context more relevant to students, sensitive to their experiences, and responsive to their needs and interests" (Course Outline, 1997/1998, p. 4). The comments of these aspiring teachers give us insights into how they understand and are taking up issues of schooling and diversity in urban school settings.

ASPIRING TEACHERS' DISCOURSES ON DIVERSITY AND SCHOOLING IN AN URBAN CONTEXT

Demographic information (February, 1998) indicates that the Westview area, in which class participants practice taught, has a population of 56,000. According to the North York Board of Education student Census, the schools in the area serve about 7,200 students, of whom about 61% were born in Canada and of the remaining%age, a significant number were children of immigrant or refugee parents coming from places such as Jamaica, Guyana, Vietnam, Sri Lanka, Somalia, Ghana, Thailand, and India. In general, the countries from which families have come total about 57, and there are about 37 languages spoken in the homes, including Vietnamese, Spanish, Cantonese, Somali and Tamil.[17] The 1991 Canadian Census, as reported by the North York Inter-Agency and Community Council (1995) indicated that

schools, an "urban area" that "tends to be characterized by low socioeconomic status, high population density, and a diversity of ethnic and racial groups, many of whom are recent immigrants and refugees" (Course Outline 1997/1998, p. 1). The class takes place in the evenings (5-8 p.m.) at a junior high school in the area. The course is part of the Partnership between the North York Board of Education and the Faculty of Education at York University. The partnership seeks to provide teacher candidates opportunities to work in "urban area schools."

[16] There are 50 students (43 females and 7 males) in the class. It is ethnically, racially, and religiously diverse with teacher candidates who reside in the area and others who come from middle class suburban areas. There are roughly 24 Whites of British, Italian, and Eastern European backgrounds, 23 South East Asians, 5 South Asians, and 9 African Canadians. Approximately two thirds of the class teach in the primary and junior schools in the area.

[17] Specifically, of the students born outside of Canada, 6% were born in Jamaica, 4.5% in Vietnam, 4% in Guyana, 3% in Sri Lanka, 2.5% in Somalia and Ghana respectively, 2% in Thailand, and 1.5% in India. The most common languages other than English spoken in the homes are Vietnamese (12.5%), "West Indian Patois" (12.65), Spanish, Cantonese, and Somali (about 4% each) and Tamil and Punjabi, Twi, and Khmer (about 3% each).

about 18% of the residents identified themselves as British (including Scottish), 23% Italian, 4% Chinese, 6% East Indian, 12% Black, 3% Vietnamese, 4% Spanish, with many speaking their respective mother tongues.[18] The Council also reported that the majority of the community members lived in apartments that they rented. With reference to the geography of the area, one class member observed that on a recent occasion as she "traveled south down" Jane, the main street that runs through the community, she noticed that "on the left side the dwellings consisted of apartment buildings and on the right side there were only houses. Jane Street is a divider like the fence near Oakdale. Also once you pass the bridge on Jane, you also enter into a new community, one which appears to be better off economically" (Kit, on-line posting, October 25, 1997). In response, another class member, Jasmine, who described herself as one who has lived "on the other side of the bridge" for most of her life, commented that she "never noticed the fact that apartment buildings only line the left side of the street. Along with the division economically comes the ethnic division, with minorities living in the area that comes before the bridge" (Jasmine, on-line posting, October 26, 1997).

The demographic and geographic profile of the Westview area is largely considered typical of the diversity to be found in Canada's "inner city" areas. It is a diversity comprised of "Other" Canadians, people who, in Canadian multicultural discourse, are identified by their race, ethnicity, language, and religion. And insofar as the communities in which these Canadians reside tend to be working class, this is seen as related to the fact that "they are new to Canada;" in other words, a product of their entrance status. How these teacher candidates, therefore, conceptualize diversity is quite significant to the project of becoming teachers and their understanding of what it takes to work in diverse "urban" communities such as Westview. I use their comments to explore the extent to which they conceptualize diversity in terms of "otherness" related to ethnicity, race, religion, language, and immigrant status—an indication of the Canadian multicultural ideology—or as an attribute of all Canadians, including themselves, where diversity is understood to constitute the complex, contextual, interrelated identities of individuals. And in terms of an educational approach to teaching in diverse settings, how do they conceptualize and think about the possibilities of multicultural education? What alternative or other approaches do they articulate?

---

[18] Apart from the students' information, this is the latest Canadian census information of the area population.

A key aspect of effective or "successful" teaching is to make the pedagogical approach and the curriculum content relevant to the interests and needs of students (Dudley-Marling, 1997). This requires not only familiarity with the communities from which the students come, and understandings of their experiences, but also teachers' consciousness of their perspectives, and awareness of the "selves" they bring to the teaching and learning process. So, although it was expected that teacher candidates would give attention to the geography and demography of the students' communities and the identities of the students, they were also encouraged to reflect on their own identities, schooling experiences, and how all of these contribute to their understanding of what it means to teach in diverse settings. Hence, within the first month of class they engaged in discussions about their own identities in terms of ethnicity, race, gender, and class. Although discussions about their respective ethnic and class backgrounds reflected the usual complications, contradictions, and lack of consensus, racial identity became one of the most problematic terms, particularly for many of the white teacher candidates and, to a somewhat lesser extent, some Chinese teacher candidates (see also Sleeter, 1993). For example, after many on-line exchanges on the question of race, Wing-Chuan, of Chinese background, asked: "What is my race?" He noted that some teacher candidates had identified themselves as "White," but because this term does not apply to him, he preferred to think of himself as "part of the human race." To this, Mohan, a South Asian of Caribbean origin, responded:

> That's nice, but let's not neglect the historical and social implications of race which have constructed stereotypes and economic oppression. For many, it is easy (and perhaps simplistic) to say that they are members of the human race. Race as a social construct is unfortunately not about how we define ourselves but how colonialism, slavery, and immigration have determined the relations between various groups that fall into categories of race. As much as we would like to define race on our own terms, we live in a world that has defined race for us, long before our individual existences here. While racial self definition is important in reconstructing problematic notions of race which currently exist, it is a futile exercise to do so without deconstructing race and therein confronting the history and reality which surrounds these ideas. (On-line posting, November 21, 1997)

During exchanges on race and racial identities, Lisa introduced something that she had observed in the high school in which she was practice teaching. This posting introduced the idea of multicultural education and in effect attempted to bring to the discussion something with which Lisa had been confronted. Lisa mentioned:

> In Westview's Library, there is a shelf off to the side which is dedicated to multi-cultural literature. On this shelf, you will find books by non-white

authors. My question regarding this is: If the literature on this shelf is supposed to be multi-cultural, shouldn't white authors be included too? I mean the very art of isolating non-white authors brings with it the connotation that non-white authors can only be viewed outside of the mainstream while emphasizing the assertion that non-white authors do not and can not belong to the literary canon. Well, if this is the case, I suggest we take the necessary steps to changing the canon so that non-white authors do not continue to be shelved in isolation. (On-line posting, November 19, 1997)

Lisa's comment on the display of multicultural books illustrates how the practice of multicultural education tends to be informed by a multiculturalism ideology of separating out bodies and their literature from the "mainstream" literature. In so doing, materials are categorized on the basis of the authors being non-white and according to subject matter, with little attention given to perspective. Picking up on the importance of content as discussed in Lisa's comment, Carmen posted the following:

Lisa, I agree with you that it's about time all literature was integrated in the canon—when I'm choosing a book to use in the class I'm looking at various categories—themes usually—and all books need to be evaluated for inclusiveness—I'd hate to see a shelf for males and a shelf for females. And just because it's "multi-cultural" does not make the book suitable. For example my class is doing a novel study of Sword of Egypt at the moment—maybe it was chosen as a multicultural book, but as I see it glorifies violence, portrays Bedouin as smelly and evil, Syrians as curly-haired and evil, slaves as stupid, merchants as stupid and self-serving, and females can only position themselves in the text as slaves or members of a harem. And then I looked at the author, and guess what, it was a white male who wrote it. Categorizing literature like this does not address the real issues in what books are used/recommended—that of good quality and inclusive literature. (On-line posting, December 5, 1997)

Both Lisa and Carmen, as well as others, as demonstrated in their postings, challenged what constitutes "multicultural books" and the uncritical way in which they are displayed and used in the school system. Their point of reference is noteworthy. Carmen, an Anglo-Canadian, makes reference to gender, indeed, an easy means of identifying with the issue. But she went on to suggest that it is not only a matter of having "multicultural books;" the content and author must also be critically examined. Lisa, an African Canadian, was concerned with how non-white authors are segregated and categorized. She seemed to suggest that being categorized as "outside the mainstream" and hence not part of "the literary canons," non-white authors are likely to remain outsiders (see Banks, 1992). In this regard, multicultural education has done little to bring non-whites into the mainstream; something that seems to be implied in Lisa's suggestion that "we [should] take the necessary steps to change the canon." This statement could also be interpreted as an appeal, borne out of her experience and desire for space for voices like hers—voices of minority group members that are not homogenized and trivialized. This point was forcefully articulated about 2 weeks later in Lisa's follow-up posting:

> Multi-cultural should be inclusive, not a way of excluding Black authors. So all of the authors and all of their respective subject matters should be included. I mean to have Black authors, simply because they're Black without paying any regard to the subject matter of the book is foolish. Not all Blacks are the same, they don't all have the same thing to say, so why categorize or segregate them as multi-cultural? I think that by doing that, you trivialize their literature, putting them to one side as if it's some amazing feat that they wrote something.... Tell me this, why do you automatically think of something negative when the subject of non-white authors are mentioned? And when I say White, I'm talking about all of the authors I've been made to read, European or North American, who did not have a thing to do with my culture. Who reflected a Eurocentric perspective. Who I have to pay $700 a pop to read or else I can't get my degree in English. Look around, there are very few literature courses which look at non-white authors. Don't we write too? Why are there only two fourth year courses that feature non-canon authors. To tell you the truth, I'm tired of this "special recognition" because of the color of an author's skin. Why can't there be a course in contemporary literature that features April Sinclair or Alice Walker or Richard Wright or Chinua Achebe? (On-line posting, December 1, 1997)

For both Lisa and Carmen, then, multicultural programs should not merely reposition the books and other learning materials, while maintaining the status quo. As they have demonstrated there is a need for "real" change. Seemingly for Lisa, the change would mean not patronizing "non-white authors" or making them tokens (through special recognition) simply because of color; but rather make them an integral part of the curriculum thus acknowledging their contributions as any other authors.

Arguing that multicultural education is not able to "address the problematic issues" of curriculum, difference, and diversity, Sabra, of South Asian origin, in response to Lisa, Carmen, and others, wrote that anti-racism offers a more transformative approach to the issues. She said that it is an approach that can "instill in the minds of children" the ability to critically think, question, and challenge stereotypes that they might face in educational literature and curriculum. And unlike multicultural literature, anti-racism literature does not present stereotypes or "picture-perfect, 'colorful' images of what goes on" in the communities of "people of color." Sabra also pointed out:

> To me, anti-racist education is not necessarily about changing the images of people of color in literature, for example. Rather I think anti-racist education is about consistently identifying, challenging and naming racism

in literature or in curriculum. It is important that it be exposed.... Through discussion, students can explore what racism can do to people. I think it is very crucial to always look at the immediate context, which for students is the school. If students can identify racism that surrounds them, are aware of racism's dangers, are encouraged to discuss what to do about it, are given the means to tackle the problem on school grounds, they would learn the real essence of what anti-racism is—a principle and not a hand-out by the board. (On-line posting, November 20, 1997)

Informed by this perspective of anti-racism, Mohan, in a number of on-line postings, kept repeating that if we are to effectively address the educational and social issues faced by the students in the area, then race, racial identification, and race privilege must be understood and "confronted" with attention to "its historical contexts." He went on to say:

Unfortunately we as educators have fallen victim to idealism of a political climate in which entire histories of racism, social, gendered and economic oppression have been neatly glossed over by words such as multiculturalism and equality. How can we possibly promote equality when it has in the past and present never even existed? It seems ludicrous that we can promote "equality" without even acknowledging or addressing the very inequality that is and has been so rampant in our society. Deconstructing race or racism therefore lies in looking at the problems of history and our society, without patronizing or sheltering our students from the real world. If school is so idealistic in promoting terms such as equality and multiculturalism while neglecting to address our historical and contemporary reality of race, sex and class based oppression, how can we in good conscience stand by and say that we are "educating" our students and how can we in reality call ourselves "teachers"? (On-line posting, November 23, 1997)

Sabra and Mohan named racism as a central issue that teachers must confront and address if they are to provide students with an education that is related to their circumstances and experiences. Despite their criticisms, multicultural education continued to be viewed by the teacher candidates as the approach that would address the issues and needs of the students in the area. This was partly because multicultural education tended to be the approach to curriculum taken by most of the teachers with whom the teacher candidates worked. In light of the on-line debate of multicultural versus anti-racism education that was taking place, Sheva asked: "Is multicultural education not achieving its purpose which is to educate and empower all students (both minority and majority group members), or is it merely emphasizing a celebration of differences among people in our society" (on-line posting, January 19, 1998). Many of the responses to this question indicated that teacher candidates felt that multicultural education, as implemented in the schools, is, as Tam stated, "unable to educate and empower ALL students" (on-line posting, January 20, 1998). Tam went on to reference

Dudley-Marling (1997), one of the class texts. She pointed out that in attempting "to empower his students by educating them about a specific culture...[Dudley-Marling] might have empowered those who did not know a lot about the culture to begin with but he disempowered the one student within the culture" (on-line posting, January 20, 1998).[19] Tam is pointing out a common error that teachers make in implementing a multicultural program. In their attempt to engage students' interests and enrich their learning, teachers will use class materials that match the students' cultural backgrounds (Dudley-Marling, 1997). As Dudley-Marling illustrated, this practice is highly problematic because the tendency to homogenize group members is based on generalized assumptions that can lead to, as Tam pointed out, disempowerment. But whereas many of the teacher candidates identified the problematic aspect of multicultural education, most did not reject this approach to education for they seemed to think the problem is one that can be fixed within the current structure of education.

Before long, and having not yet seen a definition of multicultural education in the exchanges, the question was asked, "What is multicultural education?" Alena responded by saying:

> I view it as allowing full development of abilities in all children regardless of their differences. These differences may include racial, ethnic, gender, class stratification, etc. I strongly feel that multicultural education should not be taught or implemented just for minority students. I believe that it is just as important for White students to develop a consciousness of ethnicity. White students, too, must learn about the cultures of other students. It bothers me to hear or read about students who were too ashamed and afraid to show the world their "true" identities. They felt they were not good enough to be part of the White Anglo-Saxon society. (On-line posting, January 21, 1998)

In this definition, Alena goes beyond the traditional understanding of multiculturalism, that which is informed by the multicultural policy of Canada. She sees multicultural education as incorporating issues related to factors other than race and ethnicity. This was generally the view of most of the teacher candidates who responded to the question. What is particularly significant, however, is Alena's desire that white students not learn about their own culture, but that of "other students"—non-whites. And on what seems to be a related concern, that racial minority students tend to be the focus of multicultural programs,

---

[19] Tam is referencing the story that Dudley-Marling (1997) told about reading a "Pakistani folktale" in his Grade 3 class assuming that one of the students who had immigrated from Pakistan was Pakistani. In fact, he was from Afghanistan, and was a refugee in Pakistan.

she called for attention to be paid to those white students who need to be supported in their bid to show "their true identities."

Interestingly, despite the identified weaknesses of multicultural education and the claim that it is unable to "empower" students, teacher candidates contended that it has made a difference in the educational process of the students with whom they were working. This position exemplifies the extent to which these teacher candidates' liberalism informed by multicultural ideology continues to inform their understandings of what needs to be done to transform education, and their willingness to engage in structural changes. Kim's response to Sheva's question represents this thinking:

> It may not have achieved its ultimate purpose, but what has occurred has definitely made a difference. Imagine if there had been no acknowledgement of the need for multicultural education, most people would not even have known that they were being racist, biased and discriminatory. Things can only get better as we continue to raise everyone's awareness and educate the next generation. (On-line posting, January 25, 1998)

The comments of the teacher candidates indicate a preference for, or more appropriately, comfort with a multicultural rather than an anti-racism approach to meeting the needs and aspirations of the students in the area. It was evident that the educational and social experiences of the teacher candidates played a significant role in how they understood and saw the possibilities of multicultural and anti-racism education. These two approaches to teaching in diverse classrooms were constructed as opposites. Most, particularly those of European backgrounds and to a lesser extent those of Asian backgrounds, tended to think that race was not a critical factor in identification and, therefore, was irrelevant to the personal experiences that they bring to their teaching. Similarly, they felt that the race of students was not as significant as Mohan and others, primarily those of African and South Asian backgrounds, were insisting that it was. So whereas most of the teacher candidates' postings indicated some appreciation for experiences related to ethnicity, language, race, social class, and gender—something that goes beyond the construction based on the multiculturalism policy—for most, all of these demographic factors were perceived as equally relevant. In doing so, they negate the role of the historical and social contexts and the extent to which privilege and oppression related to these factors might affect not only the experiences of the students, but also their own experiences. Those teacher candidates who argued for an anti-racism approach to education, pointing out that problems of the students in the area stem from stereotyping and essentializing as related to race and racism, did not give attention to how their narrow interpretation of anti-racism might also be problematic. They neglected to explicitly articulate the interconnections of race and the other factors.

Beyond the apparent dichotomy between multicultural and anti-racism education that seem to be represented in the discourses of these teacher candidates, are questions about their willingness to engage critically the structural and individual issues that are necessary if they are to establish equitable educational environments. It seems, therefore, that the critical framework offered by anti-racism, critical multicultural education, and redefined multicultural education must inform teacher candidates' conceptualization and interpretation of equitable practices. It will be up to teachers to ensure that their curriculum and pedagogy do not re-inscribe the dominant liberal ideology that does not address the inequitable educational contexts that today's students are expected to tolerate and survive.

CONCLUSION

In this chapter, I have tried to show that the Canadian Multiculturalism Policy/Act with its liberal ideological orientation has so informed multicultural education that its structure and practice continue to be problematic. In the early years, multicultural education was adopted as an approach that would address the needs, interests, and aspirations of ethnic, racial, linguistic, and "accented" Canadians who were constructed as "Other;" specifically, immigrants and refugees—people who over time would give up their "foreign" cultural practices and become culturally Canadians. This culture was never defined, but was implicitly understood and recognized by its practitioners, many of whom, based on the well-entrenched liberal ideology, would claim that there is no "Canadian culture." Within this context culture is conceptualized as a "problem" to overcome, and as a static element that can be represented by symbols, languages, accents, or clothing (costumes). So it is possible to "see," "identify," "practice," and "represent" culture. This ahistorical framework of multi-culturalism in Canada has limited the implementation of educational programs that address systemic issues that operate to restrict the opportunities, possibilities, and aspirations of marginalized students.

Despite the more than two decades of practice, very little has changed in the conceptualization and practice of multicultural education in Canada. This stasis reflects the difficulty in disentangling multicultural education today from its historical and liberal ideological roots. And just as the liberal multicultural ideology stifled the race relations approach to education for a racially diversified student population, so too it continues to stifle anti-racism, "redefined" multicultural education, and other critical perspectives that attempt to address and change the systemic and structural factors that operate as barriers to effective and equitable education for *all* Canadian students. That some future educators, as represented by the teacher candidates in the urban education course, give little attention to history in their attempts to contextualize their own and the students' worlds of privilege and oppression, is indicative of the extent to which the liberal multicultural ideology continues to permeate the analyses and understanding that teachers hold about effective and equitable education for a diverse population of students. If, then, today's educators and, in particular, classroom teachers who work in heterogeneous communities continue to provide educational programs without seeking to implement systemic changes, then little will be accomplished in attempts to meet the needs, interests, and aspirations of today's students. In the Canadian context, education that addresses issues of diversity must critically challenge entrenched multicultural ideology and provide marginalized students with the anti-racism knowledge and skills that make their schooling related and relevant to their social and political experiences.

REFERENCES

Adams, H. (1989). *Prison of grass: Canada from a native point of view.* Saskatoon: Fifth House.

Allen, A. (1997). Creating space for discussions about social justice and equity in an elementary classroom. *Language Arts, 74*(7), 518-524.

Amber-Belkhir, J. A. in association with 16 UWS & TSU faculty. (1996). Multiculturalism and race, gender, class in American higher education textbooks. *Race, Gender & Class, 3*(3), 147-174.

Banks, J. A. (1992). A curriculum for empowerment, action and change. In K. A. Moodley (Ed.), *Beyond multicultural education: International perspectives* (pp. 154-170). Calgary: Detselig Enterprises.

Bannerji, H. (1997). Geography lessons: On being an insider/outsider to the Canadian nation. In L. G. Roman & L. Eyre (Eds.), *Dangerous territories; Struggles for difference and equality in education* (pp. 23-41). New York: Routledge.

Black Learners Advisory Committee (BLAC). (1994). *BLAC report on education: Redressing inequality—Empowering Black learners. Vol. 3: Results of a socio-demographic survey of the Nova Scotia Black community.* Halifax: Black Learners Advisory Committee.

Brandt, G. (1986). *The realization of anti-racist teaching.* London: Falmer Press.

Cheng, M., Yau, M., & Ziegler, S. (1993). *The 1991 every secondary student survey, part 1: Detailed profiles of Toronto's secondary school students.* Toronto: Research Services, Toronto Board of Education.

Codjoe, H. M. (1997). *Black students and school success: A study of the experiences of academically successful African-Canadian student graduates in Alberta's secondary schools.* Edmonton: Department of Educational Policy Studies, University of Alberta.

Course Outline (1997/1998). Urban Education. ED.INDS 3900U.06. Toronto: Faculty of Education, York University.

Cummins, J. (1997). Minority status and schooling in Canada. *Anthropology & Education Quarterly, 28*(3), 411- 430.

Curtis, B., Livingstone, D. W., & Smaller, H. (1992). *Stacking the deck: The streaming of working class in Ontario schools.* Toronto: Our Schools/Our Selves.

Dei, G. J. S. (1994). Reflections of an anti-racist pedagogue. In L. Erwin & D. Maclennan (Eds.), *Sociology of education in Canada: Critical perspectives on theory, research & practice* (pp. 290-310). Toronto: Copp Clark Longman.

Dei, G. J. S. (1996a). *Anti-racism education: Theory and practice.* Halifax: Fernwood.

Dei, G. J. S. (1996b). Rethinking 'African-centred schools' in European-Canadian contexts. In C. E. James & K. S. Brathwaite (Eds.), *Educating African Canadians* (pp. 295-301). Toronto: Our Schools/Our Selves, James Lorimer & Co.

Dei, G. J. S., Muzza, J., McIsaac, E., & Zine, J. (1998). *Reconstructing 'drop-out': A critical ethnography of Black students' disengagement from school.* Toronto: University of Toronto Press.

Dua, E. (1999). Canadian anti-racist feminist thought: Scratching the surface of racism. In E. Dua & A. Roberston (Eds.), *Scratching the surface: Canadian anti-racist feminist thought* (pp. 7-31). Toronto: Women's Press.

Dudley-Marling, C. (1997). *Living with uncertainty: The messy reality of classroom practice.* Portsmouth, NH: Heinemann.

Evans, J., & Davies, B. (1993). Equality, equity and physical education. In J. Evans (Ed.), *Equality, education and physical education* (pp. 11-27). London: Falmer Press.

Fisher, D., & Echols, F. (1989). *Evaluation report on the Vancouver school board's race relations policy.* Vancouver: Vancouver School Board.

Gay, G. (1997, January/February). The relationship between multicultural and democratic education. *Social Studies, 88*(1), 5-12.

Gewirtz, D. (1991). Analyses of racism and sexism in education and strategies for change. *British Journal of Sociology of Education, 12*(2), 183-201.

Ghosh, R. (1996). *Redefining multicultural education.* Canada: Harcourt Brace.

Grant, C. A., & Sleeter, C. E. (1989). *Turning on learning: Five approaches for multicultural teaching plans for race, class, gender, and disability.* New York: Merrill/Prentice-Hall.

Haig-Brown, C. (1993). *Resistance and renewal: Surviving the Indian residential school.* Vancouver: Tillacum Library.

Haig-Brown, C., Hodgson-Smith, K. L., Regner, R., & Archibald, J. (1997). *Making the spirit dance within: Joe Duquette High School and an Aboriginal community.* Toronto: Our Schools/Our Selves, James Lorimer.

Henry, A. (1992). African Canadian women teachers' activism: Recreating communities of caring resistance. *Journal of Negro Education, 61*(3), 392-404.

Henry, A. (1994). The empty shelf and other curricular challenges of teaching for children of African descent: Implications for teachers' practice. *Urban Education, 29*(3), 298-319.

James, C. E. (1990). *Making it: Black youth, racism and career aspiration in a big city.* Oakville, Ontario: Mosaic Press.

James, C. E. (1995a). *Seeing ourselves: Exploring race, ethnicity and culture.* Toronto: Thompson Educational Publishing.

James, C. E. (1995b). Multicultural and anti-racism education in Canada. *Race, Gender & Class, 2*(3), 31-49.

James, C. E., & Brathwaite K. S. (1996). The education of African Canadians: Issues, contexts, and expectations. In C. E. James & K. S. Brathwaite (Eds.), *Educating African Canadians* (pp. 13-31). Toronto: Our Schools/Our Selves, James Lorimer.

James, C. E., & Shadd, A. (Eds.). (1994). *Talking about difference: Encounters in culture, language and identity.* Toronto: Between the Lines.

Jordon, G., & Weedon, C. (1995). *Cultural politics: Class, gender, race and the postmodern world.* Cambridge: Blackwell.

Lee, E. (1994). Anti-racist education: Panacea or palliative? *Orbit, 25(2),* 22-25.

Lucas, T., & Schecter, S. R. (1992). Literacy education and diversity: Toward equity in the teaching of reading and writing. *The Urban Review, 24(2),* 85-104.

Mansfield, E., & Kehoe, J. W. (1994). A critical examination of anti-racist education. *Canadian Journal of Education, 19(4),* 419-430.

McAndrew, M. (1995). Ethnicity, multiculturalism, and multicultural education in Canada. In R. Ghosh & D. Ray (Eds.), *Social change and education in Canada* (pp. 165-177). Toronto: Harcourt Brace.

McCarthy, C. (1995). Multicultural policy discourses on racial inequality in American education. In R. Ng, P. Staton, & J. Scane (Eds.), *Anti-racism, feminism, and critical approaches to education* (pp. 21-44). Toronto: OISE Press.

Ministry of Education and Training. (1992). *Changing perspectives: A resource guide for anti-racist and ethnocultural-equity education.* Toronto: Queen's Printer for Ontario.

Ministry of Education and Training. (1993). *Anti-racism and ethnocultural equity in school boards: Guidelines for policy development and implementation.* Toronto: Queen's Printer for Ontario.

Monture-Angus, P. (1995). *Thunder in my soul: A Mohawk woman speaks.* Halifax: Fernwood.

Moodley, K. (1983). Canadian multiculturalism as ideology. *Ethnic and Racial Studies, 6(3),* 320-331.

Mukherjee, A. (1993). Anti-racist education: Equity in our schools. In TVOntario (Ed.), *Anti-racist education: Selected readings and resources* (pp. 3-10). Toronto: TVOntario.

Mukherjee, A., & Desai, S. (1996). *"Some do, some don't," Implementation of a comprehensive race relations strategy: An evaluation.* Halifax: Halifax County-Bedford District School Board.

Multiculturalism Policy of Canada. (1988). *Excerpts from the Canadian Multicultural Act.* Ottawa: Heritage Canada.

National Indian Brotherhood (1972). *Indian control of Indian education.* Ottawa: National Indian Brotherhood.

Ng, R. (1995). Multiculturalism as ideology: A textual analysis. In M. Campbell & A. Manicom (Eds.), *Knowledge, experience, and ruling relations: Studies in the social organization of knowledge* (pp.32-48). Toronto: University of Toronto Press.

Ng, R., Staton, P., & Scane, J. (Eds.). (1995). *Anti-Racism, Feminism, and Critical Approaches to Education.* Toronto: OISE Press.

North York Inter-Agency and Community Council. (1995). *Demographic report on the Jane Finch area.* North York: NYIACC.

Palmer, H. (1975). *Immigration and the rise of multiculturalism.* Vancouver: Copp Clark.

Perry, T., & Fraser, J. W. (1993). *Freedom's plow: Teaching in the multicultural classroom.* New York: Routledge.

Prince, A. (1996). Black history month: A multicultural myth or "Have-Black-History-Month-Kit-Will-Travel." In C. E. James & K. S. Brathwaite (Eds.). *Educating African Canadians* (pp. 167-178). Toronto: Our Schools/Our Selves, James Lorimer.

Razack, S. (1997). Race, social work and how we know what we know: A perspective from the North. Paper presented at the Third Annual Conference of Caribbean and International Social Worker Educators. Port of Spain: Trinidad.

Rezai-Rashti, G. (1995). Multicultural education, anti-racist education, and critical pedagogy: Reflections on everyday practice. In R. Ng, P. Staton, & J. Scane (Eds.), *Anti-racism, feminism, and critical approaches to education* (pp. 3-19). Toronto: OISE Press.

Roman, L., & Stanley, T. (1997). Empires, emigres, and aliens: Young people's negotiations of official and popular racism in Canada. In L. G. Roman & L. Eyre (Eds.), *Dangerous territories; Struggles for difference and equality in education* (pp. 205-231). New York: Routledge.

Samuda, R .J., & Kong S .L. (1986). *Multicultural education: Programmes and methods.* Toronto: Intercultural Social Sciences Publication.

Schecter, S. R. (1991). L'etat, gardien de la langue: A diachronic view of language policy and planning in Quebec. In M. E. McGroarty & C. J. Faltis (Eds.), *Languages in school and society: Policy and pedagogy* (pp. 40-51). New York: Mouton de Gruyter.

Sleeter, C. (1993). How White teachers construct race. In C. McCarthy & W. Crichlow (Eds.), *Race, identity and representation in education* (pp. 157-171). New York: Routledge.

Spivey, M. (1998). *Identity politics of a Southern tribe: A critical ethnography.* Toronto: Department of Sociology, York University.

Srivastava, A. (1997). Anti-racism inside and outside the classroom. In L. G. Roman & L. Eyre (Eds.), *Dangerous territories; Struggles for difference and equality in education* (pp. 113-126). New York: Routledge.

Tanner, J., Krahn, H., & Hartnagel, T. (1995). *Fractured transitions from school to work: Revisiting the dropout problem.* Toronto: Oxford University Press.

Thomas, B. (1987). Anti-racist education: A response to Manicom. In Y. Young (Ed.), *Breaking the mosaic: Ethnic identities in Canadian schooling* (pp. 104-107). Toronto: Garamond Press.

Troyna, B. (1987). *Beyond multiculturalism: Toward the enactment of anti-racist education in policy, provision and pedagogy.* Oxford Review of Education, 13(3), 307-320.

Walcott, R. (1996). Beyond sameness: Thinking through Black heterogeneity. In K. S. Brathwaite & C. E. James (Eds.), *Educating African-Canadians* (pp. 284-294). Toronto: Our Schools/Our Selves, James Lorimer.

Yau, M., Cheng, M., & Ziegler, S. (1993). *The 1991 every secondary student survey, part 111: Program level & student achievements.* Toronto: Research Services, Toronto Board of Education.

Chapter 9

Multicultural Education in the United States: A Case of Paradoxical Equality

Joy L. Lei
Vassar College, U.S.A.

Carl A. Grant
University of Wisconsin–Madison, U.S.A.

In the United States, the field of multicultural education began in the 1960s and in the midst of social protest over civic and economic equality for segments of the population who have consistently faced structural and cultural discrimination based on their race, ethnicity, gender, sexual orientation, or disability. Multicultural education, as an educational movement, sought accordingly to transform the existing educational structure to provide equal access, representation, and outcome for all students. Since its inception, multicultural education has continued to be surrounded by controversy, criticism, and conflict. It may seem odd, especially in a country known for its ideals of liberty and freedom, that efforts to provide equal education would be met with tensions and attacks. This paradox points to the need to disentangle the various meanings of *equality* and *equal education*. In this chapter, we analyze the citation of equality in various U.S. sociohistorical contexts as strategic to the institutionalization of and the resistance to oppressive ideologies. This analysis considers the evolution of dominant ideologies that privilege particular groups of people, and oppress and marginalize others. It also considers how these ideologies have directly and indirectly influenced the education of different populations. In addition, we discuss how different groups and individuals have fought for equal education, as they define it, and use this discussion to center our chronicle of the field of multicultural education in the United States.

CONSTITUTIONAL EQUALITY

One of the most famous phrases in the United States' Declaration of Independence is: *All men are created equal.* This proclamation of equal status and rights has been cited in numerous contexts throughout U.S. history to exemplify the ideals of the nation and to support struggles for social justice. However, if we consider the sociohistorical context in which this phrase was declared, it is clear that what the "founding fathers" of the United States meant by "all men" is specifically "all White men who own property," as this was the only population who was conferred all social and economic rights during this time. Ameer (1995) argued that, as the early republic formed in the 18th century, the three main characteristics of an "American" identity were republican, Protestant, and capitalist. In addition, Ameer argued, this identity included a strong sense of American exceptionalism:

> This exceptionalism, besides reinforcing feelings of exclusiveness, also serves as a fall-back position in times of stress, a foxhole, so to speak, from which the onslaughts of change and of difficulties can be withstood and even repelled. This exclusionary aspect was further reinforced by being enshrined in the Constitution of the new republic: slaves were counted as less than fully human; women were not enfranchised; and, for a period, even freemen were denied full participation if they did not own property. (p. 16)

Thus, the writers of the Declaration of Independence believed they spoke of equality in its truest sense because of their concurrent belief that laborers, women, and people of color were inferior to them and therefore not to be included.

The Generation of Inherent Inequalities

Prager (1982) has argued that, "[E]ach time a new understanding emerges to account for racial inequality, ideology comes to be mistaken as reality. The images that are evoked concerning racial groups come to be the prism through which observation of the real social world is conducted" (p. 100). The ideology of the inherent superiority of White males and inferiority of people of color and females was so naturalized as fact that unequal treatment appeared to be, in context, equal. However, as Frankenberg (1993) pointed out,

> U.S. history is marked by an unevenly evolving history of discourses on race difference. Central to competing analyses of race have been assertions of, and challenges to, a range of claims about difference between people, including physiological or genetic differences, cultural differences, and differences in access to power. One can, in fact, identify a chronological movement in the history of ideas about race in the United States, if only to qualify and complicate the chronology immediately afterward. (p. 13)

Frankenberg (1993) described three stages of U.S. racial ideology as the following: *essentialist racism, color-/power-evasiveness*, and *race-cognizance*. It is important to note that the racial paradigms Frankenberg maps out are not exclusive of each other, nor extinct from the current racial ideology. That is, whereas the three moments can be considered as the first, second, and third phases in U.S. race discourse in the sense that they originated in that order, once past the point of their emergence they can no longer be conceptualized as unfolding chronologically in any simple sense. Instead, each tenet takes center stage, in different contexts, "as the organizing paradigm or retreats to the status of a repertoire that provides discursive elements but does not dictate overarching form or structure"; thus, "these three moments together constitute the universe of discourse within which race [is] made meaningful, with elements combined and recombined, used in articulation with or against one another, and deployed with varying degrees of intentionality" (p. 140).

According to Frankenberg (1993), the first stage, *essentialist racism*, refers to the period prior to the 1920s, when

> arguments for the biological inferiority of people of color represented the dominant discourse... for thinking about race. Within this discourse, race was constructed as a biological category, and the assertion of white biological superiority was used to justify economic and political inequities ranging from settler colonialism to slavery. (p. 13)

Thus, the normalization of essentialist racism[1] functioned to justify inequalities as fair.

This understanding of the boundaries and contradictions of equality is important for it also serves as part of the foundation of U.S. education in terms of the purpose of schooling, who taught, who was taught, what was taught, and how it was taught. As public schools came into existence in the 17th century, formal education was made

---

[1] Frankenberg (1993) argued that essentialist racism has left a legacy that continues to mark discourses on race difference in a range of ways: First, the articulation and deployment of essentialist racism approximately 500 years ago marks the moment when, so to speak, race was made into a difference and simultaneously into a rationale for racial inequality. Second, in significant ways the notion of ontological racial difference underlies other, ostensibly cultural, conceptualizations of race difference. Third, essentialist racism—particularly intentional, explicit racial discrimination—remains, for most White people, paradigmatic of racism. This renders structural and institutional dimensions of racism less easily conceptualized and apparently less noteworthy. Finally, although essentialist racism is not the dominant discursive repertoire on race difference in the United States, its corollary, racially structured political and economic inequity, continues to shape material reality (p. 139).

available exclusively for White males. However, there were individuals—freed and enslaved Africans, Native Americans, women, and their allies—who believed in the education of females and people of color from the very beginning. For example, there are numerous historical accounts of Whites and freed slaves who risked a tremendous amount to teach African slaves to read in English. Slaves themselves risked their lives and mutilation of their bodies to learn to read (see Anderson, 1988; Bullock, 1970; Weinberg, 1977). Also, as Chinese communities continued to grow, the exclusion of Chinese Americans from public education was challenged in the court case of *Tape v. Hurley* in 1884.[2] Although the U.S. Supreme Court ruled that Chinese children had a right to public education, their decision allowed the creation of separate Chinese schools. Subsequent court cases filed by Chinese individuals and communities continued to challenge the exclusion and segregation of Chinese students (see Wollenberg, 1995). In addition, due to the decentralized nature of education at the time, some education of females existed, although this education was sparse and sporadic, depending on individual parents, school leaders, and local activists (see Tyack & Hansot, 1990). The education of females became more accepted and common after the U.S. American Revolution when educated women were desired as good mothers and wives. Part of the struggle for equal education at this time then was for the *existence of* and *access to* education for females, freed and enslaved Africans, and Chinese Americans.

Although education was denied to females, Chinese children, and freed and enslaved Africans, for Native Americans and Mexican Americans, education was first denied and then considered necessary for them and later for Puerto Ricans by many political and administrative leaders of the particular period as part of the colonization process. The mostly segregated education that was imposed on the three conquered populations is described by Spring (1997) as a method of *deculturalization*.[3] This method was accompanied by the purposes of "civilizing" the Native Americans, assimilating the Mexican Americans, and winning the patriotic loyalty of the Puerto Ricans.

---

[2] Mamie Tape, a U.S. citizen, was 8 years old when she was refused admission to a San Francisco school because of her race. On January 9, 1885, Superior Court Judge ruled in favor of Mamie Tape and ordered the San Francisco School District to provide her with equal access to public education. The California legislature responded to this ruling by revising the state's school code to provide education for Chinese children in segregated schools so that they do not have to be admitted to White schools.
[3] Spring (1997) described deculturalization as "the stripping away of a people's culture and replacing it with a new culture" (p. 1).

Under these circumstances, the struggle for an equal education for many Native American tribes, Mexican Americans, and Puerto Ricans was for an education that allowed them to retain their culture and did not denigrate their peoplehood. The Cherokee and the Choctaw Indians, for example, established their own school system on Indian territory in the 1840s. These school systems were very successful—they provided bilingual education, had both White and Native American teachers, and produced a high level of literacy (Spring, 1997).

Differences in Equality

Beginning in the 1920s, the concept of ethnicity was introduced into the racial discourse and, as Omi and Winant (1994) argued, reduced the attention to the structural significance of race:

> Within this new paradigm, belonging to an ethnic group came to be understood more behaviorally than biologically. Alongside the ethnicity paradigm came an "assimilationist" analysis of what would and should happen to people of color in the United States: Like white immigrants, it was argued, people of color would gradually assimilate into the "mainstream" of U.S. society. (p. 13).

Frankenberg (1993) called this second stage *color-/power-evasiveness*, in which the dominant ideology is influenced by the color-blind theory:

> This ideology maintains that any differences in the experiences of minorities are due to their ethnic cultural backgrounds (e.g., Japanese, Polish, Puerto Rican, etc.) and not the color of their skin. While this ideology opens the racial discourse to consider the factor of ethnic culture, it diverts attention away from the structural and institutional effects of White/Anglo racism and asserts that any person of color's failure to achieve in society is due solely to the inferiority and fault of that individual.[4] Also, as McKee (1993) points out, the shift of focus from race to ethnic culture essentially meant that "racial differences translated into cultural differences, which, in turn, meant cultural inferiority." (p. 77)

Newfield and Gordon (1996) argued that the assimilationist ideology has served and continues to serve as a symbolic and cultural barrier to achieving social equality. The authors distinguish assimilation from assimilationism:

> By assimilationism we do not mean *assimilation*, the means and ends pursued by immigrants or marginalized citizens who wish to join the existing economic and political mainstream. …We are instead criticizing

---

[4] In the late 19th and early 20th century, southern and eastern European immigrants, who were arriving in the United States in large numbers, were considered by the existing Anglo-Saxon, Protestant population to be intellectually and morally inferior and, in a sense, not White.

the *terms* that *assimilationism* extracts from those who need and want its rewards. Assimilationism likes to portray itself as nothing more than the innocent desire for a good life, and indeed this is the foundation of its social influence. But as we use the term here, assimilationism refers to a specific ideology that sets the fundamental conditions for full economic and social citizenship in the United States. (p. 80, original emphasis)

Newfield and Gordon (1996) listed three main features of assimilationism: (a) it requires adherence to core principles and behaviors, (b) it rejects racialized group consciousness, and (c) it repudiates cultural equity among groups (p. 80). Thus, "The demand for a common core displaces both demands for equality and the effects of racial difference. Lacking any notion of cultural equality, assimilationism encourages functional ranking of various cultures. Downplaying the effects of racial marking, assimilationism ignores the way supposedly neutral institutions are pro-White" (pp. 80-81).

By the 1950s, through the continuous efforts of individual and community activism, education was conferred as a right to all U.S. citizens. However, there was once again a glaring contradiction to the ideals of equality in the racist Jim Crow laws of institutionalized segregation.[5] This meant that Whites and "coloreds" (a term used during this period mainly to refer to African Americans) used separate facilities (such as drinking fountains, public restrooms, restaurants) and separate areas in the same facility (such as public buses, courtrooms, and restaurants). This also meant that White students and students of color largely went to separate schools. Asian Americans and Mexican Americans at this time were placed in the category of "coloreds" when there was a significant number of them and were denied entry into White schools. In areas where there were very few Asian Americans or Mexican Americans, there was more of a chance that they would be allowed to be educated alongside White students.

Racial segregation was justified and institutionalized by the U.S. Supreme Court case, *Plessy v. Ferguson* in 1896. In this case, the judges ruled that segregated facilities were constitutional because they provided equal services. In this "separate but equal" ruling, equality was used to uphold a form of racist oppression, that is, segregation, and to ignore the fundamental racism that existed. Once again, the inherent logic behind this justification is based on the belief of the racial

---

[5] Jim Crow is a pejorative stereotype of Black men that originated from a 19th century song-and-dance act. It has been coined in U.S. racial history to refer to legal laws and traditional sanctions that enforced the institutional, residential, and public segregation of Blacks and Whites.

superiority of Whites and the inferiority of people of color. The segregated public facilities and schools for people of color were of inferior standards to those for Whites. Thus, the struggle for an equal education at this time was for an *integrated* education, with the belief that students of color should receive the better education that was received by White students.

In 1954, in *Brown v. Board of Education*, the U.S. Supreme Court reversed the ruling in *Plessy v. Ferguson*. This landmark decision in *Brown* held de jure public school segregation[6] to be unconstitutional and helped further the way to societal desegregation. In *Brown*, equality, as well as education, was cited as a fundamental social ideal and right. Chief Justice Warren wrote for the opinion of the Court:

> Today, education is perhaps the most important function of state and local governments. Compulsory school attendance laws and the great expenditures for education both demonstrate our recognition of the importance of education to our democratic society. It is required in the performance of our most basic public responsibilities, even service in the armed forces. It is the very foundation of good citizenship. Today, it is a principal instrument in awakening the child to cultural values, in preparing him [sic] for later professional training, and in helping him [sic] to adjust normally to his [sic] environment. In these days, it is doubtful that any child may reasonably be expected to succeed in life if he [sic] is denied the opportunity of an education. Such an opportunity, where the State has undertaken to provide it, is a right which must be made available to all on *equal terms*. (Quoted in Rodriguez, 1997, p. 36, emphasis added)

The Court posed the following question:

> Does segregation of children in public schools solely on the basis of race, even though the physical facilities and other "tangible" factors may be equal, deprive the children of groups of color of *equal educational opportunities*? We believe that it does…. Whatever may have been the extent of psychological knowledge at the time of *Plessy v. Ferguson*, this finding is amply supported by modern authority. Any language in *Plessy* contrary to this finding is rejected…. We conclude that in the field of public education the doctrine of "separate but equal" has no place. Separate educational facilities are *inherently unequal*. (Quoted in Rodriguez, 1997, p. 36, emphasis added)

The decision in *Brown v. Board of Education* challenged the fundamental logic of racial superiority and inferiority, which had been the basis of racial segregation in U.S. society. The case also made clear the social and economical importance of education and emphasized the significance of "equal educational opportunities," that is, equal access

---

[6] De jure segregation is that which is based on governmental—state or local—actions. In contrast, de facto segregation is that which occurs by circumstance and without governmental direction.

to educational opportunities. In addition, the Supreme Court justices refuted the "separate but equal" argument of previous Court justices by arguing that segregation conferred unequal status on White children and children of color and thus was "inherently unequal."

Although the legal barrier to integrated education had been lifted, the practice of integrated education was immediately challenged and contested by some of the White government officials, school administrators, and community members. African American children who were the first students of color to attend a previously all-White school were harassed and threatened and, in some instances, not allowed entry into their school building. In spite of the physical and psychological injury they endured, these students represented the strong and persistent fight for racial equality by continuing to arrive at their tremendously hostile school environment. The *Brown v. Board of Education* case and the ensuing opposition made clear that court-sanctioned equality did not necessarily lead to its acceptance as mainstream social ideology (Miller, 1996). However, by prohibiting segregated schooling, the Court made it difficult for schools and mainstream society to justify such acts of blatant racial discrimination.

CONTEXTUALIZING THE BEGINNINGS OF MULTICULTURAL EDUCATION

The Sociopolitical Contexts of Multicultural Education

In the third stage of the U.S. racial ideology, which Frankenberg (1993) called the stage of *race cognizance,*

> radical antiracist and cultural nationalist movements of the late 1960s and early 1970s...brought about a resurgence, reevaluation, and transformation of notions of *differentness* of peoples of color from the white dominant culture, along with an analysis and critique of racial inequality as a fundamentally structuring feature of U.S. society. (p. 14, original emphasis)

In contrast to the assimilationist/melting pot ideology of the color-/power-evasiveness stage, a social ideology of *multiculturalism* characterized the race cognizance stage. Newfield and Gordon (1996), for example, characterized the 1970s multiculturalism as having three distinguished features. First, the authors characterized this multiculturalism as *cultural democracy* built on a strong version of cultural pluralism. "While noting the continual *interdependence* of various cultures, it insisted on each culture's *independence*" (p. 95, original emphasis). A second distinguishing feature is described as *democratic pluralism*, in which group identity and individuality are seen as compatible and complementary rather than as a threat to each other. A third feature of 1970s multiculturalism is that multiculturalists were militant in their opposition to cultural supremacism and insisted on some form of *cultural equality*.

Thus, although multiculturalism had changed the way that the mainstream culture thought and talked about race, the more radical and progressive social movements' emphasis on *equity* was generally conflated with and absorbed by more mainstream struggles as *equality*. As Goldberg (1994) argued,

> ...[A]gainst the monocultural grain, the civil rights and countercultural movements of the 1960s signalled a shift from the prevailing assimilative standard to the new one of *integration*. Confronted by demographic shifts as well as by committed, vocal, and active social movements, the fragile grounds sustaining monoculturalism began to buckle. The new model of integration that emerged left cultural groups (including races) with effective control of their private autonomous cultural determinations and expressions at the sociocultural margins, while maintaining a supposedly separate, and thus, neutral set of common values (especially, but not only economic and legal ones) to mediate their relations at the center. In private, ethno-American, in public, American citizen; in private ethnic, in public American. ...The dualism of this model is reflected in its pluralist allowances at the margins with its univocal core insistences at the center. The central values continued to be defined monoculturally. ...The integrative mode has focused primarily on alleviating intergroup conflict and tension, improving ethnoracial relations. It has stressed more or less genuine attempts to define and service improvements in conditions for those who continue to be identified as "minorities," all the while serving up good subjects for the monocultural model. (p. 6, original emphasis)

The Sociohistorical Contexts of Multicultural Education

It is during this time of social change that multicultural education had its beginning. It can be argued that multicultural education grew out of several other efforts to provide equal treatment for marginalized students such as the *cultural pluralism* and the *human relations* movements. Cultural pluralism, a philosophy espoused by John Dewey and several other progressive educators in the early decades of the 20th century, has continued to maintain its presence on the education landscape. The mass immigration between 1890 and 1920 from southern and eastern Europe brought people who had cultural patterns that were somewhat different from the Anglo-Saxon culture that prevailed as the mainstream culture in the United States. Also, these newcomers were arriving in the United States not only to fulfill economic dreams, but also for religious, social, and political reasons. This mass immigration challenged the prevailing notion of "American democracy," and set off a bitter reaction because Anglo-Saxon values and culture were seen as being undermined by the cultures of, for example, Jews and Slavs. The result of the argument between those who wanted to put a stop to unrestricted immigration and those who believed the newcomers were needed to serve as workers in the developing industrial machine was the push for *Americanization*. The metaphor of the United States as a melting pot became a very popular symbol for the process of Americanization, which implied that all the various cultures would "melt down" to produce one common culture. The motto of *e pluribus unum*—out of many, one—seemed to offer the various ethnic populations the opportunity to gain a collective identity as citizens of the United States. However, in actuality, the "common" culture, one based on White, Anglo-Saxon, Protestant, capitalist beliefs, had already been established and was what new immigrants were expected to assimilate into.

Newfield and Gordon (1996) pointed out that there are different meanings of *pluralism* as it is being used in the United States. They argue that because pluralism has been translated as *e pluribus unum* in the United States, "What we usually call pluralism in this country is a pluralism of form leading to a monism of rules. It should be called *assimilationist pluralism*, where the outcome is not actually irreducibly plural, but a union or core" (p. 81, original emphasis). In this sense, the assimilationist-pluralist position is contradictory, "and yet it forms a pillar of the American Creed, standing next to its fellow pillars 'democracy' and 'free enterprise' and transforming these into elements of a core political culture" (p. 81). Similar to the ways equality has been constructed and reconstructed, cultural pluralism is acknowledged to exist in the United States but only assimilationist pluralism is accepted. In fact, assimilationist pluralism is normalized as a national ideal.

John Dewey, Horace Kallen, and others recognized that the melting pot concept did not value or accept pluralism and argued that it was undemocratic (Dewey, 1916, 1938; Kallen, 1956). The concept of cultural pluralism arose because Dewey believed democracy should mobilize the critical capacity of all people. He also believed this critical capacity was being undermined by the dynamics of the newly developing, industrialized urban society. Dewey (1916) stated that, "Democracy is more than a form of government, it is primarily a mode of associated living, of conjoint communicated experience" (p. 101). Although cultural pluralism was addressed in some social studies classes, for the most part it was not a part of the elementary and secondary curriculum. This was partly due to great political and social pressure to have immigrants assimilate into the dominant culture as quickly as possible. Also, during World War II, ethnic identification and the expression of positive feelings toward one's country of birth, especially if the country was fighting on the side of the Nazis, was denounced. Still, some educators have kept alive the philosophy of cultural pluralism and argued that, with its propensity for democracy, it is one of the fundamental principles in the evolution of multicultural education.

The effects of the human relations movement (which reached its height during the 1930s through the 1940s) in the field of education was inspired by teacher educators and teachers (from preschool through secondary school) who voiced concerns about the biased treatment of students of color and other marginalized students. Some of these educators, inflamed by the evils of World War II, argued that people needed to have greater respect and appreciation for one another. They saw school as the ideal place to teach tolerance and conflict resolution and argued for human relations training in schools. Prior to World War II, several organizations such as the Anti-Defamation League of B'nai B'rith (ADL), the Urban League, the National Association for the Advancement of Colored People (NAACP), and the National Conference of Christians and Jews, included school reform among their efforts to eliminate societal discrimination and prejudice. They offered curriculum materials, speakers, and consultants to schools to encourage and support their efforts to foster "good" human relations. The efforts by these organizations were reinvigorated due to events in Europe and the United States during World War II. Specifically, the inhumane abuse and genocide of Jews, gay men, and gypsies by the Nazis motivated many civic groups and individuals to argue for schools to teach greater tolerance and respect for all peoples. Human relations, as an educational concept, has become one of the models for multicultural education. However, it is perceived to be too weak, as the principal theory and practice, for eliminating oppression and bringing forth social justice (Sleeter & Grant, 1999).

The Theoretical Contexts of Multicultural Education

A concurrent impetus for the development of the field of multicultural education is the evolving theoretical explanations for the low academic achievement of students of color, specifically of Black students. According to Jacob and Jordan (1993), these theories on "minority achievement" include the genetic explanation, the cultural deficit explanation, the social reproduction theory, the cultural difference approach, and the cultural discontinuity/cultural ecological framework. The *genetic explanation*, which has been widely discredited, argues that social class and racial differences in IQ scores are largely the result of genetic differences. In contrast to the genetic explanation, the *cultural deficit explanation* stresses the importance of environment as a causal factor. This approach focuses on the "culture of poverty" that poor people are posited to share by virtue of their economic condition. Although proponents of this view see *all* poor people as participating in a culture of poverty, many discussions focus on the Black poor. Holding middle-class White culture as the norm, the culture of poverty is viewed as deficient in providing the experiences, attitudes, or values children need to succeed in school. Differing from these two approaches, the *social reproduction theory* shifts the focus of responsibility from the minority groups themselves to society and schools.

Two other approaches to problems associated with the education of students of color were developed in the field of educational anthropology in the 1960s. One approach, the *cultural difference approach*, argues that differences between majority and minority cultures in interaction, linguistic, and cognitive styles can lead to conflicts between school and child that interfere with effective education. Thus, the home cultures of students of color are viewed as being *different* from the school culture rather than as *deficient*. This approach encourages schools to make changes in their curriculum and methods of instruction in order to bridge the home and school cultures. The second approach, known as both the *cultural discontinuity* and the *cultural ecological approach*, differs from the cultural difference approach in two ways. First, it examines variations in school performance among populations of color. Second, it consciously looks beyond the school and home settings to the larger society in which these settings are embedded, focusing on minority groups' adaptations to the larger society (see Ogbu, 1993).

The Grassroots Context of Multicultural Education

Outside the research institutions and in the public schools, parents and community members of color, women, and their allies argued that school policies and practices were biased and based on an ideology that promoted and kept in place White and male dominance and privilege. For example, these activists argued that school policies and practices were based on a cultural deficit ideology, which is racist and promotes White, middle-class superiority. They also asserted that much of what occurred in schools was not self-actualizing for female students and students of color—for example, the curriculum materials, including textbooks, were sexist and racist. They pointed out that curriculum materials stereotyped females, African Americans, and Native Americans, and omitted people with disabilities, Asian Americans, and Hispanics/Latinos, or included them in a very limited and essentialized manner. Thus, the struggle was not only for access to the same classes, programs, and activities in which White, male, middle-class, and abled-body students participated, equality during this time for many U.S. Americans was also seen as *equal representation*, that is, more and fair representation. A major accomplishment of this activism is the establishment of ethnic studies, women's studies, and gay and lesbian studies departments and programs in colleges and universities. These departments and programs focused on producing knowledge from the perspectives of traditionally marginalized populations that can be integrated into the existing knowledge base. They also offered marginalized groups a place of their own on college campuses—that is, an academic field of study and a location where like-minded scholars could gather.

The shift in racial ideology, the preceding ideals of cultural pluralism and human relations, the Black nationalist and civil rights movements, the anthropological theories on minority achievement, and parental and community activism all contributed to the development of multiculturalism as a social ideology and the field of multicultural education. Specifically, multicultural education was spawned by several groups' determination to make schooling equal and equitable for all students.

DECIPHERING THE PHILOSOPHY AND PRACTICE OF MULTICULTURAL EDUCATION

Creating Boundaries in Multicultural Education

In the early period of the movement, those who took multicultural education as a focus of their scholarly work were united in their demand for school policies and practices that prepared students to actively work toward social-structural equality and the promotion of cultural pluralism (e.g., Baker, 1973, 1977; Banks, 1973; Gay, 1975, 1979; Grant, 1977). However, different approaches were adopted to achieve these goals. For example, James Banks (1973), in the introduction for the National Council for the Social Studies' 43rd Yearbook, *Teaching Ethnic Studies*, stated:

This is not a book written by a group of irrational radicals who use these pages for a counterproductive catharsis. Rather, it is a book penned by a distinguished group of scholars—social scientists and educators—who have spent the bulk of their lives *fighting for human rights*. Although they have experienced many frustrations in their perennial struggles—which their writing reflect—they have not despaired. They believe that change is possible and that what teachers do in the classroom, or don't do, can make a difference. This is probably the greatest significance of this book. It is bound to help every teacher who reads it to sense the *urgency of the racial crisis* in our nation, and to develop a commitment to act to resolve it. (p. xi, emphasis added)

Around the same time, the American Association of Colleges for Teacher Education's (AACTE) Commission on Multicultural Education issued the "No One Model American" statement (1972), which for years was one of the most quoted statements on multicultural education. This statement read (in part):

Multicultural education is education which *values cultural pluralism*.... Multicultural education reaches beyond awareness and understanding of cultural differences. More important than acceptance and support of these differences is the recognition of the right of these different cultures to exist. The goal of cultural pluralism can be achieved only if there is full recognition of cultural differences and an effective program that makes *cultural equality* real and meaningful. (p. 23, emphasis added)

These two framings of multicultural education represent the subtle variance and tension within the movement that reflected the variance and tension between the larger societal goals of *equity* and *equality*. Banks' quote refers to the active fight of individual social scientists and educators for equity and human rights trying to resolve the "racial crisis" in the United States, whereas AACTE's statement offers a less aggressive demand, focusing instead on equality by recognizing and valuing the various cultures in the nation, with no mention of race and racism. As we discuss later in this chapter, these subtle differences and tensions have continued to affect the evolution of multicultural education.

Also, some scholars and activists sought to expand multicultural education's focus on race and ethnicity to include concerns around gender, class, sexual orientation, and disability. The coming together of groups that represented the various interests brought with it a good deal of conceptual confusion and ambiguity regarding the meaning of multicultural education. This is partly due to the fact that there are those within the multicultural education movement who strongly believe that its focus should remain solely on race and ethnicity, and there are also others who believe the movement should include some concerns (e.g., class and gender) but not others (e.g., sexual orientation and disability). Ironically, the predominant focus on race and ethnicity has led to strong criticism of the multicultural education movement for marginalizing particular populations. To the handful of education scholars who were involved in the nascent period of the multicultural education movement, the debates over which oppressed and marginalized groups to include and which definitional terms to use for multicultural education were significant. But more important than these debates was their unity over a common objective for multicultural education—that it has at its core the elimination of social oppression, the acceptance of and value for human diversity, and the establishment of structural equality and equity for all people.

Practicing Multicultural Education

What was more difficult than defining multicultural education was determining how to *do* multicultural education—that is, how can we effectively transform the existing Eurocentric, racist, sexist, classist, heterosexist, and ableist policies, curriculum, and instruction into a democratic and multicultural education? The structural challenges to racism that Banks espoused was more difficult to translate into practices that are likely to be implemented because it challenged the entire system of education and, in effect, the dominant racial ideology of White dominance and privilege. "Celebrating diversity," however, as the AACTE's statement promoted, was a more appeasing and acceptable way of doing multicultural education. A major method of achieving this goal was by providing equal education as it was defined at this time—that is, as *equal representation*, or more and fair representation of people of color, females, and people with disabilities in the curriculum.

By framing multicultural education in terms of equal representation, the goal seemed clear: to "add" in images of and knowledge about traditionally underrepresented groups. Textbook publishers began to include more pictures of people of color, females, and maybe a picture of a person in a wheelchair in their textbooks and "multicultural" curricula became popularized as a convenient and efficient way to achieve multicultural education. Lesson plans and teaching units were created for teachers to supplement their curriculum. These curricular changes mostly occurred in the elementary grade level and in secondary grade-level subjects such as social studies and English. Added to the change in curriculum materials is the emergence of celebratory activities in schools such as "Multicultural Week" and "Black/Women's/Asian American/Native American/Hispanic History Month," which served as token attempts to include traditionally underrepresented populations. These methods are a step forward, yet they are additive and not transformative changes, and usually take a "tourist" approach of only focusing on foods, holidays, and clothes.

POPULARITY AND BACKLASH IN THE 1980s AND 1990s

The civil rights gains of the 1960s and 1970s focused on achieving equality in terms of *equal opportunity* and *equal representation*. These achievements include: affirmative action and other recruitment and retention policies; nondiscrimination laws to protect the rights of people of color, women (e.g., Title IX—a federal law making sex discrimination in schools illegal), gay men and lesbians, and people with disabilities (e.g., the Americans with Disabilities Act of 1990); and the development of ethnic studies, women's studies, and gay and lesbian studies on college and university campuses. The efforts to include traditionally oppressed and marginalized populations in the mainstream culture, along with the continuing increase in populations of color due both to high birth rates and immigration from Asia, Latin America, and the Caribbean Islands,[7] led to a surge in the popularity of multicultural education.

Scholars of multicultural education were rejuvenated by these new possibilities and opportunities, and worked to provide a more coherent understanding of multicultural education by placing it within a less ambiguous conceptual framework. Carl Grant and Christine Sleeter demonstrated that there were five approaches or concepts that educators were utilizing in their practice of multicultural education: Teaching the Exceptional and Culturally Different, Human Relations, Single-Group Studies, Multicultural Education, and Education that is

---

[7] For example, a *Time Magazine* cover story by Anderson (June 13, 1983) titled "Los Angeles: America's Uneasy New Melting Pot" was indicative of the surge in the populations of color across the country. Anderson claimed that an ethnic explosion in Los Angles had occurred between 1970 and 1983. During this period the following population demographics were noted:

	1970	1983
Mexican	822,300	2,100,000
Iranian	20, 000	200,000
Armenian	75,000	175 000
Chinese	41000	153, 000
Filipino	33,000	150, 000
Arab American	45, 000	130, 000

Multicultural and Social Reconstructionist (Grant & Sleeter, 1985; Grant, Sleeter, & Anderson, 1986; Sleeter & Grant, 1987, 1999). The *Teaching the Exceptional and Culturally Different* approach sets out to help fit people into the existing social structure and culture by teaching dominant traditional educational aims more effectively through building bridges between the student and the demands of the school. The *Human Relations* approach focuses on promoting feelings of unity, tolerance, and acceptance within the existing social structure by promoting positive feelings among students, reducing stereotyping, and promoting students' self-concept. *Single-Group Studies* focuses on promoting social structural equality for and immediate recognition of an identified group (e.g., women, Native Americans, or gays and lesbians) and attempts to promote willingness and knowledge among students to work toward social change that would benefit the identified group. The *Multicultural Education* approach seeks to promote social structural equality and cultural pluralism (i.e., the United States as a "tossed salad") through respect for those who differ and support for power equity among groups. Lastly, the *Education that is Multicultural and Social Reconstructionist* approach seeks to prepare citizens to work actively toward social structural equality, promote cultural pluralism and alternative lifestyles, and promote equal opportunity in the school. Grant and Sleeter pointed out that the majority of practices that is called multicultural education follow the first of the five approaches. In a similar vein, James Banks (1988) identified four approaches to curriculum reform: the contribution approach, the additive approach, the transformation approach, and the social action approach. Such theoretical framings by scholars such as Banks, Grant, and Sleeter provide scholars and practitioners ways of reasoning about multicultural education and ways of practicing it.

Also, during the decade of the 1980s, a second generation of multicultural education scholars were completing their graduate programs, taking university and college jobs, and beginning to contribute to the scholarship of multicultural education. Additionally, although there was still opposition to multicultural research for professors seeking promotion and tenure, this opposition slowly began to lose its force and there was a decided increase in multicultural curriculum materials and texts on multicultural education. Furthermore, teacher candidates were completing coursework that included some (although very limited in many teacher education programs) attention to multicultural education.

During the 1980s, we also saw an increase in urban school districts' demand for attention to multicultural (i.e., race, class, and gender) issues in textbooks and other curriculum materials. In addition, a growing number of teachers were more tolerant of and were requesting staff development on multicultural education. For many of these teachers, the changes in student demographics, the need to bridge the cultural differences between them and their students, the need to better manage their classes, and the need for employment demanded that they give multicultural education a chance. National education organizations, state departments of education, and local school districts began to welcome presentations, conferences, and publications on multicultural education.

At the same time, however, the increase in attention to "minority achievement," which is often associated with multicultural education, was also entangled within a Eurocentric, (neo-)nativist ideology that has persisted since the beginning of public education. According to Sleeter and McLaren (1995):

> Multicultural education frames inequality in terms of institutionalized oppression and reconfigures the families and communities of oppressed groups as sources of strength. By the early 1980s, this formulation was turned on its head in the dominant discourse about education. Discussions about education were framed mainly in terms of how to enable the U.S. to maintain international supremacy in the Cold War and the "trade war" (Shor, 1986). The early 1980s saw a wave of educational reform reports, beginning with that by the National Commission on Excellence in Education, *A Nation at Risk* (1983). In this context, students of color, those from poverty areas, and those whose first language was not English were defined as "at risk" of failure, and their homes and communities were defined as culturally deprived and morally depraved. (pp. 12-13)

Thus, along with the growth of multicultural education and the "celebration of diversity" was a concurrent regression toward blaming students of color, poor students, and their communities for the nation's lag in competing within the international arena.

For leading scholars in the field, multicultural education has always been a concept, an educational philosophy, a pedagogical process, an educational reform movement, *and* (not or) a social ideal (Gay, 1995). However, in spite of the increasing popularity of multicultural education and abundance of multicultural curriculum materials, the mainstream understanding and practice of multicultural education remained at a superficial level. This phenomenon is due to a number of factors. One is the gap that exists between the field of multicultural education—that is, the production of academic research and theoretical frameworks—and the practice of multicultural education, which reflects the chasm between educational practitioners and academics in general. Another reason is the translating of large-scale, transformative reform into acceptable and perfunctory additions.

Also, there continues to be multiple approaches to multicultural education (e.g., the approaches outlined earlier by Grant & Sleeter, 1985, and Banks, 1988). As Newfield and Gordon (1996) argued:

> When multiculturalism began to hit the news in the late 1980s, it seemed a relatively mild reform movement. It was pro-diversity *and* it defined diversity not in racial or political but in cultural terms. ...But this multiculturalism looked like curricula reforms and not at all like a social movement. ...Much criticism centered on multiculturalism's ideological timidity: since nonwhite materials were "add-ons" to white structures, they did not address the centrality and dominance of the latter. ...[M]ulticulturalism seemed to many a kinder, gentler form of assimilationism, with some expansion of a commitment to a mostly cosmetic pluralism. (pp. 86-87, original emphasis)

The various and inconsistent approaches to multicultural education—which range from superficial add-ons to structural transformations—has led to a significant amount of resistance, critique, and attacks by individuals and groups who perceive it to be a fad, a "feel-good" curriculum, lowering educational standards (by taking time away from learning the "classics" and what is considered by them as the truly important content), and as a threat to White, middle-class, male privileges.

Critiques of Multicultural Education from (the) Left and (the) Right

The popularity and development of multicultural education throughout the 1980s have led to controversy and debate over the merits and the agenda of the field of multicultural education throughout the 1990s (Banks, 1993; Nieto, 1995; Sleeter, 1995). Sleeter (1995) argued that the great majority of the critiques takes one of two opposing positions: either that multicultural education is too radical (the conservative position), or that it is too conservative (the radical leftist position). Specifically, conservative critiques of multicultural education are toward the (a) suspicious origins of multicultural education; (b) potential for divisiveness; (c) intellectual rigor of multicultural education; and (d) solutions to minority student achievement (pp. 83-85). Sleeter challenged the conservative critiques by pointing out their tendency to ignore research and theory in multicultural education, their poor analysis of present inequality, and the politics of the conservative viewpoint. Sleeter concluded that:

> The conservative critics respond not to what multicultural education scholars have said in the literature, but to actual changes in curriculum required of White students as well as students of color, and particularly changes that challenge White supremacy. Multicultural education has been around since the mid-1960s. As long as it took the form of sporadic practices in schools (largely in schools populated primarily by students of

color), scholarly writings, and occasional conference themes, conservatives could ignore it. As soon as multicultural education became the foundation for required curricula at state and university levels, it could no longer be ignored because in a "tug of war over who gets to create the public culture" (Kessler-Harris, 1992, p. 310), people of color were making gains. And they were doing so during an increasingly unstable period. (p. 88)

The struggle over who can define the knowledge base taught to students in U.S. schools, the grounds for civic socialization, signified a struggle over who defined the dominant U.S. culture and "American" identity. As Sleeter (1995) noted, the point of contention was not so much whether education should be multicultural, but what that should mean. She cites one of the conservative critics, Diane Ravitch, as insisting that the curriculum *is* already multicultural because "the common culture is multicultural" (quoted in Sleeter, 1995, p. 83). Thus, several conservative critics contrast two different forms of multicultural education: the form they advocate—which emphasizes individual rights and cultural commonality—and the form they regard as divisive—which examines group status and cultural difference. The conservatives' logic arises from a familiar privileging and normalization of White, Western ideals. According to Sleeter, "It is important to emphasize that conservatives are underscoring not only the ideals of democracy, individual liberty, and rule of law, but also the claim that these ideals are European in origin, and that their underpinnings will be compromised if Western classics lose favor" (p. 84). Thus, this constructed superiority of "Western ideals" has been so normalized into social structures and school policies, curriculum, and practices that any challenge to it is seen as "un-American," that is, un-democratic, un-liberating, and *un-equal*.[8] Ironically, multicultural

---

[8] The challenges to the normalization of institutional inequality as equality has also led to larger societal claims, mostly by White, working-class men, of *reverse discrimination*. These challenges, for example in the form of affirmative action policies and diversity initiatives, are designed to redress past discrimination and to "level the playing field" so that people of color, women, and people with disabilities are afforded the opportunity to compete for work and college and university admission on an equal basis with privileged groups. Ladson-Billings (1997) explained that, "In instances where Whites have not been hired or admitted when subordinated group members have, some Whites have claimed to be victims of reverse discrimination. This suggests that the rules put in place to provide equal opportunity and diversity have resulted in discrimination against the former beneficiaries or perpetuators of discrimination" (p. 238). Ladson-Billings went on to point out that the term "represents a curious semantic construction because reverse discrimination or the 'reverse of discrimination' means the eradication of discrimination or simply, nondiscrimination. Rather than claiming themselves to be victims of discrimination, members of the dominant group use the term *reverse*

education, with its goals of providing an equal education for all students, is portrayed as dismantling the very ideals it seeks to actualize. What is taken for granted and left unchallenged is *who* determines social and educational standards and *who* defines the common culture. As Sleeter noted, "The conservatives advocate a form of multicultural education that upholds the Western basis of U.S. institutions and thought, but incorporates diverse groups into its history and culture, with an emphasis on forging shared goals, beliefs, and allegiances" (p. 84).

In her analysis of the critiques of multicultural education, Sleeter (1995) also identified the arguments made by the radical left against multicultural education. According to Sleeter, radical critics (a) locate multicultural education within liberalism, (b) are concerned with an absence of a critique of systems of oppression; (c) find the emphasis to be on culture rather than structural inequalities; (d) fault multicultural education for putting forth psychological solutions to political and social-structural problems; and (e) regard the increasing popularity of multicultural education as a palliative White response to minority concerns that deflects attention away from structural issues such as White racism. Sleeter went on to argue that some of the radical critiques are oversimplified caricatures that dismiss the works by U.S. American scholars of color that span two decades. That is, "Critics tend to lump together everything termed *multicultural education*, including superficialities such as food festivals, without noting that established multicultural education scholars criticize the same superficialities" (p. 90).

Taking into account the conservative and radical critiques of multicultural education, Sleeter (1995) outlined their implications in her article and noted that:

> Multicultural education means a shift in decision-making power over schooling away from dominant groups and toward oppressed groups. It should be regarded as a shift in power more than a program to be implemented. ...At the level of theory, multicultural education should develop the structural and contextual analyses called for by the radical critics. ...The task of education theorists is to fuse such work with schooling issues. This theoretical work will greatly enrich the field conceptually, and has the potential to focus practice. ...At the level of activism, multicultural education needs to be "sold" to the public. ...The critiques suggest that *the work to come is political* in addition to being pedagogical. (p. 92, emphasis added)

---

discrimination or *reverse racism* to signify their *privilege*; that is they cannot be discriminated against, and what does occur is different from what subordinated or marginalized groups experience" (p. 238, original emphasis).

Leaders in the field of multicultural education such as Banks, Grant, Nieto, and Sleeter continued to emphasize the complex and multidimensional aspects of multicultural education, critiquing oversimplified practices such as the additive and tourist approaches. James Banks (1993), for example, has outlined five interrelated dimensions of multicultural education: content integration, knowledge construction, prejudice reduction, equity pedagogy, and empower school culture and social structure. Sonia Nieto (1999) reminded us that multicultural education is not something that can be "done" in a week or month, or in certain subject areas but not others; she defines multicultural education as "embedded in a sociopolitical context and as antiracist and basic education for all students that permeates all areas of schooling, and that is characterized by a commitment to social justice and critical approaches to learning" (p. xviii). In addition, Nieto (1999) pointed out that promoting human relations, helping students feel good, and preserving students' native languages and cultures, although important goals, are secondary objectives that have become the main focus for many educational theorists and practitioners. Nieto argued that the original primary objective of advancing student learning needs to become once again the focal point of multicultural education.

MULTICULTURALISM AS A PUBLIC DEBATE

The increase in populations of color, immigrant populations, attention to "minority education," and popularity of multicultural education has led to incessant, heated, and often convoluted debates in mainstream media, academic disciplines, and political arenas. Although the debates—commonly referred to as being about *multiculturalism*—often center around what to *do* with these increasing populations in terms of policies and practices, they point to deeper and larger struggles over ideology and knowledge construction. Once again, the United States as a country was deliberating what it means to be a multicultural society and what dominant ideology and knowledge should guide the country's common culture. In the 1980s and 1990s, however, people of color and women occupied more positions of economic, social, and political power, and more activist organizations and legal structures were in place to protect their rights so that the multiculturalism debates have not been as easily and quickly determined. Yet, as Goldberg (1994) argued:

> Multiculturalism and commitments to cultural diversity emerged out of [a] conflictual history of resistance, accommodation, integration, and transformation. Accordingly, no sooner had multicultural demands and aspirations begun to be articulated than they were imparted multiple and conflicting interpretations, meanings, and implications. Broadly conceived, multiculturalism is critical of and resistant to the necessarily reductive imperatives of monocultural assimilation. But this critical realignment assumes multiple forms. (p. 7)

In his edited volume, *Multiculturalism: A Critical Reader*, Goldberg (1994) provided a collection of these multiple interpretations of multiculturalism. For example: as a description of the undeniable variety of cultures inter- and intranationally; as a normative conception that stipulates the procedural and substantive principles ordering a multicultural society; and as "managed/corporate/difference" multiculturalisms—these are "the multiculturalisms of a centrist academy and multinational corporations that take themselves to be committed to the broad tenets of philosophical liberalism which are unconcerned...with the redistribution of power resources" (p. 7).

In the same volume, Peter McLaren (1994) offered a typology of the various positions held within the debates over multiculturalism.[9] He has labeled these forms of multiculturalism as *conservative* or *corporate multiculturalism, liberal multiculturalism, left liberal multiculturalism*, and *critical* and *resistance multiculturalism*. The ideology behind these positions is reflected in the critiques of multicultural education outlined by Sleeter earlier. Multicultural education and multiculturalism were terms that have been used interchangeably and often conflated with each other. This points to the interrelatedness of social ideology and educational practice, which harks back to Sleeter's (1995) statement that "the work to come is political in addition to being pedagogical" (p. 92).

McLaren traced conservative or corporate multiculturalism back to the colonialist legacy of White supremacy that is based on the belief of the cognitive and moral inferiority of Africans and African Americans. Liberal multiculturalism, in contrast, argues that a natural equality exists among Whites, African Americans, Latinos, Asians, and other

---

[9] McLaren (1994) recognized the pitfalls of fixing categories to the various positions; he argued, "These are, to be sure, ideal-typical labels meant only to serve as a 'heuristic' device ...As with all typologies and criteriologies, one must risk monolithically projecting them onto all spheres of cultural production and instantiating an overly abstract totality that dangerously reduces the complexity of the issues at stake" (p. 47).

various racial populations, and that societal inequality exists because social and educational opportunities do not exist that permit everyone to compete equally in the capitalist marketplace. According to McLaren (1994), "Unlike their critical counterparts, [liberal multiculturalists] believe that existing cultural, social, and economic constraints can be modified or "reformed" in order for relative equality to be realized," however, "[t]his view often collapses into an ethnocentric and oppressively universalistic humanism in which the legitimating norms which govern the substance of citizenship are identified most strongly with Anglo-American cultural-political communities" (p. 51). Left-liberal multiculturalism, according to McLaren, "emphasizes cultural differences and suggests that the stress on the equality of races smothers those important cultural differences between races that are responsible for different behaviors, values, attitudes, cognitive styles, and social practices" (p. 51).

The form of multiculturalism that McLaren (1994) argued for is what he calls *critical* or *resistance multiculturalism*. From this perspective, "representations of race, class, and gender are understood as the result of larger social struggles over signs and meanings and in this way emphasizes not simply textual play or metaphorical displacement as a form of resistance (as in the case of left-liberal multiculturalism), but stresses the central task of transforming the social, cultural, and institutional relations in which meanings are generated" (p. 53). As McLaren pointed out,

> From the perspective of critical multiculturalism, the conservative and liberal stress on sameness and the left-liberal emphasis on difference is really a false opposition. Identity based on "sameness" and identity based on "difference" are forms of essentialist logic.... Resistance multiculturalism doesn't see diversity itself as a goal, but rather argues that diversity must be affirmed within a politics of cultural criticism and a commitment to social justice. It must be attentive to the notion of "difference." Difference is always a product of history, culture, power, and ideology. Differences occur *between* and *among* groups and must be understood in terms of the specificity of their production. Critical multiculturalism interrogates the construction of difference and identity in relation to a radical politics. It is positioned against the neo-imperial romance with monoglot ethnicity grounded in a shared or "common" experience of "America" that is associated with conservative and liberal strands of multiculturalism. (p. 53, original emphasis)

Critical theorists such as McLaren press education theorists and practitioners, in their efforts to transform existing policies and practices, to be cognizant of the broader structural, instructional, and cultural relations in which the meanings of the policies and practices are generated. Also, in challenging the normative notions of *sameness* and *difference,* critical theorists inherently question mainstream conceptions of *equality* and *equal education.* More broadly, critical theorists interrogate the politics within which the meanings of equality are constructed to maintain the belief in a shared "American experience." For example, in outlining the various positions to multiculturalism, McLaren reveals the ways that conservative, liberal, and left-liberal multiculturalism challenge each other's version of equality without recognizing how their debates are still occurring within normative understandings of equality that are defined by dominant race, class, and gender cultural politics.

We discuss in more detail the need to disrupt these normative understandings of desireable goals such as equality and equal education in the next section of this chapter by considering how postmodernism and poststructuralist theories challenge the field of multicultural education and the multiculturalism discourse.

RE/SIGNING MULTICULTURALISM AS IDEOLOGY AND PRACTICE

The lessons learned from the critiques of multicultural education and the various interpretations of multiculturalism point to a number of important issues that needed to be re-addressed by those within the field and movement. For example: What are the goals of multicultural education? What approaches should be taken to achieve these goals? What populations are to be included within the umbrella of multicultural education? How should equal education be defined?

In the 1990s, multiculturalism debates around issues such as the ones listed above continued among scholars both within and outside of the field of multicultural education and, in some cases, became more intensified. The mainstream and popular understanding of multicultural education continued to be and became more solidified as celebratory events and the inclusion of diverse (i.e., people of color) populations in the curriculum. Some educators who work within what Sleeter and Grant (1987, 1999) would describe as the *Education that is Multicultural and Social Reconstructionist* approach found this general understanding of multicultural education to lack the necessary components for social change. These educators use terms such as *critical pedagogy* (e.g., Giroux, 1988, 1993; McLaren, 1995, 1998; Wink, 1997) and *teaching for social justice* (e.g., Adams, Bell, & Griffin, 1997; Ayers, Hung, & Quinn, 1998) to emphasize a more critical approach that addresses interrelated systems of oppression (e.g., heteronormativity,[10] anti-Semitism, sexism, ableism, racism, and classism).

Also, researchers and educators who describe their work as multicultural education continue to vary greatly in the populations of their focus. The dominant focus has remained to be on race and ethnicity, with a recognition of the significance of class and gender. This focus on race and ethnicity continues to exist within a Black/White discourse, in which the meanings of race and racism are largely understood through the experiences of African Americans (Lei, 1998). Although attention to other populations of color are increasing, this inclusion most often occurs within a Black/White framework—that is, the experiences and needs of these populations of color are understood through those of the Black population and the relationship between Blacks and Whites (Cho, 1993). At the same time, researchers and educators who challenge this dominant understanding of multicultural education and argue for the inclusion of diversity in, for example, sexual orientation *or* cognitive and physical dis/ability, generally do not address the interrelated nature of oppression either (e.g., the interrelated nature of ableism, sexism, and racism). These uneasy alliances, and the resistance to them, point to not only the ongoing tensions within the umbrella of multicultural education but also the fact that the very systems of oppression that multicultural education seeks to dismantle are operating *within* the field of multicultural education.

Can We Have a Postmodern Moment, Please?

The relatively recent application of postmodern and poststructuralist theories in the field of education offers useful guidance in considering these philosophical, political, structural, curricular, and pedagogical concerns that have existed since the development of the field of multicultural education.[11] According to Marshall (1992),

---

[10] Britzman (1998) found the term *heteronormativity* more interesting than *homophobia* "because she believes that the debates on gay and lesbian oppression need to move beyond the humanist psychological discourse of individual fear of homosexuality. "The term *heteronormativity* begins to get at how the production of deviancy is intimately tied to the very possibility of normalcy. ...Recent writing in queer theory suggests the problem is not fear of queerness but obsession with normalizing and containing queerness and, not coincidentally, otherness" (p. 152, note 25, original emphasis).

[11] Our description of postmodern and poststructuralist theories here is brief, limited, and general. For a fuller and more in-depth knowledge, we encourage the readers to look into the prolific field of postmodernism and poststructuralism.

Some of [the] concerns of the postmodern have to do with language; with how we constitute and are constituted by language; with the power of interpretation of language (who takes control of meaning). Another concern has to do with an emphasis on difference rather than on Identity: for example, people (and societies) are perceived as sites of difference, and not as centers from which pure knowledge emanates and to which absolute Truths may be made known. This notion, like everything else, must be historicized. (p. 2)

As an education movement and a field of study, multicultural education, and its appending ideology of multiculturalism, operates as a cultural framework and paradigm as it works against the dominant systems of oppression. Thus, the stated questions regarding the field of multicultural education need to be repositioned within a deconstruction of the evolved paradigm of multicultural education and the discourse of multiculturalism. That is, what are the effects of the ways we think, write, and talk about multicultural education?

In considering the language of multicultural education, we see that it is largely centered on, as mentioned, the desire for *sameness*—and through the definition of equality as sameness. For example, Jagose (1996) argued that, during the 1960s and early 1970s, lesbian and gay activists represented their social movements in terms of a *liberation model*, which focused on the radical reconception of the sex/gender system that confined individuals into mutually exclusive homosexual/heterosexual and feminine/masculine roles. However, by the mid-1970s, phrases like "sexual orientation" and the "gay minority" became a part of and began to dominate the lexicon of the movement. Jagose described this as a shift in positions to an *ethnic model*, which emphasizes community identity and cultural difference. "The ethnic model...was committed to establishing gay identity as a *legitimate minority group*, whose official recognition would *secure citizenship rights* for lesbian and gay subjects" (p. 61, emphasis added).

This "ethnic model," which is the prevailing way of addressing marginalized and oppressed populations in the United States, is supported by the majority/minority discourse and the politics of difference (or politics of diversity), both of which are pervasive in multicultural education. The *majority/minority discourse* reflects an assimilative ideology that seeks legitimation for those deemed to be part of the "minority "within the existing regulative regimes that are constructed by the "majority" and upon White, Eurocentric, male, heterosexual privilege and power. This discourse, even as it is used to address the inequalities that "minorities" face, maintains the positions and relations of those in power and those who are denied power. In effect, the discourse enacts a façade that something is being done about societal inequalities when structurally, politically, and culturally, nothing has changed.

The *politics of difference* or *politics of diversity*, which often frames multiculturalism and multicultural education, works closely with the majority/minority discourse and in a similar way. Within this discourse, diversity is a very positive thing—we want to "embrace" and "celebrate" diversity, "diversify" our schools, and make a "commitment to diversity." Diversity is used in very abstract ways that easily eludes definition even as it conjurs up warm and harmonious feelings. When we look at what is done in the name of diversity—inclusion of traditionally marginalized populations in the form of curricular materials, posters on classroom walls, and a multicultural week or month during the school year that centers on traditions, foods, holidays, and clothing from Asia, African, Latin America, and Europe—these efforts, although well intended, perpetuate the exoticization and Othering of the populations they aim to "include." Diversity has been defined within European-American ideology as people of color, foreign and exotic cultures, removed from the daily realities of U.S. life, and as fun and celebratory without attention to critical analysis or social change. Diversity is about and for the Other, and often placed on the shoulders of the Other to maintain.

These theoretical insights cast a different light on the efforts for inclusivity and equal representation in curriculum and instruction. For example, Britzman (1998) described how the arguments for the inclusion of lesbian and gay studies, which attempt to be "antihomophobic," produce the very exclusions they are meant to cure:

> Part of the tension is that there tend to be only two pedagogical strategies: providing information and techniques of attitude change. The normal view of inclusion is that one should attempt to "recover" authentic images of gays and lesbians and stick them into the curriculum with the hope that representations—in the form of tidy role models—can serve as a double remedy for the hostility toward social difference (for those who cannot imagine difference) and for the lack of self-esteem (for those who are imagined as having no self). However, the question that cannot be uttered is How different can these folks be and still be recognized as just like everyone else? Or, put differently, given the tendency of the curriculum to pass knowledge through discourses of factuality and morality, how can difference be different? And different from what? (p. 86)

The "normal view of inclusion" that Britzman wrote about has been a core component of the field of multicultural education. Although a goal is to be inclusive of differences, the dominant constructions of inclusion and of difference maintain the normalcy of sameness as equality and as desireable. The notion of an inclusive representation of diverse populations in the curriculum is also problematic because it assumes the existence of an authentic representation of a particular group—that there is a comprehensive way of accounting for the authentic experience of, for example, Asian Americans (a category that encompasses a large number of different populations with ancestry in Asia). How then, can we conceptualize equality in ways that disrupt the normative systems of oppression?

Can Multicultural Education be Queer?

Britzman (1998) introduced queer theory to pedagogy in critically reflecting on how normalcy has been defined and maintained in education and what repetitions we, in all facets of education, engage in to maintain that normalcy of equality/sameness and difference:

> Where queer theory meets pedagogy is how it conceptualizes normalcy as negation. It constitutes normalcy as a conceptual order that refuses to imagine the very possibility of the other precisely because the production of otherness as an outside is central to its own self-recognition. ...When pedagogy meets queer theory and thus becomes concerned with its own structure of intelligibility—with the education of education—and when pedagogy engages its own impertinence, the very project of knowledge and its accompanying subject-presumed-to-know become terminable despite the institutional press for closure, tidiness, and certainty. (p. 82)

A displacement of the usual repetitions within multicultural education to assert the equality/sameness of various cultures, to legitimate the rights of different (minority) groups, and the inclusion of those deemed "diverse," then, could be to question the meanings and goal of equality and equal education.

Displacing/Replacing Equality in Multicultural Education

Poststructuralist theories press multicultural educators to identify and name the regulative regimes within which they are developing their theories, policies, curriculum, and practice. The goals of being more inclusive in and diversifying the existing educational structure do not displace the performative repetitions that have naturalized Whiteness, heterosexuality, Eurocentricity, and other regulative regimes. In addition, the meaning of equal education has moved a great deal away from, but has not displaced, the normative desire to establish the declaration that: *All men are created equal.*

We can begin to displace the repetitions within the field of multicultural education and multiculturalism by displacing the recurrent and persistent questions and struggles: How do efforts to include, *exclude*? How do we *essentialize* as we attempt to diversify? What if we *cannot do* multicultural education? What if we insisted on addressing systems of oppression (heteronormativity, ableism, sexism, racism) as interrelated even as we are *not sure how to do it*? And, What would happen if we *cannot/will not identify* the race or class background of a student who is "failing" in our classroom?[12] These challenges would begin to displace the repetition of identities as natural, evident, and authentic. They also begin to displace the repetition of equality as sameness, and sameness as *normal*. Instead, as we look toward the 21st century and consider the future of multicultural education, we encourage the field to conceptualize pedagogy as "…an imaginative way to think about and to perform reading practices that still manage, however precariously, to be overconcerned with practices of identification and sociality *and* as a technique for acknowledging difference *as the only condition of possibility for community*" (Britzman, 1998, pp. 85-86, original emphasis). Rather than resigning (i.e., abandoning) the goal of equal education and the philosophy of multicultural education, we see more potential in the continued processes and relations of their re/signification (i.e., reformulation).[13] We do not see the conflicts, tensions, and inconsistencies within the field of multicultural education as necessarily negative—we see it as healthy growth, change, and reflexive critique.

We envision that the struggles occurring within the field of multicultural education will continue so that the existing normative knowledge and structure does not become replaced by another normative (though presumed *multicultural*) knowledge and structure. In saying this, we are by no means pessimistic about the future of multicultural education. What we are proposing is a way of conceptualizing multicultural education that accepts difference as difference and does not try to make it the same. We also see this difference as constantly changing, which is why multicultural education can never be *done*, it must also constantly change and disrupt normative repetitions (such as

---

[12] Here, we are not advocating for a conservative version of a "color-blind" policy; instead, we are challenging the categorizations created by the regulative regimes to maintain the positions and privileges of those in power (Nieto, S., personal communication).

[13] Our use of the term *re/signing* evokes two meanings: One meaning is to have the term resigned (i.e., disused); and the second meaning is to re-sign it (i.e., to reconceptualize it). Ono (1995), in his challenge of the term *Asian American*, wrote, "By shuttling between the two meanings: resigning (retiring) and re-signing (refiguring), I hope to enact a critical, rhetorical practice that creates slippage between using and disusing the term…" (p. 68). Ono also suggested that through critical, theoretical practices, re-signing the term may produce more effective political possibilities.

those unnatural lines that have been created to separate race, sexuality, gender, dis/ability, and class). In short, although certainly not in closure, we are interested in a multicultural education that allows equality to exist as a dynamic *community of difference*.

REFERENCES

Adams, M., Bell, L. A., & Griffin, P. (Eds.). (1997). *Teaching for diversity and social justice: A sourcebook.* New York: Routledge.

Ameer, J. P. (1995). Norm and diversity: Cultural pluralism in the history of American education. In A. Nava (Ed.), *Educating Americans in a multiethnic society* (pp. 11-30). New York: McGraw-Hill.

American Association of Colleges for Teacher Education's (AACTE) Commission on Multicultural Education. (1972). *No one model American.* Washington, DC: AACTE.

Anderson, J. (1988). *The education of Blacks in the South 1860-1935.* Chapel Hill: University of North Carolina Press.

Anderson, K. (1983, June 13). The new Ellis Island. *Time*, 18-25.

Ayers, W., Hung, J. A., & Quinn, T. (Eds.). (1998). *Teaching for social justice.* New York: The New Press and Teachers College Press.

Baker, G. C. (1973). Multicultural training for student teachers. *Journal of Teacher Education, 24*(4), 306-307.

Baker, G. C. (1977). Multicultural education: Two inservice approaches. *Journal of Teacher Education, 28*, 31-33.

Banks, J. A. (Ed.). (1973). *Teaching ethnic studies: Concepts and strategies* (43rd Yearbook). Washington, DC: National Council for the Social Studies.

Banks, J. A. (1988, Spring). Approaches to multicultural curriculum reform. *Multicultural Leader, 1*(2), 1-3.

Banks, J. A. (1993). Multicultural education: Development, dimensions, and challenges. *Phi Delta Kappan, 75*(1), 22-28.

Britzman, D. P. (1998). *Lost subjects, contested objects: Toward a psychoanalytic inquiry of learning.* Albany: State University of New York Press.

Brown v. Board of Education, 347 U.S. 483 (1954).

Bullock, H. A. (1970). *A history of Negro education in the South: From 1619 to the present.* New York: Praeger.

Cho, S. K. (1993). Korean Americans vs. African Americans: Conflict and construction. In R. Gooding-Williams (Ed.), *Reading Rodney King/Reading urban uprising* (pp. 196-211). New York: Routledge.

Dewey, J. (1916). *Democracy and education.* New York: Macmillan.

Dewey, J. (1938). *Experience and education.* New York: Macmillan.

Frankenberg, R. (1993). *White women, race matters: The social construction of Whiteness.* Minneapolis: The University of Minnesota Press.

Gay, G. (1975). Organizing and planning culturally pluralistic curriculum. *Educational Leadership, 33*, 176-183.

Gay, G. (1979). On behalf of children: A curriculum design for multicultural education in the elementary school. *Journal of Negro Education, 47*, 324-340.

Gay, G. (1995). Mirror images on common issues: Parallels between multicultural education and critical pedagogy. In C. E. Sleeter & P. L. McLaren (Eds.), *Multicultural education, critical pedagogy, and the politics of difference* (pp. 155-189). Albany: State University of New York Press.

Giroux, H. A. (1988). *Schooling and the struggle for public life: Critical pedagogy for practical learning.* Minneapolis: University of Minnesota Press.

Giroux, H. A. (1993). *Border crossings: Cultural workers and the politics of education.* New York: Routledge & Kegan Paul.

Goldberg, D. T. (1994). Introduction: Multicultural conditions. In D. T. Goldberg (Ed.), *Multiculturalism: A critical reader* (pp. 1-41). Cambridge: Blackwell.

Grant, C. A. (Ed.). (1977). *Multicultural education: Commitments, issues, and applications.* Washington, DC: Association for Supervision and Curriculum Development.

Grant, C. A. & Sleeter, C. E. (1985). The literature on multicultural education: Review and analysis. *Educational Review, 37,* 97-118.

Grant, C. A. , Sleeter, C. E., & Anderson, J. E. (1986). The literature on multicultural education: Review and analysis, part II. *Educational Studies, 12,* 47-71.

Jacob, E., & Jordan, C. (1993). Understanding minority education: Framing the issues. In E. Jacob & C. Jordan (Eds.), *Minority education: Anthropological perspectives* (pp. 3-14). Norwood, NJ: Ablex.

Jagose, A. (1996). *Queer theory: An introduction.* New York, NY: New York University Press.

Kallen, H. M. (1956). *Cultural pluralism and the American idea: An essay in social philosophy.* Philadelphia: University of Pennsylvania Press.

Ladson-Billings, G. (1997). Reverse discrimination. In C. A. Grant & G. Ladson-Billings (Eds.), *Dictionary of multicultural education* (pp. 237-238). Phoenix, AZ: Oryx Press.

Lei, J. L. (1998, April). (Op)posing Representations: Disentangling the Model Minority and the Foreigner. Paper presented at the American Educational Research Association's Annual Meeting in San Diego, California.

Marshall, B. K. (1992). *Teaching the postmodern: Fiction and theory.* New York: Routledge.

McKee, J. B. (1993). *Sociology and the race problem: The failure of a perspective.* Chicago: University of Illinois Press.

McLaren, P. (1994). White terror and oppositional agency: Towards a critical multiculturalism. In D. T. Goldberg (Ed.), *Multiculturalism: A critical reader* (pp. 45-74). Cambridge: Blackwell.

McLaren, P. (1995). *Critical pedagogy and predatory culture: Oppositional politics in a postmodern era.* New York: Routledge.

McLaren, P. (1998). *Life in schools: An introduction to critical pedagogy in the foundations of education* (3rd ed.). White Plains, NY: Longman.

Miller, L. P. (1996). Tracking the progress of *Brown.* In L. P. Miller (Ed.), *Brown v. Board of Education: The challenge for today's schools* (pp. 9-13). New York: Teachers College Press.

Newfield, C., & Gordon, A. F. (1996). Multiculturalism's unfinished business. In A. F. Gordon & C. Newfield (Eds.), *Mapping multiculturalism* (pp. 76-115). Minneapolis: University of Minnesota Press.

Nieto, S. (1995). From brown heroes and holidays to assimilationist agendas: Reconsidering the critiques of multicultural education. In C. E. Sleeter & P. L. McLaren (Eds.), *Multicultural education, critical pedagogy, and the politics of difference* (pp. 191-220). Albany: State University of New York Press.

Nieto, S. (1999). *The light in their eyes: Creating multicultural learning communities.* New York: Teachers College Press.

Ogbu, J. U. (1993). Variability in minority school performance: A problem in search of an explanation. In E. Jacob & C. Jordan (Eds.), *Minority education: Anthropological perspectives* (pp. 83-112). Norwood, NJ: Ablex.

Omi, M., & Winant, H. (1994). *Racial formation in the United States: From the 1960s to the 1990s* (2nd ed.). New York: Routledge.

Ono, K. A. (1995). Re/signing "Asian American": Rhetorical problematics of nation. *Amerasia Journal, 21*(1 & 2), 67-78.

Plessy v. Ferguson, 163 U.S. 537 (1896).

Prager, J. (1982, January). American racial ideology as collective representation. *Ethnic and Racial Studies, 5*(1), 99-119.

Rodriguez, F. (1997). Brown v. Board of Education. In C. A. Grant & G. Ladson-Billings (Eds.), *Dictionary of multicultural education* (pp. 35-37). Phoenix, AZ: Oryx press.

Sleeter, C. E. (1995). An analysis of the critiques of multicultural education. In J. A. Banks & C. A. McGee Banks (Eds.), *Handbook of research on multicultural education* (pp. 81-94). New York: Macmillan.

Sleeter, C. E., & Grant, C. A. (1987). An analysis of multicultural education in the U.S.A. *Harvard Educational Review, 57*, 421-444.

Sleeter, C. E., & Grant, C. A. (1999). *Making choices for multicultural education: Five approaches to race, class, and gender* (3rd ed.). Upper Saddle River, NJ: Merrill.

Sleeter, C. E., & McLaren, P. L. (1995). Introduction: Exploring connections to build a critical multiculturalism. In C. E. Sleeter & P. L. McLaren (Eds.), *Multicultural education, critical pedagogy, and the politics of difference* (pp. 5-32). Albany: State University of New York Press.

Spring, J. (1997). *Deculturalization and the struggle for equity: A brief history of the education of dominated cultures in the United States* (2nd ed.). New York: McGraw-Hill.

Tyack, D., & Hansot, E. (1990). *Learning together: A history of coeducation in American schools*. New York: Russell Sage Foundation.

Weinberg, M. (1977). *A chance to learn: The history of race and education in the United States*. Cambridge: Cambridge University Press.

Wink, J. (1997). *Critical pedagogy: Notes from the real world*. New York: Longman.

Wollenberg, C. M. (1995). "Yellow peril" in the schools (I and II). In D. T. Nakanishi & T.Y. Nishida (Eds.), *The Asian American educational experience: A source book for teachers and students* (pp. 3-29). New York: Routledge.

Chapter 10

Intercultural Education in the European Union: The Spanish Case

Miguel A. Santos-Rego
Servando Pérez-Domínguez
University of Santiago de Compostela, Spain

Spain, like many other countries, European and worldwide, is multicultural. However, compulsory schooling in Europe promoted, from its introduction, the development of a single language and of common values and national feeling of identity. The main objective of compulsory schooling in Europe, in order to establish clear distinctions between Spain and other countries, cultures, and languages, has been to homogenize the nations' children. This generally implied the omission of minorities,[1] especially linguistic minorities. National teacher preparation schemes were used to create and establish the basic concepts and values of the nation state.

The cultural heterogeneity that educational policies attempted to override greatly increased in many European countries with the internal and external migratory movements that accompanied economic growth since World War II. Cultural heterogeneity has extended to the Mediterranean since the shift in migratory fluxes following the economic crisis of the 1970s. Greater pluralism and heterogeneity of cultures and languages will continue to develop, affecting the work of teaching institutions at all levels as well as the educational systems themselves. Without doubt, this is an important pedagogical challenge.

The settlement of minority groups within the receiving countries demands many different social policies, especially in the field of

---

[1] In this chapter, the term *minority* refers to those who constitute a lower percentage in the population of the country as a whole, and is often associated with lack of power. We make reference to different minorities, including ethnic/racial, cultural, religious, and linguistic. Sometimes, the term "minority" is ambiguous, as minorities may constitute "majorities" within specific groups of people.

education. Multicultural or intercultural education,[2] thus has social, political, and cultural roots. It exists because there is a social need. In fact, frequently the school has been the first institution to reflect ethnic/racial, cultural, religious, and linguistic pressures. It has been the main mechanism to erase not only diversity, but also to silence these minorities' problems, difficulties, and complaints. Education for pluralism, solidarity, and respect for human rights has always been and always will be necessary (cf. Banks & Banks, 1995; Cowan & Pérez-Domínguez, 1995, 1996; Cowan, Pérez-Domínguez, & Santos-Rego, 1994; Gaine, 1995; Lynch, Modgil, & Modgil, 1992; Pérez-Domínguez, 1995a, 1995b, 1995c, 1997, 1998, 1999; Santos-Rego, 1994; Santos-Rego & Pérez-Domínguez, 1997, 1998).

This chapter seeks to outline current attitudes toward an intercultural commitment in Spain, both in schools and in society as a whole, showing how Spanish society in general, and educators in particular, have reacted to the cultural, ethnic/racial, religious, and linguistic diversity to date. José M. Esteve (1992) remarked, in a positive vein, that it seems that both politicians and educators have taken a long look at Spain's history and have sensed that, "...far from being incompatible, the cultural pluralities could form not only the foundation stones, but also important structural elements of the figurative edifice of our modern State" (p. 255). We also take note of Pumares-Fernández's opinion (1993) that we cannot close our eyes to the growth in immigration and to the social problems that immigration causes, because if we do, the problems will grow until they explode violently. Of course, we also believe that immigration does not just introduce problems. It brings together different (and also similar) views, languages/dialects, traditions, beliefs, and so on, which

---

[2] The Council for Cultural European Cooperation has agreed to use the term *intercultural* to refer to the nature of the desirable educational process. Intercultural applied to education has a normative character. It expresses an option: education toward the whole of the community, that includes both minorities and majorities of foreign origin. It also includes the indigenous/native residents, which normally constitute the dominant culture of the majority. The OECD, other national and international organizations and bodies, as well as most of the Anglo-Saxon countries, preferably use the term "multicultural education" in their works. In any case, although words are never neutral, it all depends on the real use that we make of them. More important is what is being achieved than what is being said nicely. Moreover, we would betray our beliefs in the respect for diversity if we state the pertinence of some terms instead of others. "Intercultural education" is the term used by most scholars in Spain. An interesting debate about terminology can be followed by reading the ideas of James A. Banks, Robin Grinter, Beverley Shaw, Carmel Camilleri, and Isabelle Taboada Leonetti in part two ("Multicultural, Intercultural or Antiracist: Alternative Political and Conceptual Rationales") of Volume One of the book edited by Lynch, Modgil, and Modgil in 1992, entitled: *Cultural Diversity and the Schools*.

contribute to the progress of humankind (Santos-Rego, Cowan, & Pérez-Domínguez, 1995).

We would like to point out that, although we do not deny the significance in teacher preparation institutions of the analysis of *race* and *disability*—as it is analyzed in the U.S. multicultural and antiracist literature (*cf.* e.g., Grant, 1981, 1992)—the context of Spain and its recent historical evolution from a country of emigration to one of immigration, meant that these concepts were not dealt with in Spanish multi/intercultural or antiracist literature. So, the concept of "race" it is hardly used by Spanish educators, who prefer to use *ethnicity*. Handicapped children or adults are sent to schools called "Escuelas de Educación Especial" (Special Education Schools), so it is treated as not directly related to multi/intercultural education. In turn, *gender* and *age* began to be studied in Spain when immigrant women and teenagers started to arrive in the early 1990s. The concept of *social class* has always been analyzed together with issues of cultural, linguistic, ethnic/racial, or religious diversity in the still relatively recent (but not scarce) literature on multi/intercultural education. The concept of social class has also been related to that of inequality, not only in the United States (*cf.* Cohen, 1986, 1990; Cohen et al., 1994; Sleeter, 1996), but also in Europe (*cf.* Batelaan, 1992).

In this chapter we use the concepts that serve to best describe and explain the fact that Spain is an increasingly multicultural society. The pertinence of the use of some terms instead of, or with more emphasis than, others, certainly is not the purpose of this chapter. Thus, concepts such as social class or gender, and the sociocultural and political contexts (Gay, 1994; Woods & Hammersley, 1995), will be treated with greater or lesser emphasis in the following pages, depending on how they may help to clarify multi/intercultural education in Spain.

GENERAL DATA ABOUT THE HISTORICAL, CULTURAL, AND SOCIOPOLITICAL DEVELOPMENT OF SPAIN

Spain, with about 40,000,000 inhabitants, includes the Balearic and Canary Islands, as well as five enclaves in Morocco (the cities of Ceuta and Melilla being the biggest and most representative ones). Madrid is the capital of Spain, and Barcelona, Valencia, and Seville are other major cities.

Spain is divided into 17 autonomous regions (or Autonomous Communities); each ruled by statutory law with its own parliament and government. The co-official languages with Spanish are: Galician (Galego), Catalan (Català), and Basque (Euskera), and are taught in their respective Autonomous Communities as first languages. Although

Spain's sovereign is King Juan Carlos I (1975), as it is a parliamentary democracy, there is a "Presidente" (President) who is politically responsible for Spain's future. In 1994, Spain's literacy rate was 97%, and 99% of the people declared themselves Roman Catholic. The Conservative Popular Party, which came to power in March 1996 (renewed in March 2000), governs Spain.

To understand Spain's present situation let us take a look at its history. But, let us make it clear that, as Santos-Rego and Nieto (2000) have pointed out, because of its unique historical and social processes, multiculturalism in Spain's case is quite different from what it is in the United States.

The first inhabitants were Iberian and Celts and Iberian-Celts, and the first known colonizers were Phoenicians (1100 B.C.), followed by Greeks (630 B.C.) and Carthaginians (550 B.C.). Spain became part of the Roman Empire in 206 B.C. In A.D. 412, the barbarian Visigoth leader Ataulf crossed the Pyrenees and ruled Spain. In 711, the Moslems entered Spain from Africa, and lived in Spain along with Christians and Jews. This combination of cultures was not without conflicts, although it produced a wide variety of art, languages, and cultures. In 732, the Franks, led by Charles Martel, defeated the Moslems near Poitiers, thus preventing the further expansion of Islam in Southern Europe.

The so-called "Reyes Católicos" (Catholic "Kings"—Fernando II, King of Aragón, and Isabel I, Queen of Castille) initiated the political unification of Spain through their marriage in 1469, reconquest (Granada, in 1492), and annexation (Navarra, in 1515). They also tried a religious unification, ordering all those living in Spain to convert to Christianity.

The year 1492 is relevant due to the arrival of Christopher Columbus in America. Jews were expelled by the Catholic "Kings," and the same fate awaited the Moslems of Granada in 1502. TheKings also ordered, in 1499, that Gypsies needed to have a fixed abode and a known job, otherwise they would be expelled. All this launched the infamous *Spanish Inquisition*, which sought, by every means, to secure the unity of the Catholic Church.

We consider it important to note that the outcome of the unification of Spain resulted in an expansion of the power of the throne and this imposed severe restrictions on linguistic and cultural behavior in the previous autonomous kingdoms. Esteve (1992) pointed out that this period could be classified as a period of the *melting pot policy* (p. 256).

The Second Republic movement (1931-1936) led to a constitution that declared Spain "a workers' republic," broke up the large states, separated the Church and the State, secularized schools, and proclaimed the autonomy of Catalonia, the Basque Country, and Galicia. In 1936, General Francisco Franco Bahamonde led a mutiny against the government. The civil war that followed lasted 3 years—and nearly a million people lost their lives. Several hundred left-wing U.S. Americans served in the Abraham Lincoln Brigade on the side of the Republic. The war ended when Franco took Madrid in 1939. He then became a dictator. Once again, national unity and assimilationist policies were established, and cultural assimilation was imposed. The use of local languages was prohibited.

Since 1978, after Franco's death, and the coronation of King Juan Carlos I in 1982, Autonomous Communities have been recognized as such, thanks to the Constitutional Democracy.

The cultural policies that have existed over the last five centuries have been ones of cultural assimilation and domination, and have influenced the current Spanish attitudes toward diversity.

One reaction to Franco's ideologies, which prohibited the use of languages other than Spanish, has been the increase of support for regional languages, especially in Catalonia, Galicia, and the Basque country (Arnau, Comet, Serra, & Vila, 1992).

There is no single, unique cultural policy in Spain at present. There are officially bilingual Autonomous Communities with linguistic majorities and minorities, monolingual Communities, and, as in many other countries, other languages are spoken by immigrants.

On December 30th, 1997, a law was approved in Catalonia, called *Ley del Catalán* (*Law of the Catalan Language*), which further encourages the use of the Catalan language in Catalonia, especially in schools and in official places. It substitutes the *Ley de Normalización Lingüística* (*Law for Language Normalization*) of 1983. Another *Law for Language Normalization* was passed in the Basque country in 1982 and in Galicia in 1983. The *Law of the Catalan Language*, despite being approved by 80% of the political parties in Catalonia, has created controversy due to a feeling of pressure perceived by those who are not Catalan speakers (which includes immigrants) to use the language.

THE EVOLUTION OF MIGRATION IN SPAIN

Spain's history has been characterized by two types of migratory movements, one internal and the other external. Internally, movements were made from rural areas to urban ones, particularly toward the larger industrialized areas. For instance, in just 20 years, between 1950 and 1970, more than half a million immigrants moved from the rural southern regions of Spain northeastwards to Catalonia, mainly to the province of Barcelona. External migration, nevertheless, had begun by 1492.

From a Country of Emigration . . .

Between 1882 and 1896, 360,000 Spaniards migrated to south and Central America; between 1901 and 1910, 100,000 people migrated per year. Argentina, Cuba, Mexico, Uruguay, and Brazil were the main destinations for most people, many of whom were from the region of Galicia. Hence, all the Spanish immigrants arriving in Argentina were called "Gallegos" (Galicians). Immigration restrictions in American countries, and then Franco's dictatorship (1939-1975), meant that migration to the Americas decreased.

In 1959, Franco's economic policy changed, trying to put an end to the political isolation of the country. A rise of unemployment was the result, which led to a new migration flow. People moved from the countryside to the cities, or from (a) the rural to the urban areas, as in Catalonia's case already mentioned (internal migration), and (b) a flow to the northern European countries. At that time half a million Spaniards returned to Spain. Despite this, in 1994 there were still more Spaniards living abroad (1.6 million Spaniards abroad, 52% in Latin America, 45% in other European countries) than foreigners living in Spain (Colectivo IOÉ, 1994). Generally speaking, it could be said that a strong migratory flow to America continued until the beginning of this century, lessening after the end of World War II (1945), to almost a halt at the beginning of the 1960s, particularly between 1975 (the end of Franco's dictatorship) and the 1990s.

From the 1960s onward a large number of Spaniards migrated to other parts of Europe. In accordance with Gonzalo and Villanueva (1996), between 1960 and 1973, about 3 million people went to Germany, France, Switzerland, the Netherlands, and Britain. According to Escribano (1993), from 1962 to 1976, 1,063,380 Spanish workers went to these countries.

. . . to One of Immigration

Due to the closure of frontiers and the establishment of restrictive migratory policies in other European countries, particularly in France and Italy, the 1960s saw the arrival in Spain of an important number of northern Africans (mainly Moroccans) who were seeking work.

As Gonzalo and Villanueva (1996, p. 110) have pointed out, the closure of North American frontiers also meant an influx of Philippine and Latin American people to Spain; Latin Americans were forced to leave by the military dictatorships, especially in Argentina, Chile, and Uruguay. Until 1972, however, immigrants were mainly single men, and it was not until 1986 that family groups began to arrive in Spain (Cáritas, 1987; Losada, 1988).

Statistics regarding the number of foreigners living in Spain vary substantially depending both on the source used, and on the difficulty in knowing the numbers of those who enter Spain "illegally" or, as others prefer to say, "irregularly"[3] (cf. Galino & Escribano, 1990).

According to the official statistics on foreigners with residence permits (see *Anuario Estadístico de Extranjería*, 1999) (data of December 31, 1999), Spain was home to 801,3293, of whom 361,873 were Europeans, especially British (76,402) and Germans (60,828); 211,564 were Africans, mainly Moroccans (161,870). Although the total number of foreigners with residence permits is 801,329, in Table 10.1 we only present some of the countries with the highest number of immigrants for each continent, as well as the stateless.

TABLE 10.1

Foreigners With Residence Permits

TOTAL	499,773
EUROPE	255,702
EUROPEAN UNION	235,602
- Britain	65,251
- Germany	41,942
- Portugal	36,997
- France	30,835
- Italy	19,750
- The Netherlands	12,970
- Belgium	8,904
AMERICA (North and Central)	43,928
- U.S.A.	14,889
- Dominican Republic	14,470
AMERICA (South)	65,003
- Argentina	18,426
- Perú	15,092
AFRICA	95,725
- Morocco	74,886
ASIA	38,221
- The Philippines	9,681
- China	9,158
OCEANIA	859
STATELESS	335

Note. Source: Anuario Estadístico de Extranjería (1999).

The greater proportion of immigrants in Spain is located in 6 of the 17 Spanish Autonomous Communities (Catalonia, the Canary Islands and the Balearic Islands, Valencia, Andalousia, and Madrid), which also house 61.6% of the native population of Spain. Of the immigrant

---

[3] For a number of authors the denomination of "irregular" is preferred to the one of "illegal" (cf. Galino & Escribano, 1990).

population, 52.8% is concentrated in Madrid, Barcelona, Alicante, and Málaga. Nonetheless, the number of immigrants is also increasing in all the other parts of Spain.

Gonzalo & Villanueva (1996) estimated the number of foreigners living in Spain to be 800,000 (about 2% of the total population—mainly retired people living in the south and southeast coasts of Spain)—being half from the Third World and half from European countries or North America. Official statistics from December, 1996 confirm this estimate. We believe that, if we count both legal and illegal immigration, by the end of January 2001 around 1,200,000 foreigners will be living in Spain (about 3% of the total population).

Despite the *Spanish Constitutional Law* (December 27, 1978) and the *Ley Orgánica de Extranjería* (*General Law for Foreigners*) (1985), the *Human Fundamental Rights of Foreigners Association* (1987) published a document claiming that levels of racism in Spain were high although Spanish people did not realize they had racist attitudes, especially toward Gypsies and Black Africans. Research into perceptions/attitudes of Spanish youth undertaken in Spain by Calvo-Buezas in 1986, 1993, and 1997, showed that prejudice, xenophobia, and even racism, against Spanish Gypsies, "Moors-Arabs," and Black Africans was quite significant. This negative attitude grew between 1986 and 1993, decreasing slightly in 1997. Calvo-Buezas noted that, although between 1986 and 1983 racist attitudes grew among young Spanish people, an attitude of solidarity had also emerged. As such, more youths belong to Nongovernmental Organizations (NGOs). These and further reflections can be found in *Crece el racismo, también la solidaridad. Los valores de la juventud en el umbral del siglo XXI* (Calvo-Buezas, 1995a).

Furthermore, a conflict exists in Spain, particularly in some autonomous regions. On the one hand, there is a current trend to consolidate the cultural and linguistic identities of these communities (mainly in the Basque country, Galicia, and Catalonia), whereas, on the other hand, there is a population increase through immigration and internal mobility (Arnau et al., 1992).

Racism and xenophobia are exacerbated by more immigrants entering the country. For instance, the increase in numbers of women and children in 1989 caused considerable ill feeling in Catalonia. The general opinion was that they would not contribute anything to the economy, but that they would increase the demand for additional resources to meet health, education and housing needs (*El País*, 1989).

Although a number of intercultural education programs are taking place all over Spain (mainly in Catalonia and Madrid), it has to be said that a general commitment to intercultural education does not exist as a national priority, despite the recommendations of *The Solemn Declaration of Intent for Unity* signed by heads of state and governments in Stuttgart in 1983 and the *Maastricht Treaty* (1993), the *Schengen Agreement* (signed in 1990, and put into force in 1995), and the *Amsterdam Treaty* (1997)—which promoted greater ease of movement between countries, as well as equal treatment for all and respect toward the different cultures.

Schools are microcosms of society and education should take the lead to ensure positive attitudes concerning cultural diversity (*cf.* García-López & Sales-Ciges, 1997). Mass media interpretations of ethnic issues can be confronted through education, and trends and mass thinking can be evaluated (Cowan & Pérez-Domínguez, 1996, p. 44). In this sense, as Toffler (1990) stated, "Today, our society is changing direction sharply from the idea of the 'mass society' and heading towards the 'mosaic society'" (p. 295).

Taking this into account, we would like to encourage teachers, politicians and educators to work together in overcoming constraints in policymaking and funding for relevant research. As Nieto (1992) has pointed out, both bilingual and multicultural programs for all students have to be comprehensively defined, as well as adequately and strongly supported.

THE LAWS FOR IMMIGRANTS IN SPAIN

An urgent need for legislation now exists to uphold the rights and freedom from those foreigners now living in Spain. The *Spanish Constitutional Law*, approved in 1978, created the constitutional legislative framework for dealing with foreigners.

Three years later, in November, 1984, the Council of Ministers of the Socialist Party approved the Blueprint of the *Ley Orgánica de Extranjería* (*General Law for Foreigners*). This law was approved in 1985. Minor modifications to the law were made in 1996, when the *Nuevo Reglamento sobre Extranjeros en España* (*The New Regulation of Foreigners in Spain*) came into force in August.

But, apart from the *Spanish Constitutional Law* and the *General Law for Foreigners*, foreigners, at least in theory, could also be protected because Spain had signed the *Universal Declaration of Human Rights*, the *International Pact of the Political and Civil Rights* of 1956, and the *European Convention for the Protection of the Fundamental Freedom and Human Rights*, signed in Rome in 1950. (Spain ratified the *International Pact of the Political and Civil Rights* on April 13, 1977, and the *European Convention for the Protection of the Fundamental Freedom and Human Rights*, on May 26, 1979). The fact that Spain then entered the European Community (the present European Union) on May 26, 1986, added weight to its signing of these agreements.

Once Spain became part of the European Union, those immigrants using Spain as a "gate" or transit country to other parts of Europe, mainly from Third World countries, were faced with greater difficulties due to more restrictive laws. The opposite happened and happens with immigration through Spain's northern borders, especially those from the northeast of Europe, something that could even increase the differences between the developed and underdeveloped countries.

The *General Law for Foreigners* has also been widely criticized, and it will be discussed in the next paragraph. It is clearly favorable, due to different historical ties, for Latin Americans, Portuguese, Philippines, Ecuato-Guineans, Sephardim (Spanish Jews), Andorrans (citizens from a tiny country in the Pyrenees), and native people from Gibraltar, when they are seeking work in Spain. Moroccans who live in the Spanish cities of Ceuta and Melilla (geographically placed in the north of Morocco) do not receive as favorable treatment. Those needing asylum, and refugees, have a special status, and preferential status is given to the stateless.

There are several reasons behind the criticism of the *General Law for Foreigners*. The most critical say that it is full of contradictions, dysfunctions, vagueness, and that it is even unconstitutional at times. Quick deportation is usually the "solution," meaning that an immigrant is forbidden entrance into the country for 3 years. Time is proving, however, that this is not a solution at all. In 1996, the Spanish Police and Civil Guard arrested 11,000 "illegal" immigrants as they entered the country. In 1997, a further 13,000 were caught and arrested on arrival. Many immigrants, mainly young African males, who managed to escape arrest, died while trying to reach southern Spanish coasts, principally Almería, Cádiz, and Málaga, using small boats called *pateras*. There are nowadays more women and teenagers, among "illegal" or "irregular" immigrants, and they are usually from the lowest social class (*cf.* Izquierdo-Escribano, 1993). However, despite the many who die in the attempt, immigrants continue to enter Spain, thanks to the "help" of an organized Mafia that exploits them before and after they enter Spain (*El Correo Gallego*, 2000).

Since January 11, 2000, Spain established a new immigration law. This new law was innovative with regard to key issues such as education, health, and work permits. It could be said that it was one of the most convenient laws for immigrants from all over Europe. However, after the general elections of March 2000, the government—probably due to the high number of foreigners (245,665) who wanted to legalize their status in Spain—decided to reform the law. The reform was approved on December 22, 2000 and is especially restrictive, making clear the distinctions between legal and illegal immigrants.

EDUCATION REFORMS AND ITS EFFECT ON SPANISH SOCIETY

It is our belief that educational reforms in Spain could make important contributions to expanding cultural awareness and equality. But such measures can only succeed with substantial support from the government. De Vreede's thinking (1990) supports our ideas by pointing out that "the problems that pluralistic education tries to resolve are, ultimately, political problems, and it is very doubtful if education can resolve them alone" (p. 137).

Besides, it should also be noted that current trends that try to give more power to autonomous regions in Spain are leading to increased motivation to strengthen regional languages and local traditions. This trend can easily be seen for example by observing that those moving into such regions, both from outside and within Spain, are compelled to learn local languages, especially in schools. To a certain extent one can comprehend the conflict that is sometimes created between existing and incoming groups (Delpit, 1995).

The question, then, is whether the school system truly reflects and works for the development of Spain's diversity. Although multi/intercultural education is a social need, the school curriculum does not include any subject dealing with it. It shows that, in fact, up to now multi/intercultural education has been considered a kind of "compensatory" education more than a general need (cf. Bloom, Davis, & Hess, 1965; Cueva-Álvarez, 1999; Jordán-Sierra, 1997; Jové i Monclús, 1996; Lara, 1991; Molina-Luque, 1994; Rosales-López, 1994; Swartz, 1992; Zigler & Muenchow, 1992).

The new *Education Reform Act*, from 1990 (*Ley Orgánica de Ordenación General del Sistema Educativo*—L.O.G.S.E.), establishes mathematics, foreign languages, Spanish, physical education, arts, and a new area called natural, social, and cultural environment as core curriculum areas in primary schools. The Act also establishes, for the first time, a certain number of cross-curricular areas on those relevant issues to be treated in a global way, through school activities and experiences. These issues deal with ethics and peace education, gender, equity education, health education, environmental education, and consumer education. Nothing is said about multiculturalism, except in the general aims of peace education, where the need for cultivating knowledge of and respect for ethnic, religious, and cultural diversity appears (Gonzalo & Villanueva, 1996, p. 111; Sleeter, 1996; Sleeter & Grant, 1987, 1994).

As Gonzalo and Villanueva claimed (1996, p. 108), despite being a long-established pluralistic society, Spain is now experiencing a new and more varied wave of immigration, generating predictable educational needs and some early experimentation in teacher education. Let us take a look then at teacher preparation in Spain.

TEACHER EDUCATION AND DIVERSITY

The research conducted by Bartolomé-Pina (1995, 1997) shows that, in Spain, teachers involved in multicultural education have narrowly restricted perspectives toward cultural and ethnic diversity. Outcomes of other studies show that the majority of teachers still focus on teaching effectiveness and on language, instead of (a) adapting their teaching methods to the different cultural learning styles of all children, or (b) paying greater attention to the school culture and the hidden curriculum (Cueva-Álvarez, 1999; Pérez-Domínguez, 1999). Acting as if that does not reflect the spirit of a multicultural teacher, the first step to becoming a good teacher and a good teacher educator is, as Sonia Nieto (1996) accurately maintained, to first be a multicultural person.

Such writers as Carbonell and Parra (1991a, 1991b) and Sepa-Bonaba (1993) exposed some of the teachers' perceptions associated with the increasing numbers of pupils in Spanish schools from Third World backgrounds. In the industrial areas of Barcelona, Vizcaya, Madrid, and southern Spain, cultural diversity is well pronounced, and produces feelings of lack of preparation (both preservice and in-service). In the regions with a more modest number of immigrant pupils at school, such as Galicia, teachers feel that there is a lack of preparation, but they also deny the problematic issues that arise when diversity is not treated adequately. These teachers claim that "they treat all students the same" (*cf.* Cowan & Pérez-Domínguez, 1996; Cowan, Pérez-Domínguez, & Santos-Rego, 1994; Pérez-Domínguez, 1997, 1998, 1999). Due to the fact that many immigrants live in the slum areas of large cities, problems are not only limited to cultural and linguistic issues. They are also, and perhaps more importantly, social (Bartolomé-Pina, 1995; Merino, Muñoz, & Sánchez, 1994; Vázquez-Gómez, 1994).

From these scholars we have learned that there is an urgent need to address the preparation of teachers dealing with students (mainly children, but also adults) who come from diverse cultural and ethnic/racial minority groups. Based on this urgent need, our question focuses on *what can be done and how.* Santos-Rego and Nieto (2000), based on their experience as preservice and practicing teachers and their analysis of the situation in Spain and the United States, suggested five implications for improving teacher education, as they say "by linking it [teacher education] to a more critical understanding of diversity." These implications are as follows:

1. Multicultural teacher education needs to build on the cultural differences that students bring to school.
2. Multicultural teacher education needs to be based on a reconceptualization of the relationship among teachers, parents, and other community members.

3. Multicultural teacher education needs to take into consideration the sociopolitical context in which schooling takes place.
4. Multicultural teacher education needs to be linked to curriculum transformation in teacher education courses.
5. Multicultural teacher education also needs to be tied to curriculum transform in general education courses.

We agree with Zeichner (1995) that more research should pay greater attention to listening to what teachers and teacher educators in general have to say, "incorporating the voices and practical theories of teachers" (p. 19), but also bearing in mind that, "...it is also dangerous to accept, as necessarily good, everything that teacher educators reveal in their stories about their practice" (p. 22). However, we also believe that still more scholars should conduct research directly by asking teachers for their opinions on how they would like to be prepared to teach in multicultural environments, from which they could develop further (Russell & Korthagen, 1995).

Some General Points

Micheline Rey (1986) was convinced that teacher preparation is the key to intercultural education. She believed that it is important to prepare teachers to understand pupils, their families, and colleagues from all over the world. This view is supported by San Román (1992a, 1992b, 1993, 1994, 1997) and Merino et al. (1994), among many others in Spain, including ourselves. San Román (1994) claimed that institutions have the potential to develop intercultural programs and projects along with processes for positive orientation. After all, if teachers are not involved in, or are perhaps insensitive to intercultural issues, and if they are not credited with original ideas or fail to receive appropriate preparation, any institutional policy/program will fail. Merino's work affirms that teachers are a key element in the process of change.

Despite all this theory, research carried out in 1989 by Cueva-Álvarez and Tarrow, among third-year students at the University of Barcelona, showed that students felt unprepared to teach in a multicultural setting, documenting that teacher education in Spain for the promotion of multi/intercultural education is an *ad hoc* procedure. Cueva-Álvarez and Tarrow proposed, therefore, the inclusion of multicultural education in the preparation of teacher educators for elementary schools. More recently, a number of programs of multi/intercultural education have been enclosed as optional contents in various departments of teacher education of the University.

It is encouraging, though, that the number of teachers who are gaining direct experience of different models of social behavior within the society in which they operate is on the increase. Many preservice teachers seem to have greater sensibility toward diversity; also, an increasing number of future educators from fields such as sociology, psychology, social work, or pedagogy are taking on subjects dealing with multi/intercultural education. This tendency is mirrored in the majority of other European countries. But the challenge of multi/intercultural thinking is not only to encourage the acceptance of different cultures, but also to promote, positively, the quintessential differences of each culture, so that it is not only immigrant children, but all children, who learn about the beliefs and social practices of others (Fermoso, 1992).

Furthermore, the conflict between home and school languages, social values, attitudes, and behavior creates the need for teachers to understand the very essence of what education is about. Initial teacher preparation, therefore, should encourage a continuing program for the exploration of interculturalization enhanced by a comprehensive and systematic support network to enable teachers to express fears and gain confidence (García-Parejo, 1994).

In light of social changes, the approach to pupil learning in Spain should be reexamined. Teachers are so often used to operating in the context of previous decades when nowadays social priorities and traditional values have clearly changed (Colectivo IOÉ, 1995). Teachers must be able to evaluate ethical issues in light of equal opportunity motives and with an impartiality and insight that enables a versatility of skills and a listening ear; they also need to sometimes be creative and try different teaching-learning techniques, such as cooperative learning (Díaz-Aguado & Baraja, 1993; Sales-Ciges & García-López, 1997; Santos-Rego, 1990, 1994; Santos-Rego & Pérez-Domínguez, 1997).

Racist expressions and images are still contained in many textbooks, and policies do not exist to encourage scrutiny of books in Spanish schools for discriminatory or ambiguous comments (Buxarrais-Estrada et al., 1991). In fact, a number of pejorative phrases still exist within the Spanish culture, which must be erased. Some of these expressions are, for example "to work like a Black" (meaning to work a lot, non stop), "to be a Gypsy" (meaning a false person, one who cannot be trusted, or a naughty child), "he came back looking like a Gypsy" (meaning, he came back completely dirty), "don't worry, it is not a Jewish stain" (meaning that the stain is not such a bad one), "to desire the gold and the Moor" (meaning to be too ambitious, wanting everything for oneself), "there are Moors on the coast!" (meaning "watch out!"), and so on.

Teachers need to search hard to provide practical work programs with workable objectives because, as we know, in education teachers do not have the luxury of considering and weighing the merits of different educational philosophies. If change is to take place, if fixed ideas are to be transformed, then teachers must be challenged by government directives emanating from the vision of those most closely involved in multi/intercultural work. A pack of core values, established through discussion with those most engaged in multi/intercultural work, is crucial. Commitment to and interpretation of these core values into tangible practice is, however, most important. Jordán-Sierra (1992, 1994, 1997) claimed that the defining of pluralism, within the context of education, should be seen as a positive and creative experience rather than as a way of avoiding conflict and tension. Whatever measures are taken, little will be achieved without the support of ethnic groups, educators, and the government. Lessons learned in other European and non-European countries show that moving toward intercultural thinking is a slow and painful process. It takes time and patience.

The 1990 Education Reform Act and Teacher Education

Although the Spanish Constitutional Law (1978) and 1990 Education Reform Act contain (as we mentioned earlier) generic statements about respect and tolerance toward different cultures in the country, there is no specific regulation about the preparation of teachers. As this act gives more autonomy to universities, the preparation of teachers depends on each particular university, and consequently on their economic autonomy, willingness to work in this field, or even their political and ideological dependence or independence. Many teachers show excellent efforts and have had valuable experiences, but the preparation of teachers is still often fragmented, isolated, and dispersed because of the lack of clear regulations in multi/intercultural education. It is, in the end, teachers' willingness or lack of it, that determines the sucess or failure of many multi/intercultural programs and initiatives.

The Ministry of Education first proposed a program for the integration of ethnic and cultural minorities in 1990, and this document was aimed at those schools with children from different cultures, expressing the need for introducing an intercultural perspective. For the first time, academic authorities were taking into account the fact that multi/intercultural education should be the school's responsibility and not one of individual specially trained teachers.

More concretely, and despite this autonomy for universities, all future teacher trainers must take a 3-year degree at schools of education, with a choice of different options: infant, primary, music, physical education, foreign languages, or special needs education.[4] In fact, universities are the ones that are introducing subjects dealing with diversity in both their programs in teacher education and for specialists in education. The curriculum has 60% compulsory and 40% optional subjects in the autonomous regions and, at a national level, 40% of the

---

[4] Infant education goes from 0 to 6 years, being subsidized by the state from 3 years old. Primary (elementary) education is compulsory from 6 to 12. Secondary education includes compulsory secondary education ("Educación Secundaria Obligatoria," or E.S.O.), which goes from 12 to 16. Secondary education also includes two optional educational schemes: High School ("Bachillerato") and Vocational Training ("Formación Profesional," or F.P.), from 16 to 18.

curriculum is compulsory. Each university can organize the remaining 60% of their subjects, as, for example, 40% optional and 20% compulsory, as well as to introduce particular studies. We consider that the development of multi/intercultural education is threatened not only by avoiding or rejecting multi/intercultural education programs but, perhaps more importantly, by claiming to be using an intercultural approach, when analogous or even contrary approaches are being used.

Consequently, the completed document of the *1990 Education Reform Act* has been criticized as too theoretical and impractical, and it has therefore not proved to be successful in encouraging multi/intercultural initiatives in schools despite the wide number of people involved in discussing fresh ideas for the new curriculum. Escribano (1993) believed that within the national curriculum the only gesture toward multi/intercultural education in schools is a recommendation for all those involved in education to respect diversity of traditions and to treat cultural differences in a cross-curricular way. Terms such as "equal rights," "tolerance," "discrimination," "peace," "cooperation," "solidarity among peoples," and "respect" are included, but the *1990 Education Reform Act* fails to provide specific guidelines on how immigrant children and dominant group children should be educated about diversity.

It is our belief that multi/intercultural education in teacher education should be present in all academic subjects, and teachers need also to know how economic, political, and social systems work to understand and be better prepared to face the unevenness of today's society.

THE GYPSY COMMUNITY IN SPAIN

The Gypsy community is one of the largest ethnic minorities[5] in Spain, and therefore one that most stands out among other cultures residing in this country. According to San Román (1994), there were about 500,000 Gypsies in Spain in 1994; according to Sales-Ciges and García-López (1997), there were about about 800,000. Liégeois (1998) argued that the number could oscillate between 850,000 and 1,000,000. Because of the high rate of demographic growth (for cultural and even economic reasons), we estimate that, by the end of January 2001, the number could be around 1,100,000. The Gypsy community, despite their early arrival in Spain, in 1425 according to most of the sources (*cf.* Fernández-Enguita, 1996; Liégeois, 1987), still has little social or political credibility. Public interest centers around their music and dance (Cáritas Española, 1987; *cf.* also, e.g., Fernández-Enguita, 1996).

---

[5] In the words of Pajares (1999): "We could almost say that the Gypsy population is the only ethnic minority living nowadays in Spain...[together with] the mercheros, mistakenly taken as Gypsies. And, of course, the Jews" (p. 102).

Gypsies are and feel Spanish. They say it and confirm it with pride. They do not live in hopes of moving to another "promised land."

Gypsies: A Brief History

Gypsies first entered Spain from the north. This was a safe conduct given in Zaragoza by King Alfonso V on January 12, 1425 to "Don Johan de Egipto Menor." The document orders that he be allowed to "go, stay and travel" for three months with all his luggage and those who were with him (Liégeois, 1987).

King Felipe IV proclaimed in 1633 that all representatives of authority were to be informed of the Gypsies who were in the area and to surround, capture, or kill them. Those Gypsies who, "for any fair reason" (in his words), did not warrant the death penalty or the slaughterhouse were to become slaves for the rest of their lives. The next king, Felipe V, in his day, changed to a certain extent the words of his predecessor by saying that Gypsies were to be hunted with iron and fire, even persecuted inside churches should they enter them to find sanctuary. At least he did not speak of killing them!

Another important date for Gypsies was July 30, 1749, when another king, Fernando VI, ordered the so-called *Redada General* (*General Raid*) to capture all Gypsies living in Spain. Ten or twelve thousand men and women, elderly people, and children were put in prison. The crime they had committed was "to be Gypsies," as mentioned in various official reports of that time (Gómez-Alfaro, 1993).

Even in 1942, with the dictator Franco's consent, the Civil Guard were ordered to watch Gypsies scrupulously, taking special note of their distinguishing marks, their clothes, to find out about their lifestyle, and to ascertain where they were traveling to and why.

Hunting with iron and fire has become history but exclusion and rejection continued along with inadequate administrative attention, humiliation, anathema, insults, and reproach. In short, a curse.

One of the stipulations of the Military Order of Calatrava is that no one born out of legal wedlock and of parents and grandparents who had any relationship with Jews, Moors, heretics, or peasants could be accepted in the Order.

The Present Day

Generally speaking, we could say that both previous and new attempts to improve the social and educational situation for Gypsies have not yet been successful.

Perhaps society's main concern in connection with the integration of Gypsies is that, according to some views, it would mean the integration of poverty, urban decline, unemployment, an informal economy, sexism, and drug dealing, indeed problems that also affect other marginalized groups.

Some political measures have been taken and have helped to incorporate Gypsy children into the education system, at least putting an end to generations of exclusion from it. But there continues to be an increasing inequality within the education system concerning Gypsies.

Anthropologist Tomás Calvo-Buezas (1995b) recalled, in surveys undertaken in schools over the past few years, that Gypsies have always been the most rejected and negatively stereotyped group in Spain. He pointed out that 25% of teachers would object to have Gypsy children in their classes, 17% would object to "Moors-Arabs," 10% to Black Africans, and 9% to Jews (cf. Calvo-Buezas, 1990a, 1990b).

Despite the increasing inclusion of Gypsy children in mainstream schools, there is still a high rate of underachievement, and the majority of children in fact do not go on to secondary education, let alone university. Illiteracy is very common, especially among women, as they normally abandon school at the time they begin menstruating. As Iniesta-Corredor (1986, p. 93) indicated, 72% of Gypsy females have less than elementary schooling, 27% have elementary schooling, and only 1% have gone on to further education.

Teachers who have Gypsies in their classes give three reasons for their failure at school. First, the fact is that the non-Gypsy schools do not respond to the Gypsy culture, or to the expectations and needs of Gypsies. Second, the Gypsies themselves, and especially the parents, are to blame because they outcast themselves because they do not take an interest in education. Third, there are those who attribute failure at school to a number of sociocultural factors, inside and outside the Gypsy community, including poverty and marginalization. They state that many, although not all, of the problems that Gypsies suffer are due to poverty and not to the fact that they are Gypsies (Abajo-Alcalde, 1996; Calvo-Buezas, 1995b).

One primary school teacher, Luis Romero, in an interview given for *El Semanal* magazine (March 5, 1995), stated that racism and lack of culture go hand in hand, although he believed that racism is simply an economic issue. He compared rich Muslims, called "Arabs," with poor Muslims, called "Moors," even though both belong to the same religious and cultural group. We personally believe that all these factors and especially the last ones are extremely important to understanding the Gypsy case in Spain. What is also clear is that reactionary ideas still remain, despite the passage of time. Housing, employment, political involvement, and citizenship are examples, apart from education, of situations where Gypsies find themselves outcasts. What used to be considered by some a vague social problem is now proving to be definitely a multifaceted one.

The Europe of the future is clearly destined to be a multiethnic and pluricultural mosaic. Today's children, tomorrow's European citizens, and above all, citizens of the world, must learn to live within this diversity. Otherwise, racism and xenophobia will be the norm. Now, as Spain is rapidly becoming, like other European countries, more multicultural and pluralistic, it too must take on a new identity and take steps to resolve the long-standing contentious problems that exist between Gypsies and the majority today.

On May 5, 1997, Pope John Paul II beatified Ceferino Jiménez-Malla "El Pelle," meaning "The Strong One." The news is not that a Spaniard was sanctified, but that he was Spanish and a Gypsy. He is, thus, the first Gypsy saint. In view of this, the president of the Gypsy community in Spain said: "At least now we know of one who was not bad."

THE WAY FORWARD FOR SPAIN

In the mid-1980s Husén and Opper (1984) published one of the first books in Spain (translated into Spanish) concerning multi/intercultural issues. There was no response from Spanish society at that time. Since the 1990s, important innovations and programs have been introduced in schools in some areas of Spain. Although, now, papers, articles, and books are published, seminars and conferences organized, and official monographic works ordered by the central and regional governments, qualifying chapters, doctoral dissertations, and also master's courses are and continue to be written regarding multi/intercultural education. Educational journals produce special and monographic issues about immigrants, multicultural, or intercultural education.

Moreover, new journals have appeared in Spain and other parts of Europe, such as the *Mediterranean Journal of Educational Studies* and the *European Journal of Intercultural Studies* (now *Intercultural Education*), with particular emphasis on diversity. A number of NGOs and associations, dealing with multicultural issues, have been created in each of the regions of Spain. The *Dirección General del Instituto Español de Emigración* was replaced in 1991 by the *Dirección General de Migraciones,* which deals with an increasing number of immigrants. Press, radio and television, every day or almost every day, speak or write about problems or satisfaction derived from the cultural, ethnic, and linguistic diversity of the different areas of the country.

Apart from developments and material facts of multiculturality in each autonomous region, educational projects on multi/intercultural education can be presented at a state level in the Center for Research and Educational Development (CIDE). There is a growing number of protest songs, reports, and even films against racism and xenophobia. But the growing interest in diversity also has to do with the fact that Spain now belongs to the European Union, and support and resources to investigate these issues are now available. The fact that international organizations such as UNESCO, the Council of Europe, or the OECD are also investigating and funding research is something else that has a specific importance in the development of multi/intercultural education in Spain and other parts of Europe.

All this shows that multi/intercultural thinking is being developed and has become a focus for intellectual debate with social, linguistic, and political implications. History has proved to be a controversial subject, and some autonomous regions interpret both their particular history and the history of Spain very differently. However, let us not be naïve either; this is also clearly a political issue.

Multi/intercultural education still has a long way to go, but this does not mean that programs do not exist. Educational programs for immigrant children do actually exist. García-Castaño and Pulido-Moyano (1993) highlighted two, promoted by government departments, under the already mentioned category of "compensatory education'": the MEC (the National Ministry of Education and Science; now called Ministry of Education, Culture, and Sport) and the DEGC (equivalent to the Ministry of Education and Culture, but for Catalonia). One program is directed toward Portuguese children, the other is to help immigrant students in Catalonia.

Multi/intercultural development in Spain should take note of the fact that by concentrating on immigration issues alone, more important matters such as cultural interchange will be lost. It is essential that all immigrants should be treated as individuals, each with his or her own histories, experiences, hopes, and fears. Naturally, although there will be certain groups with particular needs and problems, a generic and negative categorization of all immigrants is unfair. There are groups with special needs and abilities (all too frequently defined as "disabilities"), which require positive support systems to be set up in order to facilitate their introduction (not assimilation or integration) into an unfamiliar society (Abad, Cucó, & Izquierdo-Escribano, 1993).

But we recognize that to say that is very easy, but that it is not so easy to put into practice. The whole question of introducing immigrants into their new home country is fraught with fear and danger. The range of opinions and attitudes is virtually limitless and the positive acceptance of an unfamiliar culture into one's own context demands a great deal of sacrifice, particularly of the safe boundaries within which one has always lived. Therefore, the arrival of another culture into one's own is an opportunity to reflect on those factors in society that create a narrow vision or that lead to bigotry and rejection of certain groups. Diversity should result in an enhancement of cultural possibilities, to positive discrimination, not a blinkered defense of native customs. Positive discrimination is not an easy idea to accept, but certainly antipathy toward those who are immigrants will not enrich a society, but will create negative forces, which will limit the development of that country and produce more problems in the future (Woolard, 1989).

Commitment at both national and local levels is essential and must be manifested in the supply of appropriate human and financial resources, as well as systematic policies supported by government legislation. Immigrants need to be given the space to be responsible for their own actions and opportunities, for their voice to be heard. This is usually achieved through the setting up of support centers and representation on committees in school and in the community in general. The initiation of issues related to education, which extend into the community, employment areas, access to information and opportunity for feedback, is required.

Change, especially in education, cannot happen overnight. It requires painstaking modifications of behavior, attitudes, and beliefs, while one faces fears and misconceptions established over generations.

When change involves a transformation of cultural and social values, carrying with it a long history and tradition, then systems for implementation cannot be rushed. This is no excuse for inertia and, prior to the production of aims and policies, groundwork is required in the form of a breakdown of personal prejudice in a positive environment. An examination of the school's curriculum, books, and resources to determine to what extent negative images of other cultures are presented is another starting point, and it is proving to be a challenge facing all countries.

Naturally the needs of students are paramount in the educational climate of a school. Education for all has been the priority for Spanish schools over the past 20 years. Now it is time to address the dilemmas facing teachers, as was stated, and an adjustment of the theoretical and practical pedagogy is necessary. De Vreede (1990, 1999) claimed that it is essential for changes of attitude toward pluralistic education in order to undertake a critical revision of the whole curriculum.

TEACHERS' OPINIONS ABOUT TEACHING IN MULTICULTURAL CONTEXTS

In this section we highlight some of the results obtained from questionnaires completed by 431 teachers between 1996 and 1997. The questionnaire contained 38 items, and was entitled "The Opinions of State Primary School Teachers Regarding Teaching in a Multicultural and Multiethnic Society." The schools were located all over Spain (including two tiny Spanish cities located in northern Morocco, called Ceuta and Melilla) and Britain (England, Wales, and Scotland). (Here we refer only to Spain.) We received addresses and permission to submit 10 questionnaires to each school.

The questionnaires were divided into five main sections entitled: (a) main information about the respondent; (b) the role of the school; (c) multi/intercultural education and academic achievement; (d) teacher preparation; and (e) additional information.

There were six statements which teachers had to give their position, asking them to choose between five possible answers, which varied between "strongly agree," "agree," "indifferent/undecided/neutral," "agree," and "strongly disagree." The last question was open-ended and optional, so they could express their opinions freely.

This is part of a study on the opinions of public elementary school teachers working in schools with a minimum of 25% of the students from ethnic/racial or cultural minority groups. This research illuminates teachers' perspectives regarding the challenges, needs, and/or satisfaction they encounter in their teaching work with minority students.

In brief, four of the most relevant results were:

1. Teachers believe that the presence of ethnic/cultural minorities requires specialized training in multi/intercultural education (65.4%), and also a bit more than half of them (53.4%) consider it necessary even if they have no ethnic/cultural minorities as yet;
2. They consider that schools should be more concerned with making minority students feel integrated within the school (85.6%), and compensate possible shortfalls they may have when beginning school (89.3%);
3. They reject any kind of segregation of minority children, be it separate schools for each ethnic/cultural minority (66.1%) or receiving special separate classes within the same school (60.3%);
4. When asked whether they would like to continue teaching in multicultural schools or not (if they had the chance to choose), 69.4% of teachers said yes, and 54.1% saw teaching as a professional challenge (Pérez-Domínguez, 1999).

As for the section entitled "information about the respondent," 65.3% of them were men, 34.7% were women, and all were White Spaniards. Most of the respondents (32.4%) were between 40 and 47 years old, the lowest%age of them (5.6%) were over 56. Regarding teaching experience, 39.4% have had less than 6 years experience. Many (68.1%) were teachers and the remaining were principals (11.5%), support teachers (12.2%), and vice-principals (8.2%).

Results obtained from the research have shown that teachers feel the need to better understand the increasing diversity in Spain. Although 431 questionnaires clearly do not represent all public elementary school teachers teaching in multicultural settings in Spain with a minimum of 25% of pupils from ethnic/racial or cultural minority groups, current literature and research (see, among others, Bartolomé-Pina, 1995, 1997; Buxarrais-Estrada et al., 1991; Carbonell & Parra, 1991a, 1991b; Cowan & Pérez-Domínguez, 1996; García-Castaño & Pulido-Moyano, 1993; García-López & Sales-Ciges, 1997; Gonzalo & Villanueva, 1996; Jordán-Sierra,

1994, 1997; Jové i Monclús, 1996; Merino et al., 1994; Santos-Rego & Pérez-Domínguez, 1997; Sepa-Bonaba, 1993; Vázquez-Gómez, 1994), as well as our formal and informal talks with teachers and visits to schools, coincide with the outcomes of our research.

We believe that more research should be conducted exploring what teachers have to say about their own experience teaching in multicultural contexts.

SOME PROPOSALS AND CONCLUSIONS

We have tried to show the different aspects of intercultural education in Spain. We finish this chapter pointing out some proposals and observations for the development of multi/intercultural education. These proposals could well be grouped in four categories (a) social integration, (b) the mass media, (c) multi/intercultural education, and (d) teacher education.

Social Integration

The Gypsy Community.
1. To improve the general social conditions of Gypsies respecting and conserving their cultural identity.
2. To make social insertion easier and to promote support measures for people with more economic and social difficulties, avoiding ghettos of marginalization and poverty.
3. To encourage better relationships among citizens, in respect, knowledge, and recognition of the Gypsy culture.
4. To promote the direct participation of Gypsies in the issues that affect them, in the social, political organizations, and trade Unions; thus reducing their social and political exclusion, which makes them second rate citizens.
5. To create organisms in Public Administration (in the central administration in Madrid, and in the other autonomous regions of Spain) that take care of the protection and social and cultural development of the Gypsy community.

Immigrants and Refugees.
1. To improve the social, educational, and economic situation of cultural/ethnic minorities living in Spain. These include (a) the different groups of immigrants (to treat all immigrants the same is a great mistake, leading to the failure of the best intentioned projects/reforms) and (b) refugees' (in the same vein as immigrants) social integration policy must make sure that there is no discrimination at all, both in the development of rights and duties, as in access to social services.
2. To create new measures that end the exploitation of immigrants (especially economic exploitation of those who enter Spain because they are poor in their countries of origin and hold on to the hope for

a better future through emigration). Measures that reform the *General Law for Foreigners*, that help immigrants settle and find a job, that help families to stay together, that avoid the formation of urban ghettos and educational segregation, checking and suppressing the legal maneuvers that make it very difficult for refugees to find a job, consequently creating the conditions for illegal employment, as well as to overcome the language and schooling barriers, which make their integration difficult. Measures that also guarantee legal security in all fields and access to a dual nationality for immigrants, so that they can vote in local elections, as the European Parliament recommends.

3. To mobilize society against racism and xenophobia, facing up to the reality of prejudice against refugees and immigrants, and to create forums for debate and integration in their new "home."
4. To put an end to the intolerance toward those who are different physically, in their way of understanding the world, in their religions or beliefs, languages, and so on.

Mass Media

1. To work toward the elimination of stereotypes and prejudice in the mass media.
2. To contribute to the elimination of discrimination and the establishment of peace. International organizations, such as UNESCO or the United Nations, with their conventions and declarations, and the Council of Europe and the European Parliament, can help toward this objective.

Multi/Intercultural Education

1. To provide a critical view of reality, to develop an education that eliminates prejudice and stereotypes and that favors an active solidarity.
2. To assume that because we live in an interdependent world that is increasingly multicultural, the school and its administration and teachers have major roles and a shared responsibility toward all children and their families.
3. To develop the different government multi/intercultural school programs that demonstrate the contribution of cultural, ethnic, and social minorities to the progress of civilization, and that promote tolerance, solidarity, and the rejection of violence, xenophobia, and racism. These are also recommendations of UNESCO, the Council of Europe, and the European Parliament.
4. To aim at *all* students, both the minorities and majorities, because multi/intercultural education has to intervene with everybody, including the native people. Furthermore, multi/intercultural education is a challenge for all democracies.
5. To adapt the school to the new multicultural reality. The school texts, for example, need to be adapted to this new reality urgently by making positive reference to both majorities and minorities and their interrelation.

6. To work in close contact with the community and the NGOs and organize cultural activities for students, parents, and teachers because the school alone cannot resolve the issues derived from diversity, nor should the school turn its back on the community.
7. To promote the participation of the families of minorities in the school's activities and projects, as well as to encourage the incorporation of both children and adults in the educational process, which will undoubtedly contribute to long awaited social integration.
8. To work toward avoiding the social and political exclusion suffered by different ethnic/racial and cultural groups living in Spain.
9. To go beyond compensatory education meassures, which, although useful at times, can, at other times, produce negative effects in a student's progressive learning in the medium/long term.
10. To create an awareness in society, and indeed among teachers, that multi/intercultural education is (or should be) something more than repair work to make up for deficits in education, and in society as a whole.

Teacher Education

We consider that this is the key to the evolution and progress of multi/intercultural education. If we want change in this field (and with its projection in the other fields of society) to occur and last, we perhaps should start by hearing teachers' voices and opinions.

We are, therefore, convinced that teachers and educators in general have a very important role to play in preparing the citizens of tomorrow. If they do not receive adequate preparation to address issues of diversity, they will fail to support the needs of their students for the 21st century. This is a continuous process that starts with their own preparation. As Banks (1997) has pointed out:

> To create democratic schools for students from diverse racial, ethnic, and cultural groups, teachers must examine their cultural assumptions and attitudes, their behaviors, the knowledge and paradigms on which their pedagogy is based, and the subject matter knowledge they teach... . To develop a teacher education curriculum that reflects the myriad and emerging ethnic and cultural identities among teachers, we must make some attempt to identify them and to describe their curricular and teaching implications. (pp. 100, 107)

Bearing this in mind, we believe that teacher preparation programs should primarily be concerned with listening to what teachers/educators have to say about their perceptions of their own preparation. It is also our belief that danger exists when generalizing too much about what is or is not adequate for preparing teachers.

New studies should take into consideration the need to prepare teacher educators to first listen to the expressed demands of the teachers. In this way teacher education programs would better reflect their opinions and desires (Jordán-Sierra, 1997; Ladson-Billings, 1994; Larkin

& Sleeter, 1995; Liston & Zeichner, 1991, 1996; Pérez-Domínguez, 1999). These are ideas that coincide with those reflected in the Book *The Light in Their Eyes: Student Learning, Teacher Transformation and Multicultural Education*, edited by Sonia Nieto (1999).

Multi/interculturalism is an evolutionary process and not a sudden conversion. The introduction of multi/intercultural thinking demands a knowledge of internal and external conflict resolution, how to address prejudice and discrimination, and ways of promoting the advantages of cultural reciprocity. Commitment from those in political power must secure change through legislation, offering opportunities for the liberation of cultural expression and individual rights. This is why policy is important only if it is put into practice and is evaluated critically and in its appropriate context (Sleeter & McLaren, 1995).

ACKNOWLEDGMENTS

The authors would like to express their grateful thanks to Professor Sonia M. Nieto (University of Massachusetts at Amherst) for her useful comments on an earlier version of this chapter.

REFERENCES

Abad, L. V., Cucó, A., & Izquierdo-Escribano, A. (1993). *Inmigración, pluralismo y tolerancia* [Immigration, pluralism, and tolerance]. Madrid: Editorial Popular—Jóvenes contra la intolerancia.

Abajo-Alcalde, J. E. (1996). La escolarización de los niños gitanos. El desconcierto de los mensajes doble-vinculares y la apuesta por los vínculos sociales y afectivos [Gypsy children at school: The uncertainty created by double-meaning messages and the need for social and affective links]. *Aula de Innovación Educativa, 47*, 67-77.

Anuario estadístico de extranjería. (1999). Madrid: Comisión interministerial de extranjería, Ministerio del Interior.

Arnau, J., Comet, C., Serra, J. M., & Vila, I. (1992). *La educación bilingüe* [Bilingual education]. Barcelona: ICE Universitat de Barcelona.

Banks, J. A. (1997). *Educating citizens in a multicultural society.* New York: Teachers College Press.

Banks, J. A., & Banks, C. A. (Eds.) (1995). *Handbook of research on multicultural education.* New York: MacMillan.

Bartolomé-Pina, M. (1995). La escuela multicultural: Del diagnóstico a una propuesta de cambio [The multicultural school: From diagnosis to a proposal of change]. *Revista de Educación, 307*, 75-125.

Bartolomé-Pina, M. (1997). *Diagnóstico a la escuela multicultural* [A diagnosis of "the multicultural school"]. Barcelona: Cedecs Editorial.

Batelaan, P. (1992, September). Intercultural education for cultural development: The contribution of teacher education. Paper presented at the

International UNESCO Conference on Education "Contribution of Education to Cultural Development," Geneva, Switzerland.

Bloom, B. S., Davis, A., & Hess, R. (1965). *Compensatory education for cultural deprivation.* Chicago: Holt, Rinehart, & Winston.

Buxarrais-Estrada, M. R., Carrillo-Flores, I, Galcerán-Peiró, M. M., López-Montoya, S., Martín-García, M. J., Martínez-Martín, M., Payà-Sànchez, M., Puig-Rovira, J.M., Trilla-Bernet, J., & Villar-Martín, J. (1991). *El interculturalismo en el currículum. El racismo* [Interculturalism in the curriculum: The racism]. Barcelona: Rosa Sensat/MEC.

Calvo-Buezas, T. (1990a). *¿España racista? Voces payas sobre los gitanos* [Racist Spain? Mainstream voices about Gypsies]. Barcelona: Anthropos.

Calvo-Buezas, T. (1990b). *El racismo que viene: Otros pueblos y culturas visto por profesores y alumnos* [The coming racism: Other people and other cultures as seeing by teachers and pupils]. Madrid: Tecnos.

Calvo-Buezas, T. (1995a). *Crece el racismo, también la solidaridad. Los valores de la juventud en el umbral del siglo XXI* [Racism grows, also solidarity: Youth values at the threshold of the 21st century]. Madrid: Tecnos.

Calvo-Buezas, T. (1995b). Aprender a vivir en la diferencia [Learning to live with the different]. *Vela Mayor, 5,* 13-17.

Carbonell, F., & Parra, S. (1991a). La escuela africana de adultos Samba Kubally [The adults' African school Samba Kubally]. *Cuadernos de Pedagogía, 196.*

Carbonell, F., & Parra, S. (1991b). La Samba Kubally i l'associació GRAMC [The Samba Kubally and the association GRAMC]. *Revista de Treball Social, 123.*

Cáritas Española (1987). Los inmigrantes en España [The immigrants in Spain]. *Documentación Social, 66.*

Cohen, E. G. (1986). *Designing groupwork: Strategies for the heterogeneous classroom.* New York: Teachers College Press.

Cohen, E. G. (1990). Teaching in multicultural heterogeneous classrooms. *McGill Journal of Education, 26,* 7-22.

Cohen, E. G., Lotan, R. A., Whitcomb, J. A., Balderrama, M. V., Cossey, R., & Swanson, P. E. (1994). Complex instruction: Higher order thinking in heterogeneous classrooms. In S. Sharan (Ed.), *Handbook of cooperative learning methods* (pp. 82-96). Westport, CT: Greenwood Press.

Colectivo IOÉ (W. Actis, M. A. de Prada, & C. Pereda). (1994). La inmigración extranjera en España: Sus características diferenciales en el contexto europeo. In J. Contreras (Ed.), *Los retos de la inmigración. Racismo y pluriculturalidad* [The challenges of immigration: Racism and cultural pluralism] (pp. 83-119). Madrid: Talasa.

Colectivo IOÉ (W. Actis, M. A. de Prada, & C. Pereda). (1995). Extraños, distintos, iguales o las paradojas de la alteridad. Discursos de los españoles sobre los extranjeros [Strangers, different, equal or the paradoxes of the *alter ego.* Discourses of Spaniards about foreigners]. *Revista de Educación, 307,* 17-51.

Condena al racismo [Condemnation of racism]. (1989, January 31) *El País,* p. 19.

Cowan, B. J., & Pérez-Domínguez, S. (1996). Cultural myopia: A challenge to Spanish education. *Mediterranean Journal of Educational Studies, 1(2),* 35-52.

Cowan, B. J., Pérez-Domínguez, S., & Santos-Rego, M. A. (1994, May). An examination of multicultural policy and practice in one education authority within the U.K. and its possible implications for the present development of intercultural thinking in Spain. Paper presented at the Second International

Conference, Perspectivas da Educaçao para o ano 2000 [Educational perspectives for the year 2000] at the Portuguese University of Trás-os-Montes e Alto Douro, Vila Real, Portugal.

Cueva-Álvarez, M. J. (1999). Percepciones del alumnado de formación del profesorado y del profesorado escolar con respecto a la educación multicultural: Un estudio de casos en el ámbito catalán y otros ámbitos [Perceptions of teachers and teacher training students about multicultural education: A case study in the Catalan area and in other areas]. Unpublished dissertation. University of Barcelona.

Cueva-Álvarez, M. J., & Tarrow, N. B. (1989). Una propuesta para incluir educación intercultural en la formación del profesorado de EGB [A proposal to include intercultural education in the training of elementary school teachers]. Report presented at the Cuarta Conferencia Nacional de Magisterios, Soria.

Delpit, L. (1995). *Other people's children: Cultural conflict in the classroom.* New York: The New York Press.

De Vreede, E. (1990). What are we talking about? Plural education and teacher education. *European Journal of Teacher Education, 13*(3), 128-140.

De Vreede, E. (1999). Pluralist and intercultural education: Challenges for teacher education. Paper presented at the 24th ATEE (Association for Teacher Education in Europe) conference in Leipzig, Germany.

Díaz-Aguado, M. J., & Baraja, E. (1993). *Interacción educativa y desventaja sociocultural* [Educational interaction and socio-cultural disadvantage]. Madrid: CIDE.

El gobierno quiere reformar la Ley de Extranjería lo más rápido posible [The (Spanish) government plans to reform the Law for Foreigners as quickly as possible]. (2000, May 27th). *El Correo Gallego,* p. 9.

Encuentran 36 inmigrantes, 6 menores, hacinados en una furgoneta en Málaga—Fernández Miranda pide que se sea implacable con las redes de tráficos de personas [36 immigrants—6 under 18—are found crammed in a van in Málaga—Fernández Miranda asks for implacability with those (mafias) making business with immigrants]. (2000, June 21st). *El Correo Gallego,* p. 8.

Escribano, A. (1993). Educación intercultural: Intervenciones en la escuela [Intercultural education: Involvement at the school]. *Cuadernos de la Fundación Santa María, 11,* 7-20.

Esteve, J. M. (1992). Multicultural education in Spain: The Autonomous Communities face the challenge of European unity. *Educational Review, 44*(3), 255-272.

Fermoso, P. (Ed.). (1992). *Educación intercultural: La Europa sin fronteras* [Intercultural education: The Europe without frontiers]. Madrid: Narcea.

Fernández-Enguita, M. (1996). *Escuela y etnicidad. El caso del pueblo gitano* [Schooling and ethnicity: The case of the Gypsy community]. Madrid: CIDE.

Gaine, C. (1995). *Still no problem here.* Staffordshire, England: Trentham Books.

Galino, Á., & Escribano, A. (1990). *La educación intercultural en el enfoque y desarrollo del currículum* [Intercultural education for curriculum focusing and development]. Madrid: Narcea.

García-Castaño, F. J., & Pulido-Moyano, R. A. (1993). Multicultural education—Some reflections on the Spanish case. *European Journal of Intercultural Studies 4*(2), 67-80.

García-López, R., & Sales-Ciges, A. (1997). Educación intercultural y formación de actitudes. Programa pedagógico para desarrollar actitudes interculturales [Intercultural education and the training of attitudes. Pedagogical program to develop intercultural attitudes]. *Revista Española de Pedagogía, 207,* 317-336.

García-Parejo, I. (1994). *Enseñanza/aprendizaje de la lengua e integración: Una propuesta educativa centrada en el inmigrante adulto sobre la base de datos relativa a la Comunidad Autónoma de Madrid* [Language teaching/learning and integration: An educational proposal aiming at adult immigrants based on data from the Madrid Autonomous Community]. Madrid: CIDE (Research Project).

Gay, G. (1994). *At the essence of learning: Multicultural education.* West Lafayette, IN: Kappa Delta Pi.

Gestos [Gestures]. (1995, March 5th). *El Semanal,* p. 90.

Gómez-Alfaro, A. (1993). *La Gran redada de Gitanos* [The great Gypsy round-up]. Madrid: Presencia Gitana.

Gonzalo, C., & Villanueva, M. (1996). Training teachers for a multicultural future in Spain. In M. Craft (Ed.), *Teacher education in plural societies: An international review* (pp. 108-115). London & Washington, DC: Falmer Press.

Grant, C. A. (1981, November/December). Education that is multicultural and teacher preparation: An examination from the perspective of preservice students. *Journal of Educational Research, 75*(2), 95-101.

Grant, C. A. (1992). *Research and multicultural education: From the margins to the mainstream.* London & Washington, DC: Falmer Press.

Husén, T., & Opper, S. (Eds.). (1984). *Educación multicultural y multilingüe* [Multicultural and multilingual education]. Madrid: Narcea.

Iniesta-Corredor, A. (1986). Infancia marginada: El caso de los gitanos [Marginalized childhood: The Gypsy case]. *Educar, 9,* 85-98.

Izquierdo-Escribano, A. (1993). Los trabajadores extranjeros en Madrid: Un flujo complementario que se consolida [Foreign workers in Madrid: A complementary flux which is being consolidated]. *Política y Sociedad, 12,* 21-36.

Jordán-Sierra, J. A. (1992). *L'educació multicultural* [Multicultural education]. Barcelona: CEAC (Centro de Estudios de Aparejador por Correspondencia [Master Builder Studying Center]).

Jordán-Sierra, J. A. (1994). *La escuela multicultural: Un reto para el profesorado* [Multicultural education: A challenge for teachers]. Barcelona: Paidós.

Jordán-Sierra, J. A. (1997). *Propuestas de educación intercultural para profesores* [Proposals of intercultural education for teachers]. Barcelona: CEAC (Centro de Estudios de Aparejador por Correspondencia [Master Builder Studying Center]).

Jové i Monclús, G. (1996). *La diversitat cultural a l'escola. La investigación-acció per a la millora profesional* [Cultural diversity in the school: Action-research for professional improvement]. Universitat de Lleida: Servei de Publicacions/Manel Garriga i Bosch.

Ladson-Billings, G. (1994). *The dreamkeepers: Successful teachers of African American children.* San Francisco: Jossey-Bass.

Lara, F. (1991). *Compensar educando* [To compensate with education]. Madrid: Editorial Popular.

Larkin, J. M., & Sleeter, C. E. (Eds.). (1995). *Developing multicultural teacher education curricula.* Albany: State University of New York.

Liégeois, J. P. (1987). *Gitanos e itinerantes* [Gypsies and travelers]. Madrid: Editorial Presencia Gitana.

Liégeois, J. P. (1998). *Minoría y escolaridad: El paradigma gitano* [School provision for ethnic minorities: The Gypsy paradigm]. Madrid: Editorial Presencia Gitana.

Liston, D. P., & Zeichner, K. M. (1991). *Teacher education and the social conditions of schooling.* New York & London: Routledge.

Liston, D. P., & Zeichner, K. M. (Eds.). (1996). *Culture and teaching: Reflective teaching and the social conditions of schooling.* Mahwah, NJ: Lawrence Erlbaum.

Losada, T. (1988). La inmigración árabe musulmana en los últimos veinte años [The Arab Muslim immigration along the past twenty years]. Report presented at the Congreso Árabe-Catalán sobre Inmigración, Barcelona.

Lynch, J., Modgil, C., & Modgil, S. (1992). *Cultural diversity and the schools. Education for cultural diversity: Convergence and divergence.* London & Washington, DC: Falmer Press.

Merino, J. V., Muñoz, A., & Sánchez, I. (1994). *La educación de niños inmigrantes extranjeros en los centros escolares de la Comunidad de Madrid* [The education of immigrant children in schools of the Madrid Autonomous Community]. Madrid: CIDE (Research Project).

Molina-Luque, J. F. (1994). *Sociedad y educación: Perspectivas interculturales* [Society and education: Intercultural perspectives]. Universitat de Lleida: PPU (Publicaciones Periódicas Universitarias [University Periodical Publications]).

Nieto, S. M. (1992). We speak in many tongues: Language diversity and multicultural education. In A. F. Ada & J. Tinajera (Eds.), *The power of two languages: Literacy and biliteracy for Hispanic students* (pp. 37-48). New York: Macmillan/McGraw Hill.

Nieto, S. M. (1996). *Affirming diversity: The sociopolitical context of multicultural education* (2nd ed.). New York: Longman.

Nieto, S. M. (1999). *The light in their eyes: Creating multicultural learning communities.* New York: Teachers College Press.

Pajares, M. (1999). *La inmigración en España: Retos y propuestas* [The immigration in Spain: Challenges and proposals]. Barcelona: Icaria.

Pérez-Domínguez, S. (1995a). Etnia, escuela y comunidad: El fenómeno migratorio y multicultural en el Reino Unido y sus posibles implicaciones para el caso español. Las políticas sociales europeas como eje vertebrador [Ethnic group, school and community: The migratory and multicultural phenomena in the United Kingdom and its possible implications for the Spanish case. The European social policies as an axis]. Unpublished work for the Department of Teoría e Historia de la Educación (University of Santiago de Compostela, Spain).

Pérez-Domínguez, S. (1995b). The European dimension in education within cultural and ethnic diversity: The challenge of multi/intercultural education. Paper presented at the International Conference: 1996: A plan for Europe? Politics, Economics, Culture. Brussels (European Parliament), September 9th to 16th; Salamanca (University of Salamanca), November 25th to December 1st; Madrid (Concert Hall), December 2nd to 3rd.

Pérez-Domínguez, S. (1995c). La educación multicultural en el Reino Unido: El caso de las "white schools" [Multicultural education in the United Kingdom: The case of the "white schools"]. Unpublished paper. University of Santiago de Compostela, Spain.

Pérez-Domínguez, S. (1997, February/March). The opinions of state primary (public elementary) school teachers regarding teaching in a multicultural and multiethnic society. Paper presented at the International Conference (Second

Annual Research Conference and Fourteenth Annual International Forum): Perspectives on education: Research and practice in diverse contexts. Harvard University, Cambridge, MA.

Pérez-Domínguez, S. (1999). Teachers' attituded about the integration of Roma: The case of Spain. *European Journal of Intercultural Studies* (now *Intercultural Education*) 10(2), 219-231.

Pumares-Fernández, P. (1993). Problemática de la emigración marroquí en España [The problems surrounding Moroccan immigration in Spain]. *Política y Sociedad, 12*, 139-147.

Rey, M. (1986). *Training teachers in intercultural education.* Strasburg, Austria: Council of Europe.

Rosales-López, C. (1994). El reto de la educación intercultural en la construcción del currículum [The challenge of intercultural education in the construction of the core curriculum]. In M. A. Santos-Rego (Ed.), *Teoría y práctica de la educación intercultural* [Theory and practice of intercultural education] (pp. 43-67). Barcelona: Universidad de Santiago de Compostela.

Russell, T., & Korthagen, F. (Eds.). (1995). *Teachers who teach teachers: Reflections on teacher education.* London & Washington, DC: Falmer Press.

Sales-Ciges, A., & García-López, R. (1997, August). Implementation of intercultural education programmes based on cooperative learning. Paper presented at the International Conference "Cooperation and diversity. Cooperative learning in intercultural education—Learning to know, learning to do, learning to be, learning to live together." Södertälje, Sweden.

San Román, T. (1992a). Pluriculturalisme i minories etniques (I) [Cultural pluralism and ethnic minorities, Vol. 1]. *Perspectiva Escolar, 164*, 41-44.

San Román, T. (1992b). Pluriculturalisme i minories etniques (II) [Cultural pluralism and ethnic minorities, Vol. 2]. *Perspectiva Escolar, 165*, 51-55.

San Román, T. (1993). Reprenent marginació i racisme: Hipotesi sobre el discurs i la seva genesi [Suppressing marginalization and racism: Hypothesis about its discourse and origin]. *Perspectiva Social, 35.*

San Román, T. (1997). *La diferencia inquietante. Viejas y nuevas estrategias culturales de los gitanos* [The scaring difference: Old and new cultural strategies of the Gypsies]. Barcelona: Fundació Serveis de Cultura Popular.

San Román, T. (Ed.) (1994). *Entre la marginación y el racismo. Reflexiones sobre la vida de los gitanos* [Between marginalization and racism: Reflections about the Gypsy lifestyle] (2nd ed.). Madrid: Alianza Editorial.

Santos-Rego, M. A. (1990). Estructuras de aprendizaje y métodos cooperativos en educación [Learning structures and cooperative methods in education]. *Revista Española de Pedagogía, 185*, 53-78.

Santos-Rego, M. A. (1994). La dimensión interactiva y el aprendizaje cooperativo como vía de educación intercultural [The interactive dimension and cooperative learning as a means of intercultural education]. In M. A. Santos-Rego (Ed.), *Teoría y práctica de la educación intercultural* [Theory and practice of intercultural education] (pp. 121-142). Santiago de Compostela: Universidad de Santiago de Compostela.

Santos-Rego, M. A., Cowan, B. J., & Pérez-Domínguez, S. (1995). La política multicultural y su práctica en un área del Reino Unido. Posibles implicaciones para el caso español [The multicultural policy and its practice in an area of the United kingdom: Possible implications for the Spanish case]. *Revista Bordón, 47*(3), 317-331.

Santos-Rego, M. A., & Nieto, S. M. (2000). Intercultural/multicultural teacher education: Perspectives from the United States and Spain. *Teaching and Teacher Education, 16*(4), 413-427.

Santos-Rego, M. A., & Pérez-Domínguez, S. (1997, August). Cooperation and diversity: A new role for teachers. Paper presented at the International Conference "Cooperation and diversity. Cooperative learning in intercultural education—Learning to know, learning to do, learning to be, learning to live together." Södertälje, Sweden.

Santos-Rego, M. A., & Pérez-Domínguez, S. (1998, September). Educación intercultural y formación del profesorado: Crece la necesidad [Intercultural education and teacher preparation: The need grows]. Paper presented at the IV Congresso Galaico-Português de Psicopedagogia, Universidade do Minho, Braga.

Sepa-Bonaba, E. (1993). *Els negres catalans* [The black Catalans]. Barcelona: Ed. Fundació Serveis de Cultura Popular y Altafulla.

Sleeter, C. E. (1996). *Multicultural education as social activism.* Albany: State University of New York.

Sleeter, C. E., & Grant, C. A. (1987). An analysis of multicultural education in the United States. *Harvard Educational Review, 57*(4), 421-444.

Sleeter, C. E., & Grant, C. A. (1994). *Making choices for multicultural education: Five approaches to race, class, and gender* (2nd ed.). New York: Maxwell Macmillan International.

Sleeter, C. E., & McLaren, P. L. (Eds.). (1995). *Multicultural education, critical pedagogy, and the politics of difference.* Albany: State University of New York.

Swartz, E. (1992). Multicultural education: From a compensatory to a scholarly foundation. In C. A. Grant (Ed.), *Research and Multicultural education: From the margins to the mainstream* (pp. 32-43). London & Washington, DC: Falmer Press.

Toffler, A. (1990). *El cambio del poder* [The change of the power]. Barcelona: Plaza y Janés.

Vázquez-Gómez, G. (1994). ¿Es posible una teoría de la educación intercultural? [Is intercultural education a feasible theory?] In M. A. Santos-Rego (Ed.), *Teoría y práctica de la educación intercultural* [Theory and practice of intercultural education] (pp. 25-41). Barcelona: Universidad de Santiago de Compostela.

Woods, P., & Hammersley, M. (Eds.) (1995). *Género, cultura y etnia en la escuela* [Gender, culture, and ethnic groups in the school]. Barcelona: Paidós/MEC.

Woolard, K. A. (1989). *Bilingualism and the politics of ethnicity in Catalonia.* Stanford, CA: Stanford University Press.

Zeichner, K. M. (1995). Reflection of a teacher educator working for social change. In T. Russell & F. Korthagen (Eds.), *Teachers who teach teachers: Reflections on teacher education* (pp. 11-24). London & Washington, DC: Falmer Press.

Zigler, E., & Muenchow, S. (1992). *Head Start: The inside story of America's most successful educational experiment.* New York: BasicBooks.

Chapter 11

Post-Apartheid Education in South Africa: Toward Multiculturalism or Anti-Racism

Jeremy Sarkin
University of the Western Cape, South Africa

South Africa is a multicultural society. However, before the 1994 transition to democracy little account was taken of the multiethnic, multilingual, and multicultural nature of South African society (Sarkin, 1998b). Indeed, the state catered almost exclusively to the White, Christian, Afrikaans, patriarchal minority (Sarkin, 1998a). It is not surprising, therefore, that South Africa was a highly polarized and divided society. Many people had been dispossessed of their land, had had their language and cultures marginalized, and had suffered gross human rights violations (Varney & Sarkin, 1997). The majority of South Africans were denied access to an enormous variety of amenities, institutions, and opportunities, including many places and types of employment, particularly in state institutions. Divisions existed between Black and White but there were also divisions based on ethnicity, class, culture, religion, and language, which apartheid specifically accentuated.

The system bred intolerance, a culture of violence, and a lack of respect for life and, indeed, rights in general (Sarkin, 1998b).

This chapter examines the question of transforming school education in South Africa to redress the inequalities of the past. It begins by examining the history of education in South Africa. Under apartheid children from different cultures received separate and unequal schooling. It then describes the transition to democracy and the new constitution's emphasis on equality and multiculturalism. It looks at the government's attempts to transform school education since 1994, through legislation and a new curriculum. It also examines the debates around whether multicultural education ought to be implemented in post-apartheid schools. Finally, it asks to what extent has school integration been achieved.

APARTHEID EDUCATION

This chapter[1] uses the terms *Blacks, Indians, Coloureds,* and *Whites* to refer to different South African groups' experience of education.[2] The Population Registration Act of 1950 divided all South Africans into these four groups and subsequent apartheid legislation was based on these categories. Blacks account for approximately 75% of the population.

The first school at the Cape of Good Hope was opened by the Dutch East India Company in 1658. This was 6 years after the Dutch arrived at the Cape to build a halfway station for traders traveling between Europe and the East. This school was designed to train slaves. Thereafter, schools were founded for children of colonists as the churches recommended that slave and colonist children be educated separately (Molteno, 1988). Thereafter, separate education occurred as a matter of course.

The 1905 School Board Act sanctioned de jure segregation in education (Finnegan, 1986). This act established local education authorities with the power to establish schools, raise money for education, and own school property. No provisions were made for the education of Black children. Whereas school attendance was compulsory for White children, this was not the case for Black children. Mission schools funded by overseas churches were primarily responsible for Black education (Pells, 1954).

By 1940, less than 25% of Black children between the ages of 6 and 16 were in school. Only about one in a thousand Black children received adequate elementary education (Pells, 1954). From 1930 to 1940, education spending on Black children was minimal.

When the National Party came to power in 1948 it began the institutionalization of apartheid. General laws entrenching White supremacy were enacted in quick succession. In 1953, the Bantu Education Act took Black education away from mission churches and

---

[1] See, generally, Michael Baffoe, The African Scene: The Shifting Power in South Africa. *Community Contact*, February 29, 1997, 6(2).

[2] The terms *Black, Coloured, Indian,* and *White* were the four racial groups that South Africans were divided into during Apartheid in terms of the Population Registration Act of 1950. Black refers to indigenous South Africans whose ancestors came from Africa. White refers to people of Caucasian origin who forebears came mostly from Europe from the 17th century onward. Coloured refers to people of mixed race origin, that is, descendents of both White and Black people. Indian refers to people who are descendents of the Indian community that arrived in the 1860s to work on the sugar plantations.

gave it to the state. The act further entrenched the separate and unequal systems of education in South Africa. According to Dr. Verwoerd, the architect of apartheid, the education system in place before the coming to power of his party had been misleading by showing Blacks "green pastures of European society in which [they are] not allowed to graze" (Finnegan, 1986, p. 123). The following quote from a speech made to Parliament during the debate on the Bantu Education Act succinctly captures Verwoerd's sentiments regarding Black education in South Africa:

> If the native in South Africa today in any kind of school in existence is being taught that he will live his adult life under a policy of equal rights, he is making a big mistake...[t]he natives will be taught from childhood to realize that equality is not for them...[t]here is no place for [Blacks] in the European community above the level of certain forms of labor. (Quoted in Ormond, 1985, p. 80)

In 1953 the South African government spent US $180 on the education of each White child, whereas the amount spent on each Black child was only US $25.

After 1953, the state began to implement its plan to force Blacks to live and be educated in the homelands or bantustans. These areas were to be given "independence" so as to reduce the number of Black people living in South Africa.

By 1980, 75% of all high schools for Blacks were found in the homelands, the government spent ten times as much per capita on White as on Black students, and school buildings and educational equipment for Black children were distinctly inferior. Education was still not compulsory for Black children. Teachers in Black schools were forced to use textbooks that expressed the racial views of the South African government. More importantly, most teachers in Black schools were poorly trained and far less qualified than those in White schools. Of White teachers, 97% had professional teaching qualifications, whereas two thirds of Black teachers did not even have the equivalent of a high school diploma (Eide, 1991). Furthermore, the teacher-pupil ratio for Whites was 19 to 1. For Blacks, that ratio approached 90 to 1. The extent of the problems Blacks faced educationally is illustrated by the fact that in 1978, when there were five times as many Black children as White children in South Africa, only 12,000 Blacks passed the exit exam required to graduate from high school, whereas 36,000 Whites passed the exit exam. In 1991, the estimates of illiteracy among Blacks ranged from 33% to 50%; for Whites, the illiteracy rate was 1%.

As far as language of schooling is concerned, under Bantu Education the government introduced compulsory "mother tongue instruction" for the first 8 years of a child's education. This means that schools would teach Black children in their native language from Grades 1 through 8. Once they reached high school, Bantu Education laws forced them to learn half their subjects in English and half in Afrikaans (the two main languages spoken by Whites in South Africa). This edict was extremely damaging to Black children. Eight years of study in their native language in no way prepared these students for the abrupt change to schooling in either Afrikaans or English.

THE NEGOTIATIONS AND EDUCATION

In the late 1980s, apartheid beg, an to crumble due to international as well as domestic pressures. On February 2, 1990, then President F.W. de Klerk set in motion the process that would lead to democratization 4 years later and the reincorporation of the Black homelands into South Africa.

One of the major themes of the negotiation process was the need to provide protection for minorities and the crucial debate was whether this should occur in terms of group rights or individual rights. The fear was that without the protection afforded by a bill of rights, unrestrained majoritarianism could harm minorities or members of minority groups and that therefore a check on the power of the majority was essential.

As the country negotiated a way forward between 1990 and 1994, developments in the country influenced debates and practices in schools.

In October ,1990, then Minister of Education Piet Clase announced that White schools could lawfully admit Black students (Carrim & Soudien, 1999). Thus, as the South African state began to transform itself towards a democracy, White schools began to accept children from other racial backgrounds (Carrim, 1992). This was particularly prevalent at private schools.

MULTICULTURALISM VERSUS ANTI-RACISM

The enrollment of Black, Coloured, and Indian pupils at historically White schools forced the schools to address the question of cultural diversity. At first the schools adopted an assimilationist approach, which assumed that all pupils should emulate a White cultural approach (Carrim, 1992). As the numbers of Black children entering these schools increased, particularly after 1994, so a shift from assimilation to multiculturalism occurred (Carrim & Soudien, 1999). The shift toward multiculturism became more marked between 1994 and 1996 as the enrollment of Black students in White schools grew. Carrim (1992) saw the shift to multiculturalism entailing

> ...a displacement of racial questions into foci on ethnic and cultural differences. However, rather than working with dynamic and complex senses of cultural identities, the multicultural practices that predominate in these schools' experiences tend instead to fix, stereotype, and caricature people's identities. (p. 314)

In addition, Carrim (1992) noted that there was and still is

> ...no nationally instituted anti-racist program or package which has been put into place. There are no structured, coordinated programs to help teachers cope with multiracial/cultural/lingual/ability classrooms. There are no nationally or provincially coordinated programs for students to develop anti-racist, anti-sexist, anti-discrimination awareness or consciousness in the formal workings of the school. (p. 318)

Carrim and Soudien (1999), in their study, have shown that the multicultural approach adopted did not perceive difference within racial groups, but saw Whites, for example, as a homogeneous group and not as Afrikaans, English, Jews, Greeks, and so on.

Teachers and other educationalists began an intense debate as to what educational practices ought to be developed to address the legacy of apartheid and the multicultural nature of South African society. The debate has produced two alternative approaches: multiculturalism versus anti-racism (Moore, 1994). For example, a Black Consciousness Movement intellectual argued:

> You also ask why so many people shy away from the multicultural education discourse. I think there are three main political reasons. The first is that apartheid sits up and stares you in the face as the logical consequence of thinking about people and culture in this way. ...Secondly, the African National Congress (ANC) and its allies have as their primary political goal the creation of a united, democratic, non-racial, and non-sexist South Africa. For them multicultural education sounds suspiciously like making difference a more fundamental principle than national unity. They therefore, you will find, are more suspicious of it than downright hostile to it. It is people whose roots lie in the Black Consciousness Movement (BCM) who most commonly are openly hostile to the concept of multicultural education. Since this is a very large number of people, this is the third reason why you will find hostility to this liberal concept in this

country. ...AZAPO (Azanian People's Organisation) reflects this general BCM position. ...It argues that since culture has been distorted by capitalism and manipulated by racism it cannot be the foundation for education policy. ...Education needs to be anti-racist...and you will find that the majority of people reject the so-called "cultural boxes" into which they have been put by the Government. This would make multicultural education a health hazard for teachers in township schools. (Sebidi, quoted in Moore, 1994, p. 240-241)

Advocates of the multicultural approach argued that:

The demand for multicultural education arises out of oppression which is seen to have important cultural connotations. In countries like the United States, Britain, Canada, Sweden, and Australia, it has come onto the educational agenda as one strategy to counteract what has been seen to be a process of cultural suppression and/or cultural assimilation. It has been a struggle for the recognition of minority cultures. In South Africa the demand for multicultural education has arisen out of the struggle against segregation and apartheid education. Everywhere multicultural education owes its origins to the resistance struggles of people against oppression. It is important to recognize this because it helps us to ask of any particular multicultural education policy or program, "how will this actually help people in their struggle for justice?" (Cross, cited in Moore, 1994, p. 252)

Also arguing in favor of multicultural education, educationalist Ruth Versveld stated:

Multicultural education has a major role to play in helping us achieve a national reconciliation. What apartheid has done is elevate ethnic difference to a primary principle for organizing society. It has segregated...people into supposedly cultural enclaves. It has created monocultural schools. This whole process has hidden us away from each other and bred ignorance and mistrust. It has also fostered ethnic nationalisms which it has rewarded with measures of power. This has helped to turn ignorance into a virtue and suspicion into open violence. Now, as the old system begins to break down and people start to move out of their cultural enclaves, the urgent need is for a curriculum which helps us along the path of national reconciliation by breaking down the old myths, ignorance, suspicion, prejudice, fear and fundamental disrespect. This will not be achieved by a papering over of our ethnic differences. The post-communist experience in Eastern Europe shows us just how disastrous are the consequences of underestimating the strength of culturally defined identities and ethnically-based nationalisms. If we do not deal creatively with this issue in South Africa then people here too are likely to throw self-protecting national boundaries around themselves. We need, in South Africa, a curriculum which values diversity, tolerance and appreciation of cultural differences and which also helps students manage cultural differences productively without resorting to violence or self-protecting isolationism. Multicultural education has the phenomenally difficult task of trying to bring people out of their isolation and to help them relate to one another without suppressing their differences.... (Quoted in Moore, 1994, pp. 253-254)

THE INTERIM CONSTITUTION'S BILL OF RIGHTS

Until April 27, 1994, the date of the first non-racial elections in South Africa, the White minority parliament was sovereign. The courts, staffed largely by White males, simply interpreted and implemented the law of the land, without being able to check state power. The legislature could adopt any law and the courts had only a procedural reviewing function. This changed when the interim Constitution came into force in April, 1994.[3]

The interim Constitution included a chapter on fundamental rights. This was the first time in South Africa's history that a bill of rights had been part of the legal order.

In addition to forbidding discrimination on the basis of "race" and "gender," the Bill of Rights also prohibited discrimination on the basis of sex, ethnic or social origin, color, sexual orientation, age, disability, religion, conscience, belief, culture, or language.[4]

The Bill of Rights insulated from constitutional challenge "measures designed to achieve the adequate protection and advancement of persons or groups or categories of persons disadvantaged by unfair discrimination."[5] In a similar vein, it provided for the "right to respect for and protection" of dignity, which has generally been deemed to be the right of individuals to be treated with dignity by the state.

The central importance of notions of equality can be seen in the provisions on religion, belief, and opinion. The Bill of Rights guaranteed the right to freedom of conscience, religion, thought, belief, and opinion. These provisions effectively reduced the power and influence of the church (particularly the Dutch Reformed Church, which partnered the apartheid regime), giving equal place for the first time to other religious denominations as well as to opinions and beliefs outside of organized religion (Sarkin, 1995a). A much stricter

---

[3] Section 251 of the Constitution of the Republic of South Africa Act 200 of 1993.
[4] Section 8(2).
[5] Section 8(3).

differentiation and separation between church and state was brought into being and, although the church is still able to influence individuals, it does not have the power to affect government policy.

In the past, despite the multilingual character of the population, South Africa had only two official languages—English and Afrikaans. One of the proposals during the negotiations was that the new democratic South Africa should officially recognize only a single language (English) in order to facilitate national unity, communication, and easier and cheaper administration. Those whose languages would have been excluded resisted this proposal and their view found favor with the drafters of the interim Constitution (Sarkin, 1999). Section 3 of the interim Constitution thus provided for 11 languages at national level and stated that "conditions shall be created for their development and for the promotion of their equal use and enjoyment." In addition, provision was made for the establishment of an independent Pan South African Language Board to develop South African languages as well as German, Greek, Gujerati, Hindi, Portuguese, Tamil, Telegu, Urdu, and other languages used by communities in South Africa, as well as Arabic, Hebrew, and Sanskrit, and other languages used for religious purposes.[6] In addition, the Bill of Rights provides that: "Every person shall have the right to use the language and to participate in the cultural life of his or her choice."[7]

The interim Constitution established a number of institutions to promote democracy and human rights. These structures were seen to be crucial, given the prior absence of human rights and the need to entrench a human rights culture and act against state repression, corruption, and anti-democratic practices. The institutions provided for included the Human Rights Commission,[8] the Commission on Gender Equality,[9] the Commission on the Restitution of Land Rights,[10] and the Public Protector.[11]

---

[6] Section 3(10)(c).
[7] Section 31.
[8] Sections 115-18.
[9] Sections 119-20.
[10] Sections 121-23.
[11] Sections 110-14.

THE BILL OF RIGHTS IN THE FINAL CONSTITUTION

The final Constitution came into force in February, 1997. The Bill of Rights in the final Constitution protects more rights than the interim Constitution did.

Clauses similar to those contained in the interim Constitution protect cultural, religious, and language rights. Among the provisions of the languages clause[12] is the duty of the Pan South African Language Board to "promote and create conditions for the development and use of" all official languages, the Khoi, San, and Nama languages, and sign language. The rights of cultural, religious, and linguistic communities are protected,[13] as is the right to freedom of religion, belief, and opinion.[14] It is noteworthy, however, that the exercise of cultural and religious rights is explicitly subject to conformity with the Bill of Rights.

A new body called the Commission for the Promotion and Protection of the Rights of Cultural, Religious, and Linguistic Communities was also established. This body was the result of compromise to accommodate the National Party's demands for special protection of language and cultural rights.

THE EFFECT OF THE CONSTITUTION ON EDUCATION

Education was necessarily affected by the constitutional changes (Sarkin, 1995b, 1996). Article 32 of the interim Constitution stated that every person shall have the right:

1. to basic education and to equal access to educational institutions;
2. to instruction in the language of his or her choice where this is reasonably practicable; and
3. to establish, where practicable, educational institutions based on a common culture, language, or religion, provided that there shall be no discrimination on the ground of race.[15]

---

[12] Section 6.
[13] Section 31.
[14] Section 15.
[15] The rights to practice one's culture, language, and religion, in addition to being considerations within the education clause, are fundamental rights of their own in the Interim Constitution. Freedom of religion is protected in Article 14, and Article

South Africa faced a massive overhaul of the educational system in order to afford all of its citizens the educational opportunities that had previously been granted only to Afrikaners (Enslin & Pendlebury, 1998). As with other major aspects of the country's transformation, the right to education was negotiated during the drafting of the interim and final constitutions (Sedibe, 1998).

To date, there have been two Constitutional Court cases examining education and the provision of it in relation to culture. In re Dispute Concerning the Constitutionality of Certain Provisions of the Gauteng School Education Bill of 1995[16] it was argued that certain clauses in the Gauteng province's School Education Bill violated the Constitution. It was contended that the Constitution imposed a positive obligation on the state to establish public schools based on a common culture, language, or religion. The court found that there was no such obligation.

The Final Constitution also has provisions regarding the right to education. Article 29 states:

1. Everyone has the right:
   (a) to a basic education, including adult basic education; and
   (b) to further education, which the state, through reasonable measures, must make progressively available, and accessible.
2. Everyone has the right to receive education in the official language or languages of their choice in public educational institutions where that education is reasonably practicable. In order to ensure the effective access to, and implementation of, this right, the state must consider all reasonable educational alternatives, including single medium institutions, taking into account:
   (a) equity,
   (b) practicability, and
   (c) the need to redress the results of past racially discriminatory laws and practices.
3. Everyone has the right to establish and maintain, at their own expense, independent educational institutions that:
   (a) do not discriminate on the basis of race;
   (b) are registered with the state; and
   (c) maintain standards that are not inferior to standards at comparable public educational institutions.

---

31 guarantees a person the "right to use the language and to participate in the cultural life of his or her choice."

[16] See In re School Education Bill of 1995 (Gauteng), 1996 (4) *Butterworths Constitutional Law Reports (BCLR)* 537 (CC). The other case was In re National Education Policy Bill 83 of 1995, 1996 (4) *BCLR* 518 (CC).

4.   Subsection 3 does not preclude state subsidies for independent educational institutions.

NEW EDUCATION LEGISLATION

Before April, 1994 there had been in all sectors much debate about what post-apartheid South Africa should look like. There were fierce debates as to what system and what processes ought to be developed to undo apartheid education.

The Creation of a National Ministry of Education

Before 1994 there were nearly 20 different authorities in charge of schooling in South Africa. The different racially and regionally separate departments of education administered different standards of education for the different racial groups.

In 1994 a National Ministry of Education was established to administer a unitary school system. The Department has responsibility for developing educational policies for the Republic of South Africa, monitoring educational progress of South African citizens, and setting educational norms and standards for the entire country. The new system made education compulsory for all children for the first time. Whereas South Africa's new system of education is a single national system, the nine provinces still have local control over school management. Provincial legislation affects the management and local funding of schools within each province.

The Reconstruction and Development Program providing free school lunches and launched in 1994 saw its role in education as ensuring that the education system would equalize the disparity between Black and White schools (Perkins, 1997). This program was eventually reduced in profile and has had little effect. As far as the discrepancy between White and Black schools is concerned, Jonathan Jansen, a Professor of Education, noted (1998a) that, "...measured in terms of net available onsite resources, the distance between Black and White schools has increased in this short period since the legal termination of apartheid in the early 1990s" (p. 7).

In 1996, Parliament passed the National Education Policy Act. The Act's objectives were to: a) provide for the determination of national education policy by the Minister of Education; b) mandate that the Minister of Education engage in consultative efforts prior to the determination of policy; c) provide for the publication and implementation of national education policy; and d) order the monitoring and evaluation of education.

The Schools Act

Parliament's next major step toward fulfilling the educational mandates of the new South African Constitution was the passage of the Schools Act in 1996. The Act's purpose was to provide a uniform system for governing and funding schools, so that all citizens may receive a quality education. Additional provisions of the Bill included: a) compulsory attendance for all children aged 7 to 15; b) all students have the right, free from racial discrimination and in accordance with the new Constitution, to receive an education in the official language of his or her choice; c) admission to public schools must not conflict with the Constitution—meaning, among other things, race should not hinder admission to a public school; and d) the state must fund all public schools on an equitable basis.

This Act was important because it set standards for the transformation of South Africa's educational system. This legislation abolished old apartheid education laws, established new laws, and "wiped the slate clean" for a fresh start in the reconstruction of education.

Curriculum 2005

In March, 1997, the Department of Education announced South Africa's new school curriculum: Curriculum 2005 (Duke, 1997). South Africa will phase in its Curriculum 2005 plan over an 8-year period, between 1998 and 2005 (Department of Education, March 1997). The new scheme will attempt to abolish the old apartheid educational system that encouraged passive and rote learning. Curriculum 2005 aims to produce critical thinkers and active learners by introducing new ways of learning (Department of Education, April 1997). It shifts from a content-oriented curriculum to one based on objectives or "outcomes." Peer learning will occur by questioning, debating, and finding viable solutions to problems. There will be eight broad learning categories that cover literacy and language learning; numeracy and mathematics (Cellier, Scheppers, & Glover, 1997); life orientation; human and social sciences; physical and natural sciences; arts and culture; economic and management sciences; and technology.

Students will no longer take a single exit test or examination at the end of their career. Instead, schools will now evaluate students progressively.

Curriculum 2005, based as it is on Outcome Based Education (OBE), has been criticized for a number of reasons (Jansen, 1997, 1998b). Jansen (1997), conducting research on Curriculum 2005 and OBE in South Africa, found that, "Almost every official I interviewed for the paper was privately critical of OBE. The same officials, though, would defend OBE in public as if it was the best discovery on the education landscape" (p. 8). Jansen (1998b) outlined the main criticisms of OBE in the South African context:

1. it is driven by political imperatives which have little to do with the realities of the classroom;
2. it is implicated in problematical claims and assumptions about the relationship between curriculum and society;
3. it is based on flawed assumptions about what happens inside schools, how classrooms are organized and what kinds of teachers exist;
4. there are strong philosophical reasons for questioning the desirability of OBE in democratic school systems;
5. there are important political and epistemological objections to OBE as curriculum policy;
6. OBE with its focus on instrumentalism...sidesteps the important issues of values in the curriculum;
7. the management of OBE will multiply the administrative burdens placed on teachers;
8. OBE trivializes curriculum content even as it claims to be a potential leverage away from the content coverage which besets the current education system;
9. An entire re-engineering of the education system is required to support the innovation. There is neither the fiscal base nor the political will to intervene in the education system at this level of intensity. Yet nothing less is required to give the policy a reasonable chance of success.

Exploring the racial dimension of teachers' acceptance of OBE, Jansen (1997) stated that:

Few black [sic] teachers were against OBE, although they expressed reservations about their level of preparedness to implement this new policy. More training and time was needed, they said. Among most white [sic] teachers I encountered there was general cynicism about OBE, largely because it was read as a strategy to undermine the privileges embedded in the status quo. OBE, among some white [sic] teachers, meant automatic passes for black [sic] students; the collapse of multiple grades or standards into one classroom; the loss of status for English; and the dropping of standards. (p. 8)

Thus, many believe that no matter how dynamic Curriculum 2005 is it will not succeed, because of pupil-teacher ratios, under-qualified teachers, and language barriers in and among the provinces. The high costs of implementing Curriculum 2005 are also seen as problematic (Mutume, 1998b).

In addition, the realization of Curriculum 2005 has been impeded by insufficient direction and supervision from the various levels of government. Whereas the national education department must design policy frameworks and set "norms and standards," it is the regions who must legislate on all aspects of education government. But, as each province has its unique context and issues, so each system has evolved differently (Education Policy Unit, 1998). Teacher strikes have also occurred because of the retrenchment of teachers, the deficiencies in service delivery in schools, and the proposed system for funding schools.[17] These strikes, and boycotts by teachers, parents, and pupils, have impeded the implementation of education, as has the unavailability of textbooks and other materials.

Funding of Schools

On the positive side, the National Norms and Standards for School Funding[18] was regulated in October 1998. These regulations handle the norms and standards in the distribution of finance to public schools and subsidies to independent schools. They provide for school fee exemptions for the poorest families. Also enacted was the Employment of Educators Act,[19] which specifies who employs each group of teachers, and makes the national level government responsible for many issues in education. It also contains the conditions of service of teachers and regulates appointment, incapacity, misconduct, promotion, transfer and terminations, and the role of school governing bodies in decisions around teachers.

---

[17] See Memorandum from SADTU to the National Economic Development and Labor Council, April 10, 1998.
[18] *Government Gazette* No. 19347.
[19] Act No. 76 of 1998.

HAS INTEGRATION BEEN SUCCESSFUL?

South Africa's transition has not always been easy.[20] Many sectors have experienced resistance to integration. Although schooling is becoming more integrated, this mostly applies to historically White schools. In the main, White children do not attend historically Black schools. Black schools still suffer from overcrowding, inadequate funding, under-qualified teaching staff, and various other problems ("South Africa's pupils...," *The Washington Post*, March 25, 1998). Pupil-teacher ratios in Black schools are extremely high. Teachers in Black schools are still poorly trained; two thirds of the teachers in Black schools do not even have the equivalent of a high school diploma. Resources for teaching in Black schools are scarce (Mutume, 1998b). Lack of proper supplies, books, and adequate libraries, and dilapidated facilities are just a few of the problems that plague Black schools. Despite the textbook shortages, the budget for these items was cut by 40% (Mutume, 1998a) and the education budget as a whole was cut by 6% for the year 1997/1998 (Mutume, 1998b). However, an extra R200 million was eventually or had to be eventually allocated for more textbooks ("Some of the...," *The Star*, November 3, 1998).

Although the integration of historically White schools has mostly proceeded smoothly, there have been a few well-publicized cases where White parents have resisted integration. For example, in January, 1996 in Potgietersrus, a group of Afrikaner parents tried to prevent African children from enrolling in the local school. In response, government officials joined the parents of the African schoolchildren in bringing a court action against the Afrikaner parents in February 1996.[21] The parents asserted that the presence of English speakers would negatively affect the quality of the Afrikaans-medium education and would erode the culture of the Afrikaners. The Supreme Court rejected this argument and ruled in favor of integration. The Afrikaner parents threatened to appeal the suit, but in the end did not, opting instead to protest at the school and to withdraw their own children from the school rather than tolerate an integrated education. Police officers

---

[20] There was, however, euphoria initially indicated by this comment of a citizen noted during the transition: "We are the happiest nation today...and if our new government can provide the promises they made—jobs, housing—I'm sure we will remain the happiest nation" ("The World's Happiest Nation...," 1994).

[21] See *African Review*, 2/1/97,1997 WL 10204067.

were stationed at the school to ensure the safety of the African children and their access to their constitutionally entrenched right to an education (This Weekend...," *The Guardian*, March 1, 1997).

Also in 1996, a White school in Trompsburg refused to allow Black children to register. A sit-in was held at the school to protest and White children moved to an all-White building on the school grounds, leaving the main building to the Black students ("Hopeful Notes...," *The Star*, April 24, 1998).

In February 1998, White parents attacked Black students at Vryburg High School who wanted to register at the school and who wanted to be instructed in a language other than Afrikaans, which was the primary medium of instruction at the school ("South Africa's Pupils...," *The Washington Post*, March 25, 1998).

Although many communities throughout South Africa have been able to adapt to the new schooling system, these incidents are not isolated. Some Afrikaners resist the change to racial integration by arguing that they will lose their culture. In face of the constitutional mandate regarding public schools, however, many Whites would rather send their children to school elsewhere than send them to a local integrated school. Thus, "White flight" has begun to occur in some communities. For example, when segregation ended in 1994, the White families of the small town of Philippolis sent their children away to attend private schools in Bloemfontein as weekly borders ("Where the Whites...," *Financial Times*, March 14, 1998).

CONCLUSION

This chapter has examined the transformation of school education in South Africa. Although the constitution and new legislation provide the conditions for free compulsory education of an equal quality for all South Africans, the reality is that the government is struggling to solve the problems inherited from the previous regime—that is, the poor quality of teaching and learning in black education due to a legacy of scarce spending on black education. The national education department recognized the crisis facing education in a February, 1998 submission to the Parliamentary Portfolio Committee on Education. In this document Trevor Coombe, Deputy Director General of Systems and Planning in the national department of education, conceded that the education department was "far from achieving our vision for education" and that the goal of remedying the past inequalities was "in danger of being sidetracked."[22] It was also acknowledged that administrative shortcomings, management indiscipline, and budgetary limitations seriously jeopardized service delivery and qualitative reform.

REFERENCES

African Review. (1997, September 21). WL 10204067. Act No. 76 of 1998. Saffron Walden, Essex, England: World of Information.

Baffoe, M. (1997). The African scene: The shifting power in South Africa. *Community Contact, 6*(2), 42-59.

Carrim, N. (1992). *Desegregating Coloured and Indian schooling.* Johannesburg: University of the Witwatersrand.

Carrim, N., & Soudien, C. (1999). Critical antiracism in South Africa. In S. May (Ed.), *Critical multiculturalism: Rethinking multicultural and antiracist education* (pp. 153-171). London: Falmer Press.

Celliers, N., Scheppers, N., & Glover, C. (1997). The learning locomotive: Curriculum 2005. *Numeracy Grade 1: Teachers Guide.* Hatfield: Nasou.

Department of Education. (1997, March). *Outcomes based education in South Africa: Background information to educators.* Pretoria: Government Printer.

Department of Education. (1997, April). *Curriculum 2005: Specific outcomes, assessment, criteria, range statements for Grades 1 to 9.* Pretoria: Government Printer.

Duke, L. (September 30, 1997). South African children embrace post-apartheid education: Schools in poorest areas struggle with new curriculum. *The Washington Post,* A01.

Education policy unit. (1998, May 15). *Quarterly Review of Education and Training, 5*(3), 333-349.

Eide, L. (1991). Current crises facing children in South Africa and efforts to overcome it. *Howard Law Journal, 34,* 37-40.

Enslin, P., & Pendlebury, S. (1998, November). Transformation of education in South Africa. *Cambridge Journal of Education, 28*(3), 333-349.

Finnegan, W. (1986). *Crossing the line: A year in the land of apartheid.* New York: Harper & Row.

Hopeful notes amid a land of flux. (1998, April 24). *The Star.*

In re National Education Policy Bill 83 of 1995, 1996 (4) *Butterworths Constitutional Law Report (BCLR),* 518 (CC).

In re School Education Bill of 1995 (Gauteng), 1996 (4) *Butterworths Constitutional Law Report (BCLR),* 537 (CC).

Jansen, J. (1997, September). Professor stands by his OBE paper. *The Teacher, 7,* 23-32.

---

[22] See Submission to the Parliamentary Portfolio Committee on Education, by the Department of Education, February, 1998. See further, *The Star,* February 25, 1998.

Jansen, J. (1998a). Why policy creates inequality. Address to the CHRI/IDASA Symposium. Cape Town, South Africa.

Jansen, J. (1998b). Curriculum reform in South Africa: A critical analysis of outcome based education. *Cambridge Journal of Education, 28*(3), 321-323.

Molteno, F. (1988). The historical foundations of the schooling of Black South Africans. In P. Kallaway (Ed.), *Apartheid and education: The education of Black South Africans* (pp. 44-107). Braamfontein, Johannesburg: Ravan Press.

Mutume, G. (1998a, February). Education—South Africa: Fewer funds for a system in shambles. *Inter-Press Service.*

Mutume, G. (1998b, June). Economy—South Africa: Macro-economic policies will hurt Education. *Inter-Press Service.*

Ormond, R. (1985). *The apartheid handbook.* Harmondsworth, Middlesex, England: Penguin Books.

Pells, E. G. (1954). *300 years of education in South Africa.* Cape Town, South Africa: Juta & Co.

Perkins, O. (1997, November 24). Unfulfilled promise: After apartheid South Africa. *Plain Dealer Reporter,* 1A.

Sarkin, J. (1995a). Abortion and the courts. In S. Liebenberg (Ed.), *Towards a final constitution: A gender perspective* (pp. 217-247). Cape Town, South Africa: Community Law Centre, University of the Western Cape.

Sarkin, J. (1995b). A study of the effect on corporal punishment of the South African transitional constitution and bill of rights. *International Journal of Children's Rights, 3*(1-17), 369-389.

Sarkin, J. (1996). Problems and challenges facing South Africa's constitutional court: An evaluation of its decisions on capital and corporal punishment. *South Africa Law Journal, 103,* 71-93.

Sarkin, J. (1998a). The effect of patriarchy and discrimination on apartheid South Africa's abortion laws. *Buffalo Human Rights Journal, 4,* 141-175.

Sarkin, J. (1998b). The development of a human rights culture in South Africa. *Human Rights Quarterly, 20*(3), 628-665.

Sarkin, J. (1999). The effect of constitutional borrowings on the drafting of South Africa's interim Bill of Rights and the role played by comparative and international law in the interpretation of human rights provisions by the Constitutional Court. *Journal of Constitutional Law, 2,* 34-59.

Sedibe, K. (1998). Dismantling apartheid education: An overview of change. *Cambridge Journal of Education, 28*(3), 269-282.

Some of the key allocations. (1998, November 3). *The Star.*

South Africa's pupils failing to graduate: System remains scarred by apartheid. (1998, March 15). *The Washington Post,* A18.

Submission to the Parliamentary Portfolio Committee on Education by the Department of Education. (1998, February 25). *The Star,* 11.

This weekend last year: February 23, 1996—Apartheid lost stand at the school gates. (1997, March 1). *The Guardian,* 14.

Varney, H., & Sarkin, J. (1997). Failing to pierce the hit squad veil: An analysis of the Malan trial. *South African Journal of Criminal Justice, 10,* 141-161.

Where the Whites.... (1998, March 14). *Financial Times*, B6.

World's happiest nation: Mandela's oath, event to treasure. (1994, May 11). *Cincinnati Post*, 5.

Chapter 12

Color Me Black, Color Me White: Teacher Education in the Aftermath of the Apartheid Era—In Search of a Critical Multicultural Perspective Among a Complexity of Contradictions

Patti Swarts
Lars O. Dahlström
National Institute for Educational Development, Namibia

. . . as the saying goes, tribalism is the last refuge of a scoundrel!

—Minister Nahas Angula, Ministry of Higher
Education, Vocational Training, Science
and Technology, Namibia
NEW ERA (October 10–12, 1997, p. 9)

A HISTORICAL AND SOCIAL CONTEXT

This chapter[1] addresses teacher education in Namibia from a broad cultural, social, and political perspective. It is our belief that it is necessary to apply an approach that analyzes the broad contextually based forces affecting life and implementation of educational policy to create an understanding from which further educational development can emerge.

In Namibia, as in other African countries, education can be divided into three periods: (a) pre-colonial; (b) colonial; and (c) post-independence (Halls, 1990). Even though this chapter concentrates on the colonial and post-independence periods, we start with some reflec-

---

[1]The title of this chapter refers to a song by Steve Kekana, a South African artist, who recorded *Noma Ngi Nyama*—Color Me Black—in 1981.

tions that bring us back to the pre-colonial period and the contextual development since then

As in most parts of the world, the social struggle for power and hegemony between ethnic groups has also taken place in pre-colonial southern Africa. The early migration of Africans from central parts of the continent resulted in the arrival of most Bantu groups, including the largest group of Ovambos, in the 16th century to the areas that are now part of Namibia, which at that time was the home of the San people (Bushmen). Already the names of the different tribes indicate an early social order, as the name *Ovambo* is derived from Ajamba, meaning "the rich," whereas the name *Ovahimba* stands for "poverty." The very fact that the names of the Ovambos and Ovahimbas were developed from the Herero language is another indication of the historical social stratification, where the power to name ethnic groups reflects a powerful social position by the Hereros and a position that also gave the Hereros the power to semantically discriminate between the Ovambos and the Ovahimbas on economical grounds as one being richer than the other (Tötemeyer, 1978).

Although the common understanding is that the basis for the present social order was created during the colonial period through the exploiting and "divide and rule" policies by the colonial powers of Germany and South Africa, many researchers claim that poverty and a massive social stratification already existed before the colonial period. Pankhurst (1996) claimed that a strata of economically strong herders developed in parts of the country even before independence by stating that "such herders had accumulated such a degree of wealth and control over land that in Hereroland, at least, they resembled a black [sic] rural bourgeoisie" (p. 419). Even though the Ovambos were named as "the rich," it has been shown that poverty and related sufferings in the northern part of Namibia were widespread even before the colonial era and that communities "were already under stress from famine, drought, cattle and human epidemics, and all these problems continued throughout the early colonial periods" (p. 415). The pre-colonial constraints are also addressed in a handbook produced by SWAPO (South West Africa People's Organization) of Namibia in 1984:

> Education in pre-colonial Namibia expressed the interests of the semi-feudal ruling chieftaincy and the like. The subject people were assimilated into the culture of deliverance to, and reverence for the ruling chieftaincy. Popular culture transmitted through the family, the peer group and society at large, was the main form of education. Such societies were firmly cemented together by the feeling of collective insecurity. The low technical base, matched by an unyielding ecology, militated against meaningful

surplus production. Hunger and famine were not, therefore, unfamiliar experiences in pre-colonial Namibia. (SWAPO, 1984, p. 5)

The stratification of the society accelerated especially during the second colonial phase under the South African apartheid regime and through its institutionalization of racist policies following the German rule over Namibia, which, among other atrocities, also included the genocide of a large portion of the Herero communities.

The people in the North were in a specifically vulnerable situation. "In fact the search for alternative sources of income besides farming, including employment away from home, pre-dated colonialism, which arguably made some communities more susceptible to state efforts to obtain cheap migrant labor than others" (Pankhurst, 1996, p. 415). The extreme patterns of inequalities in Namibia accentuated and manifested through the apartheid subjugation were reasons enough for the resistance against the apartheid regime and the start of the armed liberation struggle in the mid 1960s, which led to independence in 1990.

The larger social and historical context for multicultural education in Namibia is one of a dichotomy between the "haves" and the "have-nots." This dichotomy has its roots in the history of the country manifested through decades of official racist practices instituted by the state and its agents and is still today, years after independence, the main obstacle for the development of a democratic social and economic order in Namibia.

A recent report by UNDP (United Nations Development Program) (1996) expresses in its foreword in relation to the publication of data on the Namibian Human Development Index that "a shocking picture of 'poverty in the midst of plenty' emerges. In fact, Namibia is the most unequal country in the world, outdoing both South Africa and Brazil for this dubious honor." The Gini-coefficient, which according to a UNDP report in 1997 is a widely accepted measure of income distribution, is 0.67 for Namibia. The report (UNDP, 1997) characterizes the Namibian economy as a bi-modal income distribution and states that a reference to an average income is meaningless as hardly anybody is an average income earner. Another report on the Namibian economy published in January 1998 states that "Although government sets aside significant proportions of its budget for education and health every year, the overcoming of inherited deficiencies is a long term process, and has not yet been reflected in significant changes" (Hansohm, Mupotola-Sibongo, & Motinga, 1998, p. 1).

A tentative assessment of the present social structures of the Namibian society indicates that "Namibia is still characterized by socioeconomic dualism inherited from the apartheid colonial system"

(Jochem, 1998). Jochem stated that the economy is service oriented, expresses a dualism with poor links between the rural and urban economies, constitutes large numbers of low-skilled, unemployed, and under-employed members in the labor force (of which 60% were unemployed or underemployed in 1996, according to the National Household Income and Expenditure Survey), and that over 70% of the country's national income is generated by 5% of the population, mainly Whites (Jochem, 1998).

Linking this description of the Namibian society to the often positive attitudes amongst the privileged people toward the policy of reconciliation (see, e.g., Basson, 1998), a reflection is that reconciliation has manifested the continuation of a social and economic dichotomy.

In an article on the education system after independence, //Gowaseb (1998) referred to an interview with Henning Melber, Director of the Namibian Economic Research Policy Unit (NEPRU), who said that "Namibia's education model is derived from the questionable blueprint of industrialized capitalist societies" and an exclusion policy effectuated through a doubtful approach that supports the survival of the fittest. Melber is a proponent of a home-grown education system that applies an inclusion policy, which is in line with the general educational policy but might not always be the case when it comes to implementation. Melber's view is supported by Diphofa (1995, pp. 35-40) who stated that in South Africa the crisis in education was not due only to unequal capital and per capita expenditure, but also to the irrelevance of the curriculum and the illegitimacy of the system. Teachers were trained and expected to facilitate the legitimization of a racial-capitalist order. They were taught that the type of authority exercised in education was a "derived" authority: that the authority of teachers over learners, of principals over teachers, and of departments over schools, was derived from elsewhere. At the heart of this view was the assumption that nobody was to challenge the authority, even when they were excluded. In fact, everyone in the system was conditioned to accept exclusion, especially Black teachers. Because the same educational paradigm and the same policies applied in Namibia before independence, this situation was also found in Namibia.

A critical multicultural perspective has to consider these historical, social, and economical realities and their strong impact on the lives of Namibians beyond the political slogans of reconciliation and affirmative action.

EDUCATION DURING THE COLONIAL PERIOD

In the colonial period, education was segregated along racial and ethnic lines, and as a result was organized in three systems of education: one for the *Blacks* (of African origin), one for the *Coloureds* (of mixed origin), and one for the *Whites* (of European origin). "The implications were one form of education for whites [sic], a reduced form for the Coloured population and an even more reduced education for the black [sic] population" (Storeng, 1994, p. 86). Racial discrimination was the basis for government policies in Namibia during the apartheid years, and was used to exaggerate intergroup differences while minimizing intragroup differences.

The segregation of society along racial lines ensured that schooling was the privilege of a few, based on the philosophy to educate elites. The concept of human nature with certain individual characteristics of different ethnic groups was reflected in the type of education deemed to be necessary for especially the Black groups to fashion them into "hewers of wood and drawers of water."

After their victory in South Africa in 1948, the Afrikaner National Party set about entrenching their policy of apartheid, reinforcing racial separation and domination by the White minority over the Black majority in all spheres of life. Christian National Education became the official policy for Whites as a means to protect their cultural and economic interest, whereas for the Blacks the colonial government introduced Bantu Education (Swarts, 1998). The adoption of Bantu Education meant a very restricted curriculum for Blacks, ensuring that they would be literate in their mother tongue and be able to make basic calculations, as well as having a basic knowledge of Afrikaans and English. In this way they would only be equipped to perform unskilled work in line with Verwoerd's policy, which stated very clearly:

> There is no place for the native in the European [white] community, above the level of certain forms of labor.... When I have control of native education I will reform it so that natives will be taught from childhood to realize that equality with Europeans is not for them. (Quoted in Ellis, 1984, p. 23)

Teaching, nursing, the police, service in the church, public service, and local government were the only fields available to Blacks with some schooling. The missions established six teacher training institutions at which entry was after Standard 6 (eight years of schooling). The qualifications of teachers were lower than those of the Whites and Coloureds, as were the salaries. Because the education at secondary level was inadequate, too few of the teacher trainees had the necessary preparation for teacher training.

Concerning educational opportunity, the Coloured learners did not have much more scope than the Black learners who were severely restricted in the choice and scope of career opportunities. Coloureds, however, were not restricted to 4 years of education, as was the case for Black learners. Their curriculum was similar to those of the Whites, but the resources available to them were little more than those for the Blacks, resulting in very limited opportunity to progress beyond the lower grades (Cohen, 1994).

The White privileged position was entrenched and reinforced by the apartheid system and great inequities and disparities in terms of educational provision, quality of provision, and provision of resources were created. According to Cohen (1994) the "greater government financial backing they enjoyed meant high quality facilities, while the admittedly superior education they were exposed to inculcated leadership and elitist values and prepared them for dominant roles in the society" (p. 104).

As a result of these conditions, by the late 1950s young Namibians started to flee the country in search of education and to fight for independence. The South West African People's Organization (SWAPO), now the ruling party but then in exile, recognized that after attaining independence the educational system would have to undergo fundamental changes to serve the interests of all Namibians. Within the general framework of SWAPO's policy for national independence and social reconstruction, education was given a central role (Swarts, 1998).

The National Education Act (Act No. 30 of 1980) replaced the Bantu Education Act (Act No. 47 of 1953) and brought control to the Department of National Education (DNE) of all primary and secondary education that did not fall to an ethnic authority. In instances where the ethnic authorities chose not to exercise their educational responsibilities, these could be performed by the DNE. The DNE was also to provide professional services at primary and secondary school level to the ethnic authorities on request.

In 1985 the DNE appointed an Education Committee to look into the issue of improvement of education and to submit proposals in that regard. The report observed and noted inequality and discrepancies in the provision of education and the distribution of financial resources as well as in access to qualified teachers. However, recommendations put forward could not in any way "make education available to the impoverished African majority" (Amukugo, 1993, pp. 93-94) as the

DNE and the ethnic authorities had some say in educational matters, but no real political power to effect real change. Amukugo referred to this as colonial "oppression in an invisible way" (p. 99). This was the state of affairs in education when Namibia gained its independence in 1990.

SWAPO, totally opposed to the kind of education experienced by the majority of Namibians, was adamant that a new education system had to be an antithesis of the colonial system and therefore started to prepare for social and political programs that could help Namibians to overcome the colonial legacy and to participate in the creation of a new society.

TEACHER EDUCATION DURING THE COLONIAL PERIOD

Before independence teacher education, like education in general, had been controlled and regulated by the different ethnic authorities. The teacher training programs were designed to produce teachers for the ethnic administrations that controlled them and therefore differed considerably in terms of scope, structure, content, sequence, duration, philosophy, entry requirements, and exit competencies. The White and Coloured groups had their own colleges of education, offering programs exclusively for teachers belonging to their specific groups and preparing them for teaching in the schools under their specific ethnic authorities report. The Academy for Tertiary Education, through its satellite campuses at Ongwediva, Rundu, and Katima Mulilo, provided teacher training for the Black authorities. Thus Namibian teachers belonging to the three main ethnic divisions were trained in isolation from each other and worked in isolation from each other. Even where they taught in the same schools (as a result of not enough qualified Black teachers to teach in Black schools), they stayed within their subgroups with very little and superficial contact with teachers from other ethnic groups.

The statistics for teachers employed from 1982 to 1990 show a steady increase in the numbers of teachers employed by the DNE. Because no reliable statistics are available from the different ethnic administrations, the DNE figures in Table 12.1 are used to illustrate the trend.

TABLE 12.1
Teachers According to Ethnic Groups, 1982-1986

Population Group	1982	1986
Bushman	2	0
Caprivian	1	3
Coloured	40	81
Damara	325	370
Herero	210	271
Kavango	16	81
Nama	36	45
Rehoboth Baster	4	9
Tswana	73	67
Ovambo	41	160
White	81	315
Other	36	41
TOTAL	1,065	1,375

Note. Source: DNE statistics.

Because there is a definite connection between the level of formal education and professional training of teachers, and the quality of teaching, it can therefore be concluded that poor instruction and low-level performance was the trend in the majority of Black schools. Table 12.2 indicates teacher qualifications for the different ethnic groups in 1990.

TABLE 12.2
Teacher Qualifications According to Former Ethnic Authority, 1990

Authority	Std 10	Std 10+	Total
Admin. for Whites	6	1,109	1,115
Admin. for Caprivians	513	269	782
Admin. for the Damara	256	165	421
Admin. for the Herero	593	103	696
Admin. for the Kavango	1,190	90	1,280
Admin. for Coloureds	173	472	645
Admin. for the Nama	295	214	509
Admin. for the Tswana	17	23	40
Admin. for Ovambo	4,754	422	5,176
DNE	871	1,062	2,033
Gov. of Rehoboth	166	368	534
TOTAL	8,934	13,231	4,297

Note. Source: EMIS, Ministry of Education, Culture, Youth and Sport, 1990.

EDUCATION AFTER INDEPENDENCE

When Namibia gained its independence from South Africa on March 21, 1990, it entered into a social transformation process. SWAPO assumed power and started to challenge and replace the ideologies and power bases supporting the colonial social system. As education was seen to be in a position to play a pivotal role in nation building and in healing the wounds of apartheid, the entire education system had to be transformed and reformed in line with the visions, major goals, and policies of the new government. However, the transformation of the educational system did not take place without resistance from the privileged minority, and the ideological struggles are still continuing as any change, and therefore also educational change, is accompanied by ideological struggle (Swarts, 1998). The post-independence goals of access, equity, pedagogical effectiveness, internal efficiency, and democratic participation, as spelled out in the policy document "Toward Education for All" (MEC, 1993), necessitated a paradigm shift from a content-based education for a few, to a learner-centered system for all, which required dramatic and radical changes in the content and processes of teacher education.

POST-INDEPENDENCE REFORM OF TEACHER EDUCATION

Even before independence the unevenness of the teacher education programs caused concern. In 1989 SWAPO organized an international conference in Lusaka to discuss teacher education and the role it needed to play in an independent Namibia. Dahlström (1995) stated that, "... perhaps the most important aspect of the conference was that it catered for the first major official confrontation between the educational philosophy and practices carried out by SWAPO in exile and representatives from the old establishment, thus preparing the ground for the new system after independence" (p. 279).

Important fact-finding missions preceded the Lusaka conference like Callewaert and Kallos (1989) and program reviews like Dahlström and Janson (1989), which together with a later report by Andersson, Callewaert, and Kallos (1991) came to have an impact on the new policies after independence.

After independence the government followed a policy of national reconciliation to foster national harmony and mutual understanding to pave the way for effective integration. Those who had belonged to different ethnic authorities and who had become used to working in unrelated systems, as well as those who had been in exile for many years, were brought together and were expected to work together in establishing a new education system. Dahlström (1995) stated in this regard:

> The reform process started in a situation where many civil servants from one day to another were supposed to implement a policy in sharp contrast to the old one. Many of these civil servants, with a few significant exceptions, did not appreciate the need for change and were reluctant to administer the new policy and advocated "improvements" of the old system. (p. 275)

The contradictions in the Namibian situation after independence were also reflected in the development process of teacher education. Although there was a strong need for a national agenda as opposed to the previous "divide and rule" policy, the new democratic order also called for decentralization and the implementors' participation in decision making. The National Institute for Educational Development (NIED), assigned to be the innovative center in the reform, was caught in between these disparate demands. NIED was commissioned to lead the reform efforts in teacher education, and the new national program, Basic Education Teacher Diploma (BETD), was introduced at all four colleges of education in 1993. The first stage in the transition period after independence was characterized by a strong urge for nation building and to create a common foundation for teacher education among the previously divided colleges. Measures like a number of national seminars when all teacher educators met in different parts of the country was part of this strategy, which at times could be experienced as rather frustrating. Many initiatives and activities emanated from NIED and the central administration in Windhoek during this period and it was not until later that the second stage of a more shared responsibility for the development of the program was implemented. There are certainly different opinions about the timing of these two stages both from a nation building and a decentralization perspective, but the general assessment of this process is that the new leadership after independence recognized the need to unite the previously divided and ethnic-oriented institutions under a national educational policy.

The BETD is a unified program for all teachers in basic education, that is, Grade 1 to 10, and BETD graduates receive a broad competency to teach either in Grade 1 to 7 or in Grade 5 to 10, with a specialization in one of the phases in basic education, i.e., Grade 1-4, Grade 5-7, or Grade 8-10. One significant reason for creating this broad competency among teachers in basic education is that it can cater to the needs of education in small and marginalized communities. All BETD graduates also get the same salary, thus breaking the long tradition in formal education to reward teachers with better salaries the higher they serve in the education system.

The development of the BETD was based on the Namibian Constitution and guided by the four goals of *access, equity, quality,* and *democracy.* It is based on a democratic pedagogy, a methodology that promotes learning through understanding, and practice directed toward empowerment to shape the conditions of one's own life (MBEC & MHEVTST, 1998, pp. 1-2). This is consistent with Dewey's vision of democracy that sees a community of various groups and individuals in dialogue. Lasch (in Kaplan & Kaplan, 1997, p. 425) called Dewey's vision "civic equality" that calls for equal participation of all citizens in identifying, discussing, and solving community problems. This "civic equality" of the educational fraternity is in sharp contrast to the pre-independence authoritarian conception of teaching and learning that legitimized the actions of the state and excluded the teacher from participation and decision making.

Namibia has taken a strong stand against the previous rote learning and authoritarian practices in African schools, which has its roots in a mixture of traditional and conservative Western and religious schooling. The BETD Broad Curriculum also spells out that the teachers "must be able to meet the challenges of the realities of an educational system in change and development" and that the main aim is "to promote change toward the goals of the educational reform in Namibia" (MBEC & MHEVTST, 1998, pp. 2, 4). This represents some of the evidence of the strong bias toward change in the official policy directives for the educational reform in Namibia. However, the contradictions between the policy directives and the way the broader social development since independence is perceived is sometimes striking, which we attend to later in this chapter, from a multicultural perspective.

Most of the 19 specific aims of teacher education expressed in the BETD Broad Curriculum can provoke questions related to the diversity of the Namibian society. A few examples are given as follows:

Key words from the BETD Aims	Questions related to the diversity of the Namibian society
Cultural Values and Beliefs	• How are the different Namibian cultural values and beliefs, traditional as well as modern, taken into consideration in teacher education? • Which values and beliefs flourishing in the Namibian society cannot be accepted in teacher education?
Human Dignity and Needs	• How can teacher education support and develop a perspective that answers to the needs and human dignity of all citizens, including AIDS victims, Bushmen (San people), and other marginalized groups, who are treated like outcasts or servants by others?
Social Responsibility	• What kind of social responsibility should teacher education encourage? • Social responsibility toward whom? • A social responsibility that is based on solidarity with others beyond your own social group?
Gender Awareness and Equity	• In what way can teacher education develop awareness beyond the stereotyped and traditional gender attitudes? • What is the role of teacher education in affirmative actions toward gender equity in education?

The same type of questions can be asked about key words such as Social and Individual Needs and Abilities, Attitudes toward Individual Differences, Partnership between School and Community, Namibian Languages, Creative and Expressive Abilities and Skills, Learning is Interactive, Shared, and Productive, Different Ways of Knowing, and Knowledge about Intellectual, Emotional, Social, Aesthetic, Moral, and Spiritual Development.

The BETD program is delivered at the four colleges of education in the country with the following number of teacher educators and students, as shown in Table 12.3.

TABLE 12.3
Staff and Students at the Colleges of Education

Category	CCE	RCE	OCE	WCE	Total
Professional Staff	24	14	53	55	146
BETD Students	383	367	834	544	2,128

Note. CCE = Caprivi College of Education; RCE = Rundu College of Education; OCE = Ongwediva College of Education; WCE = Windhoek College of Education. Data from January, 1998.

The BETD is the only program that the colleges are offering, and the program is still in a developmental stage. A revised BETD Broad Curriculum has recently been approved by the two educational ministries, and revised subject syllabuses are implemented from this year, which have been developed during the last 2 years by teacher educators and coordinated from NIED, through a national appraisal process based on a network of subject groups across the four colleges. There is still a lot of work to be done on the implementation on classroom level in relation to the new philosophy of learner-centered and democratic education, even though Andersson and Murangi (1997) found that BETD graduates have a fairly good understanding and capacity to implement the new philosophy in their own classrooms.

Other data confirms that much of the college-based studies are still subject-content oriented; a large proportion of the studies are based on individual assignments, class work, and lectures; the study material is in most cases handouts from the teacher educator, and the studies are mostly organized as secondary education with a number of isolated lessons taking place during the day. When BETD students were asked how the studies were related to the new philosophy their answers indicated that their perceptions of the BETD philosophy included central concepts like participation, sharing, working together, and research-related activities (Dahlström, 1997).

Although there was a broad consensus among the majority of Namibians after independence that the prevailing educational practices had to be changed, we believe that there was only a small number of Namibians, partly because of the isolations during the apartheid era, who had had a possibility to broaden their perspectives beyond the traditional educational practices and develop perceptions of the "new order" through models for alternative practices and to develop new theoretical and practical understandings of pedagogy. The introduction of a national and full-scale "piloting" of the BETD program created a period of educational conceptualization integrated with the actual implementation of the program at all levels. This was probably an unintended, but in retrospect, necessary, dynamic, and integrated process of implementation and conceptualization, which created many frustrations along the road as it did not follow a linear development process, which most practitioners, policymakers, and a number of external advisors and donors did expect and were trying to identify in their appraisal of the development process. Instead the development process was characterized by a search and "re-search" for appropriate representations and conceptualizations in the attempts to create a common understanding of the pedagogical issues and policies. This kind of growth process was a new experience for many of the people involved in the reform efforts at all levels (Dahlström, 1998a).

A Namibian knowledge base about education and the development process after independence is emerging from the experiences of and practitioner inquiries carried out by students, teacher educators, and education officers. This knowledge base is important to nurture as it is a way to bring to the surface the frustrations and lost opportunities, but even more important, the successes and creative ideas, which have been allowed to develop in this complexity of contradictions, as the legacy of the apartheid system continues to trouble the country 10 years after independence.

This legacy contains elements of mistrust on the sides of both the White minority and the Black majority. Thus, two "societies" are identified with very different perceptions and expectations of the education system and what it can or cannot do for them (Avenstrup & Swarts, 1992). It is within the context of these two, or multiple, "societies" that we are examining a critical multicultural perspective, which can address the complexity of the Namibian society. Examples are drawn from one of the four colleges of education to illustrate how the battleground for reconciliation, affirmative action, control, and hegemony still affects the reform of teacher education and the possibilities to develop Namibia into a democratic and people-centered society.

TOWARDS CRITICAL MULTICULTURAL PERSPECTIVE

A range of policy documents for education produced by SWAPO before independence and by the ministries of education after independence have touched on culture and education. SWAPO's policy objectives on education included the goal to "unite all the people of Namibia, irrespective of race, religion, sex, or ethnic origin, into a cohesive, representative, national political entity" as well as to "combat all reactionary tendencies of individualism, tribalism, racism, and regionalism" (SWAPO, 1984, p. 9). In one of the first documents produced by the Designated Minister for Education, Culture, and Sports, the goals of education were summarized in six points:

1.   Provide education to all the children up to the age of 16.
2.   Ensure that such education is free and compulsory.
3.   Enhance the cultural rights of individuals.
4.   Devise educational programs that are based on the ideals of the universality of human knowledge, culture, and technology.
5.   Articulate educational programs that enhance the development of the full potentialities and personality of the learners.
6.   Put into motion an administrative structure that will promote the achievement of such goals. (SWAPO, 1990)

In a contemporaneous workshop address, the Designated Minister expressed that "without cultural enhancement of the social forces one cannot expect the full development of democracy as enshrined in our Constitution" (Angula, 1990, p. 3). Angula continued and stated:

Moreover, without equal access to meaningful education for all, the concept of equal opportunity will remain a hollow slogan.

Education is, therefore, an arena of competing claims to access to national power and wealth. If the national education system is not fair to all its citizens so will it be likely that power and wealth will be unfairly distributed within society. The situation in our country today is precisely characterized by this phenomenon.

Namibia today is a country of two nations; the well educated section, highly remunerated...the so-called "first world nation"...; and the ill-educated section...with low standard of living...the so called "third world nation." (pp. 3-4)

In a recent position paper (Dahlström, 1998b) for a suggested staff development program for teacher educators, we have pointed to the effects of the so-called globalization, which should be considered from the cultural and social dichotomy described in different ways earlier. One of the most basic features of schools in Africa is that they are operating in an environment that for the great majority consists of forms of life, work, economy, family, and conviction which are different from the transnational modernistic way of life and culture spreading over the world, and affecting the local way of life everywhere. This transnational modernistic culture is spread based on the claim to be the expression of the universal truth about humans and society. It eliminates the chance of a constructive growth process involving other cultures and ways of life. Schooling under independence in Africa has to a great extent continued the colonial schooling and therefore supported this transnational modernistic culture. Now it has to take a drastic turn in order to become the place where a new way is invented out of the confrontation between tradition and modernism, reversing the process of being an instrument of unconscious destruction of civilizations, without allowing people to participate in this globalization process in other ways than as victims, except for an urban middle class minority.

The globalization of this transnational modernistic culture is based on a super-individual and egoistic perspective, whose extreme way of life can be exemplified by the relationships between computer users and the artificial cyberworld, a perspective that is totally disassociated with social realities. Less obvious, but more common, are the alienating images of an unrealistic lifestyle that is also penetrating African societies through the international entertainment and advertising media. The obsession with beauty contests in Namibia is furthering this individualistic perspective in a situation where solidarity and collective perspectives are needed to meet the threats from the "two-nation-society" and other factors like AIDS, which has already created major social trauma and obstacles for societal development. There are strong indications that the HIV/AIDS epidemic could become the most important macroeconomic and social determinant of human welfare and poverty in Namibia over the next few years. (Dahlström, 1998b; UNDP, 1997)

A draft policy document on educationally marginalized children in Namibia estimates that 12% of each cohort of children never enter or do not complete primary education, that is, Grade 1 to 7, and that these children are from marginalized groups like children of farm workers, children in remote rural areas like San and Ovahimba children, street children, children in squatter camps, children with physical or mental impairment, children over-aged according to existing policies, and children of families in extreme poverty. This policy document attributes the main reasons for educational marginalization to poverty and attitudes, that is, poverty among the marginalized and attitudes among the others (Kann, 1997).

The educational reform in Namibia is based on certain goals outlined in policy documents like Toward Education for All (MEC, 1993), as mentioned previously. The concept of learner-centered education has been chosen to represent the new philosophy of education through which Namibia will reach these goals. As a philosophy of education, learner-centered education goes beyond teaching methods and includes views on how teaching and learning processes can contribute to the democratization and restructuring of the Namibian society. The education policy also recognizes that the concept of culture goes beyond cultural artistic expressions and includes peoples' "values, world views, and ways of knowing and understanding...culture is a shared way of living, not a fossil from the past but a vibrant, dynamic, constantly changing complex of ideas and interactions" and expresses the aim to develop a true Namibian culture as an enriched unity in diversity. At the same time as the policy is to develop this conflict-free perception of culture, it is also expressed that "it would be naive to assume that the cultural superiority and cultural prejudice of the past will disappear easily" (pp. 46, 51).

We started this chapter with a reference to how the names of some of the tribes in Namibia were created. Language is still a strong social marker in the Namibian society and is even today used as a symbolic marker of tribal and social stratification. The common reference to the majority of Black people in Namibia by the White minority mirrors this historical influence on the minds and attitudes of the people in social and financial power. A very common expression referring to the Black majority by Whites in Namibia today is "these people." "These people" has been used when referring to the chosen color of the seats in the dining hall at an official institution, as well as in statements like "You can't trust these people!" The following description clearly reflects how entrenched cultural prejudices are in the use of language in Namibia:

> When we came back from the urban city in the neighboring country to our work place for the national reform efforts in education we told our colleagues that we had been assaulted and robbed by a group of young men in the city. One of our colleagues expressed her worry about the increasing crime rates after independence in Namibia and South Africa and asked if the robbers were Black. Our answer was, "Yes, of course," to indicate that the majority of people are Black and poor and therefore also the most plausible to commit crimes on pure statistical grounds. Based on the fact that we are not Namibians and working in the country to support its educational development, our colleague, who is set to develop the educational system based on democratic and certain moral principles, responded with the words: "Why do you struggle for these people?" (Personal experience, 1996)

The Namibian society is still, a decade after its political independence, heavily entrenched in its colonial and racist past. Although tranformative infrastructural changes have taken place on certain levels in the society, for example, in the areas of communication, information, and the overall national administrative functions, the common social and human forces are still, to a large extent, a matter of class, gender, ethnicity, and color interphased with ideological interpretations and the social functions of general political policies—like reconciliation and affirmative action—in the struggle for influence, power, and economic gains.

There are a number of multicultural perspectives prevailing among the complexity of contradictions that we have tried to illuminate. McLaren (1995) has explored different forms of multiculturalism, some of which we refer to in our description of the Namibian situation. In his attempts to "formulate a theoretical grid that can help discern the multiple ways in which difference is both constructed and engaged," McLaren explored what he has termed *conservative multiculturalism*, *liberal multiculturalism*, *left-liberal multiculturalism*, and a *critical multiculturalism* (p. 35).

We interfuse the multicultural perspectives with evidence based on official documentation from and interviews with staff and students at one of the colleges in Namibia. To create a contextual understanding for the readers of this report we make a brief historical retrospect.

This college was established in 1978 as a college for White student teachers only. The spacious and well-equipped campus was situated in one of the White suburbs to the capital. As one teacher educator expressed it:

> I never realized how important that building was for the teacher educators at that time. I never realized the psychological effects of working and living in a beautiful surrounding and a wonderful nature. It created an ivory tower problem. We were so physically removed from everything that we did not realize what was happening around us. (Interview, teacher educator, 3/2/1998)

It should be noted that the White community of teacher educators was never united as a political entity. There was always a White minority of teacher educators who welcomed Black students and who tried to use educational material that applied an educational perspective beyond the "approved racist propaganda," even though many of them never stayed for long at the college. A confession from one teacher educator is a sign of a rare awareness among the White teacher educators at this college: "You think you are liberal and you think you understand, but you are really fooling yourself. As a White/middle-class/teacher educator I cannot understand how it is to be a Black student at this college in 1998. I must respect my ignorance."

After independence the college merged with the college for Coloured students and a few years later it was moved to a different site in the opposite direction from the center of town to give room for the newly established University of Namibia (UNAM). The merging of the two colleges for Whites and Coloureds was based on a political decision, but created a situation where the White hegemony continued. "One college had to die" and that was the case for the previous Coloured college with effects that are emerging today.

In addition to the physical move to a less-prosperous campus in one of the Black suburbs, the introduction of the new teacher education program, BETD, became problematic for the conservative teacher educators, regardless of color, whereas others realized that the learner-centered and democratic educational policy was not something invented by the previous "terrorists," but part of a global change that had already taken place years ago in other parts of the world.

Another significant change was related to the students. From being a college for White students only, new cadres of students of color entered the college who were politically mature as opposed to the "politically naïve" students before independence. Even though the student leadership is composed of highly competent student leaders, the political and social maturity of many other students are questioned by their own leaders. Referring to the problems of uniting the students and its relation to ethnic issues, one student expressed: "This place is sometimes called a glorified high school, but because many students are drinkers and are mostly after girls, it will soon be changed into a glorified kindergarten, because that's all they want to do. Give them alcohol, and they will have something in common!" The overall impression is that everyone at the college is aware of the conflicts and that these conflicts are related to ethnic matters and matters of color. When referring to the policy of reconciliation, a student expressed:

> I am asking myself the question about reconciliation and integration, and it brings me to the question of tribalism and what it is. We have reconciled with the mouth. Deep down people are still what they used to be. We have not moved to a situation when we accept one another as people with our hearts and our minds. That's why this college is not going to move very far given the current situation and in terms of contributing the way it should.

Conflicting Perspectives on Multiculturalism

A conclusion we make from our previous historical, social, and political descriptions, being the context within which a new and innovative model for teacher education has emerged, is that there are two strong and conflicting perspectives on multiculturalism permeating the Namibian society: A *conservative* perspective, which lately has accentuated in different ways and from different quarters, and a *critical* perspective, which is still struggling against the grain.

A Conservative Perspective. McLaren is tracing conservative multiculturalism to colonial views of African Americans, the slave trade, Christian imperialism, and right-wing organizations that in the United States created the legitimacy of publications like *The Bell Curve.* Conservative multiculturalism in the U.S. context is a proponent of a common culture that annuls deviations from the mainstream White culture of the dominant class. Linguistic hegemony is used as a means of social stratification and a drive toward linguistic conformity. White ethnicity is not recognized as the hidden norm from which other ethnicities are judged and diversity is used as a smoke screen for the assimilation policy (McLaren, 1995, pp. 35-37). According to McLaren:

> Conservative multiculturalism wants to assimilate students to an unjust social order by arguing that every member of every ethnic group can reap the economic benefits of neo-colonialist ideologies and corresponding social and economic practices. But a prerequisite to "joining the club" is to become denuded, deracinated, and culturally stripped. (p. 38)

The conservative multiculturalism which McLaren refers to in the U.S. context has its parallel in Namibia. The fact that the majority of Namibians are Black confirms that the real issues in multiculturalism are related to power, economic positions, class, and social position, which at times, when they suit the objectives, follow racial and ethnic lines. The Namibian version is rooted in the previous apartheid policies, the historical and ethnic stratification as well as the "racial bigotry" that that system bred. A Black teacher educator assessed the present situation as follows: "The feeling of racism is very, very strong right across the college amongst students and lecturers alike."

The liberation struggle created a strong political consensus to overthrow the apartheid regime, across different political affiliations, even though they often followed ethnic lines. When independence came and SWAPO won an overwhelming election victory, a position that the ruling party has consolidated in recent years, it seems as if the ethnic affiliations started to override the political preferences, and that tribalism and ethnicity have become the means to aspire to social positions of hegemony and power. The liberation struggle brought many Namibians together under the banners of unity and social justice. However, when the struggle was won individualism replaced the collective efforts for a common good, and the individual ambitions could easily be related to and supported by racial and ethnic perspectives in line with nepotism. There are amble examples expressed by students and teacher educators where individual gains are coupled with racial or ethnic perspectives, when the issues at hand become less important than the concern to side with your own "clique." This practice seems to be common among students as well as teacher educators.

This conservative multiculturalism has as its major goal to replace one subjugation with another, based on felt supremacy. That is why there have been calls from a specific ethnic group among the students that their college should become their own, that is, an ethnic college of education! Claims have also been made that manipulations with the students' hostel places have made it possible for a certain ethnic group to monopolize the hostel places, which has created problems for students from other areas. As one informed teacher educator put it: "This noble idea to give educational opportunities to everybody, also from outside this region, is really sacrificed in favor of ethnic belonging."

This type of division and hostility is also apparent among the teacher educators. People are covering up for each other in the same ethnic group and you do not support a suggestion from another ethnic group even though it might be a good suggestion. A practice of "secret meetings" is flourishing and individuals are promised certain benefits if they join these meetings. It is not so much the fact that people with the same interests choose to meet to be able to organize their forces on matters of importance, but the way people talk about these "secret societies" shows that it is something different from political or labor meetings.

Affirmative action in the Namibian context means that special measures are taken to create possibilities for the Black majority, for example, to reach certain positions and to influence decision making at the institutional level. Appointments have been made to equalize the possibilities of influence and those opposed to these appointments have claimed that it undermines the professional ethos as it does not recognize good work: "There were better people, Black and White, that could have been promoted. Now it does not matter if you do a good job."

The general opinion among the students is that the White group of teacher educators is still in power: "The Whites are still the bosses here, Blacks are just in office." On the other hand, students also recognize that changes are taking place, which is affecting the distribution of power among the teacher educators. Referring to a new militancy among the students, developed from experiences as detainees and freedom fighters, it is recognized that the reactions from those who represent the previous establishment is a sign of lack of control and power: "Currently the Whites are pushed in a corner and they will do anything to get out. The more you push the tiger in the corner the more 'tigerish' will the response be!"

Many students and teacher educators are concerned about the destructive effects these types of perspectives have on the situation, unless you believe that it is only from chaos that a new progressive and constructive professional development can gain support.

Teacher educators are describing the present situation as full of suspicion, mistrust, omission, neglect, and a division among themselves. Some teacher educators are even accused of openly instigating and using the weaknesses among colleagues for their individual ambitions and gains. Situations sometimes erupt where pure racist remarks are made by both teacher educators and students.

Students express their concern about the future of the college, they call for a new leadership with an "ironfist," "because that's where the Whites come from." A critical self-reflection also includes the misuse and misunderstanding among students of the concept of democracy, for example, when claiming that students should be able to negotiate "if we can come 20 or 30 minutes late to classes." As one student expressed it in despair: "This place is stupid to some degree.... It is very stupid."

A picture emerges where expressions for conservative multicultural perspectives are allowed to dictate the common discourse at this tertiary institution and conflicts about petty issues are becoming the official order of the day, while the real issues are hidden in the cupboards or manipulated behind the scene.

A Critical Perspective. Taking into account that it is through a long historical struggle between social forces since the pre-colonial period, from which the strata where people are placed today have emerged, it takes a strong vision that an opposite process can take place, one that is based on a commitment to social justice beyond political independence. As one of the political leaders both during the liberation struggle and today expressed it some time after independence: "It is now that the real struggle starts!"

The components of a critical multicultural perspective are related to the basic assumption that it is possible to build a society on social justice, solidarity, and an economic democracy that takes into account people's different social positions and the possibilities and limitations these positions create. In a sense, difference is closely related to capitalist exploitation, profit, and individual gains, and a critical multicultural perspective will therefore always be a swim against the stream in capitalist societies.

McLaren (1995) pointed to the role of language and representation in the construction of meaning and identity, some of which we have quoted in this chapter as an example. Diversity is not a goal in itself but has to be placed within a critical perspective on the cultural and social positions of difference, which are products of history, power, and ideology.

Rizvi (1991) referred to the distinction between the *phenomenal* form in which the world is represented in human experiences, and the *essential* relations that go beyond what appears to be the issues at the surface to the underlying social structures that create the basis for the phenomenal surface understanding. A critical multicultural perspective is concern with the essential relations and would, for example, lead to the identification of class divisions also within the culturally distinct ethnic groupings referred to in this chapter. An ethnic petit bourgeois and a working class are also found within the different ethnic groups in Namibia. The rhetoric of globalization is also infected with a phenomenal form that obscures the fact that this globalization is only meant for a few.

The role of teacher education in a critical multicultural perspective is to move the critical intellectual inquiry of social analysis beyond ethnicity and tribalism, and beyond a compensatory perspective that does not recognize the social and cultural norms that are embedded in the dominant culture (Swartz, 1992). Such a critical multicultural perspective can be supported through the development of critical practitioner inquiry practices in teacher education carried out by both student teachers and teacher educators. The result of such practices can then be made public and part of the emerging knowledge base of education in Namibia.

Some people would claim that Namibia is not ready for a critical multicultural perspective and for critical inquiries into multicultural issues, due to the tensions between reconciliation and affirmative action, the tensions created by the dual society, and the lack of a common vision of a future society building on social justice, solidarity, and a different economic and social order. Contrary to that claim, one of the first steps toward such a vision is to recognize what Amin (1997) has said in his critique of what he calls "the ineluctability of globalization":

> ...to understand that development is not synonymous with market expansion. But the dominant discourse always refuses to make this

distinction. It implies that market expansion necessarily "leads to" social progress and democracy, and that the "difficulties" (the "pockets" of poverty, unemployment and social marginalization, as they are called) are really only "transitory." No one gives much thought to whether the transition will last a few years or several centuries! (p. xii)

Another step is to start asking the following: Who decides what is the acknowledged understanding of multicultural issues and how and on what basis are the official as well as unofficial discourses about the Namibian society established?

A FINAL NOTE ON EDUCATIONAL POLICY IN NAMIBIA

Although Namibia has made great strides in trying to meet the needs of all its citizens in the various sectors, it is clear that the attitudes and practices ingrained by the colonial regime will take a long time to be erased, if at all. However, it is the clearly articulated policy of the government not to retreat from the aspirations of equity, justice, democratic participation, and respect for human dignity, and to continue with nation building and national reconciliation. Education is perceived to be the primary vehicle in this endeavor. In trying to achieve this an egalitarian educational system is envisaged where,

> ...the competence of teachers, the availability of materials, and the quality of learning do not depend on race, or gender, or family origin. Books and other curricular materials in an egalitarian system do not have images that portray the world from only one group's perspective or that suggest that one group is better suited for particular occupations or positions in life (Development Brief, MEC, 1993, p. 35).

However, the government has also recognized that to simply abolish discrimination by race, or religion, or gender would not bring about the desired change, as segregation was not just a matter of law, it was also a matter of the allocation of resources and of everyday practices. It has therefore embarked on a policy of affirmative action the intention of which is not to exclude any one, but to include those who have been systematically disadvantaged. Measures in this regard will include making it "...the responsibility of our institutions and their staffs to diversify their recruitment and to ensure that their enrolment matches the rich heterogeneity of our country" (Development Brief, MEC, 1993, p. 36).

Democracy, as stated previously in the chapter, is one of the major goals of education. Although the laws and regulations under the previous regime had been phrased in the language of democracy, they had effectively excluded most Namibians from it. It is therefore necessary for the principles of democracy to be firmly established to enable all Namibians to participate in civil society, to know their rights, and to accept their responsibilities. In this regard the preparation of teachers has an important role as stated in the Development Brief: "Our learners must understand that democracy means more than voting. Malnutrition, economic inequality, and illiteracy can be obstacles to democracy that are far more powerful than barriers to participate in elections" (1993, p. 41).

REFERENCES

Amin, S. (1997). *Capitalism in the age of globalization.* London: Zed Books.
Amukugo, E. M. (1993). *Education and politics in Namibia: Past trends and future prospects.* Windhoek, Namibia: Gamsberg Macmillan.
Andersson, I., Callewaert, S., & Kallos, D. (1991). *Teacher education reform for Namibia.* Location: Department of Education, University of Umeå; Department of Education, University of Copenhagen.
Andersson, S. B., & Murangi, V. K. (1997). *National evaluation of the Basic Education Teacher Diploma: Professional issues.* Namibia: NIED.
Angula, N. (1990, February). Our schools today: Problems and prospects. Paper presented at the Education Forum by the Rössing Foundation, Windhoek, Namibia.
Avenstrup, R., & Swarts, P. (1992, November). We, the people of Namibia. Paper presented at the Comparative Education Conference, University of Oslo, Norway.
Basson, D. (1998, March 21). Reconciliation policy is magic prescription. *NEW ERA—8th Anniversary of Independence Special.*
Callewaert, S., & Kallos, D. (1989, September). Teaching and teacher training in Namibia: today and tomorrow. In *SWAPO/UNIN, International conference on teacher education for Namibia* (pp. 23-70), Lusaka, Zambia.
Cohen, C. (1994). *Administering education in Namibia: The colonial period to the present.* Windhoek, Namibia: Namibia Scientific Society.
Dahlström, L. (1995, July) From the liberation struggle to a national agenda for teacher education—consensus and contradictions in independent Namibia from a participatory perspective. Paper presented at the ICET World Assembly.
Dahlström, L. (1997). *National evaluation of the Basic Education Teacher Diploma: Subject area issues, Report 1. What's going on during college-based studies.* Namibia: NIED.
Dahlström, L. (1998a). At the crossroads with teacher education reform in Namibia. Unpublished manuscript.
Dahlström, L. (1998b). A position paper for an integrated in-service staff development program for sustainable capacity building in teacher education for basic education in Namibia. Unpublished manuscript.
Dahlström, L., & Janson, G. (1989, September). The integrated teacher training program (ITTP): 1986-89. In SWAPO/UNIN, *International conference on teacher education for Namibia* (pp. 154-161), Lusaka, Zambia.
Diphofa, M. (1995). Teacher participation in curriculum development: Views from the Ground. *Multicultural Teaching, 13*(3), 35-40.
Ellis, J. (1984). *Education, repression and liberation: Namibia.* London: Catholic Institute for International Relations.

//Gowaseb, M. (1998, March 21). Is Namibia's education system still a failure? *NEW ERA—8th Anniversary of Independence Special.*

Halls, W. D. (1990). *Comparative education: Contemporary issues and trends.* London/Paris: UNESCO.

Hansohm, D., Mupotola-Sibongo, M., & Motinga, D. (1998). *Overview of the Namibian economy, January 1998.* Windhoek, Namibia: Namibian Economic Policy Research Unit (NEPRU).

Jochem, J. (1998, March 21). Black empowerment: Namibia still characterized by socioeconomic dualism, *NEW ERA—8th Anniversary of Independence Special.*

Kann, U. (1997). *A national policy for educationally marginalized children* (draft). Namibia: Ministry of Basic Education and Culture.

Kaplan, L. D., & Kaplan, C. (1997). Democracy, meritocracy and the cognitive elite: The real thesis of the bell curve. *Education Theory, 47*(3), 425-431.

McLaren, P. (1995). White terror and oppositional agency: Towards a critical multiculturalism. In C. E. Sleeter, & P. McLaren (Eds.), *Multicultural education, critical pedagogy, and the politics of difference* (pp. 33-70). Albany: State University of New York Press.

Ministry of Basic Education and Culture & Ministry of Higher Education, Vocational Training, Science, and Technology. (1998). *The broad curriculum for the Basic Education Teacher Diploma (BETD), Pre-Service.* Okahandja: NIED.

Ministry of Education and Culture. (1993). *Toward education for all, a development brief.* Windhoek, Namibia: Gamsberg-Macmillan.

Pankhurst, D. (1996). Similar but different? Assessing the reserve economy legacy of Namibia. *Journal of Southern African Studies, 22*(3), 405-420.

Rizvi, F. (1991). The idea of ethnicity and the politics of multicultural education. In D. Dawkins (Ed.), *Power and politics in education* (pp. 161-195). London: Falmer Press.

Storeng, M. (1994). *Ideological changes—Educational consequences: How is education evolving in Namibia from a perspective of liberation? Report No. 6.* ELI, University of Oslo, Norway.

SWAPO. (1984). *Education for all—National integrated educational system for emergent Namibia.* Luanda, Angola: SWAPO Department of Education and Culture.

SWAPO. (1990). *The national integrated education system for emergent Namibia—Draft proposal for education reform and renewal.* Namibia: SWAPO.

Swarts, P. (1998). *The transformation of teacher education in Namibia: The development of reflective practice.* Unpublished dissertation. Oxford Brookes University.

Swartz, E. (1992). Multicultural education: From a compensatory to a scholarly foundation. In C. A. Grant (Ed.), *Research & multicultural education* (32-43). London: Falmer Press.

Tötemeyer, G. (1978). *Namibia old and new.* London: Hurst.

UNDP. (1996). *Namibia—Human Development Report 1996.* Namibia.

UNDP. (1997). *Namibia—Human Development Report 1997.* Namibia.

Chapter 13

International Perspectives on Education: The Response of the Mother Country

Harry Tomlinson
Leeds Metropolitan University, United Kingdom

THE POST-WAR SCHOOL SYSTEM IN THE UNITED KINGDOM

The 1944 Education Act[1] in England and Wales created the tripartite system that mirrored and sustained the British class system. It was nevertheless in some ways idealistic, offering, for the first time, secondary education for all according to "age, aptitude, and ability." The Act provided a moral rationale for education in Britain. In practice, however, this meant grammar schools for the academically able 20% and secondary technical and secondary modern schools for the rest. The 80% who "failed" the 11-plus entry test to grammar schools were substantially failed by the system. The examination system throughout the 1950s was essentially for grammar school children only, who largely came from, and would be absorbed into, the middle class (Verma, 1998). This was the form of schooling Commonwealth immigrants found in Britain and that was sustained for 20 years until comprehensive schools were developed in the 1960s. In comprehensive schools all children, except those attending private schools, were to be educated together. However, these schools that, in theory, would achieve equity, failed to ensure that ethnic minority pupils achieved. The schools remained socially stratified because of the communities

---

[1] The 1994 Education Act produced a tripartite partnership between central government, local government, and the organized teaching profession. In the immediate post-war years the power of central government was used sparingly. Policy was implemented by educational professionals and administrators with very little party political input.

they served. Within schools equity was not achieved because the values and organization usually reinforced classism and racism.

Between 1944 and 1988, governments were mainly concerned with the structure and organization of the system as a whole, and schools and teachers with the curriculum and learning. The tripartite system of the government, local education authorities, and schools sharing responsibility confirmed a cozy consensus that assumed that this system would ensure that all children reached their full potential (Cashmore & Troyna, 1990). There was no sufficiently rigorous examination of current practice, and, though parents achieved some influence in school governance from the 1970s, central government exercised very little authority in schools until the Education Reform Act of 1988. In the late 1970s two significant events sowed the seeds for subsequent reform. William Tyndale, a primary school in Islington, was a dramatic example of what could go dreadfully wrong in government schools if they were left uncontrolled.[2] More politically significant was a speech at Ruskin College, Oxford by the then Labor Prime Minister James Callaghan (1976) when he criticized the achievements of the education system, and made it clear that he judged it necessary for the government to intervene in the affairs of teachers and the curriculum. Teachers were letting down the country and the economy. These two events raised the issue as to who should have control over schools and what the appropriate balance of power should be (Riley, 1998). The election of Margaret Thatcher's conservative government in 1979 began the process of serious reform.

ASSIMILATION AND INTEGRATION

Within a few years of the early attempts to recruit labor for Britain from the New Commonwealth, symbolized by the arrival from Jamaica of the Empire Windrush in 1948, the right to enter and settle for immigrants were being steadily reduced by a succession of legislative control measures. This was associated with the early *assimilationist* strategy that involved, for example, busing children, but not White children, from their home areas to ensure that no more than 30% of children at any school was of ethnic minority origin. This was eventually abandoned only because of cost and increased parental

[2] The Auld report on the Public Inquiry (1976) into the teaching, organization, and management of William Tyndale Junior and Infant Schools censured the headteacher, teachers, managers, and local education authority, all of whom were severely criticized for their intransigence in damaging the school.

resistance, not because of the unthinking denial of the cultural inheritance. *Integration* was seen as the way forward with a monocultural education attempting to ensure that all children adopted the cultural values of the "host" community. The process of integration was based on the denial of ethnic, linguistic, and cultural differences (Pumphrey & Verma, 1990). Hence the problem with language centers set up to provide teaching of English as a second language. They were established to enable immigrants to learn English and to become British, it was hoped, by unlearning their own languages. These assimilationist approaches were dropped in the 1960s because of resistance and because they were failing, not because they were perceived as ethically wrong. Integration is now widely perceived to have been an irrelevant and degrading process.

Multicultural education, which emerged in the 1970s, was a part of a White liberal response to the racial disadvantage and discrimination to which ethnic minorities were being subjected. Its focus was on coordinating the goals of each ethnic group while encouraging them to maintain and develop their own distinctive cultures. Talk about education for a just and harmonious society seemed to imply that such a society existed, conflating the aim with the reality. What was not recognized sufficiently in this development was the social and political context in which multicultural education was becoming publicly acceptable. The traditional industries in the inner cities where immigrants had settled had already fallen into decline and the high unemployment of Black youth was demonstrably disproportionate. The school that the author was head of from 1975 to 1981, Birley High School, was in Hulme, Manchester. The form of multicultural education developed in this school, with approximately 60% White children, 30% of Afro-Caribbean, and 10% South Asian origin, was perceived as being exemplary in the Rampton Report (1981) and in the Manchester City Council Report on the Moss Side Uprisings presented in 1982. Arguably, however, by 1980 when it was accepted as an ideal model, it was already outmoded and inappropriate. The multicultural curriculum, in particular in the humanities, encouraged all the children to learn about different cultures and lifestyles. The intention was that such knowledge would bring about better race relations in school. An opportunity for six children of Jamaican origin to visit Jamaica for the first time, with the headteacher, provided a further opportunity that might have been more fully considered. The opportunity to understand the reality of present day Jamaica and the exploration of individual "roots" in a wider context may have been limited because it remained multicultural rather than exploring its relevance for anti-racism. A visit to an independent (private) school intended for mutual understanding resulted in the Black pupils from Birley High School being racially harassed, abused, and bullied in the school playground.

This cultural pluralist approach asserts that each ethnic group has an equal right to retain and develop its individual characteristics and culture. This builds in assumptions about equality including equality of access to power. It was precisely this lack of access to power for minority groups that required the change from multiculturalism to anti-racism. There were also problems in the assumption that exploring the Jamaican cultural inheritance in the curriculum would be educationally advantageous. White pupils saw the Jamaicans colonizing their curriculum. Pupils from other Caribbean islands were also not particularly interested in Jamaica. It might have been better to focus on a re-interpretation of British history that considers the racism manifested in the relationship between the "mother country" and the colonies.

The state had manifestly failed to respond to demands required by the increasingly heterogeneous nature of society by the early 1980s. There remain even now concerns about how institutions and the curriculum can meet the challenges of cultural plurality. The state is assumed to espouse equality with a commitment to equity as a central pillar of the law. There are ambiguities in the word "equality." It can mean equality of input (formal equality), equality of opportunity, and equality of outcome. Formal equality under the law, the first of these, is incompatible with the other two. The development of equal opportunities for ethnic minorities required positive discrimination to overcome structural and historical disadvantage (Verma, 1998). What was happening was that young Blacks were taking to the streets to protest in the early 1980s because of the impact of racism on their lives. The overt discriminatory behavior of the White majority was changed by legislation that criminalized such acts in employment, for example. However, the racist structures in society were not addressed and therefore the underlying values and attitudes were not challenged. There was no commitment to equality. Britain is, however, the only country in the European Community that has enacted primary legislation with the clear purpose of ensuring its ethnic minority individuals are not discriminated against.

IMMIGRATION

The Royal Commission on Population (1949) asserted that the balance of desirability of making up manpower losses by importing workers and creating racial or ethnic tensions by so doing "could only be welcomed without reserve if immigrants were of good human stock and were not prevented by their religion or race from intermarrying with the host population and becoming merged in it." After the era of excess demand for labor of the 1940s and 1950s, the legislation in the 1960s and 1970s to control New Commonwealth immigration was badly mismanaged. Immigration increased substantially in 1961 to four times the number from Pakistan and 10 times the number from India over the 1960 figures in anticipation of the 1962 legislation (Braham, 1987). Migration had previously followed the economic cycle but the botched legislative process ended up by making temporary migration permanent. That migration had been previously determined by needs of the economy was shown by how rapidly it fell after the 1962 Act when only one third of work vouchers available for issue were utilized.

In the decreasing urban cores of what had been expanding industrial areas, in the twilight zones, the lack of facilities, decay, multi-occupation, and overcrowding were compounded by the loss of jobs. In 1963, Enoch Powell, the then Minister of Health, was actively recruiting nurses in Barbados. Five years later he was complaining that "numbers are the essence" and that, if there were too many immigrants, Britain would have "rivers foaming with blood." The management of immigration control was clumsy and enhanced the racism that was already endemic in society. Immigrants who came for work, a better standard of living, and education were finding only unskilled work, the standards of living they had hoped to achieve were not accessible, and the education service was providing a poor education for their children.

IMMIGRATION LEGISLATION

Legislation has continuously limited the freedom of potential immigrants to enter the country and the rights of ethnic minorities in the country. This is shown in the following brief analysis of the major policy issues in the legislation:

- The *Commonwealth Immigrants Act 1962* removed the right of the majority of New Commonwealth citizens whose passports were not issued by the U.K. government to settle and enjoy full citizenship rights. Thereafter, with the exception of dependents of those already settled, permission to enter Britain depended on obtaining an employment visa from the Ministry of Labor.

- The *Immigration White Paper of 1965* then reduced the number of vouchers to 8,500 per year.

- The *Commonwealth Immigrants Acts 1968* restricted the entry of East African Asians to those in possession of U.K. passports issued by the U.K. government and not by the colonial authorities, at a time when they were being driven from Kenya and Uganda.

- The *Immigration Act 1971* distinguished "patrials" who had a "substantial personal connection" with Britain through parents or grandparents (these were almost entirely White) who retained the right of entry, and "non-patrials" who must obtain work permits and, if admitted, may apply for British citizenship after 5 years of residence.

- The *British Nationality Act 1981* abolished the "Citizen of United Kingdom and Colonies: British Subject" status. Those with right of abode became British citizens. Others were assigned to other categories. The concept of nationality was subordinated to a framework of immigration control.

- The *1988 Immigration Act* abolished "guarantees" given to long-settled Commonwealth citizens and reversed earlier court decisions favorable to immigrants.

Britain's traditional role in receiving those suffering political repression and in fear of their lives is now permanently threatened by the complexities of further extensions of immigration procedures. This incessant legislation with its obsessive focus on providing a rationalization for keeping out Black immigrants undermined any race relations legislation intended to be more constructive as it was seen to be so manifestly racially discriminatory. The word "Black" was now being used to define relationship with the state by some members of the ethnic minorities whose skin was not black. This is sustained today in attempts to prevent the entry of Moslems from Bosnia.

RACIAL DISCRIMINATION AND RACE RELATIONS

In the 1960s there was substantial evidence that race relations legislation was politically inevitable. Daniel (1968) found that there was racial discrimination in housing, employment, and the provision of services "varying in extent from the massive to the substantial." Asians were discriminated against on cultural grounds, but prejudice against West Indians was based on "physical and racial grounds" and hence was "most deep rooted and widespread." The label immigrant was in practice extended to redefine Blacks born in Britain as an inevitable rationalization. The expectations of young Blacks that they would not have to perform the sort of jobs that their parents were obliged to accept were not met. The assumption that all ethnic minorities are immigrants has been sustained through the last 50 years partially because of the legislation but more significantly because racism has not been tackled directly.

Legislation against gender and race discrimination emerged in the mid-1970s at the same time as multicultural education was beginning to be perceived as the way forward. The relationship between the Equal Opportunities Commission and the Commission for Racial Equality has not always been mutually supportive.

Equal Opportunities Commission (EOC)

Racism and sexism were seen as mutually reinforcing. The approaches in principle were similar but women in positions of greater influence were more successfully able to challenge current ideologies. The EOC, which is the expert body on equality between men and women in the United Kingdom, was created by Parliament in 1976 with three main tasks:

1. working to end sex discrimination;
2. promoting equal opportunities for women and men; and
3. reviewing and suggesting improvements to the Sex Discrimination Act and the Equal Pay Acts.

The EOC leads the way in areas such as employment practices, equal pay, retirement and pensions, and rights for pregnant women and part-time workers. The Sex Discrimination Act (SDA) came into force in 1975. It was amended and broadened in 1986. Specifically sex discrimination is not allowed in employment, education, and advertising or when providing goods, services, or facilities. It is unlawful to discriminate because someone is married. Women must be paid the same as men for equal work. Indirect discrimination means setting unjustifiable conditions that appear to apply to everyone, but in fact discriminate against one sex. The Equal Pay Act (EPA) took effect in 1975 and was amended in 1984. It applies when a woman and a man are doing like work, work that has been rated as equivalent and work that is of equal value.

Legislation about gender and race has arisen from the same political environment and at the same time. There is an argument that there have been inadequate improvements in both these areas in the last 25 years because the initial legislation was insufficiently strong, and has certainly not been developed.

Commission for Racial Equality (CRE)

The CRE was established to enforce the Race Relations Act in 1976, which covers Great Britain except for Northern Ireland. It works through local committees for race relations. The CRE has three main duties:

1. to work toward the elimination of racial discrimination and to promote equality of opportunity;
2. to encourage good relations between people of different racial backgrounds;
3. to monitor the way the Race Relations Act is working and recommend ways in which it can be improved.

It is unlawful to discriminate in employment, training, housing, education, and the provision of goods, facilities, and services. There is again the issue of direct and indirect discrimination. The Race Relations Act does not cover discrimination on grounds of religion but Sikhs and Jews have been defined as racial groups for the purposes of the Act. Racially motivated acts or threats of violence are covered by the criminal law. The Home Office has accepted that there may be as many as 130,000 racially motivated acts in a year, even though it is an offense for anyone to publish or distribute written materials, or to use in public language that is threatening, abusive, or insulting and likely to stir up hatred against any racial group.

In the early 1980s the author was principal of a school/college that was for girls only up to the age of 16, and then for young men and women of college age. He attempted to provide a program for the 30% of girls from the school who were Moslem that would be culturally based and ensure they could continue their education. This initially had strong support from the girls and their mothers. As interpreted by the author this eventually had to be abandoned because of the influence of men in the Moslem community, but then also Manchester City Council, the Equal Opportunities Commission, and the Commission for Racial Equality. All these agencies saw the program as racist and sexist. The girls lost their education. The role of the school leader in such a highly politicized environment can be difficult to fulfil.

MULTICULTURAL OR ANTI-RACIST APPROACHES

There have been major problems associated with the use of appropriate language. The word "Black" in Britain for example is arguably a political construct not used so much for skin color but to describe personal and political experience (Troyna, 1993). This has developed in response to the early *immigrant perspective* that was associated with low social status, general inferiority, unskilled labor, and poor education derived from the long and unequal history of slavery and colonialism. The Empire was only just disappearing after World War II with its association of color with conquered and therefore subordinate peoples. Hence this was transferred to Black immigrants. However, pupils in the author's school in Hulme, Manchester, with parents from different "races," were anxious not to deny either parents or their cultural heritage, and children from other ethnic backgrounds refused to be described as Black. Language remains a difficult issue.

Though here the author is concentrating on the impact of race on education, race, gender, and class issues operate simultaneously at the personal, cultural, institutional, and structural levels. These all need to be recognized because they mutually reinforce each other. What was significant was how all were marginalized at the time of the Education Reform Act (1988). Now, however, when there is a growing concern about the underperformance of boys, this is attracting significant priority, attention, and resources.

The debate on multicultural versus anti-racist approaches originated in the early 1980s (see Klein, 1993). Multicultural approaches (Stone, 1981) that focused exclusively on cultures were too absorbed with "saris, samosas, and steel bands." An academic of Afro-Caribbean origin, Stone (1981) argued that Black pupils were further disadvantaged by multiculturalism. The outcome was racist, despite the good intentions, and working directly against the interest of Black children. Roy Jenkins, the Home Secretary, had earlier (1966) described multiculturalism as "not a flattening process of assimilation but equal opportunity, accompanied by cultural diversity, in an atmosphere of mutual tolerance." He assumed that people started from an equal base, ignoring the racial injustice that was pervasive in British society. Anti-racist approaches provided alternatives to multiculturalism in that they incorporated issues of power and injustice. Klein (1993) suggested that it is possible to take into account power issues while still supporting cultural activities. She argued that educationalists need to understand the causes and processes of racism. It was the failure to engage with understanding the processes and dynamics of racism with its roots in the 17th century that had led to confused practice.

The Schools Council, a government agency, set out to identify good practice in multicultural education with reports that reviewed the nature and development of multicultural education (Little & Willey, 1981), extrapolated the principles and made recommendations to schools about curriculum delivery (Willey, 1982), and identified the theoretical and research literature, guidance for teachers, and curriculum materials (Klein, 1982). As late as 1989 the National Curriculum Council, a successor to the Schools Council set up a task group that produced a report that proposed a rationale for multicultural education, planning a whole school policy, curriculum planning, and the implementation in terms of school organization with some exemplary materials (see following). In retrospect the debate on curriculum policies for a multicultural society were undermined throughout the 1980s and early 1990s by a sustained and determined attack on multicultural education from New Right groups such as the Center for Policy Studies, the Hillgate Group, and the Salisbury Group.

In addition to the Commission for Racial Equality there were other organizations campaigning for a more anti-racist approach. The Institute of Race Relations, the Runnymede Trust, and the teachers' associations, in particular the National Union of Teachers, publicly stood against racial discrimination and racist practices in their members.

Mullard (1984) was perhaps the person who seminally crystallized the issues and led to NAME, the National Association for Multiracial Education, changing its title to the National Anti-racist Movement in Education. From the mid-1980s those who understood the issues were working for anti-racist education in schools.

Anti-racism is contrasted with multicultural strategies that focus excessively on curriculum content and "positive images" but do not engage with power and racism in interpersonal and institutional contexts. Barry Troyna in numerous publications (Troyna, 1993; Troyna & Carrington, 1990) campaigned to clarify the centrality of anti-racism if there was to be change. In practice, policy has been deracialized in the 1990s. Gillborn (1995) argued that this is demonstrated in three themes. There is a "racist" obsession with national identity and culture. The discourse subsumes "race" issues with deracialized concepts such as "disadvantage" and "inner cities." Thirdly, racism in education is defined as a personal issue of ignorance and prejudice. This results in the systematic bias in institutional structures and norms of racism being defined out.

REPORTS AND RESEARCH

Established in 1978, the Committee of Inquiry into the Education of Children of West Indian Origin produced an Interim Report in 1981. The Rampton Report (1981) revealed the racism in society and schools and recommended steps to eradicate it in and through education. Its primary focus was on the growing underachievement of African and Caribbean children in mainstream education. The report was equivocal as to how racism and indeed underachievement could be eliminated. There was a focus on "cultural tolerance" rather than the curriculum and assessment issues. This focus on children and disadvantage rather than racism, on the cultural and linguistic characteristics of the immigrants rather than racism in schools and society, was inevitably limited. At this time Maureen Stone (1981) was challenging assumptions about Black children's poorer self-image and that they were less well motivated. The "immigrant" language problem that resulted in Section 11 Home Office monies for language needs similarly focused on a deficit model.

The Scarman Report (1981) was published in the wake of Black "uprisings" or "riots," depending on the political perspective, in Brixton, Southall, Liverpool, and Manchester in 1981. These were attributed to the "ill-considered, immature and racially prejudiced actions of some (police) officers in their dealings on the street with young people" (Scarman, 1982, p. 63). This defined the problem as the prejudice of thoughtless, uneducated, and individual police. This implied that these individuals could have their attitudes changed with training. Institutional racism, then as now endemic in the police force, was not challenged significantly and the individual policemen and policewomen were themselves arguably victimized. This period in 1981 was the most profound manifestation of Black outrage at the continual and continuing racial discrimination, prejudice, and injustice to which young men in particular were subjected. Since then there has been an adequate response from the state to control racism sufficiently to largely maintain order on the streets.

The Swann Report, *Education for All*, which was published in 1985, built on the work of the Rampton Committee that was set up to deal with the problems of all Black children and provided a wider perspective. This is the main report on multicultural education that

Britain has produced. It was in theory about education for all. This was the time that multicultural education had its highest profile. The report however looked backward to cultural diversity rather than forward to an analysis and attack on structural racism. Multicultural education, as interpreted by Swann, has two strands—educational provision for children from ethnic minorities groups, but also a concern to educate the majority White pupil population for a multicultural society. Both the Rampton and Swann reports tend to support the model that makes racism individual. Thus institutional racism continued to be legitimated, sustaining the image of Britain as essentially a tolerant society with some extremists.

The School Effect (Smith & Tomlinson, 1989), with which the author was associated as a member of the Steering Committee throughout the 7-year project, was the book resulting from the DES (Department of Education and Science) research project, Factors Associated with Success in Multi-Ethnic schools. It is still arguably the most sustained piece of research on school performance. This confirmed that, in schools at which pupils' academic performance is better than might be expected, Black pupils do well. The differences between schools, and, in particular, departments in schools, were astonishingly different, however. The same child would achieve highly significant grade differences in examinations. The school effect is about the progress that pupils make, the added value provided by the school. The variation in school performance became more of a focus than how well Black children were achieving. The government is only now slowly moving toward presenting school performance in an added value format.

The McDonald Inquiry investigated the murder of a 13-year old Asian pupil, Ahmed Ullah, in 1986 by a White boy, Darren Colbourn, also 13. The report stated that there were lessons to be learned about different forms of oppression. Ahmed was a victim of racism. Darren, convicted of murder, was a victim of class oppression. The police denied there was any evidence of racism in the crime. The school's anti-racist approaches were confined to working with and supporting Black pupils and parents. White parents and pupils were therefore part of the problem. Two lessons emerged from Burnage High School: firstly, the struggle against racism needs to be equally a struggle against other forms of inequality, and secondly, as racism damages both Black and White people, both have to be brought into the fight against racism. The recommendations included the setting up of anti-racist training and political education, particularly for White youths, and a range of actions to build links with all parts of the community, not forgetting

White parents. The report entitled "Murder in the Playground" (McDonald, Bhovani, Khan, & John, 1989) was broadened into a inquiry into racism and racial violence in Manchester schools. Of the headteacher the report stated, "We feel that the man has become so obsessed with the ideology of anti-racism that he has become unable to see what was needed." Manchester City Council having alerted the press they were going to publish the report withdrew it because they claimed the report defamed a number of individuals who might sue the Council.

The murder of Stephen Lawrence , a Black sixth former in London, in April, 1993, has not resulted in those allegedly guilty being brought to justice. The effects of a liberal perspective is still evidenced in responses to the continuing issue of racism in the police force. The Lawrence inquiry report, by Sir William Macpherson, was published early in 1999. The Chief Constable in London, where the murder occurred, Sir Paul Condon, had insisted that there was no institutional racism in the police. The report suggests the investigation was "flawed and incompetent." After publication of the report, the Chief Constable accepted that there was institutional racism on the definition in the report, that is, that it did not mean that every individual officer was racist. This has continued to be a high-profile racist murder because it is clear that the gross mishandling within the criminal justice process is responsible for those thought to be guilty being brought to justice. This report is significant for this analysis because it demonstrated how racism remains endemic in British society.

NATIONAL CURRICULUM

The National Curriculum was developed in Britain after the Education Reform Act (ERA) of 1988. The setting up of separate subject groups and the decision that multicultural education was a cross-curricular dimension guaranteed that even multiculturalism did not inform the curriculum significantly. The absence within the curriculum of social studies and politics in the national curriculum also meant that there was no real commitment to tackling racism despite the rhetoric. The 1988 Act was intended to restructure for the future with the reforms ensuring the achievement of more ambitious educational goals. A more multicultural, multilingual, multifaith Britain might have been recognized in the process. In the 1988 Act the government had taken, for the first time, direct responsibility for the curriculum and assessment. The National Curriculum Council decided not to issue formal guidance on the multicultural cross-curricular dimension (King & Reiss, 1993). The Task Group set up for this purpose in 1989 was disbanded after 18 months amidst considerable controversy. The Council's publications did indirectly encourage schools to engage with the issues of racism, racial disadvantage, and discrimination, and to eradicate racism and prejudice within schools. The cultures, languages, and religions of ethnic minorities were to be treated with respect. Moral issues such as social justice and equality were to be considered by pupils. One might argue that official action had attempted to greatly reduce the multicultural dimension.

Multicultural education is, one might suggest, simply good education. It is about higher standards and achievement—quality as well as equality. The Education Reform Act (1988) led to the establishment of a highly prescriptive curriculum. There was also concern that the new national assessment procedures would in fact discriminate against bilingual pupils because they were not culturally or linguistically appropriate. There was an argument that the introduction of the market into education was similarly antipathetic to multicultural and anti-racist education because it was individualistic, competitive, and racist. Power was taken from the local education authorities, some of whom had been pacesetters in anti-racist developments, passed to the central government, and simultaneously devolved to schools where the atomized parent consumers tended to concentrate on examination results rather than broader social issues. The greater freedom for parents to opt out of the local education authorities was inevitably going to produce greater inequalities between schools. The National Curriculum was divided into subjects and therefore there was a danger that the interdisciplinary, collaborative work with more democratic and participatory teaching and learning styles would be lost. There were so many new initiatives that commitment to multicultural anti-racist education was in practice significantly reduced.

CURRICULUM SUBJECTS

There was considerable public controversy about many subjects, including history, mathematics, modern languages, and English (King & Reiss, 1993). The history curriculum debate focused on the balance between British, European, and world history. The New Right asserted that this was central to British identity and demanded a much more central place for the traditional British culture and values. It was not just British history, but a particular interpretation of that history that was to be imposed. There should be significant emphasis on the zenith of Empire and its civilizing mission, and little exploration of the destructiveness of slavery and the undermining of the economies of Commonwealth countries. Mathematics was a site of particular controversy, seen to be unimaginative in its treatment of the multicultural dimension. The modern languages documents appeared to assert a hierarchy of languages with European languages given the highest status, and with little provision for the development and sustaining of heritage languages. The English debate was focused on the debate about forms of teaching but this spilled over into which books should be given priority. Religious education was not part of the national curriculum, though it was a statutory requirement. It had to be of a "broadly Christian nature" and the compulsory act of collective worship every day had to be "wholly or mainly Christian." The effect of the whole was to downgrade the significance of multicultural anti-racist education.

The cross curricular themes (education for economic and industrial awareness; careers education and guidance; health education; education for citizenship; environmental education) and dimensions (countering racism in British education; personal and social education: a Black perspective; gender issues in education for citizenship; children with special educational needs; European community understanding; cultural differences and staff development; accountability and local management of schools) (Verma & Pumphrey, 1993) were to be developed across the curriculum. The incessant changing of the curriculum and assessment has not led to significant improvements in quality because teachers were not able to plan due to changing policies and an incoherence in the curriculum model.

There has been little opportunity to evaluate the National Curriculum and even the one major review (Dearing, 1993) that affirmed that the National Curriculum and assessment and testing is the key to raising educational standards stated, five years after teachers had said so, that urgent action was needed to (a) simplify and clarify the programs of study, (b) reduce the volume of material to be taught, and (c) reduce prescription so as to give more scope for professional judgment. We are aware of the turbulent environment and the pace of change but the mess of the implementation of the National Curriculum was due to sheer bad planning.

ACHIEVEMENTS AND PERFORMANCE OF ETHNIC MINORITIES

The Office for Standards in Education (OFSTED), the Government's Office for inspecting schools, published a report in 1996 called Recent Research on the Achievements of Ethnic Minority Pupils. A major issue in Britain has been educational performance in relation to race, class, and gender. Driver (1980) published research based partially on the school the author was headteacher of, which controversially showed how West Indians, and in particular girls, were overperforming. The OFSTED research shows that if ethnic diversity is ignored and if differences in educational achievement and experience are not examined, then considerable injustices will be sanctioned and enormous potential wasted. Social class and gender both clearly affect school performance, but when these are controlled for African Caribbean pupils, both sexes achieve below the level of other groups, the boys in particular. There have been significant improvements nationally in the last 10 years, but in some parts of the country the achievement of African Caribbean boys has worsened. Asian pupils achieve better than Whites of the same class and gender, with those of Indian origin achieving more highly than those of Bangladeshi origin. There is evidence that some secondary schools are more effective for certain ethnic minority groups in achieving high performance in school. This is measured against anticipated performance that takes account of socioeconomic factors. However, in schools that are effective in achieving high measured performance above expectations, not all pupils benefit equally. South Asian pupils suffer harassment in greater degree than other groups, but Black Afro-Caribbean boys are six times more likely to be excluded from school than White boys. Qualitative research indicated a relatively high level of conflict between White teachers and African Caribbean children. There is a considerable gulf between the daily reality experienced by many Black pupils and the stated goal of equal opportunities for all. This analysis by a government agency deserves serious consideration. This evidence shows how little progress there has been since Coard's (1971) book, *How the West Indian Child is Made Educationally Sub-normal in the British School System.*

There is research on how schools achieve good interethnic relations (Verma, Zec, & Skinner, 1994). There is little that is unexpected. Teachers are creatively engaged in responding to cultural diversity. Schools are constantly focused in their determination to implement equal opportunities. They recruit, retain, and promote ethnic minority teachers. They concentrate on behavior and insist on justice and mutual respect. They have many extracurricular activities and live democratic values. They repudiate staff who behave inappropriately and acknowledge and accept evidence of racist attacks. There is little here that could not be anticipated and that occurs in all good schools.

In the 1980s and 1990s there were extraordinary changes to education in Britain in the funding and management of schools; the curriculum; the assessment of children's learning; and the school's relationship with parents and the community.

These massive changes have not resulted in the addressing of issues associated with race, indeed arguably they have diverted attention. In the last 10 years there has not been the commitment within the education service to anti-racism that appeared to be emerging in the mid-1980s because of the pressures of coping with other changes including a totally new and changing national curriculum, new national assessment procedures, local management of schools, and open enrollment creating the marketization of education. Teachers need to be trained to have this as a priority (Verma, 1993). In addition, however, this may be because anti-racist approaches, with a broader challenge to current orthodoxy, have proved more difficult to accommodate.

The European Year Against Racism, which was 1997, was about seeking new ways of collaboration to combat racism and xenophobia across Europe. The central issue during the year was why, in an age of mass education, it had proved impossible to create a society that was liberated and free from the fears, hatred, and prejudices that fuel and feed racism, xenophobia, and other forms of oppression. The globalization of the world economy and intense competition is creating insecurity. In these circumstances it is insufficient simply to educate young minds about honesty, tolerance, cooperation, caring, and other such values. Unemployment, miscarriages of justice, racial attacks, bad education, and poor inner-city housing demonstrate how racial discrimination and hatred have not been challenged. The education system, which is itself a product of this increasingly performance-driven competitive society, cannot concentrate sufficiently on social justice without challenging many of the assumptions central to society. Leadership is the key to equity and it is still not sufficiently clear what the New Labor Project actually is. Old Labor appears to have been more aligned to removing inequalities. We shall have to see if the new government will have the courage to tackle racism in society and in schools.

ACKNOWLEDGMENTS

With thanks to Gajendra Verma for his wisdom and in memory of Barry Troyna for his passion.

REFERENCES

Auld, R. (1976). *William Tyndale, junior, and infant schools public inquiry, a report to the inner-London education authority.* QC, London: Inner London Education Authority.

Braham, P. (1987). *Migration and settlement in Britain* (Unit 2 of the Open University Course, E 354, Ethnic Minorities and Community Relations). Milton Keynes, England: Open University Press.

Cashmore, E., & Troyna, B. (1990). *Introduction to race relations.* London: Falmer Press.

Coard, B. (1971). *How the West Indian child is made educationally sub-normal in the British school system.* London: New Beacon Books.

Daniel, W. (1968). Racial discrimination in England. Harmonsworth, England: Penguin Books.

Dearing, R. (1993). *The national curriculum and its assessment.* London: School Curriculum and Assessment Authority.

DES. (1965). *The Education of immigrants.* DES Circular 7/65. London: HMSO.

DES. (1985). *The Swann report.* London: HMSO.

Driver, G. (1980, November). How West Indians do better at school. *New Society.*

Gillborn, D. (1995). *Racism and antiracism in real schools.* Buckingham, England: Open University Press.

King, A. S., & Reiss, M. J. (Eds.). (1993). *The multicultural dimension of the national curriculum.* London: Falmer Press.

Klein, G. (1982). *Resources for multicultural education: An introduction.* London: Longman for Schools Council.

Klein, G. (1993). *Education towards race equality.* London: Cassell.

Little, A., & Willey, R. (1981). *Multicultural education: The way forward.* York, England: Longman for the Schools Council.

McDonald, I., Bhavani, R., Khan, L., & John, G. (1989). *Murder in the playground: The Burnage report.* London: Longsight Press.

Mullard, C. (1984). *Anti-racist education: The three O's.* Cardiff, Wales: National Anti-racist Movement in Education.

Pumphrey, P. D., & Verma, G. K. (Eds.). (1990). *Race relations and urban education.* London: Falmer Press.

Rampton, A. (1981). *West Indian children in our schools.* Cmnd 8273. London: HMSO.

Riley, K. A. (1998). *Whose school is it anyway?* London: Falmer Press.

Scarman, L. (1981). *The Brixton disorders 10-12 April 1981.* London: HMSO.

Smith, D., & Tomlinson, S. (1989). *The school effect: A study of multiracial comprehensives.* London: Policy Studies Institute.

Stone, M. (1981). *The education of the Black child in Britain: The myth of multiracial education.* London: Collins Fontana.

Troyna, B. (1993). *Racism and education.* Buckingham, England: Open University Press.

Troyna, B., & Carrington, B. (1990). *Education, racism, and reform.* London: Routledge.

Verma, G. K. (Ed.). (1993). *Inequality and teacher education: An international perspective.* London: Falmer Press.

Verma, G. (1998, July). Inequality and multicultural education: Challenges for the 21st century. Keynote Address, University of Alberta, Canada.

Verma, G. K., & Pumphrey, P. D. (1993). *Cross curricular contexts: Themes & dimension in secondary schools.* London: Falmer Press.

Verma, G., Zec, P., & Skinner, G. (1994). *The ethnic crucible: Harmony and hostility in multi-ethnic schools.* London: Falmer Press.

Willey, R. (1982). *Teaching in multicultural Britain.* York, England: Longman for the Schools Council.

Chapter 14

Education, Social Class, and Dual Citizenship: The Travails of Multiculturalism in Latin America

Carlos Alberto Torres
University of California–Los Angeles, U.S.A.

THE ENLIGHTENMENT, CITIZENSHIP, AND A CRITIQUE OF NEOLIBERALISM IN LATIN AMERICA

Both the notion of citizenship and the notion of modern education are related to the basic premises of the Enlightenment. The movement of the Enlightenment suggests that there is a historical and social construction of human identities and therefore the individual socialization in rational principles is considered important. Educational institutions—as key institutions of the Enlighten-ment—have played a pivotal role in the constitution of citizenship in the liberal states in Latin America. It is precisely the liberal definition of citizenship that has profound implications for any discussion of multiculturalism.

There are three elemental aspects of a theory of citizenship for the Enlightenment. First, the Kantian proposal, which sustains the hypothesis that socialization processes, especially as related to cognitive thinking, have a place within structures that precede the coming to age of individuals becoming knowledgeable. Second, the Hegelian proposition, which suggests that the capacity to be socialized should be recognized as a civilizing technique, that is, as part of a process that depends, to a large extent, on the circumstances that inhibit or facilitate progressive social change. Third, the Marxist contention, which suggests that without access to the production and distribution of resources, that is, without access to the material benefits of the economy, it is impossible to sustain citizenship in political terms.

With the Hegelian reconstruction of Kant, a philosophy of consciousness—which later found in Marx and in the entire historical materialistic tradition an emblematic position—begins. This philosophy includes a notion of consciousness that surpasses the Kantian image of a universally abstract subject whose capacity to understand reality was measured a priori by cognitive categories enabling learning and science. For Hegel and the Enlightenment tradition—which granted importance to the non-positivistic educational humanism that predominated in the development of educational systems of the 20th century—the origins of consciousness emanate from a process of mutual recognition of self-consciousness and of the "other" as exteriority. Self-consciousness, according to Hegel, exists in and for itself, and for this reason, exists for another. In other words, it exists only to be recognized as such. Hence a philosophy of consciousness is the basis for the constitution of a liberal theory of citizenship.

An anthropology and a philosophy of consciousness point out the possibility of intersubjective recognition and the necessity to establish a philosophy of the rights of individuals within a framework of tolerance of difference. It was only within this framework of a political-philosophical interpretation advanced by diverse thinkers, from Plato, Aristotle, and Machiavelli, to the 17th- and 18th-centuries' contributions of Locke, Hobbes, and Rousseau, up to the 20th century work of Dewey, Freire, and Habermas, that it was possible to develop a theory of citizenship in the Enlightenment—which obviously did not remain uncontested. Critics argue that the philosophy of the Enlightenment is based on a comprehensive master narrative that is too abstract, ahistorical, and cannot understand the discourse of peoples situated in their temporality and location. Thus the Enlightenment is, "...a self-conscious—indeed belligerently self-conscious--antihistorical, antinarrative, anti-relational, naturalistic conceptual frame" (Somers, 1992).

Taking this critique seriously, it is necessary to acknowledge that a theory of citizenship based on a philosophy of consciousness runs the risk of considering all citizens as subject to the same rights and obligations because they are inherently similar in their cognitive abilities, social conditions, and ethical endeavors. In other words, the liberal theory of citizenship sees reality constituted by a totality of homogeneous individuals (insofar as they all confront work, nature, and fear) but with a diversity of interests. It will be naive, however, to conceive of the liberal perspective as one attempting the inclusion of large segments of the society in citizenship. On the contrary, it was built on a process of systematic exclusion of certain groups rather than inclusion. Considering the practical implications of a theory of citizenship that historically excluded women, the working class, or ethnic minorities, to name but a few, it is clear that the complex configuration of social reality is different from any homogenizing rhetoric.

The diverse identities of class, gender, race, ethnicity, sexual preference, religion, regionalism, and many other differences in the perceptions, preferences, and experiences of the social actors, cannot be easily subsumed under a "diversity of interests" perspective nor can they be encapsulated into the notion of "the citizen" as a concrete particular reflecting a universal abstract notion. This critique challenges any essentializing notions of citizenship, and invites us to undertake the analysis with a historical-structural nuance and, paraphrasing Ricoeur, with an epistemology of suspicion. This is particularly important in discussing the role of the liberal states in the constitution of education and citizenship.

As creatures of the Enlightenment, the liberal states in Latin America promoted public education. In their design of public education systems, they sought to incorporate all sectors of the population under the same institutional framework (including a hegemonic language, centralized curriculum and school governance, and prescribed, top-down national values), conferring to the educational system the responsibility to educate all people or, as the leading Latin American school reformer Domingo Faustino Sarmiento put it, "educating the sovereign."

The question of citizenship and democratic education cannot and should not be separated from the question of who are the citizens to be educated, how these citizens change over time in terms of their own demographic, political, cultural, and even symbolic configuration, and how citizens perceive these changes—what David Tyack called the public culture in the construction of difference (Tyak, 1990). Therefore, the discussion of multicultural democratic citizenship appears as central for theories of citizenship.[1] Moreover, it is fundamental to understand how the figure of the citizen itself changes in the context of the changes of the state and the process of economic, political, and technological globalization. Finally, it is fundamental to discover how

---

[1] This is not the place to outline the principles of a theory of democratic multicultural citizenship. Given the purpose of this chapter, I choose to emphasize the contradictions of citizenship building facing the issue of class, and particularly poverty in Latin America. For an analysis of theories of citizenship, theories of democracy, and theories of multiculturalism, see my work *Democracy, Education and Multiculturalism: Dilemmas of Citizenship in a Global World* (Torres, 1998).

the institutional settings in which citizens' virtues are played out change, implying, by definition, serious challenges to the role that the educational system and the political culture should play in citizenship building.

In short, the relationships between democracy, citizenship, and education cannot be treated in isolation from the question of multiculturalism, a theme that, by and large, was ignored by the liberal state. Yet, the liberal state sustained public education (free, mandatory, massive public education) as a "common ground," as a key component of the civil minimum, and as part of a process of integration of the population into the polity. The original intentions of the liberal state were expanded with the development of the welfare state; a state form that albeit incomplete, limited, and with few distributional resources compared to their industrial advanced counterparts, took shape in Latin American societies in this century.[2]

From the Welfare State to the Neoliberal State

The welfare state represents a social pact between labor and capital. Its origins can be found in the institutional reorganization of capitalism at the beginning of the 20th century in Europe, especially in the European social-democracies, such as the Scandinavian countries. Later in the century, the New Deal engineered during Roosevelt's administration in the United States represents a form of government in which citizens can aspire to reach minimum levels of social welfare, including education, health, social security, employment, and housing. These things are considered a right of citizenship rather than charity. Another central aspect is that this model operates under the assumption of full employment in an industrial economy following Keynesian models. For many reasons, such as the populist experiences and the extreme inequality of income distribution in Latin America, state formations with a strong element of intervention in civil society have some similarities with the model of the welfare state. However, there is also an important divergence, especially in the lack of state unemployment benefits. The state, which played an important role as the modernizer of society and culture, is also a state that undertook protectionist activities in the economy, supported the growth of

---

[2] One may be tempted to begin a systematic theoretical and historical analysis on the characteristics of the Latin American states, their corporatist and populists traits, and some of the historical peculiarities in the implementation of welfare policies. However, I refrain from doing so given the limited space available and different purpose of this paper. (For a treatment on the question of populism and corporatism, see, for instance, Torres, 1990; Torres & Morales-Gómez, 1990.)

internal markets, and promoted import substitution as a central aspect of the model of articulation between the state and society.

It is important to point out that the expansion and diversification of education took place in Latin American states sharing traits similar to the welfare state. These were interventionist states that considered educational expenditures as an investment, expanded educational institutions, including the massification of enrollments, enormously expanding educational budgets and the hiring of teachers.

The role and function of public education was magnified, following the premises of the 19th-century liberal state that consolidated the nation and markets.[3] In this liberal model of the state, public education postulated the creation of a disciplined pedagogical subject, hence the presence of an authoritarian substratum in the educational system that Paulo Freire so aptly described as "banking education." Thus, the role, mission, ideology, teacher's training models, as well as prevailing hegemonic notions of school curriculum and official knowledge, were profoundly influenced by a political philosophy that was, despite its liberal origins, state-oriented (Carli, Galiano, Puiggrós, Rodriguez, & Ziperovich, 1992; Puiggrós, 1986, 1990). The fiscal and external debt crisis of the 1970s and 1980s in Latin America, and the need to reorient, restructure, and stabilize the Latin American economies, brought into play the notion of a neoliberal state, with important implications for the educational systems.

Revisiting the Premises of the Neoliberal State

Neoliberalism, or the neoliberal state, are terms used to designate a new type of state that emerged in Latin America in the past two decades. They are tied to the experiences of the neoconservative governments such as those of Margaret Thatcher and John Major in England, Ronald Reagan in the United States, and Brian Mulroney in Canada. The first experience of neoliberalism implemented in Latin America is the neoliberal economic program carried out in Chile after the fall of Salvador Allende under the dictatorship of General Pinochet. More recently, the market models implemented by the governments of Carlos Saœl Menem in Argentina, Carlos Salinas de

---

[3] In the 19th century, the consolidation of the nation-state implied the end of civil war with the triumph of one of the warring elite factions and the constitution of a national army, the control of political borders of the nation and hence the control of labor and to some extent capital, the articulation of a jurisprudence with the linchpin of liberal constitutions regulating exchanges in the different markets and political networks, and sustainable cultural and educational policies usually associated with the development of compulsory, massive, and free educational systems.

Gortari and Ernesto Zedillo in Mexico, and Fernando Henrique Cardoso in Brazil, to name a few, represent, with the particularities of the Argentinean, Mexican, and Brazilian circumstances, neoliberal models.[4]

A central element for understanding the development of neoliberalism is the globalization of capitalism (Torres, 1998). The phenomena of globalization is based on the transformation of capitalism that alters the principles of the functioning of capitalism of petty commodity producers. It has been progressively built through several processes that analysts have characterized in several ways. Analysts have emphasized several traits, such as that of the imperialist expansion as the ultimate phase of capitalism (in the vision of Lenin), or the presence of monopoly capitalism analyzed by theoretical currents tied to the New Left in the United States (Paul Baran and Paul Sweezy), or what Claus Offe has denominated late or disorganized capitalism, with its problem of democratic ingovernability (Offe, 1985). From a postmodern perspective, globalization is linked to Fredric Jameson's definition of the characteristics of postmodernism as the cultural logic of late capitalism (Jameson, 1991). In short, globalization is central to understanding the transformation of contemporary capitalism. Although globalization cannot be equated with neoliberalism, the process of globalization provides a key historical framework for the neoliberal transformation.[5]

Neoliberal governments promote notions of open markets, free trade, the reduction of the public sector, the decrease of state intervention in the economy and market deregulation. Lomnitz and Melnick pointed out that historically and philosophically neoliberalism is associated with structural adjustment programs (Lomnitz & Melnick, 1991). Structural adjustment is defined as a set of programs, policies and conditionalities that are recommended by the World Bank, the International Monetary Fund, and other financial organizations. Although the World Bank distinguishes between stabilization, structural adjustment, and the policies of adjustment, it also recognizes that the use of these terms are "imprecise and inconsistent" (cited in Samoff, 1990, p. 21). These programs of stabilization and adjustment

---

[4] Without attempting to make a theoretical excursus, it is useful to point out that the notions of neoconservativism and neoliberalism have been identified by Michael Apple as two factions of the same movement of the right (Apple, 1993). (See Torres, 1995 for a discussion of the position of Apple and some of the differences between the two ideologies.)
[5] See Torres, 1998 for a detailed discussion of the implications of the transformation of the post-Fordist model for education.

have given rise to a number of policy recommendations, including the reduction of state spending, the devaluation of currencies to promote exports, reduction of tariffs on imports, and an increase in public and private savings. Thus, structural adjustment and stabilization policies seek to free international exchange, reduce distortions in price structures, do away with protectionism, and facilitate the influence of the market in the Latin American economies (Bitar, 1988).

The political rational of the neoliberal state is made up of a mixture of theories and interest groups that are tied to supply-side economics, monetarism, neoconservative cultural sectors, groups opposed to the redistributive policies of the welfare state, and sectors worried about the fiscal deficit at all costs. It is a contradictory alliance. These state models respond to fiscal crises and the crisis of legitimacy (real or perceived) of the state. In this way, the crises of confidence in the citizens are seen undermining the exercise of democratic representation and confidence in governments. In this culturally conservative and economically liberal model, state interventionism, and state enterprises are part of the problem, not part of the solution. For the neoliberal ideology, the best state is a small government.

In contrast to the model of the welfare state in which the state exercises a mandate to uphold the social contract between labor and capital, the neoliberal state is decidedly pro-business; that is to say, it supports the demands of the business world and drastically diminishes the regulatory and interventionist role of the state. Nevertheless, as Daniel Schugurensky rightly pointed out, this departure from state interventionism is not total but rather differential (Schugurensky, 1994). It is not possible to abandon, for symbolic as well as practical political reasons, all of the state's social programs. It is necessary to diffuse conflictive and explosive areas in the various realms of public policy.

This is the reason why even in neoliberalism there are programs of social solidarity in Costa Rica and Mexico, or why Brazil and other Latin American countries have passed very progressive legislation that protects street children. Furthermore, the state does not abandon the mechanisms of discipline and coercion, nor the employment of populist strategies of distribution of wealth (or promises of such), in order to obtain political consensus, especially during electoral campaigns. That is, the dismantling of the public policies of the welfare state are selectively, not indiscriminately, directed at specific targets.

There are important contradictions in the neoliberal and neoconservative models that are reflected in various domains. On the one hand, the neoliberal and neoconservative models promote individual autonomy (that is, in the realm of capital accumulation possessive individualism). On the other hand, they suggest that all citizens have public responsibilities, a fact that is not reconcilable with possessive individualism. In the economic realm, a similar dilemma exists in regard to promoting individually conceived preferences and searching for an alternative selection of public policies based on "rational public social choice." If markets are aggregates of individual preferences totally independent of any notion of the public good, this mechanism only functions when there is considerable convergence in the order of preferences of individuals. This model of political philosophy cannot easily reconcile possessive individuals with autonomous individual preferences and the state as an arena of negotiation of such preferences.

Furthermore, it is impossible to advance this reconciliation without presuming that there is a set of norms of behavior that are stable, supported by a mature state structure, a rational public policy based on a legal-rational approach, and in the context of consensual bases that are widely accepted in the political culture of society. These conditions are obviously rather different from the everyday reality of the majority of the countries in the world and specifically in the analysis of the Latin American countries; more so when growing poverty in Latin America offers a clear-cut class distinction in the social structures of the Latin American societies vis-à-vis industrial advanced societies (Williams & Reuten, 1993).

CITIZENSHIP, POVERTY AND MULTICULTURALISM: SOCIAL CLASS AND THE DUALIZATION OF CITIZENSHIP

To discuss theories of citizenship and their importance to education, it is important to move beyond historical or legal considerations in the definition of citizenship. That is, it is important to move beyond the notion of citizenship as a kind of personal status, a combination of rights and duties that all legal members of a nation-state hold. The discussion of theories of citizenship requires stating a premise from the outset: A theory of a good citizen should be relatively independent from the formal premises of the legal question of what it is to be a citizen. This is so because of the dual theoretical concerns of citizenship: citizenship as identity and as civic virtues—a theme which I do not have the time nor the space to discuss in detail in this chapter (see postscript in Torres, 1998). However, without considering the political economy dimension, and the need for a historical structural analysis of citizenship, any suggestion that citizenship is primarily a function of the civic virtues could be see as an idealistic undertaking. Civic virtues need a civil minimum that can only be found in a historical-structural context where these civil minimums overlap with basic material conditions. These material conditions should serve as basic premises in the constitution of citizenship. Hence the importance of social class, and particularly poverty, affecting the definition and practice of citizenship, and by implication education, in the region.

Poverty and Social Class

Recent data shows that there are 210 million people below the line of poverty in Latin America. Moreover, the situation is also linked to the question of employment and salary level in the region. The Economic Commission for Latin America (ECLA) has pointed out that 1995 salaries are below the 1980 salaries, and that the minimum salary in 1995 for 13 of the 17 Latin American countries studied are below those in 1980. For instance, in 1996 in Chile, the 20% richer strata of the population received 57.1% of the national income whereas in 1992 they had 52.4% of the income. The 20% poorer strata received in 1996 only 3.9% of the national income whereas back in 1992 they received 5%. Of the 14 million Chilean citizens, 3.3 million live below the poverty line. Argentina is not very different: The 20% richer received by May, 1997 52.9% of the national income whereas the 20% poorer received only 4.3%. Twelve years before, the 20% richer received 49.4% of the income and the 20% poorer received 5.9%. Hence, not only has the disparity in income distribution between rich and poor has widened, but salaries for the poor have become lower and employment more precarious.

The problem of poverty in Latin America appears to be intractable given the onerous hegemony that is evident in the neoliberal economic reasoning of the dominant classes. Several studies have pointed out the dangerous contradictions that arise when an exclusionary and marginalizing economic model, which permits previously unknown forms of social apartheid, is juxtaposed with a democratic regime whose legitimacy rests on expectations of political integration or real citizenship by the masses (Boron, 1991).

The relationship between citizenship and class, particularly the issue of poverty, is important for a number of reasons. If the process of globalization, and particularly neoliberal programs, assigns to the state a less prominent role in the construction of citizenship and the provision of social services to large segments of the population, this implies a loss of solidarity implicitly embedded in welfare policies. If there is a loss of solidarity in the community attributed to the changing role of the state, this poses important problems for democratic theory. Similarly, growing segments of the population becoming impoverished creates a quagmire for public policy and citizenship.

Dual Citizenship

From a political perspective, power is fragmented and diffused, as several versions of postmodernism argue. Looking at the moral crisis of contemporary societies, a central element in the analysis is that the distinctions of *difference*—to paraphrase Bourdieu—led people to construct the categories of *otherness*. By placing the blame and responsibility of the perceived economic, social, or moral crisis on "the other" as scapegoats, the ethical and political dilemmas emerging in the constitution of working and caring communities are diffused or ignored. Thus, shifting the blame to "others" (illegal immigrants, lazy workers, people of color, etc.) facilitates a pedagogical discourse that relocates the responsibility of providing high-quality education to all citizens from the hands of the state to the invisible hand of the market. After all, the market, as a *deus ex machina*, will discriminate against less able individuals. Hence, the most rational means of resource allocation (i.e., the markets' supply and demand dynamics) will identify means and ends, making it possible for the most motivated, best educated, and "productive" individuals to succeed.

With the logic of the market prevailing, the argument goes, individuals will then be free from state intervention and from clientelist and patrimonialist state practices. They will be able to pursue their free will without outside intervention in the context of a freer exchange of goods and services regulated by market mechanisms. This position may be considered a philosophy of libertarianism with its exacerbation of individualism, and it does little to develop forms of solidarity beyond kinship and small groups. An unqualified market orientation will pit individuals and the social representation of the notion of free individuals against socially constructed notions of community and collective attempts for social change. The construction of community in contemporary and fragmented capitalist societies, given the exclusionary nature of capitalist development, demands the creation of social inducements—beyond individual ethics—to foster generosity and solidarity. In addition, it requires notions of social contracts that can be achieved—even though operational notions of individual autonomy and freedom may be, following the Rousseaunian dilemma, qualified and, occasionally, restricted, so the whole community could access to higher convivial levels of freedom. In the same vein, following the postmodern notion that the state is mostly social regulation, any crisis of social regulation refers to deep fractures in society—for instance, what Habermas called legitimacy deficit in late capitalism. Yet these crises may also refer to typical problems of the state in late capitalism (Acker, 1988; Apple, 1982, 1988, 1993; Connell, 1985). The paradox is that crises of social regulation, and by implication drastic changes in the role of the state, may explain the decline in solidarity.

There are several indications of serious dislocations in schools systems in Latin America. For instance, teachers may find students aloof, with no interest in learning cognitive skills or pursuing public deliberation. Students may find teachers (and the adult society in general) distant from their own interests and social construction of knowledge—a knowledge base that is the result of the appropriation of a global mass culture. Another example, closer to the experience of the United States, relates to debates on the politics of identity. Taken in one of its most extreme versions, the politics of identity and representation of minority groups in schools and universities may agree with the theory of a zero-sum society. With a zero-sum approach, the affirmation of rights of one group of underrepresented individuals, and the appropriation of resources to satisfy a historical grievance or modify an identifiable process of discrimination, will imply, by definition, that resources are taken from one group at the expense of another group of underrepresented individuals. Thus, the result is the continuous conflict among diverse constituencies representing minorities, women, class-based, ability, and other underrepresented groups, given the implicit (and widely accepted notion) that resources are fixed or inelastic.

What are the implications of dislocations of this magnitude for the relocation of the politics of identity and difference in Latin America? Is it possible to find a framework of solidarity that does not depend entirely on the performance of the welfare state, or any reconstructed notion of state intervention that could be made sharply distinct from the neoliberal state? This question requires different levels of analysis. To begin with, the notion of social regulation set forth by Foucault is very useful to link the workings of structures and the process of reception, adaptation, resistance, and re-elaboration of knowledge by individual actors. Can social regulation operate independently from competing ideologies? If this is the case, then the gap between generations or the declining state intervention in sponsoring solidarity should not be an issue. The rules of regulation and the instruments of regulation will simply have changed hands, giving a more prominent place to market exchanges. Knowledge will not only be fragmented but segmented by social hierarchies. Those who can afford to pay growing user fees will continue to send their children to schools, and their offspring will be able to access the "pool" of knowledge that society has to offer. Those who will be unable to pay the growing out-of-pocket expenses will simply become marginal to mainstream knowledge and societal structures.

The same can be said regarding the socialization of children and youth who are introduced to new technologies, computers, or advanced communications devices. Technological literacy will become a central component in the context of social differentiation in the region. The best-endowed private and (to a much lesser extent) public schools will be able to take advantage of the reception of these new technologies in terms of both teaching and learning. This, in turn, increases the exposure of middle-and upper-class students to the most creative and productive—not to mention the most profitable—technologies. Public schools that do not have access to additional funding to modernize their technological structure, to hire specialized teachers and technicians, and to attract the best students in their areas of influence, will remain quite distant from the avant garde training and socialization.

With these increasing processes of differentiation, the educational system will then be another form of exclusion rather than inclusion, reflecting the dualization of society. Dual societies reflect in dramatic ways how individuals differ in their access to wealth, power, influence, and political representation. There is no reason why, with the withdrawal of the state from its public mandate, society will provide free and compulsory education to its citizens. Schooling will become segmented and inequality will increase.

Citizenship, Social Class, and Multiculturalism

Latin American societies have become increasingly dual, with rich and poor sectors growing very much apart. This dualization of class structures is not exclusive of Latin America but a phenomena of worldwide proportions. Therefore, there are serious contradictions, tensions, and imbalances between the social citizenship and the political citizenship. The social citizenship is expressed by the effective access to a certain quantity of goods and services, both material and symbolic, which decisively condition the quality of life of individuals. The political citizenship is expressed by means of equal and universal suffrage, and the exercise of rights and obligations. This schism between both types of citizenship, so insightfully argued by T.

H. Marshall (see Marshall, 1950, 1963, 1965, 1981, 1983), will propitiate the proliferation of attitudes, beliefs, and values antagonistic to the democratic stability and the legitimation formulae on which democratic regimes are founded. Needless to say, with teachers' perceptions that they need to transmit the collective values of the nation to children and youth, there is no surprise that teachers' leaders and rank-and-file in Latin America are visibly upset with diminishing investment in public education, which is seen as one more trend in this process of dualization. In this context, it is legitimate to ask if the disequilibrium between these two citizenships may explain the withdrawal of state investment in education and compulsory schooling. This withdrawal, perhaps forced by structural adjustment conditionalities, is reflected in educational budgets and eventually in declining enrollments, particularly in public secondary education (see Torres, 1993).

The dualization of schooling will result in, and be an example of, the constitution of at least two broad types of citizens: triple A (AAA) citizens, to use a term in vogue in Latin America resembling the nomenclature to classify the quality of bonds and credit ratings of institutions, and "dispensable" citizens or class B citizens. AAA citizens are those who can exercise any model of political representation and participation they wish, not only through their vote but also through political action because they are connected to the networks of power. They can achieve information quickly through new cybernetic technologies—and the navigation of the growing "information super highway"—and can manipulate the symbols of the highbrow cultural capital. Dispensable citizens are those whose marginality is constructed through the process of representation of mass media coupled with their political isolation and fragmentation. They are also suffering serious economic pressures, many of them are already part of a poverty belt surrounding the metropolitan areas of Latin America, or located in deteriorating sectors of cities, particularly inner cities. Their strategies for survival in their everyday life takes precedent over any other activity, including politics. Both types of citizens are exposed simultaneously to the multiple messages of a growingly inter-nationalized mass media committed to the construction of the possessive individualism, to use the term popularized by MacPherson in his insightful critique of liberal theories of democracy (Popkewitz, 1991, p. 75). In Latin America this is what a cultural critic called "the unilateral North-Americanization of the symbolic markets" (Canclini, 1993).

SOCIAL CLASS, DUAL CITIZENSHIP, AND POVERTY: THE PERILS OF MULTICULTURALISM

Who must ask for forgiveness and who can grant it? Those who, during so many years, sat in front of a full table and satiated themselves while we sat with death, so daily, so ours, that we are no longer afraid of it? Those who filled their pockets and their souls with formal statements and promises? The dead, our dead, so deadly dead of "natural" death, that is, of measles, flu, dengue, cholera, typhoid, mononucleosis, tetanus, pneumonia, malaria, and other gastrointestinal and pulmonary goodies. Our dead, so completely dead, so democratically dead. Our dead who died without anyone counting, without anyone saying at last "THAT'S ENOUGH." That would give meaning back to those deaths so that someone would ask of the common dead, our dead, that this time they come back to live rather than to die again? Those who denied the right and the ability of our people to govern? Those who denied the respect of our customs, of our color, of our language? Those who treated us as strangers in our own land and who asked us for papers and to obey a law whose existence and righteousness we ignore? Those who tortured us, imprisoned us, and disappeared us for wanting a piece of land, not a large piece, not a small piece, only a piece where we could reap something to fill the stomach? Who must ask for forgiveness and who can grant it? (SubComandante Marcos, 1994, front page)

This issue of dual citizenship poses the perennial question of who is being included and who is being excluded from compulsory schooling and the benefits of the social systems. The epigraph by SubComandante Marcos, discussing the situation of the indigenous people in Chiappas, is telling. SubComandante Marcus' sharp criticisms reflect historical conditions that are not idiosyncratic of the Chiappas region or Mexico per se, but of a more generic situation throughout the region.

The inclusion or exclusion of social groups from schooling should be discussed in light of increasing user fees, decentralization, privatization, and municipalization policies. These policies are not restricted to Latin America, and therefore this discussion has an intellectual and political appeal that goes well beyond idiosyncratic or regional considerations. As has been pointed out, a disturbing factor regarding the establishment of citizenship and education is the accelerated impoverishment of large sectors of Latin American societies (Boron & Torres, 1995; for an interesting pedagogical and political analysis, see Romío, 1997). This situation bears serious consequences for democracy, the implementation of economic modernization, social reform projects, and indeed, educational reform.

This contradiction between neoliberalism and democracy is far from being a mere theoretical or rhetorical problem. Rather, it reflects the tremendous difficulties that await Latin American democracies in their efforts to reconcile three fundamental imperatives of this type of political regime: equity, access, and representation. Boron and Torres (1995) argued that there are three main problems in the relationship between poverty and democracy and that these problems have a direct impact on the role that education plays in the fight against poverty and in citizenship. The first is of an ethical nature: the serious attack on justice that is produced by the neoliberal policies that have burdened the lower socioeconomic classes with the costs of stabilization and structural adjustment. Despite different styles, the basic principles of these policies have been similar in the different Latin American countries: a general reduction in social expenditures, an increase in tax revenues through the increase of indirect taxes that further aggravate the regressive nature of tax structures, the freezing of wages and salaries, especially in the public sector, and the "flexibilization" of labor markets, a euphemism for justifying massive layoffs, unemployment, and underemployment. This euphemism is used to such a point that there are countries, such as Nicaragua, in which it is possible to say that there are more unemployed than employed persons in the formal labor markets. The poor are increasing in number and poverty is growing to previously inconceivable levels (McMahon, 1995).

The second problem is of an economic nature. Until what point are growing poverty levels compatible with the need to improve the macroeconomic "rationality" of Latin American capitalisms? To what extent will the economic reforms, directed toward the attainment of certain objectives, continue to condemn the popular sectors by diminishing their income and consumption patterns and reducing their expectations for individual and collective progress? It is not necessary to adhere to a catastrophic vision of the world to understand that an impoverished society would have a difficult time expanding its consumption or being in conditions to achieve increased competition, which would permit it to compete in the turbulent waters of international markets—markets in which the "competitive advantages of nations" are based on higher levels of education, health, and the quality of life of their labor forces.

The third issue is related to the effects of structural adjustment on the ideological foundations of new democracies. In several Latin American societies, the principles of democratic legitimacy have been missing the strength that can be found in other regions. This weakness in the ideological principles of democracy is a serious obstacle for the consolidation of democracy, especially given that for its effective functioning, it is necessary to count on a relatively high level of credibility in its administrative efficiency and a positive opinion of its capacity to represent the "general interests" of society.

Nevertheless, these menacing tendencies are not necessarily destined to endanger the collapse of democracy. The "economic reductionism" dominant in certain domains of social sciences during the 1970s, both on the Right and on the Left, has been disputed by the perpetuation of Latin American democratic regimes during the tumultuous decade of the 1980s. Empirical investigation has convincingly shown that, at least in the short run, economic crises do not necessarily precipitate the desarticulation of democratic regimes. Furthermore, Latin American democracies have been shown to possess a surprising strength (Remmer, 1991). Yet, even though these conclusions may serve to extinguish the fires of premature anxieties, it is still the case that democratic governments, insensitive to the urgent needs of the poor and indifferent to the growth of poverty, could very well be digging their own graves.

The tradition of Western political thought speaks with one voice: generalized indigence is incompatible with the spirit and the practices of democracy and liberty. Plato criticized oligarchic governments of the polis, because they resulted in the violent coexistence of two cities: that of the poor and that of the rich, joined "in a permanent conspiracy against each other, mother of the disorder which would put an end to liberty" (Plato, 1963 version, paragraphs 551.d and 552.d). Almost two thousand years later, Rousseau theorized about the conditions that would assure the existence/coexistence of democracy and liberty. To achieve this objective, he recommended reducing the differences between the "different classes, as much as possible," so that there would be neither beggars nor magnates. These groups, two faces of the same coin, were considered dangerous for the future of democracy because, "it is among them that the business of public liberty would be determined: some buy it and others sell it" (Rousseau, 1968/1980).

Identity and diversity cannot be subsumed exclusively into class supremacy but neither can they be separated from it. Cornel West would agree with this because he argued that: "...this historical process of naming is part of the legacy not just of white supremacy but of class supremacy" (West, de Alva, & Shorris, 1996, p. 57).

The epigraph that animates the conversation in this conclusion, taken from the indictment by SubComandante Marcos to the Ladino Mexican system and written in the Lacandona tropical rain forest of Chiappas, is a sobering reminder of what is at stake in considering multiculturalism and the political challenges to the politics of culture and identity. Add to these historical grievances the growing presence of poverty and the lack of satisfaction of growing segments of the population in achieving the laudable goals that the educational systems under liberal states in the region had outlined, and we have a most explosive social issue that cannot be simply addressed with technical recommendations of public policy. It will require a serious and concerted effort for the social transformation of class structures; a revolutionary effort in searching for a genuine democratic multicultural citizenship.

REFERENCES

Acker, S. (1988). Teachers, gender, and resistance. *British Journal of Sociology of Education, 9*(3), 307-322.

Apple, M. W. (Ed.). (1982). *Cultural and economic reproduction in education.* London and Boston: Routledge & Kegan Paul.

Apple, M. W. (1988). *Teachers and texts: A political economy of class and gender.* New York: Routledge.

Apple, M. W. (1993). *Official knowledge: Democratic education in a conservativeaAge.* New York and London: Routledge.

Bitar, S. (1988). Neo-conservativism versus neo-structuralism in Latin America. *CEPAL Review, 34,* 45.

Boron, A. (1991). *Estado, capitalismo y democracia en América Latina* [State, capitalism, and democracy in Latin America]. Buenos Aires: Imago Mundi.

Boron, A. A., & Torres, C. A. (1995). Educación, pobreza y ciudadanía en América Latina [Education, poverty and citizenship in Latin America]. In E. Pieck & E. A. López (Eds.), *Educación y pobreza: De la desigualdad social a la equidad* [Education and poverty: From social inequality to equity] (pp. 89-120). Zinacantepec, Mexico: Colegio Mexiquense & UNICEF.

Canclini, N. G. (1993, October/December). Una modernización que atrasa: La cultura bajo la regresión neoconservadora [Backward modernization: Culture under the neoconservative regression]. *Revista de Casa de las Américas,* 3-12.

Carli, S., Galiano, R.S., Puiggrós, A., Rodríguez, L., Ziperovich, R. (1992). Escuela, Democracia y Orden [School, Democracy and Order]. In A. Puiggrós (Ed.), *Colección Historia de la Educación en Argentina III* [Series: History of Education in Argentina III]. Buenos Aires: Editorial Galeana.

Connell, R. W. (1985). *Teachers' work.* Boston: Allen & Unwin.

Jameson, F. (1991). *Postmodernism or the cultural logic of late capitalism.* Durham, NC: Duke University Press.

Lomnitz L., & Melnick, A. (1991). *Chile's middle class: A struggle for survival in the face of neoliberalism.* Boulder and London: Lynne Rienner.

Marcos, Sub-comandante. (1994, January 18). Carta de Marcos [Letter by Marcos]. *La Jornada.*

Marshall, T. H. (1950). *Citizenship and social class and other essays.* Cambridge, England: Cambridge University Press.

Marshall, T. H. (1963). *Sociology at the crossroads.* London: Heinemann.

Marshall, T. H. (1965). *Social policy in the twentieth century.* London: Hutchinson.

Marshall, T. H. (1981). *The right to welfare and other essays.* London: Heinemann.

Marshall, T. H. (1983). Citizenship and social class. In D. Held, J. Anderson, B. Gieben, S. Hall, L. Harris, N. Parker, B. Turok, & M. Robertson (Eds.), *States and societies* (pp. 248-260). Oxford, England: The Open University.

McMahon, C. (1995, January 17). Weak peso hurts poorest Mexicans. *Chicago Tribune,* p. 1.

Offe, Claus. (1985). *Disorganized Capitalism*. Trans. J. Keane. London: Hutchinson.

Popkewitz, T. S. (1991). *A political sociology of educational reform: Power/knowledge in teaching, teachers education, and research*. New York and London: Teachers College.

Puiggrós, A. (1986). *Democracia autoritarismo en la pedagogía Argentina y Latinoamericana* [Democracy and authoritarianism in Argentine and Latin American pedagogy]. Buenos Aires: Galerna.

Puiggrós, A. (1990). *Sujetos, disciplina y curriculum en los orígenes del sistema educativo Argentino* [Subjects, discipline, and curriculum in the origins of the Argentine educational system]. Buenos Aires: Galerna.

Remmer, K. L. (1991). The political impact of economic crisis in Latin America in the 1980s. *American Political Science Review, 85*(3), 777-800.

Romío, J. E. (1997). *Dialética da diferencía. O projeto da escola bésica cidadí frente ao projeto pedagógico neoliberal* [Dialectic of difference. The basic urban school project vis à vis the national political project]. Doctoral dissertation, Universidad de Sío Paulo, Facultade de Educacíon, Sío Paulo, Brazil.

Rousseau, J.-J. (1968/1980). *The social contract*. Baltimore: Penguin.

Samoff, J. (1990, June). More, less, none? Human resource development: Responses to economic constraint. Unpublished manuscript.

Schugurensky, D. (1994). *Global economic restructuring and university change: The case of Universidad de Buenos Aires*. Doctoral dissertation, University of Alberta, Edmonton, Alberta, Canada.

Somers, M. (1992, Winter). Narrativity, narrative identity, and social action: Rethinking English working-class formation. *Social Science History, 16*(4), 593.

Torres, C. A. (1990). *The Politics of nonformal education in Latin America*. New York: Praeger.

Torres, C. A., & Morales-Gómez, D. A. (1990). *The state, corporatist politics and educational policy making in Mexico*. New York: Praeger.

Torres, C. A. (1993). *Public education, teachers' organizations and the state in Latin America*. Prepared for the conference on "Educational Reform. Changing Relationships Between the State, Civil Society, and the Educational Community," at the University of Wisconsin—Madison.

Torres, C. A. (1995). The state and education: Or why educational researchers should think politically about education. *Review of Research in Education, 21*, 255-331.

Torres, C. A. (1998). *Democracy, education and multiculturalism: Dilemmas of citizenship in a global world*. Lahman, MD and Boulder, CO: Rowman & Littlefield.

Tyack, D. (1990). Restructuring in historical perspective: Tinkering towards utopia. *Teachers College Record, 92*(2), 170-191.

West, C. de Alva, J. K., & Shorris, E. (1996, April). Colloquy: Our next race question. The uneasiness between Blacks and Latinos. *Harper's Magazine*, p 57.

Williams, M., & Reuten, G. (1993, Spring). After the rectifying revolution: The contradictions of the mixed economy. *Capital and Class, 49*, 82.

Chapter 15

Addressing Equity and Social Justice Concerns in Chile's Formal and Informal Education: An Historical and Contemporary Analysis

Guillermo Williamson C.
Universidad de La Frontera, Temuco, Chile

Carmen Montecinos
University of Northern Iowa, U.S.A.

This chapter provides a description and an analysis of efforts, over the last 30 years, within the formal educational system (the state) and the informal sector (the civil society) to promote equal educational opportunities for Chilean citizens. Although informal and formal initiatives in the areas of youth development, adult education among peasants, workers, and women, indigenous first-nations, and human rights have not coalesced in a progressive educational movement, collectively and individually each represents concerns, issues, and goals similar to those that have driven the multicultural education movement in the United States. These are all efforts that recognize that equitable educational practices must be rooted in the historical, cultural, and social specificity of distinct social groups. These are projects that seek to position each of these groups to be on an equal status as they embark in a common national project that purports to further democratic participation, equity, pluralism, and social and economic justice for each group and individual.

There has been widespread consensus among citizens and educators alike that the primary entity responsible for the education of all citizens—and upward social mobility—is the state itself. In fact, since the 1930s and until 1980, with the Primary Instruction Act of 1936 and the first Popular Front government (with the slogan, "To govern is to educate," 1938), the primary educational agency in Chile was the State. Three factors converged then, and now, to afford a high profile to education: (a) the need of the ruling class to disseminate and validate to society its ideology and worldview, (b) a political sense held by the progressive elements that public education is an essential component of a democracy, and (c) the popular perception that education is, par excellence, the route to individual and collective social and economic advancement. Currently, although the state has given the administration of schools to municipalities and private corporations, 92% of all Chilean students attend free schools that are subsidized by the government, with a 96% coverage in the basic, compulsory education level (Grades 1 through 8).

The educational processes in Chile have experienced significant changes over the last half of the 20th century as the country has undergone important political, economical, and sociocultural transformations. Three distinct periods can be identified: the development and leftists movements of the 1960s and early 1970s; the military dictatorship from 1973 to 1989; and the transition toward the restoration of democracy beginning in 1990. In this chapter we give an overview of the specific proposals the government of each period offered as it understood the role of education in such tasks as deepening democracy, promoting economic development, and the welfare of Chilean citizens. We also describe important educational initiatives through which various sectors of the civil society sought to broaden access to job-skill training as well as their social and political organization. Within the context of the last period of educational reform, currently underway since 1991, equity has been a guiding principle in resource allocation. Whereas the government analysis first identified social class discrepancies in achievement as the target of equity efforts, women's and indigenous groups' activism have led to the institutionalization of policies that speak to these groups' plight for equity. These policies are also described. As a conclusion, we reflect on some of the limitations and contradictions in the current educational scenario in Chile. These signal new possibilities for deepening democracy and pluralism in the education that Chile offers to its citizens.

1960 TO 1973: PERIOD OF THE DEMOCRATIZATION OF EDUCATION

In Latin America, two historical movements of tension and contradictions, from which Chile was not exempt, shaped this period. One was the movement toward development, driven by the U.S. Agency for International Development (US/AID) and the Inter-American Conference held at Punta de Este, Uruguay, in August, 1961. At this conference, situated in the context of the Cold War, development was thought to entail (a) the implementation of reforms in revenue, education, and agrarian matters; (b) the technological modernization of productive and government structures; and (c) new policies for integrating the marginalized sectors of society. The second movement represented the leftist social and political forces of the period, which flourished under the influence and example of the Cuban Revolution. These latter forces sought to deepen the reforms started by the Development Movement, or to overcome capitalism. This tension is seen in Chile's progression from a liberal rightist government (that of Jorge Alessandri R., 1958-1964), to a centrist development/reform government (of Eduardo Frei M., 1964-1970), ending with a government transitioning into socialism (Salvador Allende G., 1970-1973).

Formal Education

During this period education was viewed as one of the most important democratic reforms. Consequently, the state apparatus under the rule of the Christian-Democratic party first and the Popular Union later devoted much attention to it. For conservative elements of the Chilean right, private education was a matter for the elite and public schooling was oriented toward paternalism, in response to the need to cover the growing and varied demands for semi- and skilled laborers for the economic sectors as well as for assuring an ideologically aligned social base.

The two governments of that period pushed for different approaches to educational reform. The first one, the Christian Democratic government (1964-1970), designed and implemented an educational reform that began in 1965 and ended, for all practical purposes, in 1980 when the military regime imposed a general reconstruction of the educational system. The second one, the Popular Union government (1970-1973), only formulated the design of its proposal for a Unified National School. Even in its initial stage, this proposal generated such a strong negative reaction among sectors of society that opposed this government, it never got to be fully discussed, much less implemented, before the military coup in 1973.

Educational Reform of 1965. Within the Development and leftists movements the state's responsibility for modernizing the educational system was widely understood as just another task within the state's political obligation of integrating citizens into society (the principle of democratization) by means of one of the primary instruments that it had available for such a task (education). The Educational Reform was oriented toward two main objectives: (a) increasing educational access at the different levels of schooling, and (b) updating the national curriculum and the necessary didactic resources to support the new curriculum. By 1960, preschool enrollment covered 2% of the 0 to 5 age group, primary enrollment covered 80% of the 6 to 13 age group, and secondary enrollment covered 14% of the 14 to 17 age group (Arancibia, Edwards, Jara, Jelvez, & Nuñez, 1998). Increasing enrollment entailed building new schools and using existing school buildings in double shifts of 5 to 6 hours of school time each.

To achieve the second objective in a manner coherent with the demands of the economic and sociopolitical developments in Chile, the school system's structure was also modified. The old system of 6 years of primary school and 6 years of secondary school was replaced with a system of 8 years of obligatory basic school and 4 years of high school. High school students were asked to choose between a Humanistic-Scientific track and a Technical-Professional track. New curricular standards and contents were also developed, as well as textbooks and teaching materials. Extensive professional development programs and an institutional restructuring of the Ministry of Education were implemented. The Reform incorporated adult education, which, associated with the Agrarian Reform or the Popular Promotion Program, became very important in rural and urban areas. Here, the work of Paulo Freire made substantial contributions to state policies of education and training on a theoretical basis as well as on a methodological one, especially in the field of literacy and in the training of social educators.

The Reform represented an advance in democracy as it widened the social sectors of the population who had access to broader opportunities for basic training (e.g., people in rural areas or youth). Nevertheless, the general emphasis on increasing coverage, coupled with a technological-behaviorist perspective guiding curricular changes, largely failed to produce the improvements in academic achievement expected by the Reform. An excessive operational design of the curriculum and programs (in accordance with Skinner, Bloom, and Tyler) had the effect of inhibiting teachers' creativity and innovative possibilities, orienting them basically toward an application of predesigned practices.

The reform spirit in education, and in society in general, was manifested in several important social-educational movements. Especially important was the teachers' movement, which led to the formation of the Single Union of Education Workers (SUTE in Spanish). During this period, the teachers' union struggled for better salaries and working conditions. Others included the high school students' movement, resulting in the formation of the Federation of Secondary Students (FESES), and the university students' movement, which drove the University Reform (1968), beginning in the Catholic universities and then extending throughout the system. In addition (and perhaps unprecedented until then), private, elite schools joined in the process, generating innovations in their school culture and in the orientation of their educational projects. Markedly, starting in 1969 to 1970, these groups' mobilizations became increasingly politicized, articulating their actions with the ideals and political conflicts that were posed with much tension and contradictions in the life of the society.

Education became a field of disputes and political struggle among the different sectors that sought power and influence within the state apparatus. In the face of this process of social change that was becoming more and more sharpened, reformism (educational, agrarian, political, social) clearly showed its limits and impossibilities vis-à-vis a greater radicalization of popular demands and the ideological and social contradictions that the society was facing.

Unified National School (1973). In 1970, the presidential candidate for the Popular Unity, a coalition of parties from the left of differing shades of socialism, was democratically elected. The coalition's main platform was the strengthening of democracy and a peaceful transition to socialism. One of the projects that the government tried to enact during its second year was a change in the educational system. This change cohered with the policy of the cultural formation of a "New Man" for a more democratic and socialistic society. This Unified National School (ENU in Spanish), although only at the proposal stage, drew such vehement protest from the business, religious, and private education sectors, and from the political opposition groups that the government was forced to withdraw it from public consideration.

In its conception, ENU deepened the relationship between the educational system and the changes that were taking place in the economic, social, and ideological structures of Chilean society. Among its goals was to convert education into an instrument for the exercise of democracy, for critique, reflection, and the valuing of the popular culture. It wanted to make education closer to the work of scientists and artists as well. Another goal was to decrease the achievement gap between classes. Educational inequalities between a private education that prepared dominant elite classes and a public education for the rest of the country's majority was seen as contributing to inequities in other areas. Public education, according to the Popular Unity, was preparing them more for subordination and proletarianization, rather than for a certain upward social mobility. The state, they argued, was responsible for strengthening public (state) education and reorienting high school's focus from humanistic-scientific training toward technological (or technical-professional, as it is called in Chile) training.

In the face of the growing political, social, economic, and cultural demands of the popular sectors for their integration and participation in the benefits of development and for democracy itself, the State of Compromise generated in the 1930s and the reformism of the 1960s showed their shortcomings. The subversive actions of the dominant classes, associated with U.S. interference, the discontent of other sectors of society, the critical economic situation, as well as errors committed by Popular Unity itself in the areas of political strategy, sectarianism, and dogmatism, all led up to the military coup of 1973. ENU never went further than the proposal stage.

Informal Education

In the field of non-formal education, one could still not speak of any massive experiences, as was the case later in the 1980s with the experiences in popular education conducted by Non-Governmental Organizations and social movements. Still, some important formative actions do stand out. Headed up by university groups or their student federations, the universities, which were themselves in the midst of a reform process, generated rich and broad educational programs. Young people attending high schools and universities lived, especially from 1969 on, with a deep sense of solidarity, idealism, and social commitment, especially concerning the extremely poor and the transformation of society. In this process we can see experiences of political education conducted by traditional political parties; participation in social, university, or youth pastoral activities promoted by the Catholic Church; and the appearance of Scout groups, cultural groups, and other options that stimulated sociability in youth. Among the many expressions of non-formal education for young people, two are particularly noteworthy.

The University/Worker/Peasant Department of the Pontifical Catholic University of Chile (DUOC in Spanish) was created by university students (primarily Social-Christian reformists) with the objective of providing free training services to poor urban and rural communities. The students did training in slums, communities, or rural areas on topics that were related to the majors they were studying. This initiative was greatly broadened so that in 1975 it was reaching almost 80,000 adults and young people who were studying (now for a nominal fee) different courses and skill training programs, including those at the middle technical level. Technicians and professionals from certain fields joined the students as teachers, as did certain skilled members of slums (e.g., barbers, dressmakers). The DUOC turned into a flexible pedagogical experience, made up of volunteers oriented toward solidarity, and a very basic curriculum oriented toward specific job-related skills. Classes were delivered by the university students wherever the minimum conditions could be found. In 1978 the military dictatorship took over the DUOC and converted it into one of the principal centers of private, technical training in the country.

A second innovative and massive educational initiative led by young people was the so-called Voluntary Jobs. These were service experiences organized by the High School and University Student Federations, and by youth or university pastoral groups. Students engaged in voluntary service in specific areas (health, literacy, family gardens) helping outlying economically deprived urban and rural communities build up their social infrastructure (i.e., community centers, schools, first aid stations). Service experiences were carried out during summer vacation, a few days during the winter vacation, and on weekends. Although it was intermittent and there was not necessarily a perspective of political commitment present on a permanent or sustained basis, it was a type of social pedagogy. In the absence of such political commitment, these service activities could be viewed as an expression of a certain paternalistic idealism on the part of the young people. Nevertheless, they were a determining factor in the education of urban youth, and children of the middle class and skilled laborers. Its impact in generating political consciousness and organization among youth was quite significant. Both experiences established a dialogue between the youth/university world and the most economically disenfranchised sectors of Chilean society. This dialogue, among other factors, contributed to an active political participation by youth/university students during the Christian Democrat government and later during the Popular Unity government.

As for the peasants, the processes of rural development and agrarian reform of the period generated the conditions for an active policy of adult education, oriented toward literacy and training in aspects of production, social and cultural issues, and especially in terms of organizing. One of its strategic components for change was the different educational processes: formal and informal education, education of adults, and training of leaders and advisers. Their primary objective was to structure a peasant social movement, through unions and cooperatives, which would be able to sustain politically and socially the agrarian changes that were occurring. The proposals of Paulo Freire and his psychosocial method constituted a conceptual and pedagogical milestone for the period, in that it inspired many pedagogical practices in literacy, as well as the training of advisers and peasant leaders, adult educators, and social workers. This work was conducted in the private sector of educational institutions linked to the Catholic church and, basically, in public institutions. The agrarian reform broke down the relationship between the large land estates and the small farmsteads within the Chilean agrarian structure, and pushed for rural development.

1973 TO 1990: THE MUNICIPALIZATION AND PRIVATIZATION OF EDUCATION

September 1973 saw the military coup that brought down the Constitutional President, Salvador Allende G., and his Popular Unity coalition. An authoritarian regime was established, oriented by the principle of national security. Inclined toward developing the privatization of many public services as a condition for the development of capitalism, Chile became one of the first wholesale followers of neo-liberal economics. Significant changes in education were implemented. The changes included above all the State's role in relation to education and, consequently, to society, and were aligned with the redefining and all-encompassing inspirational doctrine of the regime.

Formal Education

Initially, and in the context of the Doctrine of National Security, repressive measures were taken against those who had been linked to the previous government: directors, teachers, students, public officials, and individual schools and staff in the Ministry of Education. Books considered subversive were withdrawn from libraries. Modifications were made to the Plans and Programs of Study. Weekly civic ceremonies were organized. The Parents' Associations were placed under the protection of officials of the new regime. The board members of Students' Federations were appointed by decree. This military control of the system lasted directly or indirectly throughout the military period. However, in the latter years of the regime there were some organizations, in the context of social mobilizations and the progress of democratic forces, that achieved a certain degree of autonomy from the authorities.

In the context of embedding neo-liberalism into all aspects of society, the institutional organization of Chilean education was completely restructured in 1980. With this regime, the notion of the State of Compromise ended, replacing it with the notion of an authoritarian and subsidizing state. This had a direct consequence on formal education. The guiding principle in education that had existed since the 1930s, the state as educator, gave way to the subsidizing state. Specifically, this meant that the state (through the Ministry of Education) would no longer be directly responsible for the administration of the schools. Responsibility for the administration of the schools was given to the municipalities or, in the case of Technical-Professional Education, to business corporations.

The privatization of education was established through different mechanisms: (a) incentives and competition, (b) legal means, (c) de-professionalizing and de-organizing the teachers' unions, and (d) through use of financing. The state's financing of the municipal and private system was called "subsidizing," and was based on an Educational Subsidy Unit calculated on the average number of attending students per grade and school. The state kept for itself the functions of technical supervision (i.e., curriculum development) and control of the standards that guided the educational system.

At first the Plans and Programs of Study were reorganized by Presidential Directives, by which new curriculum was developed, with content and pedagogy reflective of the regime's overall ideology and worldview. With the democratic triumph of the Plebiscite of 1987 calling for presidential elections in 1989, the military regime ended in 1990. One day before the new democratically elected president representing a coalition of center and leftist parties was to take office, the military regime passed the Constitutional Organic Law of Education (LOCE in Spanish). In effect, this law locked in not only the political institutional nature of the existing system, but also the rationale and normative ideology of the educational system. The LOCE laid out goals and governing principles for education, as well as for institutionalizing the financing system, educational management, and ownership. It also confirmed the state's subsidizing role, through its functions of technical supervision and regulation of standards.

The LOCE was structured in connection with the principles of Educational Liberty and Educational Decentralization, which meant that: (a) local schools had total freedom and autonomy to define their own educational projects and internal regulations, and only had to keep the Ministry of Education informed; and (b) the state could not control the use of subsidies, which became part of the assets of the supporter (i.e., the private or municipal owner of a given school). This law offered no legal mechanisms for protecting the right to a quality education, nor the rights of students and their families. Although the right to education was stated in the Constitution, it was not spelled out in any law or regulation. Schools were to be owned and managed by educational entrepreneurs who received financing from the state but were not accountable to it nor the educational community. The state control of schools was not allowed, except in very specific instances. As a consequence, the constitutional right that makes parents the primary educators and gives them choice in deciding what education their children received was not achieved. The logic of the system set up a type of large supermarket of competing educational options that, obviously, were beyond the reach of the middle and lower classes (except for religious options).

Given the country's tradition of the state as educator, LOCE was a revolution in education. It was a process begun in 1980 in the context of the set of neo-liberal modernizing actions taken on by the military regime (others being legislation regarding labor, health, revenue, social security, access to foreign investment, etc.). The decentralization of education, in an authoritarian context, did not generate substantive changes in the quality of education, but it did generate an institutional context that the democratic governments, since 1990, have used to drive the current Educational Reform.

From the perspective of the resistance of teachers to this process, the Reform was lived out in the framework of the professional organizations. The *Colegio de Profesores* (a labor association that legally replaced the dissolved Single Union of Education Workers [SUTE in Spanish]) was organized by the military regime in the mid-1980s. In some regions, the regional boards of the Colegio were taken over by opponents to the military regime. Its board had official status until the coming of democracy, when opposition forces gained national leadership through free elections. At the same time the democratic educators started their own formal organization, the Labor Association of Educators of Chile (AGECH in Spanish), which opposed the imposed policies. Completely against the municipalization and privatization of Education, the AGECH promoted internal communication among educators, and sociopolitical training for teachers. Later the AGECH was dissolved and its directors, through elections, went on to occupy several board positions in the Colegio de Profesores.

Informal Education

In this period, an alternative educational mobilization was developed through Non-Governmental Organizations (NGOs) and the pedagogical work of Social Organizations (SOs). These organizations made up, more or less organically, the social movement of the time. This alternative educational mobilization was rich, varied, broad, active, and articulate.

Some of the social activists came together, legally, in a group of associations or organizations that integrated, at the beginning, the democratic resistance against the dictatorship. Chief among these activists were teachers and technicians who had remained in Chile and who had been fired or forced to leave the universities, governmental institutions, or private organizations that had been taken over by the military regime. The restructuring of the social fabric of society was achieved through social and political training of traditional and young leaders, and through training the core of the SOs. Later they evolved into the construction of alternative propositions from different scopes and topics of contingency or strategic projection, in accordance with global tendencies.

NGOs were orienting their work toward the environment, intercultural and indigenous issues, alternative agriculture, popular economics, types of popular education, gender studies, social and educational studies and research, and so on. Their work was linked to Latin American and global networks that developed similar activities in different educational contexts in different countries, especially in the poorest ones. This work also permitted the survival of persons, families, and social groups, in that it provided financial and social support to those who had lost their jobs for political reasons or as a consequence of the economic restructuring that resulted in high unemployment among middle- and lower-class urban workers. Active international cooperation and solidarity financed their activities and programs. In addition to contributing toward the lowering of the risk associated with rising poverty in broad sectors of the society, NGOs gave intellectuals, professionals, technicians, and social leaders who had remained in Chile an opportunity to reconstruct their ideals based on new social practices.

In the case of education, many NGOs were created, operating throughout the country with informal education and training. NGOs with objectives that were not strictly educational (such as those advancing women's rights and the rights of indigenous groups) also incorporated educational work as a key strategic element.

At that time, education, as well as training, leadership development, innovative experience development, research, seminars, study and discussion groups, and so on. all formed part of an important strategy of resistance to the dictatorship. However, they also played a role in the production of useful knowledge for constructing new categories of social analysis and praxis, which were becoming integrated into the task and demands of the Social Organizations. In addition, these activities played a role in the proposals that the political opposition was building as an alternative program of government. In this process the notion of human rights was being reconstructed and affirmed, as a guiding axis of this variety of pedagogical practices. Education was thus linked with the greater democratic struggle centered in the recovery of democracy as a condition for the full exercise of human rights. At the same time, it called for justice in relation to human rights abuses that had been committed since the day of the military coup.

One field that continued to flourish during this time through the work of NGOs is what is known as popular education. Popular education's roots are found in the following sources: (a) autonomous Latin American experiences of popular education, especially in indigenous areas as well as urban and rural popular culture; (b) the thinking of Paulo Freire and others who promoted his ideas; (c) the cultural thought of A. Gramsci and the Frankfurt School in the thinking of the political and educational; (d) the contribution of Orlando Fars Borda, from Colombia, whose thinking was important for the field of participatory investigation; (e) ideas of several representatives of critical pedagogy, such as Bernstein and Apple, which made a contribution in relation to the cultural construction of the curriculum, which was then extrapolated to popular education; and (f) the Catholic church, especially the church in Brazil, which contributed a new pedagogical conceptualization, generated from a confluence of Liberation Theology, the guidelines of the Continental Episcopal Conferences of Medellin in 1968, and Puebla (1979).

This new pedagogical concept was put into practice in millions of Core Church Communities (CEBs in Spanish) throughout the continent, which had a great impact on the participation of Christians in the progressive social and political mobilizations of the period. In this period there was practically no social sector untouched by these institutions: peasants, owners of small plots of land through the agrarian reform, teachers, popular educators, settlers, women, young people, popular businesses and cooperatives, the health sector, indigenous communities, alternative cultural expressions, political education, core church communities, high school and university students, human rights, and legal, medical, and psychological support of victims of the dictatorship and their families.

1990 TO 1999: IMPROVEMENT IN QUALITY AND EQUITY IN EDUCATION

In 1990, the first post-dictatorship democratic government came into power, headed up by an alliance of center-left parties. Their primary objective was to bring about the transition to democracy. Other objectives included improving Chile's entrance into the globalized economic scene, overcoming poverty, and "canceling the social debt" toward those sectors that had been the most excluded by the policies enacted by the military regime. Among these was education. Funding for education declined steadily from 1981, reaching its lowest point in two decades by 1990 when it represented only 2.8% of the GNP (Arancibia et al., 1998).

Formal Education

In the field of education the government diagnosed that the problem in Chile was not one of coverage. By 1996, 96% and 82%, respectively, of school age children and youth attended primary and secondary school (Arancibia et al.,1998). In Chile there is an undisputed difference in the quality of education available to different social classes. The quality of education diminishes substantially as one moves down the economic ladder. The indicators of inequalities and poor quality of public schools are many. For example, 20% of the children from the upper income group attend preschool as compared to 2% of those from the lower income groups. On a nationwide assessment of students' performance in math and Spanish, by 1992 children from the bottom 5% schools were achieving half of their counterparts attending the top 5% schools. By 1996 this difference has narrowed to 40 percentage points, a figure reflecting the persistence of social inequities in education. This unequal social distribution of knowledge has as its consequence the impossibility of equal opportunity, which is a basic condition for the existence of democracy.

For this reason, a priority for both governments since 1990 has been the program Improvement of the Quality and Equity in Education (MECE in Spanish). Three principles have guided this program. First, quality that is understood to mean a sustained improvement of learning (cognitive learning as well as other types of skills), in which differences in minimum achievement standards would be decreased among student groups of differing economic backgrounds. Second, equity, or the equitable social distribution of knowledge, is considered an ethical requirement referring to the role of the state in supporting those who are economically disenfranchised. The term, "positive discrimination" has translated into programs for those schools or social groups who are seen as the most vulnerable. For example, the Program of the 900 Schools, which addressed the needs of the 10% of the schools with the lowest academic achievement results (which coincided in the vast majority to the poorest schools of the country), was implemented. Initially, this program relied on financing from international solidarity from Sweden and Denmark. Third, participation is associated with the concept of educational decentralization and autonomy on the part of teachers and schools. Educators can now freely restructure curricula according to the local context. In addition, schools now have access to a set of instruments, primarily competitively awarded grants, for school improvement projects through which they could further their initiatives.

The first priority was to invest in the improvement of elementary education (since 1990). The policies have broadened progressively to high school education (1994-1995), preschool (1997), and university education (1997). The 1990s began with the design and implementation of improvement programs and ended with an Educational Reform fully underway as of today.

Starting with the second government of the Unification of Parties for Democracy (1994), education came to be a priority of the government. In 1996, the president called on Chilean society and the government to bring about an Educational Reform, with a new curricular framework—Basic Objectives and Obligatory Minimum Contents (OFCMO in Spanish) for Elementary and High School Education. This framework sets a common national curriculum while leaving room for schools to develop an additional differential curriculum. It also calls for extending the school day and school facilities through the introduction of the Complete School Day. The Reform, begun in 1997 with first and second grade, will gradually incorporate the whole system by 2003. Another pillar of the reform is the extensive deployment of a computer network, Enlaces, which purports to link 50% of all state-funded elementary schools and 100% of the high schools by the year 2000. This network gives teachers and students access to the incorporation of information technologies in instructional planning and delivery.

These policies imply a substantial improvement in pedagogical resources (textbooks, libraries, computers, teaching materials) associated with professional development, new teaching proposals for changing teaching practices, and movement from a standardizing supervision to one that is technical-pedagogical. To this are added policies for improving schools' infrastructure and equipment, for school health and food services, and for improving the subsidies that finance the system, all by means of a massive, sustained increase in public investment in education. A sustained increase in teachers' salary, above the national average, is understood by most as key to the success of this Reform.

For teachers, a policy of professional development is being implemented through two main channels: (a) the Teaching Profession Statute, which provides municipal teachers with guarantees in conditions of national salary negotiation and job stability; teachers' salaries will be set according to factors such as difficult duties, seniority, and professional development; and (b) the provision of in-service education is now decentralized in the hands of universities and other private corporations, with individual school owners purchasing services from these entities. Additionally, since 1996 almost 4,000 schoolteachers mostly from low-income communities have gone abroad to study and have specialized in various fields.

In general, these policies have implied an effective, sustained improvement in learning among students in economically deprived areas, narrowing the gap with wealthier sectors; nevertheless, the gap is still significant. Sectors that had been outside the system have been progressively incorporated, especially from seventh grade up through high school. The scholastic level of the population over 15 years of age has risen, in contrast to the declining trend during the authoritarian government. There has been a broadening of actions centering on groups that had never had programs oriented toward them, for example, multigrade rural schools and indigenous groups.

The period of transition and restoration to democracy has involved significant changes in the social issues that the government and society have been asked to confront, and, consequently, the issues that formal education must confront. A major and persistent problem nine years into the restoration of democracy has been how the society will deal with human rights abuses committed during the military dictatorship (reconciliation, punishment, reparative justice, etc.). Two social groups that have been historically marginalized and subordinated within Chilean society, women and indigenous people, emerged from the years of dictatorship with a well-articulated agenda. Unprecedented in the history of this country, these groups' organizing and activism were instrumental in securing institutional attention, on the part of the Ministry of Education, to gender-fairness in schooling and a recognition of the need to offer intercultural bilingual education to the meet the needs (demands) of indigenous groups. In other words, these groups have been effective in creating an awareness that in addition to social class, gender, and ethnicity are significant factors impinging on the possibility that all Chileans students have access to equal educational opportunities.

Equal Opportunities for Women in Education. In tracing the history of the production of knowledge about women's issues in Latin America, Teresa Valdés (1995) identifies a number of "moments" that have shaped approaches taken to articulate spaces and strategies for women's emancipatory struggles. In Chile, like many other many Latin American countries that found themselves under the rule of military dictatorships, women's movements were at the forefront in the struggle for human rights and the restoration of democracy. Therefore, when the transition to democracy began in 1990—the context of significant United Nation's proclamations on behalf of women's rights—women had positioned themselves to propose an agenda for the transformation of social, political, and cultural practices that had historically subordinated them. As noted by Valdés, in many countries this took the form of creating government structures that afforded women's struggles visibility within the political institutions. In 1991, the Chilean government created an office, *Servicio Nacional de la Mujer* (SERNAM) (Women's National Service), with its director having the rank of a minister. This government agency was charged with assisting in the development of public policies that would favor women's development in the context of a new social relation based on democracy, equality, and nondiscrimination.

The government's rationale for creating this office was that deepening democracy and promoting the economic development of the country and its efforts toward modernization made overcoming the discrimination of women a political imperative. Thus, the focus of governmental policies has been to develop equal opportunities and rights for women and men. To this effect, SERNAM was charged with proposing an equal opportunity plan (*Plan de Igualdad de Oportunidades*, 1994-1999), which would outline specific objectives and action plans in key institutional areas, including education. Although carrying out these action steps was the responsibility of each ministry, SERNAM was charged with coordinating, doing follow-up, and the monitoring of the measures proposed in the plan.

SERNAM (1995) commissioned a number of studies that sought to examine how education might serve the purpose of reproducing gender inequities as children and youth were socialized in ways that restricted women's access to the public sphere of power and decision making and men's access to the "domestic" or family terrain (Bilbao, 1996; Micheli & Edwards, 1995). Research in Chile coincided with findings from studies done elsewhere as they documented the invisibility of women in school textbooks, their limited representation in contexts that reinforced women's primary roles as mothers and wives, school socialization practices based on hierarchical relations among men and women (women subordinated to men), differential teacher expectations that reinforced women's passivity rather than creativity and their dependency rather than independence, the protagonist role teachers afforded male students in class discussions and school functions, the denial of opportunities for males and females to enroll in high school courses or programs deemed gender "inappropriate," and so on (García Huidobro, 1996). In addition, clear gender differentiation in students' choices for vocational training in high school as well as career choices at the university level have been documented. In high school, girls enroll in vocational classes such as hairdressing, seamstress, and as preschool paraprofessional. Boys, on the other hand, will enroll in auto mechanics and other "industrial" as well as agricultural training. In college, women make up the vast majority of students in teacher education, nursing, and other service-oriented jobs, and men tend to enroll in engineering and other fields linked to the production of goods. These differences, of course, later translate into differences in earning potential.

The picture just described is rooted in cultural values that education is on the one hand designed to honor and at the same time designed to challenge when these values interfere with giving every person, regardless of their gender, equal opportunity for developing their potential. Education, therefore, is a major focus of the Plan for Equality. It proposes the following seven objectives, each accompanied by a series of actions, some of which are described for illustrative purposes:

1. Incorporate the principle of equality of opportunities for women and men into educational policies affecting each level of the educational system. Examples of actions leading to the attainment of this objective include that gender equity be formulated as an explicit objective in the MECE program, and that the curriculum framework include elements that guarantee that education will promote equal opportunities for women.

2. Eliminate sexist bias from curricula and educational resources. Examples of actions leading to the attainment of this objective include the inclusion of women's contributions to the development of culture and society, promoting the elimination of gender division in courses in the areas of physical education and technological education, ensuring that sex education is taught from a nonsexist perspective based on the principles of equal opportunities, and ensuring that textbook adoption guidelines include an item related to gender equity and nonsexist content.

3. Create awareness so teachers can eliminate from their own practices those that are sexist and can improve their professional performance toward effective equality between men and women participating in the educational process. Examples of actions leading to the attainment of this objective include incorporating into preservice teacher education the study of gender and equal opportunities for women and men, providing staff development for school counselors such that they inform and motivate women to explore a wider range of occupational choices and conducting workshops to help teachers identify sexism in language, attitudes, and interactions within the classrooms.

4. Give special attention to risk factors faced by female students and that impinge on their future development under conditions equal to those of males. Among these, special attention must be given to pregnancy prevention. Examples of actions leading to the attainment of this objective include evaluating compliance with Circular No. 247, which prohibits schools from expelling students who become pregnant (a directive routinely ignored in too many privately administered schools), and implementing mechanisms for denouncing sexual harassment of students in primary, secondary, and higher education.

5. Development of educational programs for adult women that will take into consideration their needs and interests, which will reduce illiteracy and facilitate their participation in the culture and labor market. Examples of actions leading to the attainment of this objective include conducting a study to evaluate current adult education programs and their accessibility to women, and developing curricular materials that are specific to the population of adult women.

6. Promote a research program regarding equal opportunities, gender, and women, looking at the social and biological dimensions.

7. Improve the production and dissemination of statistical data that reflect the situation of women and men and their evolution in various spheres of social life.

How far did these proposals travel? At an international seminar on the status of women in education organized by SERNAM, Juan Eduardo García Huidobro (1996), Chief of the Department of General Education in the Ministry of Education, outlined his Ministry's response to SERNAM's call for action. We must add that the initiatives mentioned by García Huidobro provide opportunities for addressing the concerns and problems identified. There is no evidence that these opportunities are being appropriated by school personnel and that these professionals are in fact engaging in new curricular practices and social relations that promote gender equity. Some of these initiatives include:

1. The new curriculum framework establishing the minimum standards (common curriculum) gives schools freedom to create curriculum (differential curriculum) that is pertinent to their student population and community. The implication of having only minimum standards is that schools can now, if they wish, have courses on gender studies, women's literature, and so on. Schools are also being encouraged to use educational strategies that involve active participation of students in the construction of knowledge and meaning. Placing attention on students' interests and concerns also has the potential for creating opportunities to make curricular content and pedagogy more responsive to the needs of female students.

2. The new curriculum framework also includes Fundamental Cross-sectional Objectives, which provide the value framework for teaching and learning. These objectives orient students' personal, moral, and social development. Prominent among the values that schools are expected to teach are respect for diversity, equality, and no discrimination. In fulfilling these objectives, teachers can develop content and activities that promote social interactions that explicitly teach children and youth not to discriminate on the basis of gender, among other status characteristics.

3. Since 1994, textbook adoption/purchasing policies by the Ministry of Education include guidelines that allow reviewers to assess the material on the basis of gender-fairness and nondiscrimination criteria.

4. New sex education programs that addressed the importance of establishing a relationship of respect and equality among women and men. In developing these programs, the Ministry of Education is working jointly with agencies such as the SERNAM and the national Institute for Youth (*Instituto Nacional de la Juventud*). These also address pregnancy prevention and school retention of adolescent mothers.

5. Professional development. SERNAM workshops are being offered to teachers to make them aware of gender equity issues in their own practices. Unfortunately, in our extensive work in teacher education reform in Chile we have seen little indication that questions of gender equity have the centrality that is needed if Chile's new teachers are to be prepared to guide their practice by the principle of equal opportunities for women and men. It is our experience that professors of education need to be a significant part of the groups targeted for the types of "awareness" workshops described in the SERNAM Plan. They are a group that is not currently targeted by the education efforts of SERNAM or the Ministry.

García Huidobro (1996) noted that the technical-vocational schools have been particularly resilient to changing their rigid views regarding what gender should receive what type of technical preparation. In this way they contribute to the gender division of work that places women in service (lower paying) rather than product-oriented jobs. This is a major problem given the large number of working-class youth who enroll in these types of high schools.

An important limitation of current educational reform in Chile is that it has been designed and driven by the Ministry of Education with little participation of teachers. This lack of participation not only has fostered resistance among many teachers but also has created little ownership over the cultural transformations they have been asked to foster. Embarking in a cultural project that purports to alter gender relations and social practices is a project of transformation that will take place over a long period of time, so one must remain hopeful.

Intercultural Bilingual Education. According to the census of 1992, 10.33% of the Chilean population self-describes as an indigenous person (998,385 persons of various ethnicities). Given that people under the age of 14 were not counted in that census, it is estimated that the real number of indigenous people is about 1,000,300. The Mapuche constitute the largest ethnic group, totaling about 800,000. According to the 1992 census, the Rapa Nui, a population originally from Easter Island (a Chilean territory in Polynesia), include 21,848 persons (*Corporación Nacional de Desarrollo Indígena*). A third group, the Aymara, live predominantly in the Andes highlands and extreme northern Chile. The last census of population and housing (1992) recorded 48,477 Aymaras living in Chile.

These three ethnic groups have developed within the occidental culture and their integration into the social, cultural, linguistic, and economic fabric of the wider society has been marked by their subordination. Indicators of quality of life among indigenous groups are lower than those of the general population: less income, higher rates of illiteracy, less years of schooling, less availability of potable water and electricity, less access to agricultural credits, and so on. In terms of achievement, data show that students from these groups achieve below the general population of students.

The presence of their distinct cultural and linguistic characteristics is quite scarce among these groups. Nevertheless, their cultural roots have not disappeared, representing a living patrimony signifying the pluralistic and multilingual character of Chilean society. It is this patrimony that each group has called on education to rescue and preserve.

Until very recently, Chile did not recognize itself as a multilingual country. Even though some legislation in this area has been passed, mostly as a result of strong indigenous activism throughout Latin America and in Chile, nationally this does not represent an awareness of ethnic consciousness in Chilean society. Nevertheless, since 1990 indigenous people have been able to gain some significant spaces in response to demands they have placed on the government and the civil society.

Socially and politically, indigenous groups were among the few social groups that emerged from the period of dictatorship well organized and with an agenda for their demands for economic, cultural, and political revindications. This led in 1993 to the promulgation of the Indigenous Law (No. 19.523 of 28.9.1993, known as *Ley Indígena*), which sought both the protection and development of indigenous people. The law created the National Corporation of Indigenous Development (*Corporación Nacional de Desarrollo Indígena*, CONADI). This Corporation is located within the Ministry of Planning and is charged with coordinating national policies that will benefit the indigenous groups. The Law spells out some specific articles pertaining to education. Among these:

Article 28. The recognition, respect, and protection of the indigenous cultures and languages will involve:

1. The use and maintenance of indigenous languages, together with Spanish, in areas where there is a high concentration of indigenous population;
2. the establishment in the national curriculum of programs that allow students to have access to adequate knowledge of the indigenous cultures and languages, preparing them to value these positively;
3. the promotion of television and radio programs in indigenous languages in the regions with high concentration of indigenous population and support for the creation of indigenous radio stations and other mass communication outlets; and
4. the establishment of courses in history, culture, and indigenous languages in higher education institutions.

Article 32. In the areas of high concentration of indigenous people, the Corporation in coordination with other agencies of the state that are appropriate will develop a system of intercultural bilingual education, for the preparation of indigenous students who can function effectively in the communities of origin as well as in the global community.

Article 33. Indicates that special funding will be given to the Ministry of Education to provide scholarships for indigenous students.

It is important to note that by introducing the concept of intercultural bilingual education, the state, for the first time in Chile, acknowledged that quality and equity in education must involve respect for cultural differences, the development of curricular materials that are pertinent to the cosmovision of various ethnic groups, and that members of ethnic groups themselves have an important role to play in deciding educational matters that affect their survival as a distinct cultural and linguistic group. It is also important to note that intercultural bilingual education does not have a transitional character by which Indian languages are used as a bridge to help children learn faster and better Spanish or mainstream curricula. Rather, intercultural bilingual education programs seek to maintain and strengthen indigenous students' cultural knowledge and language, fostering their full ethnic identities. Additionally, these students are expected to become skillful in using the cultural codes and technologies of mainstream or hegemonic culture (Barnach-Calbó, 1997).

What have been the implications of this law for the provision of educational services to indigenous populations? Here we can report the case of one region. As Regional Minister for Education in the area that concentrates about 250,000 Mapuche, one of the authors (Williamson) was charged with overseeing a number of projects that were developed under the auspices of this law. There are number of things that this legislation made possible; however, one must recognize that not enough has been done. Any analysis must keep foremost in mind that it was only in 1996 that the Ministry of Education created a Program for Intercultural and Bilingual Education (*Pograma de Educación Intercultural Bilingüe*, PEIB). In 1997, the first measures were taken, a national coordinator was appointed, a budget was allocated, a program of action was developed, agreements with CONADI were signed, and a representative from the Ministry of Education joined the National Advisory Board for CONADI. That is, only 2 years have passed since the topic of indigenous education was institutionalized within the Chilean Ministry of Education.

As in the case of the proposals drafted by the Plan for Equality of Women and Men, the Reform offers a number of opportunities to implement the articles of the Indigenous Law that pertain to education. Beyond sanctioning the use of indigenous languages as legitimate means of instruction, schools serving indigenous communities have been developing school improvement plans and receiving grants to make their practices more intercultural. Workshops on how to develop culturally appropriate curriculum have been offered to teachers and there is at least one university that offers a teacher preparation program in intercultural education. Textbooks have been revised to eliminate ethnocentrism and also to eliminate historical errors and recover subjugated histories. In adult education, a number of indigenous organizations are developing courses in agricultural topics. In term of cultural activities, the Ministry of Education has awarded a number of grants to poets, writers, plastic artists, musicians, and researchers who further the living patrimony of various ethnic groups.

Regardless of these important efforts and advances, much more remains to be done. Most significantly, a lack of teachers who are members of these ethnic groups or who can speak the languages severely limits the provision of bilingual education. Second, most of the work done in intercultural bilingual education has been experimental in nature and in elementary grades. The needs of secondary students have been largely ignored. The inclusion of interculturalism and bilingualism into vocational high schools with the idea of preparing them to create and manage small business or cooperatives is missing; they're mostly being trained as laborers. Most importantly, perhaps, there needs to be a greater effort placed on integrating the interest and perspectives of indigenous communities to education in ways that foster their political and economic organization. Another significant task that is pending is addressing the needs of indigenous people who have migrated to the cities in search of better economic opportunities. The majority of the

Mapuche people live in Santiago, where they are highly vulnerable to losing their ethnic identity and traditions. Improving the economic conditions that sustain life in rural areas must become an important task for the national and regional governments, if education is to fulfill its promise of maintaining ethnic and linguistic diversity among Chilean ethnic minorities.

Informal Education

Non-governmental organizations, universities, and social organizations, with few exceptions, have been either slow in becoming involved in the tasks of educational change, or in fact have decreased their involvement. In the case of the universities and their teacher education programs, the return to democracy and the new educational policies found them, in general, in a state of crisis and disconnected with the political and new pedagogical proposals of MECE and the Reform. In practice the ideas of educational change were generated within the state, designed and executed by political and technical staff who came from the NGOs, independent research centers, from abroad, and, only in a few cases, from the universities.

As international aid for NGOs dwindled in light of the country's improved economic indicators, many ceased to exist. Others began to operate as institutions in collaboration with the state. As extensions of the government, NGOs have become ever more dependent on state resources and therefore on its policies. In fact their alternative and critical role toward the overall system has been replaced by an effort to try to influence the state with ideas, all within the framework of the freedom of movement that the government afforded them. Public criticism has been transferred to several nuclei of university, public, and private centers, or to NGOs that have their own operating resources. With the exception of the reforms in preservice teacher education, the civil society has not offered substantive criticism and alternative proposals to the state's reform initiatives. A coherent, alternative, integrating thought with respect to the government's proposal for the Educational Reform or its social programs is missing.

CONCLUSION

As of 1999, when we are writing this chapter, there is a great national consensus regarding the priority that educational reform has in furthering Chilean development. There is, however, less consensus as to the relative importance that different social actors within education and in the broader political scene afford to the three principles guiding current reform efforts: quality, equity, and participation. Particularly problematic is the attainment of equity when culturally relevant curricula and pedagogy are developed mostly at a cultural artifacts level rather than at an ideological level. Participation is also problematic because the Reform has been centrally driven and largely imposed on teachers. Decentralization and choice assumes parents who can make demands as consumers of educational services. In Chile, however, parents have not had experiences in organizing themselves as consumers and partners in education, thus they are not making demands for quality and equity.

As Chile has transitioned to democracy, emphasis has been placed on consensus rather than on criticism. But criticism will come, and is coming. Education always plays two simultaneous roles: the role of preservation and the role of change. This is a dialectic movement through which the generated tension liberates energies at the least expected times. In this sense, solidarity as well as resistance is always building within society's cultural and pedagogical acts rooted in the economy or in the urban life of the population. In the context of globalization, information moves beyond the citizens' everyday context and they begin to look for new forms of communication, encounters and social recognition, and of dialogue. This situation creates new forms of social organizations and demands for the integration of groups that refuse to be assimilated or to continue to be excluded.

REFERENCES

Arancibia, S., Edwards, V., Jara, C., Jelvez, M., & Nuñez, I. (1998). *Reform in progress: Quality education for all.* Santiago, Chile: Ministerio de Educación, República de Chile.

Barnach-Calbó, E. (1997). La nueva educación indígena en Iberoamérica [The new indigenous education in Iberoamerica]. *Revista Iberoamericana de Educación, 13.*

Bilbao, J. (1996). Discurso inaugural [Inagural speech]. En Servicio Nacional de la Mujer (Ed.), *Igualdad de oportunidades para las mujeres en la educación* [Equal opportunities for women in education] (pp. 9-15). Santiago, Chile: Servicio Nacional de la Mujer.

Corporación Nacional de Desarrollo Indígena [Corporation for Indigenous Development]. http://www.conadi.cl.

García Huidobro, J. E. (1996). Hacia la igualdad de oportunidades de la mujer en educación: La experiencia Chilena [Towards equal opportunities for women in education: The Chilean experience]. En Servicio Nacional de la Mujer (Ed.), *Igualdad de oportunidades para las mujeres en la educación* [Equal opportunities for women in education] (pp. 86-93). Santiago, Chile: Servicio Nacional de la Mujer.

Micheli, B., & Edwards, V. (1995). Discriminación de genero en la educación media [Gender discrimination in secondary education]. *La Piragua, 10,* 62-71.

SERNAM. (1995). *Plan de igualdad para las mujeres* [Plan for the equality of women]. Santiago, Chile: Servicio Nacional de la Mujer.

Valdés, T. (1995). La producción de conocimientos sobre la mujer en América Latina [The production of knowledge regarding women in Latin America]. *La Piragua, 10*, 1-10.

Contributors

Cristina Allemann-Ghionda, of Italian origin, has been a Senior Lecturer at the Universities of Zürich, Berne, and Geneva (Switzerland). She earned the *Venia Legendi* for comparative education from the Westfälische Wilhelms—Universität of Münster (Germany) in 1998, and has been a Professor of Education at Cologne University (Germany) since 2000. The topics of her books and papers include: comparative research on aspects of the educational systems of European countries, intercultural education in theory, policies, and practice, and inquiry into the contents of, as well as curriculum development for, teacher education. She also studied the reception of John Dewey's educational theory in post-World War II Italy.

Desmond Cahill is Professor of Intercultural Studies in the Faculty of Education, Language, and Community Services at RMIT University in Melbourne. As one of Australia's foremost authorities on immigrant and intercultural education, he has conducted, for the Australian government, the 1984 Review of the Commonwealth Multicultural Education Program, the Ethnic Minority Youth Studies in 1987 and 1992, and the Immigration and Schooling Evaluation in 1996. He has also conducted numerous studies on Australia's immigrant communities. His current interests are focused on globalization and cross-cultural professional practice.

Sveta Davé Chakravarty works for a not-for-profit agency, the Centre for Education Management and Development (CEMD), which is engaged in the facilitation of change in education. The goal of the organization is to bring about quality education through systemic reforms, at all levels of education, by focusing on the impact of individual educators, institutions, and change of schools and state systems on student learning. Sveta Davé Chakravarty is Coordinator of CEMD's School Reform Program in the Delhi government system of schools, covering 11 Districts, 1,200 schools, and about 720,000 students. She did her undergraduate work at Mount Holyoke College and graduate work at the University of Virginia, and taught at Bryn Mawr College and Yale University before returning to India in 1994.

Lars O. Dahlström teaches at Umeå University in Sweden and is Coordinator of the Teacher Education Reform Project in Namibia. He has been involved in teacher education reforms in Southern Africa for twenty years.

Inés Dussel is Director of the Education Research Unit at the Latin American Faculty for the Social Sciences (FLACSO) in Argentina. She is also an author of several books and articles on the history of education in Argentina and on contemporary educational theories. Her research interests are poststructural theories, histories of curriculum, and the history of the regulation of bodies in schools. She earned her Ph.D. at the University of Wisconsin-Madison.

Carl A. Grant is Hoefs-Bascom Professor of Teacher Education in the Department of Curriculum and Instruction at University of Wisconsin-Madison. He has written and edited numerous books and monographs on multicultural education and teacher education, as well as more than 100 articles, chapters in books, and reviews. He has received numerous awards for his research, writing, and teacher education programs, including the School of Education Distinguished Achievement Award in 1997. He has been a classroom teacher, an administrator, a Fulbright Scholar in England, President of the National Association for Multicultural Education (NAME), and Editor of *Review of Educational Research* (*RER*).

Chuen-Min Huang earned her Ph.D. from the University of Washington in 1997. She conducted research and taught courses on multicultural curriculum and instruction, educational anthropology, and educational ethnography at the Institute of Education, National Chung Cheng University in Chiayi, Taiwan for two years. Currently, she is Assistant Professor in the Department of Education at National Taiwan Normal University in Taipei, Taiwan.

Leena Huss is Research Fellow and Associate Professor at the Centre for Multiethnic Research and Lecturer in the Finno-Ugric Department, Uppsala University (Sweden). She is the editor of *Many Roads to Bilingualism* and author of *Reversing Language Shift in the Far North: Linguistic Revitalization in Northern Scandinavia and Finland*.

Álvaro Moreira Hypolito is Assistant Professor in the School of Education at the Federal University of Pelotas, Brazil, where he teaches courses in sociology of education and educational policy studies. His research interests include curriculum theory, teachers' work, and gender, class and race relations and education. In Brazil, he has written many articles on these issues, as well as a book entitled *Teachers' Work, Social Class and Gender relations*, published in 1997. He is currently working on his Ph.D. in Curriculum & Instruction at the University of Wisconsin-Madison.

Carl E. James is an Associate Professor in the Faculty of Education and in Social Work and Sociology at York University. He is also an Associate in the Faculty of Physical Education and Health at University of Toronto. He teaches courses in urban education, foundations and models of education, and practitioner research. His research and publications explore issues related to equity in relation to race, class, and gender, youth and sports, anti-racism, and multiculturalism. He has worked as a youth and community development worker with local, national, and international organizations and has been a visiting lecturer in the Teacher Training Department at Uppsala University, Sweden since 1997, where he lectures on multicultural education. He has also worked in continuing education at the Institute of Adult Education, Dar es Salaam, Tanzania. James holds a Ph.D. in sociology and, in addition to his many journal articles, is the author and co-author of several books and educational resources.

Joy L. Lei holds a M.S. in the Department of Curriculum & Instruction and a Ph.D. in the Department of Educational Policy Studies at the University of Wisconsin-Madison. Her research and teaching interests include multicultural and anti-oppressive education, racial and ethnic identity construction, race relations, and Asian American Students in U.S. schools. She is an Assistant Professor in the Department of Education and American Culture Program at Vassar College.

Carmen Montecinos is a professor in the Department of Educational Psychology and Foundations at the University of Northern Iowa. She has authored numerous journal articles and book chapters on the topic of multicultural teacher education.

Servando Pérez-Domínguez is a Researcher at the University of Santiago de Compostela (Spain) and holds a BA in Philosophy and Sciences of Education. He teaches subjects related to multi/intercultural education and comparative education. His current research focuses on comparing the opinions of teachers regarding teaching in multiethnic and multicultural settings in the United Kingdom and Spain. He was an Erasmus Grantee at the University of Reading (Britain) in 1991-1992 and was an Honorary Visiting Scholar at the same University between 1994 and 1998. In 1995 he participated in the European Projects: *Erasmus Network for Lesser-Used Languages* (LULs) and *Mercator Education Project for Minority Languages*. During the academic year of 1996-1997, he was a Visiting Scholar at the Harvard Graduate School of Education. Since 1997, he has been the coordinator in Galicia (Spain) for the European

Project *Dialogue for the Future*, which explores the opinions of European Youth about issues of racism.

Miguel A. Santos-Rego holds a BA and a Ph.D. in Sciences of Education at the University of Santiago de Compostela (Spain), where he is Senior Lecturer in the Department of Theory & Sciences of Education. He has been Visiting Professor at the Universities of Illinois, Southern Mississippi, and Johns Hopkins, U.S.A. His academic works include books and articles in specialized pedagogical journals, both in Spain and abroad. Most of his publications deal with issues related to educational policy, intercultural education, and motivational processes in education. He is a member of the Academic and Editorial Board of several educational research journals. Positions that he has held, among others, include Director of the UNED (State University for Distance Education) in A Coruña, Vice President of Universities and Research in the Xunta de Galicia (Galician Autonomous Government), and Vice Chancellor of Academic Affairs at the University of Santiago de Compostela. He is a member of the Board of Governors of Schools in Galicia. Presently, he is the Director of the ICE (Institute of Sciences in Education) at the University of Santiago de Compostela.

Jeremy Sarkin is Professor of Public Law and Deputy Dean of the Law Faculty at the University of the Western Cape in Cape Town, South Africa, where he teaches constitutional law, international human rights, and humanitarian law, as well as transitional justice. He is an attorney of the High Court of South Africa, and an attorney of law in the State of New York, U.S.A. He has a BA and a LL.B. from the University of Natal in South Africa, a LL.M. from Harvard Law School, and a Doctorate of Law degree from the University of the Western Cape. He served as the National Chairperson of the Human Rights Committee of South Africa from 1994 to 1997. He has written widely in the fields of human rights, constitutional law, private and public law, and transitional justice. He is an editor of the journal *Law, Democracy and Development* and is at present editing an issue on transitional justice. He has been working recently on the truth and reconciliation process in Rwanda as well as the trial process in Ethiopia. He is also assisting the constitutional process in Burma.

Patti Swarts is Director of the National Institute for Educational Development (NIED) in Namibia. NIED is responsible for innovation and renewal in education through research and curriculum and professional development. She holds a Ph.D. in Teacher Education from Oxford Brookes University, United Kingdom. She was a high school teacher for English as a Second Language, and a teacher educator at the Khomasdal and Windhoek Colleges of Education.

Harry Tomlinson was a headteacher and principal in four schools/colleges in the United Kingdom, two of which had a strong multicultural ethos. He is now a Professor at Leeds Metropolitan University, where he is responsible for managing two government contracts for the National Professional Qualification for Headship (NPQH) and for Performance Management Consultancy in the Yorkshire and Humber Region. He is also project director for one of the consortia delivering the Leadership Programme for Serving Headteachers (LPSH). He has been involved in contracts in Malaysia and Hong Kong, and written widely on a range of education matters. His most recent edited book is *Living Headship: Voices, Values and Vision.*

Carlos Alberto Torres is a political sociologist of education and is Professor of Social Sciences and Comparative Education and Director of the Latin American Center at University of California, Lost Angeles. He is the author of several books, including (with Nick Burbules) *Education and Globalization: Critical Concepts* and *Education, Democracy and Multiculturalism: Dilemmas of Citizenship in a Global World.*

Guillermo Williamson C. is a professor in the Department of Education at the Universidad de La Frontera, Temuco, Chile. He has authored several articles and books on the topics of popular education, rural education, and intercultural education. He has also coordinated a number of governmental and non-governmental programs in these areas.

Author Index

A

Abad, L. V., 258, 264
Abajo-Alcalde, J. E., 256, 264
Acker, S., 347, 353
Adams, H., 180, 201
Adams, M., 229, 235
Afshar, H., 102, 111
Åhl, H., 138, 139, 158
Ahmed, L., 100, 101, 111
Aikio-Puoskari, U., 144, 156
Alia, J., 99, 111
Allardt, E., 141, 146
Allemann-Ghionda, C., 2, 3, 4, 8, 19, 23
Allen, A., 184, 201
Ambasht, N. K., 65, 82, 88, 90
Amber-Belkhir, J., 190, 201
Ameer, J. P., 218, 235
Amin, S., 313, 315
Amuchastegui, M., 106, 111
Amukugo, E. M., 296, 315
Anderson, J. E., 208, 220, 235, 236
Andersson, I., 299, 315
Andersson, S. B., 303, 315
Angula, N., 305, 315
Anzaldúa, G., 110, 111
Apeltauer, E., 5, 24

Apple, M. W., 165, 166, 169, 171, 172, 347, 353
Arancibia, S., 357, 377
Archibald, J., 180, 183, 202
Arnau, J., 243, 246, 264
Audard, C., 98, 111
Auld, R., 318, 334
Avenstrup, R., 304, 315
Ayers, W., 229, 235

B

Baffoe, M., 272, 287
Baker, G. C., 217, 235
Balto, A., 138, 143, 151, 156
Banks, J. A., 68, 86, 90, 128, 129, 130, 132, 160, 171, 195, 201, 217, 222, 223, 225, 235, 263, 264
Bannerji, H., 178, 180, 191, 201
Barcelos, L. C., 163, 164, 172
Barnach-Calbo, E., 374, 377
Barros, F., 164, 171, 172
Bartolomé-Pina, M., 250, 264
Basson, D., 294, 315
Bell, L. A., 229, 235
Bennett, J. M., 17, 24

Y

Z

Subject Index

A-B

Aboriginals
    in Australia, 27, 50, 57-58
    in Canada, 180
    in Taiwan, 115, 125
Academic resources, 130
Access to education, 79
Access to Equity Strategy, 43
Additive biculturalism, 135
Affirmative action, 4, 71, 107, 311
Afrocentric pedagogy, 187
Alternative pedagogical perspectives, 175
American identity, 224
Anti-multicultural position, 108
Anti-racism curriculum, 186, 189, 325-327
Apartheid, 271-274
Assimilation, 4, 6, 11, 36-39, 105, 122, 135, 137, 159, 209-210, 274, 318-321
Assimilationist pluralism, 214
Australian ESL Program, 39, 51
Bamti edicatopm. 272-273, 275
Bilingual teaching, 15, 32
Black Focus School, 187
Black/White binary, 230, 328

C

Census, 28
Citizen identity, 339, 345
Citizenship
    as civic virtues, 344
    as political, 348
    as social, 348
Civic equality, 301

Civil society, 355
Colonialism, xi, 27, 64
Colonial policies, 314
Commercial textbooks, 116, 125-126
Commission for Racial Equality, 324
Compensatory programs, 5, 106, 249, 313
Composite identity, 61
Constitutional Equality, 206-212
Construction of difference, 339
Critical pedagogy, 229
Critical tradition, 160, 228
Cultural deficit, 216
Cultural democracy, 177, 186, 212
Cultural diversity, 1, 7, 45, 125, 175
Cultural equality, 213
Cultural identity, 3-4, 67, 136
Cultural informants, 149
Cultural knowledge and suppression, 139
Cultural maintenance, 319
Cultural pluralism, 98, 213, 320
Cultural policies, 123
Cultural relativism, 136
Cultural resource center, 150
Cultural revitalization, 144, 146
Cultural struggle, 55-56, 121, 166
Cultural studies, 191
Cultural tolerance, 327
Culturally relevant education, 82
Culture and control, 225, 325
Curriculum, 15, 16, 43, 138, 282
    and content, 80
    and culture, 45, 165, 185
    and Eurocentricism, 183
    inclusiveness of, 83
    that is latent, 68
    relevance of, 294
    standards of, 116

D

Decentralization, 73, 85, 300, 363
Deculturalization, 208
Deficit hypothesis, 6, 11
Deliberative universalism, 18
Democracy, 118, 278, 366
Democratic education, 301, 303, 339
Democratic pluralism, 212
Derived authority, 294
Devolution, 46
Difference
    and discourse, 178
    and management, 178
    and denial, 319
Dual schooling, 349-350
Dual societies, 348
Dysconsciousness, 162

E

Economic development, 44, 118
    and culture, xv, 11-12
    and segregation, 295
    and structure, 13
    as colonization, 208
    as universalist, 12
Educational control, 180, 296-297, 318
Educational expansion, 341
Educational reform, 249, 307, 358
Educational rights, 279-280
Emagratory movements, 28
Endangered language, 147
Enlightenment, 337-340, 338
Equality
    vs. equity, 79, 176, 213, 218, 320
    See also Constitutional Equality
Equitable multiculturalism, 47
Equity, 57, 176, 189
    See also Equality versus equity
Ethnic activists, 143
Ethnic community schools, 37, 46
Ethnic minority success, 52
Ethnic revitalization, 62, 118, 122, 141
Ethnicity, 121-123
    as multilayered, 61
    as racial discourse, 209
Examination system, 317

F-G

Feminization, 160
Funding, 282-284
Gender, 63, 69-70. 123-124, 323, 332, 369
Gender equity education, 126
Genetic explanation, 215
Globalism, xi, xiii, 12, 48, 104, 94, 305,
    313, 341, 366
Gypsy community, 254

H

Hegemony, 345, 339
Heritage classes, 182
Heterogeneous immigration, 11, 13, 32
Hierarchies of legitimacy, 95
History of oppression, 178
    in Australia, 37
    in Canada, 179-180
    in Chile, 356-366
    in Europe, 5
    in India, 62-64, 66-69
    in Namibia, 291-297
    in South Africa, 272-274
    in Spain, 241-247
    in Taiwan, 117-124
Homogenization in France, 98

I

Identity, 6, 10, 15, 43, 44, 61, 95, 166
    See also Composite identity and
    Organic identity
Ideological struggle, 226, 299
Ideology as naturalized, 206
Illegal immigrant children, 35
Immersion, 5
Immigrant in-take cuts, 33
Immigration
    in Argentina, 104
    See also Heterogeneous
    immigration
Inclusive pedagogy, 176
Indigenous people, 135
Individualism, 346
Informal education, 360-361, 364-366,
    376

Instructional materials, 116, 120-121,
   122
Integrated education, 145, 210
Integration, 3, 80, 253, 299, 318-321
   resistance to, 285
Intercultural education, 1-2, 240, 373
Intercultural marriages, 31
Intercultural studies, 40
International language, 182
International power relations, 94
Intersecting disadvantage, 53

L

Language, xi, 30, 64, 118-121, 252
   and insecurity, 140
   and policy, 179
   and prohibition, 137
   as symbolic affirmation, 121
   maintenance of, 153
Languages and hierarchy, 331
Liberal theories of citizenship, 338
Literary canons, 195
Literate citizenship, 104
Local knowledge, 152

M

Marketization, 4, 46, 341, 361-366
Migrant students and special
   education, 14, 126
Migratory movements, 239
Minorities
   and identity, 135, 140
   and school failure, 38, 164, 183, 327
   and streaming, 175
Miscegenation, 159
Mother tongue instruction, 126, 139,
   274
Multicultural education
   and critics, xv, 218, 223
   as difference, 181
   as empowerment, 197, 330
   as transformative, 130
   in Australia, 39
   five approaches to, 220-221
   goals of, 229
   research in, 217
Multicultural school, 129, 143

Multiculturalism
   and backlash, 220
   and ideology, 176
   and social class, 350-352
   as conservative, 310
   as critical, 190, 312
   as reproducing inequities, 95, 103,
      195, 325
   as systems management, 30
   See also Redefined multiculturalism
   and Resistance multiculturalism
Multicultural policies, 2-6
   in France, 3
   in Germany, 4
   in Italy, 3
   in Namibia, 291, 299, 305
   in South Africa, 281-284
   in Spain, 247
   in Taiwan, 116
   in the United Kingdom, 321-322
Multilingualism, 7, 10, 40
Muslim veils, 97-104

N

National curriculum, 165, 170, 254-257,
   329
National development, 67, 299
National identity, 41, 94, 105, 117, 182,
   239
National reconciliation, 314
Neo-liberalism, 170, 341-344, 362
Neocolonialism, 103
Non-Governmental Organizations, 75,
   246, 364
Normalization, 106

O-P

Official languages, 278
Oral tradition, 149
Organic identity, 61
Otherness, 139, 177, 338, 346
Outcome Based Education, 283
Participatory process, 73
Pedagogy, 16
   and diversity, 11
People's Movement, 76-77
Permanent Ethnic Minority, 34
Pluralism, 17, 96, 143

Policies
  and immigrants, 256
  and leverage, 88
  in Australia, 32-36
  in Canada, 176
  in Chile, 367-368
  in India, 65, 69-78
  in Latin America, 343
  See also Colonial policies and
    Multicultural policies
Political asylum, 35
Politics of identity, 347
Positive discrimination, 14
Postmodern theories, 230
Pre-colonial hegemony, 292
Productive diversity, 56
Public versus private, 99

Q-R

Queer theory, 232
Race and income, 163
Race cognizance, 212
Racial categories, 160
Racial data in Brazil, 159
Racial democracy myth, 159, 162
Racial discrimination, 163, 246, 322-323
Racial ideology, 207
Racial violence, 328-329
Racialized curriculum, 165
Redefined multiculturalism, 189
Refugee families, 33, 35
Relevant education, 190, 194
Religious affiliation, 30
Republican contract, 98
Residential schools, 71
Resistance movement, 141-142
Resistance multiculturalism, 228

S

School autonomy, 4
School segregation, 144
School structure, 318
Social justice, 44, 180
Social regulation, 347
Social reproduction, 79
Social stratification, 293

Socioeconomic class, 42, 52, 108, 160,
  332, 345
South West Africa People's
  Organization (SWAPO), 296
Special education
  See Migrant students and special
    education
State power, 277
Structural issues, 219, 293, 308, 351
Subject areas, 150, 330-331
Suburbia, 31-32
Systemic racism, 184, 188
Systems approach, 86

T

Teacher education, 19-22, 39, 85, 105,
  131, 169, 191-200, 249-254, 291, 301
Teacher strikes, 284
Teachers
  and race, 160
  and social class, 166
Teachers' perceptions, 42, 68, 80, 175,
  250, 259-261, 309, 332, 347
Teachers' Union, 107
Teaching and standardization, 170
Temporary migration, 36
Textbooks, 84, 116, 252
  See also Commercial textbooks
Theories of citizenship, 337
  See also Liberal theories of
    citizenship
Tokenism, 83
Total Quality Management, 54
Tourist approach, 219
Transnational culture, 306

U-W

Uniforms, 106
Value relativism, 17
Welfare state, 340-343
White aprons, 105-108
White hegemony, 168
White immigration, 161
Whitening, 159
World War II, 9, 27, 37, 141, 214, 239